Precarious Passages

UNIVERSITY PRESS OF FLORIDA

Florida A&M University, Tallahassee
Florida Atlantic University, Boca Raton
Florida Gulf Coast University, Ft. Myers
Florida International University, Miami
Florida State University, Tallahassee
New College of Florida, Sarasota
University of Central Florida, Orlando
University of Florida, Gainesville
University of North Florida, Jacksonville
University of South Florida, Tampa
University of West Florida, Pensacola

PRECARIOUS PASSAGES

The Diasporic Imagination in
Contemporary Black Anglophone Fiction

Tuire Valkeakari

University Press of Florida
Gainesville · Tallahassee · Tampa · Boca Raton
Pensacola · Orlando · Miami · Jacksonville · Ft. Myers · Sarasota

Publication of this paperback edition made possible by a Sustaining the Humanities through the American Rescue Plan grant from the National Endowment for the Humanities.

Copyright 2017 by Tuire Valkeakari
All rights reserved
Published in the United States of America

First cloth printing, 2017
First paperback printing, 2022

27 26 25 24 23 22   6 5 4 3 2 1

Library of Congress Cataloging-in-Publication Data
Names: Valkeakari, Tuire, author.
Title: Precarious passages : the diasporic imagination in contemporary Black Anglophone fiction / Tuire Valkeakari.
Description: Gainesville : University Press of Florida, 2016. | Includes bibliographical references and index.
Identifiers: LCCN 2016049594 | ISBN 9780813062471 (cloth) | ISBN 9780813069463 (pbk.)
Subjects: LCSH: English literature—Black authors—History and criticism. | Caribbean literature—Black authors—History and criticism. | American fiction—Black authors—History and criticism. | Blacks in literature.
Classification: LCC PR120.B55 V35 2016 | DDC 820.9/896041—dc23
LC record available at https://lccn.loc.gov/2016049594

The University Press of Florida is the scholarly publishing agency for the State University System of Florida, comprising Florida A&M University, Florida Atlantic University, Florida Gulf Coast University, Florida International University, Florida State University, New College of Florida, University of Central Florida, University of Florida, University of North Florida, University of South Florida, and University of West Florida.

University Press of Florida
2046 NE Waldo Road
Suite 2100
Gainesville, FL 32609
http://upress.ufl.edu

Contents

Note on Usage   vii

Acknowledgments   ix

Introduction: Passages to (Be)Longing   1

1. An African American Journey to Black Diasporic Consciousness: Charles Johnson's *Middle Passage*   33

2. Early Black Atlantic Crossings: Lawrence Hill's *The Book of Negroes*   62

3. War, Trauma, Displacement, Diaspora: Toni Morrison's and Caryl Phillips's African American Soldiers   99

4. Journeys to the Heart of Empire after World War II: George Lamming's, Caryl Phillips's, and Andrea Levy's Caribbean Migrants   131

5. Roots, Routes, and Returns: Caryl Phillips's, Cecil Foster's, and Edwidge Danticat's Caribbean Returnees   177

Epilogue   222

Notes   229

Bibliography   291

Index   321

Note on Usage

This book, which discusses the diasporic imagination in post–World War II and contemporary black Anglophone fiction, uses the terms "African diaspora" and "black diaspora" interchangeably. Some academics pick one of these options and stick to it, choosing either the former to stress the importance of the African continent for their interpretive frameworks or the latter to highlight "blackness" as a sociocultural construct developed in the Western world. Although this distinction can be very useful, I do not find it systematically sustainable in this book. The two meanings overlap frequently both in the materials that I examine and in my discussions of them; hence my preference for interchangeability.

English vocabulary about "blackness" and black ethnicities is not the same everywhere; terminological preferences vary from region to region and from individual to individual. For example, should one use "African Caribbean" or "Afro-Caribbean" as a synonym for "black Caribbean"? As I was writing this book, I started out with "Afro-Caribbean," which US scholars employ frequently, but I ran into problems when I began to think about black Caribbean immigrants to Canada. "Afro-Caribbean" seems antiquated in Canadian contexts—as does "Afro-Canadian," for that matter. In studies of British culture and society, "Afro-Caribbean," "African Caribbean," "West Indian" (a designation that has not died, contrary to what one might have expected), and the more comprehensive "black British" are all in use. In transnationally oriented academic texts, "African Caribbean," following the example of "[US] African American," is an increasingly common choice. I recognize the possible ambiguity inherent in "African Caribbean" (its suggestion, to some, of "African-born"—the same problem that many initially had with "African American," before the term achieved its current standard status), as well as the difficulty caused by the different terminological preferences in different regional and national contexts. However, since I could not reasonably opt for

"Afro-Caribbean" in some chapters and for "African Caribbean" in others, I chose one variant, the latter, while also frequently employing "black Caribbean" and, at times, "West Indian."

Whenever the term "West Indian" appears in this study, it means the same as "Anglophone Caribbean." In chapter 4—more specifically, in the discussion of collective West Indian identity formation among Caribbean individuals and groups living in Britain during and after World War II—the adjective "West Indian" has, for contextual reasons, at times been a more natural choice than the somewhat unwieldy "Anglophone African Caribbean" or "Anglophone black Caribbean," in part because the chapter includes a reference to the short-lived political entity known as the West Indies Federation.

I use the word "black" rather often (a practice that resonates particularly well with British usage) because it is a practical term in comparative contexts—for example, in discussing black British, black Caribbean, black US, and black Canadian writing in the same breath. Also, since there is no terminological alternative for the socially and culturally constructed abstraction articulated by the noun "blackness," it hardly makes sense to shy away from the adjective either. I should add that particularly in the 1970s and 1980s, "black," in addition to meaning "of African descent," was also used by Britons to refer to various Asian immigrant groups living in Britain. This usage can still be found in many theorizations of "black British literature," especially in studies that focus on the legacies of Empire and highlight interracial solidarity among the decolonized. However, although this book is attuned to the intersectionality of postcolonial and diaspora studies, I consistently use "black" synonymously with "of African descent," regardless of national context.

Ethnoracial terminologies are constantly changing and evolving, both nationally and transnationally. Choices that seem appropriate today may appear outdated tomorrow. However, regardless of such provisionalities of language use, this book places a set of Anglophone novels originating in various African diasporic contexts in dialogue with each other. In so doing, it seeks to make a contribution to scholarly discussions about postwar and contemporary literary representations of black diasporic identity formation.

Acknowledgments

I am deeply indebted to the Department of African American Studies and the Program in American Studies at Yale University for providing me with the intellectual inspiration, instruction, and resources that made this project possible. I had the good fortune to be mentored by two extraordinary scholars, Robert Stepto and Hazel Carby. I am extremely grateful for their expert guidance and their wonderful generosity and kindness. My heartfelt thanks are also due to Elizabeth Alexander, Paul Gilroy, and Matthew Jacobson. The opportunity to train under them was a transformative experience that will always stay with me.

I am, moreover, truly thankful to the Department of American Studies at Brown University, especially Robert G. Lee, then chair, for allowing me to use Brown's excellent libraries as a visiting scholar in fall 2012. I benefited immensely not only from the library privileges but also from conversations with fellow scholars in literary studies and beyond. Beverly Haviland, for example, did me a wonderful favor by discussing trauma theory with me from an angle I had not considered previously.

I thank warmly all my colleagues in my current academic home, the Department of English at Providence College, for camaraderie, intellectual sparring, and good cheer. Friends in American Studies (especially Jeff Johnson, Peggy Reid, Margaret Manchester, Keith Morton, and Eric Bennett), History, Black Studies, Global Studies, and Women's Studies have graciously included me in a broader, interdisciplinary community of passionate and dedicated teacher-scholars. To single out just a few particularly enthusiastic and knowledgeable fellow travelers, at various stages of this project Bruce Graver, John Scanlan, Adrian Weimer, Ted Andrews, Bob Reeder, and Elliott Stevens kindly read portions of this work or took the time to discuss the changing world of academic writing and publishing with me. Jamie Warren, whom I met when he was a visiting scholar at Brown, selflessly did the same.

A special shout-out goes to the librarians at Phillips Memorial Library at Providence College, who always help me out, no matter how much I test their patience. The staff at Sterling Memorial Library at Yale also deserve special commendation for their unfailing assistance over the years. At the University Press of Florida, Shannon McCarthy, Catherine-Nevil Parker, and the rest of the editorial team have been terrific to work with; I thank them for their enthusiasm and seasoned professionalism. Olakunle George and two other external readers solicited by the Press made excellent suggestions that improved the manuscript at key stages of the process. My warmest thanks to them all.

Sarianna Metso Ulrich and Eugene Ulrich have, as always, been extremely kind, supportive, and patient. They have not only talked shop with me in all sorts of useful ways but have also been loyal and untiring friends. Bo Pettersson, Mark Shackleton, Keith Byerman, and Kathy Patterson never fail me, no matter how mundane my questions or requests may be. Many others, too, have been generous fellow-academics-cum-friends—Tom King, Françoise Hamlin, Abigail Brooks, Elliott Gorn, Darra Mulderry, and Sylvia Karlsson-Vinkhuyzen among them. Moreover, special thanks are due to all my Finnish friends; Skyping with them is my lifeline.

Earlier versions of some portions of this book have previously appeared in the following articles: "Beyond the Riverside: War in Toni Morrison's Fiction," *Atlantic Literary Review* 4.1–2 (2003): 133–64; "The Politics of Perception in Herman Melville's *Benito Cereno* and Charles Johnson's *Middle Passage*," *Studies in American Fiction* 33.2 (2005): 229–50; "Through a Black Traveler's Eyes: Claude McKay's *A Long Way from Home*," *American Studies in Scandinavia* 38.1 (2006): 78–98; "Between Camps: Paul Gilroy and the Dilemma of Race," *Post-National Enquiries: Essays on Ethnic and Racial Border Crossings*, edited by Jopi Nyman (Newcastle, UK: Cambridge Scholars Publishing, 2009), 8–29; and "A Journey to 'Partial Cosmopolitanism' in Michael Ondaatje's *Anil's Ghost*," *Studies in Canadian Literature/Études en Littérature Canadienne* 38.2 (2013): 67–87. Such previously printed materials have been reframed and revised for this publication. I thank each journal and publisher most kindly for permission to reprint. I also thank the estate of Claude McKay for permission to quote from his 1920 poem "I Shall Return."

Finally, I dedicate this book to my students, past and present. The questions they ask of texts, of academic approaches, and of the world remind me, on a daily basis, that intellectual life is indeed about passages and border crossings. Grateful for the journey that the task of writing this book took me on, I look forward to what comes next.

Introduction

Passages to (Be)Longing

In the Canadian author Lawrence Hill's 2007 novel, *The Book of Negroes* (named after a 1783 British military ledger), the African-born narrator-protagonist, Aminata Diallo, undergoes the Middle Passage as a child in the winter of 1756–57, spends her youth in South Carolina, escapes from her master during a trip to New York City in the revolutionary spring of 1775, participates in Black Loyalist migrations to Nova Scotia and Sierra Leone, and eventually spends the first years of the nineteenth century in London advocating for the abolition of the Atlantic slave trade. "We are travelling peoples," she remarks more than once in the novel's course, referring to Africans and their descendants.[1] This innocent-sounding word, "travelling," takes on a variety of meanings during her journey through life: the Middle Passage, escapes, evacuations, and voluntary migrations—in brief, a myriad of border crossings, geographical as well as psychological, involuntary as well as willed. Hill gives metaphorical expression to the theoretical concept and empirical reality of the African diaspora by always keeping his protagonist moving, always in a mental and geopolitical space that can never truly become "home" for her. Throughout her forced exile in the New World, Aminata suffers from severe homesickness for the village of her childhood, situated in present-day Mali.[2] However, even after her eventual, hard-won return to West Africa, she once again finds herself in a geographical and ethnic context foreign to her. The locals of Sierra Leone, whose language, ethnicity, and customs are different from hers, never accept her as a "native." After attempting in vain to find the village where she was born and raised (located in a region vastly altered by the slave trade since her childhood), Aminata finally leaves the continent of her origin again, this time voluntarily, in order to participate in the abolitionist movement in London. This turn of the plot, which forms one of the novel's pivotal paradoxes, succinctly captures the diasporic individual's difficulty in defining, establishing, or returning "home." Poignantly, "home" is the novel's last word; yet home remains, even in the final scene, ephemeral and elusive.

Attentive to this diasporic elusiveness of "home," this book, *Precarious Passages*, thematically focuses on black movement and migration, on passages and routes, and on the diasporic longing of the dispersed to belong. On a level beyond thematics, it investigates how one type of cultural production, fiction written in English, participates in the ongoing transnational construction of black diasporic identity within the old Anglophone black Atlantic diaspora.[3] The "old Anglophone black Atlantic diaspora," synonymous with the "old Anglophone African Atlantic diaspora," here denotes the English-speaking descendants, in the Western world, of those Africans who were enslaved in the Americas.[4] This Atlantic group, a product of post-Columbian modernity, consists of most US African Americans, Anglophone African Caribbeans, also known as West Indians (including, in this study, those who have migrated from the Caribbean to other destinations in the Western world, such as Britain, the United States, or Canada, thus creating Caribbean "sub-diasporas" within the old Anglophone black diaspora), and those English-speaking black Canadians whose ancestors experienced perpetual servitude on Canadian soil, particularly as a result of the arrival of Loyalists in Nova Scotia after the American Revolutionary War.

In discussing "consciousness, community, and identity" as key elements of most definitions of diaspora,[5] Aisha Khan notes that "diaspora refers to population movements and displacements and the creation over time of *literal and symbolic communities*."[6] Maureen Warner-Lewis, furthermore, accurately observes that the dispersed communities of the African diaspora (unlike, for example, those of the Jewish diaspora) "are united around no venerable scripted text or texts, nor do they share codified and institutionalized religions."[7] This being the case, secular culture, in its various forms, plays a major role in producing and reproducing the African diasporic imaginary—that is, in creating symbolic communities, in the sense suggested by Khan, and in keeping alive the sentiment that there *is* something that can be called a black diasporic community and something that can be called a black diasporic identity, however loosely and nonprescriptively defined. In order to examine one cultural form that reproduces this imaginary, this book analyzes eleven historically informed novels written by eight contemporary novelists of African or African Caribbean descent, reading these narratives as cultural mediators and interpreters of a collective (that is, African diasporic) memory.[8] Taken together, Charles Johnson's *Middle Passage* (1990), Hill's *The Book of Negroes*, Toni Morrison's *Sula* (1973) and *Tar Baby* (1981), George Lamming's *The Emigrants* (1954), Caryl Phillips's *The Final Passage* (1985), *A State of Independence* (1986), and *Crossing the River* (1993), Andrea Levy's *Small Island* (2004), Cecil Foster's *Sleep On, Beloved* (1995), and Edwidge Danticat's *Breath, Eyes, Memory* (1994) give multifaceted expression to the cultural, socioeconomic, and psychological consequences that involuntary and voluntary migrations have had for black communities and individuals in North America, the Caribbean, and Britain during various stages of black Atlantic history. In so doing, they actively contribute to black diasporic identity formation, which this book understands both as a theme that these novels depict and as a constitutive process in which they participate as cultural products.

Transnational in scope, this study seeks to advance our understanding of contemporary black Anglophone diasporic literature by placing novels usually classified as "African American," "black Canadian," "black British," or "postcolonial African Caribbean" in dialogue with each other. Works falling into these categories are traditionally read, interpreted, and anthologized separately, but this book adopts an integrative approach: rather than, for example, pairing African American fiction either with black Canadian or with black British or with black Caribbean fiction, it reads samples of all these national/regional varieties of black Anglophone diasporic fiction together.[9] This comparative reading strategy demonstrates that the concept of the African diaspora (adapted from Jewish thought and pregnant with the need to remember, mourn, and commemorate the original dispersal) points to a foundational common denominator among the varied cultural identities within the old African diaspora in the Western world—namely, to an awareness, throughout this diaspora, of its historical origin in an ur-event (the Middle Passage and black enslavement in the New World), the memory of which is passed on from generation to generation through education and other cultural practices and products, including novels. In other words, the fiction examined in this book indicates that if cultivating something called African diasporic identity is still a meaningful endeavor within the old black Atlantic diaspora (and they suggest that it is), then the Middle Passage and slavery continue to represent a "usable past" for the purposes of such transnational identity formation.

This book is not intended as a systematic, let alone comprehensive, literary-historical overview of black diasporic fiction. Instead, it demonstrates that the novels analyzed here (even if they focus on *current* imaginaries of "home," belonging, and unbelonging) contextualize black diasporic dilemmas of (be) longing within the political and socioeconomic legacies of the original major propellers of the African Atlantic diaspora—the Atlantic slave trade, slavery, colonialism, and imperialism. *Middle Passage* and *The Book of Negroes* are set in the era of slavery, and sizeable portions of both books address the slave trade and its consequences. The other novels, primarily depicting later eras, include brief references to the Middle Passage and/or slavery in their fabric even when they describe contemporary migrations that do not fit the familiar "from West Africa to the New World" pattern, such as moves from Barbados or Trinidad to Britain or from Jamaica to Canada. That is, even when they discuss antiblack racism in post–World War II and present-day societies, they subtly link their depictions of black diasporic identity formation to the foundational, tragic developments of the history of the black Atlantic, covert as such linkages and allusions may be. Of course, not every single black-authored novel published in the contemporary Anglophone Atlantic world uses the strategy of referencing the Middle Passage and enslavement to depict present-day structural antiblack racism. However, the novels analyzed in this book do, and in employing this method they exemplify a larger trend[10] and call attention to their shared self-understanding as novels of the African Atlantic diaspora.

To elaborate, four interrelated arguments inform this book. First, I claim that as my selected novelists reimagine the lives of uprooted groups and individuals in various stages and settings of black history, they actively contribute to the ongoing transnational formation of black diasporic identity. (I understand "black diasporic identity" fluidly and use the term nonnormatively. "Black diasporic consciousness" and "black diasporic awareness" would be equally appropriate lexical choices.) It is common knowledge that novels have, in many countries, significantly participated in shaping national identities. What is acknowledged less often is that novels can have a similar role in forming transnational identities as well. Transnational communities were not what Benedict Anderson had in mind when he famously called modern nation-states "imagined communities,"[11] but much of the logic that he articulated applies to transnational contexts, too. While national identities indeed are, in many ways, "product[s] of collective imagination," as Arjun Appadurai elaborates in *Modernity at Large* (1996),[12] the same is also true of their transnational counterparts, as Martin Sökefeld emphasizes in "Mobilizing in Transnational Space" (2006).[13] Black diasporic identity formation is a prime example of an ongoing, dynamic construction of a transnational awareness and self-understanding. Fiction—particularly historical fiction, broadly defined—plays an important role in this process because it is, as a medium and genre, extremely well suited to portray the ambivalences that characterize the diasporic longing of the scattered and displaced to belong.

Second, in depicting black diasporic (be)longing and identity formation, my selected novels evoke (some quite subtly) slavery and colonial modernity, which ushered in the post-Columbian African Atlantic diaspora, and examine their oppressive legacies. By summoning the Middle Passage and enslavement as a past that is "usable" in the process of forging, maintaining, and developing a black diasporic identity, these novels place themselves in a continuum initiated by poetry and activist nonfiction written by African-descended Anglophone authors in the latter half of the eighteenth century. As Michelle M. Wright observes in *Becoming Black* (2004), black diasporic identity has, from the very beginning, "been produced in contradiction"[14] because, as James Sidbury notes in *Becoming African in America* (2007), "[t]he terms 'Africa' and 'African' and the perception that the continent of Africa (or the sub-Saharan portion of it) comprises a unified cultural and/or 'racial' unit are European in origin."[15] As a result of chattel slavery in the New World, "African" quickly became a pejorative term, a *tabula* onto which Europeans and American-based white colonists started to project an essentialist—and tragically offensive— understanding of "racial" blackness.[16] During the latter half of the eighteenth century, however, African-descended writers living in the West began providing Anglophone readers with an alternative understanding of black, or African-derived, identity,[17] as Sidbury points out in discussing Phillis Wheatley and Ignatius Sancho:

> Both [writers] were aware of the ethnic diversity on the [African] continent and understood that it undercut any notion of an indigenous "African" identity. Both responded by creating *a narrative of African identity that took its meaning from the diaspora* rather than from the conditions on the continent, a narrative that began with enslavement and the experience of the Middle Passage. Peoples of various ethnic backgrounds became "African" together by virtue of sharing the oppression of Atlantic slavery. The resulting sense of African identity was forged through the common experience of slavery and did not rest on a notion of an essential difference between "Africans" and other peoples.[18]

Similarly, my selected novelists' allusions to the Middle Passage and enslavement speak to the choices that these authors make while participating in the continuing construction of black diasporic identity, regardless of whether they belong to the civil rights generation of African American novelists, or to the cultural-nationalist generation of Caribbean authors, or to a later generation of contemporary transnational British, Canadian, American, or Caribbean writers.

My third argument is that much can be gained through a dually focused thematic approach that *both* examines black novelists' representations of diaspora *and* explores their depictions of more temporarily and loosely understood experiences of displacement or dislocation. The concept of diaspora reveals an awareness, across the old African diaspora in the West, of how and why Africans were scattered circum-Atlantically during post-Columbian modernity. It also facilitates reflections on the ever-complex relationship between transnationalism, national identity, and other modes of belonging. More fleetingly construed instances of temporary displacement, in turn, in diasporic fiction often illuminate, point to, or metaphorically represent predicaments that are, ultimately, diasporic in nature. That is, an inclusive approach to black novelists' treatment of uprootedness reveals that diasporic sensibilities frequently emerge at unexpected junctures, manifesting themselves in narratives of various types of black displacement and thus informing passages in which their presence might not be anticipated. Morrison's and Phillips's stories of African American troops' experiences overseas, discussed in chapter 3, illustrate this logic.

Another example of the same logic, from a novel that falls beyond the scope of this book, helps to clarify my point: Morrison's sixth novel, *Jazz*, which is mainly set in Harlem in 1926 but also offers flashbacks to the slavery era, ultimately casts the early-twentieth-century Great Migration of African Americans from the rural southern countryside to northern cities as an episode in the centuries-long and untraceably complex sequence of events propelled by the forced ur-migration of black people to the New World. Morrison's rendering of the Great Migration resonates, in other words, with time-transcending concerns about the multiple ways in which community and communality can be lost under the pressures caused by various "by-products" of modernity—whether such pressures are brought on by slavery and its legacies, by black participation in wars initiated by white Others and fought on foreign soil, or by early-twentieth-century forms of urban individualism.[19] My discussion in chapter 3 addresses similar concerns in *Sula* and *Tar Baby* and in Phillips's *Crossing the River*, particularly from the angle of how Morrison and Phillips connect African Americans soldiers' experience of war as a temporary traumatic dislocation with the diasporic ur-trauma of forced displacement and dispossession.

My fourth claim is that the novels discussed in this book reflect what I term, referencing W.E.B. Du Bois's intellectual and terminological legacy (and Paul Gilroy's and Samir Dayal's dialogues with it), a "diasporic double consciousness."[20] On the one hand, my selected novelists portray the possibility of belonging—of any uncritically embraced national belonging, in particular—as if it were, in itself, a "fiction" for them or their protagonists.[21] In practice, this dilemma often translates as a character's sense of being caught, legally or emotionally, in a no-man's-land between diasporic identification and national citizenship. As Gilroy remarks, "Diaspora identification exists outside of, and sometimes in opposition to, the political forms and codes of modern citizenship."[22] In fact, some scholars have experimented with the term "African diaspora citizenship," which seeks to elevate black diasporic belonging to the status of a metaphorically understood "citizenship."[23] On the other hand, my selected authors depict their geographically rerouted characters' desire to have a framework of identification transcending temporary, fleeting social roles as a fundamental human need that cannot be suppressed without incurring emotional or psychological damage. To the extent that it is possible at all to identify any shared dynamics characterizing the diverse body of contemporary black diasporic literature, such dynamics coalesce around this thematic duality: the dis-/relocated protagonists' sense of not belonging *and* their simultaneous yearning to experience fulfilling human connection and communion in a place they could call "home."

Language, Geography, and the Old and New African Diasporas

Five further remarks on language and geography will help to clarify the scope of this book and the limits of the claims that the text makes. First, I fully recognize, of course, the existence and significance of the old Francophone, Hispanophone, Lusophone, and Dutch-speaking African diasporas, as well as the presence of myriad new African diasporas in Europe and in the Western Hemisphere. However, these diasporas fall beyond the purview of this book (with the relative exception, explained below, of the inclusion of the debut novel of Haitian-born Edwidge Danticat, whose native context is Francophone). A single study could hardly do justice to the nuances of all these linguistic, literary, and intellectual traditions. Moreover, I do not possess a universal definition of "the" black diaspora applicable to all diasporic populations of African descent, nor do I have much faith in the viability or usefulness of pursuing such a totalizing definition. Today, even the old Anglophone African Atlantic diaspora is characterized by considerable ethnic, national, socioeconomic, sociocultural, religious, and political diversity, as well as by markedly different interplays of race, class, and gender in different locations and microcontexts;[24] hence my interest in a common denominator that may supply the term "black diasporic identity" with *a* shared referent in the context of *this* diaspora but does not undermine this diaspora's polyvocality, which is powerfully evident both in real life and in its literary representations.

Second, although this book investigates black diasporic identity formation within Anglophone parameters, my goal is not to try to inappropriately universalize the Anglophone experience. Rather, my focus on the English language and on the geographical triangle of North America, the Anglophone Caribbean, and Britain indicates that the former British Empire and its racial practices constitute the historical and geopolitical background for this book—as does, relatedly, the contemporary status of the United States, once an assortment of British settler colonies, as a neo-empire. As Michelle Ann Stephens argues in *Black Empire* (2005), "diaspora is precisely that space of blackness that has been shaped by empire's international reach and global designs."[25] Although the theoretical discourses and experiential realities of diaspora and empire are not identical, this book—while foregrounding diaspora—acknowledges their intersectionality.

Third, while Britain is only one of the former European empires relevant to the study of the past and present of the African diaspora, the role that the British had in shaping "the enslaved Atlantic" was pivotal, as James Walvin notes in *Making the Black Atlantic* (2000), because "at the height of the Atlantic slave system, the British shipped more Africans than any other nation; their slave colonies disgorged produce (and its associated prosperity) on an unparalleled scale, and Britain itself benefited from slavery to a degree which largely goes unrecognized."[26] Indeed, despite the multidisciplinary attention that the English-speaking African diaspora and its cultures have already received, exploring how contemporary black Anglophone authors grapple with the complex legacy of the British Empire is still a relevant intellectual endeavor.

Fourth, even though black Anglophone novelists have traditionally originated from countries or regions that once were part of the British Empire, this situation is changing rapidly, or rather, has already changed. The United States, in particular, is now home to novelists of the African and African Caribbean diasporas who write in English but are first-generation or 1.5-generation[27] immigrants from ex-colonies of former European empires other than Britain. Edwidge Danticat, from Haiti, and Junot Díaz, from the Dominican Republic, are among the best-known examples of this development. Acknowledging this shift, this book concludes with a brief discussion of Danticat's first novel, which, while partly concerned with a Kreyòl-speaking community in a former colony of the French Empire, was written in English and converses with US immigration and socioeconomics. The inclusion of a brief discussion of *Breath, Eyes, Memory* in this book's final chapter tests and expands the boundaries of the black Anglophone diasporic novel and points to a future that has, in effect, already arrived.

Fifth, the Western world is, as noted, also home to what many now call "new African diasporas" (the title of a 2003 book edited by Khalid Koser),[28] including new Anglophone African diasporas. Although the new African diasporas are beyond the purview of this book, it is important to at least mention them here, however briefly. This term refers to Africans who are recent arrivals—or offspring of relatively recent arrivals—in Europe or the Western Hemisphere, rather than descendants of those who experienced the Middle Passage and slavery. Some are refugees; others are voluntary migrants, although they have, in many cases, left behind circumstances marred by the various legacies of colonialism. The presence of these populations in the West poses new questions for those who create typologies of diasporas and research demographic distributions within the African diaspora. Critically acclaimed Anglophone novelists (beyond such canonical examples as Wole Soyinka and the late Chinua Achebe), including ones who write about movement and migration, have already emerged from these groups—Nigerian-born, US-based Chimamanda Ngozi Adichie and Okey Ndibe, for instance. On the one hand, the works of these authors are rapidly changing the face of the black Anglophone diasporic novel. On the other hand, as these writers live and work in the Western world, they operate in a racialized West where pejorative stereotypical notions of blackness, created in the era of colonialism and slavery, are not extinct. The new African diasporas are therefore connected to the old, in the sense that all individuals of African descent are at the risk of facing antiblack racism in the West, regardless of the genealogies of their (or their families' or ancestors') arrival in Europe or the Americas. For this reason, some or much of what this book discusses is also relevant, albeit indirectly, to the study of the new African diasporas.

Diasporic Interrogations

As even the brief remarks above demonstrate, it is no longer possible to explain what the key concept of this book, "diaspora," means by simply referencing the word's ancient origins or the notion of the "victim diaspora."[29] As Jana Evans Braziel and Anita Mannur remark in their introduction to the 2003 anthology *Theorizing Diaspora*, "theorizations of diaspora have emerged in area studies, ethnic studies, and cultural studies as a major site of contestation."[30] Their word choice, "contestation," is apt. In the revised 2008 edition of his 1997 landmark study, *Global Diasporas*, Robin Cohen identifies four phases of diaspora studies,[31] starting with the study of "victim diasporas,"[32] also known as "forced," "classical," or "prototypical" diasporas; this terminology refers, as is well known, to diasporas that have their historical origin in a traumatic or catastrophic event. While this first phase began with examinations of the Jewish experience, from the 1960s and 1970s onward—"[e]xcluding some earlier casual references," as Cohen concedes[33]—the designation "victim diaspora" has been extended to apply to the African, Armenian, and Irish diasporas, in particular.[34] What Cohen regards as the second (the 1980s and onward) and third (from the mid-1990s) phases saw a gradual broadening and diversification, and eventually an explosive expansion, of meanings applied to "diaspora."[35] What for Cohen distinguishes the third phase, which he sees as being driven by radical social constructionism, was its attempt "to decompose two of the major building blocks previously delimiting and demarcating the diasporic idea, namely 'homeland' and 'ethnic/religious community.'"[36] Although Cohen is highly critical of this development, he nevertheless acknowledges that the positive impacts of third-phase scholarship included a new drive toward a "more sophisticated understanding of shifts in the homeland-diaspora relationship, the ways in which a diaspora is mobilized and how diaspora studies connect to post-colonial studies."[37] Finally, what Cohen calls the ongoing "consolidation" phase is characterized by a renewed search for definable criteria for "diaspora"—not a simplistic return to the first phase, but a complex conceptual negotiation that seeks to *both* incorporate the second- and third-phase emphases on inclusivity, hybridity, and deterritorialization *and* prevent "diaspora" from becoming such a comprehensive umbrella term that almost all humans may find themselves to be diasporic, in which case the concept is no longer useful as an analytic tool.[38]

The following aspects of this book build on third- and fourth-phase scholars' emphases: an interest in the intersectionality of diaspora and empire, which is elaborated in chapter 4, in connection with the postwar black Caribbean diaspora in Britain; attentiveness to gender, especially to women's diasporic experiences (discussed in chapters 2, 4, and 5), rather than an overvalorization of "the mobility of masculine subjects as the primary agents of diasporic formation,"[39] to quote Tina Campt and Deborah A. Thomas's stern 2008 critique of masculinist "diasporic hegemonies";[40] an examination of lateral diasporic connections within the old Anglophone black Atlantic diaspora; an exploration of the complications embedded in potentially teleological narratives of "return" (a topic addressed in chapters 1, 2, and 5); a relinquishment, to quote Campt and Thomas again, of "any claim to a *universal* or shared definition of diaspora"[41] and, consequently, a humble acknowledgement of the necessarily limited scope of this volume. However, rather than seeking to deconstruct all the elements of "diaspora" that were deemed constitutive during the first and second phases, I agree with Cohen that the focus on an ethnic or religious community (in this study, on the Anglophone African diaspora in the West) and the sense that "diaspora" in *some* way includes *some* kind of reference to ancestral origins (however mythologized, unlocatable, or deterritorialized such origins may be) provide the basic building blocks for discussing "diaspora."

My approach to "diaspora" also resonates with Paul Gilroy's following remark in *Against Race* (2000), although neither Gilroy nor I seek to reduce all aspects of diaspora to the "victim" model:

> [The word "diaspora"] identifies a relational network, characteristically produced by forced dispersal and reluctant scattering. It is not just a word of movement, though purposive, desperate movement is integral to it. Under this sign, push factors are a dominant influence. The urgency they introduce makes diaspora more than a voguish synonym for peregrination or nomadism. As the biographies of Equiano and [Phillis] Wheatley suggest, life itself is at stake in the way the word connotes flight following the threat of violence rather than freely chosen experiences of displacement. Slavery, pogroms, indenture, genocide, and other unnameable terrors have all figured in the constitution of diasporas and the reproduction of diaspora consciousness.[42]

Current discussions of diaspora frequently—and fully legitimately—transcend issues of oppression and victimization; as Geneviève Fabre and Klaus Benesch remarked in 2004, "with globalization in full swing, attention is shifting to the global dimensions of diaspora, to traveling circuits, border crossings and constant geographical dispersal and redistribution."[43] But even so, and while acknowledging the full spectrum of life experiences (across any imaginable socioeconomic, gendered, educational, cultural, and geographical boundaries) within the contemporary African diaspora, my primary sources nevertheless concur with Gilroy that it is vital not to lose sight of the history and consequences of the confluence of imperialism, preindustrial capitalism, and antiblack racism that originally propelled this diaspora into being. Gilroy's deliberately poignant and strongly worded reminder that the African diaspora was initially brought into existence by terror, rather than by the attractive pull of globalization, is foundational for this book's examination of the black diasporic imagination in postwar and contemporary fiction.

Overall, my approach to the African diaspora particularly aligns itself with the theorizations of James Clifford, the late Stuart Hall, and Gilroy. Of these three, I owe my most acute intellectual debt to Gilroy, although I seek to emphasize diasporic women's experiences and the intersectionality of gender, race, and class more than *The Black Atlantic* (1993) did.[44] Three aspects of Gilroy's diasporic theory are particularly important to my project. I have already mentioned the first, the importance of keeping in sight the origin of the old black Atlantic diaspora in post-Columbian slavery and colonial modernity. The second is Gilroy's emphasis on cultural hybridity—which, in fact, demonstrates how strongly his insights on diaspora have been inspired by Clifford and especially by Hall. Clifford's foundational work on traveling culture, including his pioneering insistence on routes rather than roots, is extremely well known,[45] and Hall's various articulations of diaspora and identity formation, including his consistent insistence on hybridity and diversity as key concepts of black diasporic interrogations, are among the most often quoted expressions of the field's fundamental ideas. Gilroy's writings, too—resonating with Hall's emphasis on hybridity and with the spirit of James Clifford's "The Pure Products Go Crazy" (a chapter subtitle that Clifford borrowed from a poem by Williams Carlos Williams)[46]—argue against any type of racial, ethnic, nationalist, and cultural purism.

Third, I wish to spotlight Gilroy's antiessentialist understanding of race.[47] When Gilroy, in *The Black Atlantic*, discusses the problems that any excessive romanticization of Africa and African-derived connectedness may cause,[48] he in effect presents a critique of the Afrocentric movement of the 1980s and early 1990s and, in the process, criticizes racial essentialism. He advocates "diaspora" as an alternative, emphasizing this concept's "ability to pose the relationship between ethnic sameness and differentiation: a *changing* same."[49]

In Gilroy's usage, the term "changing same," borrowed from the late LeRoi Jones/Amiri Baraka,[50] suggests not only that black identities are malleable and individually unique, but also that "[b]lack identity . . . is lived as a coherent (if not always stable) experiential sense of self."[51] That is, he argues that diasporic identification provides a unique way of navigating between the Scylla of racial essentialism and the Charybdis of *the* kind of antiessentialism that only sees division, difference, and fragmentation when observing "the fragile psychological, emotional, and cultural correspondences which connect diaspora populations [of African descent]."[52] In Gilroy's view, the lexicon of diasporic identification facilitates discussions about black identities and their formation without the dead weight of racial absolutism. This is the key, and my approach in this book, which emphasizes antiessentialism, taps into the potential of this insight.

Admittedly, the caveat that Brent Hayes Edwards offers in *The Practice of Diaspora* (2003) is ever important and relevant: "The use of the term *diaspora* . . . implies neither that it offers the comfort of abstraction, an easy recourse to origins, nor that it provides a foolproof anti-essentialism."[53] The search for precise articulations of the relationship between racial antiessentialism and black diasporic identity is an ongoing process, not a finished one. (Hence, for example, Edwards's 2003 conceptual experimentation with the French term *décalage*,[54] which has since been engaged by some scholars but has not been taken up by the academic community at large.) Edwards is on the mark when he says that the concept of diaspora "forces us to articulate discourses of cultural and political linkage only through and across difference in full view of the risks of that endeavor."[55] As this book examines literary representations of black migrations through the Door of No Return and beyond, it conceptually relies on "diaspora" yet all along acknowledges that articulating connectivity "through and across difference" is a fragile enterprise and a complex, continuing process.

"Blackness" and Racial Antiessentialism

Because this book's diasporic hermeneutics are in part inspired by racial antiessentialism, which here translates as a desire to focus on cultural memory rather than to reify "race," a few words about "blackness" are warranted. The humanities and social sciences have by now proceeded beyond the phase of vainly (and, more often than not, oppressively) attempting to theorize an "ontological blackness," or of trying to argue that all persons of African descent share some universal "black essence." No one has ever been able to define either "the black essence" or "the white essence" in any objective or universally applicable manner. The present scholarly consensus, of which I fully approve, is that neither "blackness" nor "whiteness" is anything ontologically definable. Both are semiotic constructs whose meanings are defined, and constantly redefined, socioculturally.[56]

Many scholars nevertheless want to keep "blackness" on the cultural and social agenda: they emphasize black diversity *and*, at the same time, view "blackness" as a signifier that can and should be filled with a content (or, more accurately, with an endless multiplicity of contents), rather than as a term that is rendered unnecessary by its very plurality and indefinability.[57] There are others who, while fully acknowledging black diversity and polyvocality, remain unconvinced of the future usefulness of either "blackness" or "whiteness" for the global human community. For example, the legal scholar Harlon L. Dalton notes that "Whiteness is meaningless in the absence of Blackness; the same holds in reverse," and he adds, sarcastically yet seriously, that "race itself would be meaningless if it were not a fault line along which power, prestige, and respect are distributed."[58] Gilroy, moreover, whose first three monographs can be read as an internally evolving project on diaspora, nation, and race,[59] in *Against Race* offers a substantive book-length argumentation against race-thinking[60]—paradoxical as this may seem to some, given that Gilroy is a leading theorist of the black Atlantic. (It is crucial to note, though, that while Gilroy critiques essentialist understandings of "race," he also stresses, throughout his oeuvre, that it is necessary to have analytical tools and language for critiquing past and present rac*isms* and their oppressive consequences.)[61] In yet another twist to the color-coded language of "race," in the contemporary United States such racial concepts as "redness" and "yellowness" seem crude and are seldom used in everyday speech; not much empowering discourse exists today that celebrates either of these two terms.[62] With Native and Asian Americanness, prevalent US discourses now avoid the lexicon of "color," which inevitably emphasizes "race," and instead foreground ethnocultural heritage. As this example demonstrates, respectful recognition of ethnocultural difference and distinctiveness is entirely possible without recourse to racialization.

Yet, there is no doubt that the lexicon of "blackness" and "whiteness" currently persists in the United States and beyond. The past and present racial power relations and their various sociocultural ramifications, including both (the blatantly racist) white pride and (the more culturally celebratory) black pride, have kept these two racially charged concepts alive.⁶³ All literary authors discussed in this book have, therefore, so far lived their lives in an era when the terms "blackness" and "whiteness" have been actively used both in common parlance and in scholarly discourse. Particularly in essays and interviews, the authors themselves employ them too, or at the very least use the vocabulary of "black people" and "white people" or some other related variation of the race-inflected language of "blackness" and "whiteness." The racial terms "black" and "white" are still with us, and it is difficult to have discussions about culture without them.

Under these complex circumstances, and in the midst of the boundless diversity that characterizes the old Anglophone African diaspora in the West, what is it, then, that in this context might provide "black diasporic identity" with a minimalistically defined common denominator differentiating this term from a completely free-floating signifier? My book's response to this question resonates with the Trinidadian Canadian author Dionne Brand's eloquent reference, in her self-designed epigraph to *A Map to the Door of No Return: Notes to Belonging* (2001), to "the Door of No Return which is illuminated in the consciousness of Blacks."⁶⁴ This means, first of all, that in one way or another each novel analyzed in this study keeps in sight the old African diaspora's origin in a violent uprooting; and, second, that I read these novels as reflecting an antiessentialist understanding of black diasporic identity that draws on collective remembrance of the originary event. This originary "event," of course, in actuality consisted of a long series of events spread across centuries during the Atlantic slave trade and slavery. In Brand's usage, "the Door of No Return" synecdochically represents the entire history of the Middle Passage and enslavement.

In discussing migration, Aisha Khan offers a conceptually important remark on diaspora: "The difference between 'diaspora' and 'migration' is not simply about . . . the creation over time of communities symbolically connected to ancestral origins. It is also about consciously interpreting one's culture as indelibly marked . . . by the experience of being uprooted."⁶⁵ My diasporic hermeneutics reinforce Khan's emphasis on diasporic groups' deliberate and persistent cultural self-representation as uprooted communities. Rather than essentializing "race" or getting mired either in controversies about black cultural "authenticity" or in debates about "roots" in a geographically locatable sense, my approach to the post-Columbian African Atlantic diaspora highlights the originary event (the Middle Passage and New World slavery) and the ongoing cultural mediation of its collective remembrance.

Diaspora, Collective Memory, and Cultural Mediation

Brand above employs the term "the consciousness of Blacks," and I, too, use the phrase "black diasporic consciousness" in discussions of individual and collective diasporic self-identification. In my usage, "consciousness" denotes not an ontologically or mystically conceived layer of the human psyche, but, rather, an outcome of both education and sociocultural mediation/interpretation. The latter, in turn, covers a broad spectrum of cultural activity and production, including literary art. My approach, in other words, highlights the role of cultural mediation in the emergence and development of collective memory and identity. Admittedly, articulating what we actually mean when we speak of the "memory" of a collective—here, the "memory" of a large diasporic population, the old Anglophone African Atlantic diaspora—is a complex enterprise that remains a work in progress in the humanities and humanistically oriented social sciences. Kerwin Lee Klein's magisterial overview of what he, in *From History to Theory* (2011), terms "the emergence of *memory* in historical discourse"[66] makes this processual and incomplete state of affairs very clear. While my goal in this book is not to arrive at a comprehensive definition of "collective memory," I actively avoid what Klein, less than appreciatively, terms "indulging mystical transpositions of individual psychological phenomena onto imaginary collectives."[67] Rather than postulating a Jungian collective unconscious, I refrain from hypothesizing any ontologically conceived "overarching group mind"[68] with a life or essence of its own and, instead, underscore the importance of the cultural mediation of trauma as I examine the role of the Middle Passage and slavery in black diasporic memory and in the ongoing construction of black diasporic identity. In the realm of cultural mediation, literary art, notably, plays an important role as a reconstructor and interpreter of history.

More specifically, the way in which I use and interpret "collective memory" is inspired by Ron Eyerman's *Cultural Trauma: Slavery and the Formation of African American Identity* (2001). Eyerman writes as a sociologist, not as a psychoanalytically oriented literary critic; the latter have their own distinguishable takes on trauma theory (including Cathy Caruth's influential approach to trauma, which will be evoked in chapter 3). Rather than focusing on individual memory, Eyerman, taking his cue from such second-generation Durkheimian sociologists as Maurice Halbwachs, theorizes "collective memory" with reference to collective identity[69] and to the question of "how societies [or groups within them] remember."⁷⁰ Eyerman writes about the emergence of African American identity in the United States after the Civil War, but the gist of his argumentation is applicable to black identity formation within the old African diaspora more generally. He suggests that even though post–Civil War African American generations had not experienced the trauma of slavery directly, it nevertheless "came to be central to their attempts to forge a collective identity out of its remembrance."⁷¹ Most importantly, he discusses slavery as a trauma that, "[a]s cultural process, . . . is mediated through various forms of representation and linked to the reformation of collective identity and the reworking of collective memory."⁷² In other words, Eyerman emphasizes the importance of cultural mediation: after the fact, trauma is not inscribed in collective group consciousness in any automatic or mechanical way, but needs to be passed on actively and given meaning culturally if it is to become part of a group's collective identity; the same point has been made repeatedly in Holocaust studies. Such mediation always involves interpretation or "meaning-making," or what Eyerman terms a "meaning struggle."⁷³ Groups, like individuals, actively construct their identities by determining what a past traumatic experience means for their self-understanding.⁷⁴ My book reinforces this valuable point, whose significance is not limited to the United States but also applies to black diasporic contexts more universally.

Eyerman particularly highlights the role of "intellectuals" as cultural mediators of the "socially constructed, historically rooted collective memory [that] functions to create social solidarity in the present."⁷⁵ He elaborates that "[i]ntellectuals in this sense can be film directors and singers of songs"⁷⁶—that is, artists, including novelists, one might add. Caryl Phillips says as much in his 1987 travelogue, *The European Tribe*: "[I]n a situation in which history is distorted, the literature of a people often becomes its history, its writers the keepers of the past, present, and future. In this situation a writer can infuse a people with a sense of their own unique identity and spiritually kindle a fire of resistance."⁷⁷ Even though the novels examined in this book cannot be reduced to representatives of any single cause, they do portray moments of community/solidarity based on black diasporic identification or, alternatively, depict fictional characters' struggles with the question of what, if any, practical conclusions one should draw from one's identification with the African diaspora. In so doing, these novels, as cultural products, participate in the larger sociocultural process of shaping black diasporic identities.

Possible Pitfalls of the "Middle Passage Epistemology"

Because of my frequent references to the Middle Passage as a culturally and transgenerationally transmitted originary trauma, my intellectual position may at first glance seem identical with what Michelle M. Wright, both in "Middle Passage Blackness and Its Diasporic Discontents" (2013) and in *Physics of Blackness* (2015), terms the "Middle Passage epistemology"[78]—an "epistemology" that she critiques sternly. I here respond to two criticisms that she presents in her important and thought-provoking 2013 article.

Wright expresses, first of all, the legitimate concern that the Middle Passage epistemology may too monolithically view "all Africans and peoples of African descent as victims of slavery and/or racism" and therefore disregard "all forms of black agency."[79] I emphasize, in response, that although my approach highlights the African diaspora's origin in trauma, my discussions of black diasporic self-definitions extend beyond narrowly addressing literary representations of past and present victimization. *Both* poles of the dialectic of victimization and black agency are present in the very impulse, characteristic of much of the fiction analyzed in this book, to trace the birth of modern black diasporic subjectivity back to the Middle Passage. Arlene R. Keizer argues in *Black Subjects* (2004) that "[r]ather than using representations of slavery primarily to protest past and present oppression ... black writers have begun to represent slavery in order to explore the process of *self-creation* under extremely oppressive conditions."[80] The point that she makes about contemporary narratives of slavery applies to contemporary literary representations of the Middle Passage as well.

That is, on the one hand, fictional Middle Passage narratives—as well as the often brief and covert allusions to the Middle Passage found in black fiction set in later eras—mourn and lament what was historically lost as a result of the slave trade and depict the emergence of a socially constructed and oppressively racialized "blackness" in the New World. On the other hand, the same texts also celebrate black agency and highlight the radically innovative strategies of survival, sociocultural acclimatization, political resistance, and identity formation that enslaved Africans and their descendants developed in the Americas and Europe. This duality is tangibly present, for example, in *Feeding the Ghosts* (1997) by British Guyanese, US-based Fred D'Aguiar. A fictional retelling of the horrific *Zong* massacre that took place in the Caribbean in November 1781, the novel not only depicts the horror but also celebrates the courage, resourcefulness, and resilience of the fictive female survivor Mintah.

Similarly, both aspects of the dialectic of suffering and agency are foundational for my selected novelists' understanding of black diasporic identity, informing their treatment of the Middle Passage as well as later black migrations.

I would like to add, parenthetically, that in *Forging Diaspora* (2010) Frank A. Guridy remarks that at an early stage of his project he was primarily interested in "the dynamics of racialization" in Cuba, but as he was composing his book, his focus shifted "away from a history of racialization to a study of diaspora-making."[81] I, too, initially believed that my book would concentrate on literary representations of racializing encounters—that is, on contemporary fictional equivalents of those passages in Olaudah Equiano's *Interesting Narrative* (1789) in which he relates how his early encounters with whites "made" him black on the slave ship and beyond. As Hazel Carby observes, Equiano's memoir depicts his "transformation into a racialized subject": Equiano "steps into the place of the recognitions given to him by others" while being "forcibly inducted into modernity as a subject."[82] However, although examining racialization remains an important part of this book's texture, this study has evolved to emphasize more broadly what Guridy calls "diaspora-making"—that is, the formation of black diasporic identity on diasporans' own terms. In the novels examined here, such active "diaspora-making" is represented by black characters asserting agency against oppressive forces, establishing meaningful and existentially rich lives in the New World against all odds, and challenging any pejorative definitions of blackness created by the racializing white Others.

As Carby's comment on Equiano implies, racialization (here primarily understood as white-authored victimization) can be viewed as an example of interpellation, in the sense explained by Louis Althusser in "Ideology and Ideological State Apparatuses" (1970/1971), if his conceptual apparatus—in particular, his pivotal point that "Ideology Interpellates Individuals as Subjects"[83]—is applied to "race."[84] On the one hand, such applied Althusserianism suggests that New World Africans and their descendants were compelled, through naming ("hailing") and oppressive use of force, to "recognize" what society's ideology of race considered their blackness, and they then internalized this imposed identity position and became "black subjects" internally, too. On the other hand, Judith Butler, in discussing Althusserian interpellation in relation to sex/sexism and race/racism in *Bodies That Matter* (1993), asks a vital question: "If one comes into discursive life through being called or hailed in injurious terms, how might one occupy the interpellation by which one is already occupied to direct the possibilities of resignification against the aims of violation?"[85] She goes on to argue that such subversive "occupying" and "resignification" (reflective of agency and cunning resistance) *is* possible through a repetition, displacement, and reversal of the interpellation's original aim: "The compulsion to repeat an injury is not necessarily the compulsion to repeat the injury in the same way or to stay fully within the traumatic orbit of that injury."[86] Indeed, even when the novels examined in this book reference the Middle Passage and enslavement, they participate in a process of affirmative black diasporic identity formation: they highlight black agency as well as emphasize that black subjectivity's nuances and complexity transcend any simplistic dichotomy of victimization and celebration. Such contributions can be read as examples of the type of displacement of an interpellation's original aim that Butler postulates and encourages, and they directly address Wright's first concern.

Wright's second concern is that the Middle Passage epistemology "rejects ... black difference."[87] Although this book focuses on fiction produced in the old Anglophone black Atlantic diaspora, I do not pit "Middle Passage blackness" and other types of black diasporic experiences against each other or ideologically marginalize the diasporic experiences of those individuals and groups of African descent whose ancestors did not leave Africa on slave ships. Also, despite my emphasis on a common black diasporic cultural *memory*, I all along acknowledge that "the" black diasporic *experience* contains a vast amount of internal diversity because of factors related to gender, socioeconomic class, and contextual sociocultural differences, and also because of constant cross-cultural cross-pollination in most regions where black diasporans live. As Stuart Hall famously wrote in "Cultural Identity and Diaspora" (1990), "The diaspora experience is defined ... not by essence or purity, but by the recognition of a necessary heterogeneity and diversity; by a conception of 'identity' which lives with and through, not despite, difference; by hybridity."[88] Diasporic sensibilities, rather than being monolithic or static, necessarily keep renewing and transforming themselves in response to the immense variety of life experiences in the diaspora. The range of fictionalized migration experiences discussed in this book attests to my emphasis on black diversity and difference: the analyzed experiences vary in terms of geographical and temporal settings, the migrating subjects' gender and class positions, and the migrants' individual responses to their changing circumstances.

However, rather than merely highlighting black diversity and polyvocality for its own sake, my analyses frequently bring the discussion back to the original propellers of the old African diaspora, in order to underscore the coexistence of the past and the present in black diasporic identification and consciousness. I concur with Gilroy that "diaspora is a concept that problematizes the cultural and historical mechanics of belonging" and "destroys the *naive* invocation of common memory as the basis of particularity by drawing attention to the contingent political dynamics of commemoration."[89] Nevertheless, by choosing to highlight narrative acts that pass on this very "common memory," this book demonstrates that literary referencing of the tragic past of the African diaspora does not have to result in a mechanical or naive repetition of a shibboleth. Rather, it can serve—and, in the treatment of the novelists studied here, does serve—as an inquiry into the complex dynamics of diasporic (be)longing and as an insight into the genealogies of various current black predicaments, socioeconomic as well as existential.

Africa and "Return"

No matter where one goes with diasporic interrogations in the era of globalization, Africa (albeit real Africa, in its multiplicity, or a "rememoried" and possibly mythologized homeland in diasporans' cultural imagination) can never be ignored. One way or another, Africa is always part of the relevant cartography and empirical and mental geography. Hall's comment, in "Negotiating Caribbean Identities" (1995), on the role of Africa in black diasporic identity formation is highly perceptive: "The [black] political movements in the New World in the twentieth century have had to pass through the reencounter with Africa. The African diasporas of the New World have been in one way or another incapable of finding a place in modern history without the symbolic return to Africa."[90] True, what Edwards in "The Uses of 'Diaspora'" (2004) terms the "quagmire of origins"[91] surely *is* a quagmire, considering the centuries that have passed since the Atlantic slave trade began. Nevertheless, Africa—named or unnamed, real or mythical—hovers in the background of diasporic interrogations and needs to be engaged and considered.

The consideration of Africa has gone through multiple, and in part chronologically overlapping, phases in scholarship on black people's history and sociocultural experience in the New World. In the eyes of many current African Americanists, much of the work of the prominent sociologist E. Franklin Frazier (1894–1962) epitomizes the now antiquated paradigm that placed a strong emphasis on the Middle Passage having all but completely disconnected the black people of the Americas from Africa, not just physically but also culturally.[92] Such a denial of African survivalisms in the Americas has long been an outdated intellectual position. In the United States, the rise of academic black studies programs and departments in the aftermath of the civil rights movement gradually led to what can be called an Africanist turn in scholarship; the anthropologist Melville J. Herskovits (1895–1963), particularly well known for *The Myth of the Negro Past* (1941), was an early precursor of this development. The Africanist turn means, first of all, that the emphasis has shifted to the connections that New World black cultures have with Africa. The focus is now more on continuity and connectivity than on rupture. Contemporary scholarship recognizes the persistence of Africanisms in many areas of social and cultural life, such as religion, music, the visual and performing arts, and certain linguistic features of the English(es) spoken in African America.[93] Another vital aspect of the Africanist turn in black/Africana studies is a strong interest in Africa—that is, Africa as understood on its own terms, in all its mind-boggling multiplicity (which is racial, among other things, as Achille Mbembé reminds us),[94] and with the help of any multi- and interdisciplinary tools that the humanities, social sciences, and other relevant scholarly fields can offer.

Afrocentrism,[95] which was popular in many African American communities and in some US academic institutions especially in the 1980s and early 1990s (although many of its main ideas were older),[96] should also be mentioned here. In contrast to the current emphasis on Africa's internal diversity and plurality, Afrocentric intellectuals and artists ahistorically romanticized a mythically refigured and unified pan-Africa. In the process, they reenvisioned the idea of "returning" to Africa in a way that both harkened back to early back-to-Africa movements and to Marcus Garvey's cause and, at the same time, thoroughly reformed and reconceptualized them. That is, Afrocentrism offered a spiritually envisioned and culturally materializable "return" that was accessible to any diasporic individual of African descent, regardless of means or mobility: the movement encouraged black diasporans, especially African Americans, to embrace aspects of the culture of an alleged pan-Africa by adopting African-inspired cultural practices in their diasporic environments—such as the celebration of Kwanzaa, created by Maulana Karenga in the United States in 1966. The adoption of such attitudes and practices was cast as a spiritual return to "roots," to the African origins of black diasporic subjects.

Prior to the rise of Afrocentrism, the idea of "return" had been rekindled more specifically and concretely among African Americans, as Kevin Gaines reminds us in *American Africans in Ghana* (2006), by Ghana's 1957 independence and by Kwame Nkrumah's vision that black diasporans should come "home" and help to build the new nation. However, African Americans had, from early on, noticed that diasporans' physical returns to Africa often resulted in a deep disappointment for those expecting to be embraced as "Mother Africa's"[97] lost children who had been sorely missed during their forced absence. In his 1940 autobiography, *The Big Sea*, Langston Hughes wryly recalled an experience that had repeatedly astonished him during his 1923 trip to Africa: sub-Saharan Atlantic Africa "was the only place in the world where [he had] ever been called a white man."[98] This shock undoubtedly served as important inspiration for his poignant poem "Afro-American Fragment" (1930), which eloquently expresses a diasporic longing for Africa but also wonders whether any existentially meaningful connection can be reconstructed in the present.[99] Furthermore, Richard Wright's *Black Power* (1954), an account of his trip to the Gold Coast just a few years before the country transformed itself into an independent Ghana, is a markedly undecided narrative, permeated by an anxious ambivalence about Africa and its significance for those living in the diaspora.[100]

No wonder, then, that Hall, in "Negotiating Caribbean Identities," responded to romantic, transhistorical Afrocentrism by deploying a demythologizing approach and advising caution: "Africa is not waiting there in the fifteenth or seventeenth century, waiting for you to roll back across the Atlantic and rediscover it in its tribal purity, waiting there in its prelogical mentality, waiting to be woken from inside by its returning sons and daughters."[101] This comment by Hall could easily serve as an epigraph to Saidiya Hartman's story of her diasporic "return" to Ghana in *Lose Your Mother* (2007). As the title indicates, Hartman's book is no tale of an idealized homecoming. Instead, she narrates her encounters with the scarce records of slavery on both the American and African sides of the Atlantic. In terms of approach and politics, her project is akin to Michel-Rolph Trouillot's Haitian-focused *Silencing the Past* (1995), although the two books are vastly different in style. *Silencing the Past* is, in Trouillot's words, "about history and power," about "the many ways in which the production of historical narratives involves the uneven contribution of competing groups and individuals who have unequal access to the means for such production."[102] Inspired by Michel Foucault, Trouillot, in writing about how power operates in the production of knowledge, particularly historiography, focuses on what he calls "[t]he general silencing of the Haitian Revolution by Western historiography."[103] Hartman, in her more autobiographical narrative, similarly records her process of listening to the sounds of silence—about the lives, personalities, and final fates of individual slaves—in her family, in the archives, and in slave castles along the coast of West Africa.

However, even as Hartman interrogates the silencing of slave voices on both sides of the Atlantic, she by no means dismisses the significance of the time that she spent in Ghana. On the contrary, her book by its very existence demonstrates the validity of Hall's above-quoted remark on the need of diasporans to reencounter Africa, physically or symbolically, in order to clarify their place in modern history.[104] Hartman emphasizes how important it was for her, professionally and personally, to make this pilgrimage (however demythologized) "back" to the sub-Saharan Atlantic Africa of her ancestors. When she traveled to Ghana, she was not seeking a glorious African past in which to anchor her personal identity but, instead, stories of those who had been outsiders and outcasts on both sides of the ocean:

> Torn from kin and community, exiled from one's country, dishonored and violated, the slave defines the position of the outsider.... I traveled to Ghana in search of the expendable and the defeated.... I would seek the commoners, the unwilling and coerced migrants who created a new culture in the hostile world of the Americas and who fashioned themselves again, making possibility out of dispossession.[105]

In the end, Hartman does not find what she is looking for (a stored, storied, or memoried presence of those who had ended in the diaspora)—or so she believes, until she encounters a group of children singing a song about those taken, those sold into slavery, a song about the diaspora: "Here it was—my song, the song of the lost tribe. I closed my eyes and I listened."[106] This carefully crafted narrative moment can be read in dialogue with two canonical African American literary texts: Hughes's above-mentioned "Afro-American Fragment" and Toni Morrison's *Song of Solomon* (1977). In "Afro-American Fragment," the narrator longs to connect with Africa by accessing collective memories viscerally transmitted by African songs—songs with lyrics that the narrator cannot comprehend, songs "Of bitter yearnings lost."[107] Hartman initially encounters a similar language barrier, but she soon finds an interpreter who tells her (indeed, shouts in her ear) what the children's song is about. Hartman casts this fleeting connection as a sign of hope that, after all, points to the possibility of black Atlantic solidarity and reconnection. In *Song of Solomon*, similarly, the Michigan-based African American male protagonist connects with his past and intuits something important about his home and (be)longing when, in a small rural locale in Virginia, he unexpectedly hears a group of children sing about an ancestor of his who, according to oral tradition, flew back to Africa as one of the "flying Africans" of black southern folklore.[108] In both *Lose Your Mother* and *Song of Solomon*, a connection between Africa and the New World, however fragile, *is* discovered—not in history books, not in archives, and not in museums, but in a cultural performance, in a song sung by children that points both to the past (by serving as a repository) and to the future (through the identity of the young performers).

Hartman's experience of listening to the African children sing "her song" resonates with the profoundly diasporic sensibility of her concluding meditation on the African dimension of her African American identity. For her, most importantly, "losing her mother" does not mean losing her brothers and sisters. Hartman discovers very few archival traces of her ancestors; nor does she find faith in the meaningfulness of a *mythologized* relationship with "Mother Africa."[109] However, she does not lose either her need for or her utopian faith in black Atlantic solidarity:

> If an African identity was to be meaningful at all, at least to me, then what it meant or was to mean could be elaborated only in the fight against slavery, which . . . was not about dead people or old forts built by white men but the power of others to determine whether you lived or died. . . . For me, returning to the source didn't lead to the great courts and to the regalia of kings and queens. The legacy that I chose to claim was articulated in the ongoing struggle to escape, stand down, and defeat slavery in all of its myriad forms. It was the fugitive's legacy. . . . It was a dream of autonomy rather than nationhood. It was the dream of an elsewhere, with all its promises and dangers, where the stateless might, at last, thrive.[110]

These eloquent remarks attest to the importance of the hermeneutic principle, emphasized throughout this introduction, of remembering the traumatic origins of the African diaspora. At the same time, Hartman's discourse demonstrates that an awareness of early African Atlantic history does not have to result in a defeatist affirmation of a black victim status. Black Atlantic interconnectedness, however difficult to define in exact terms, can point to a fight against any form of enslavement, to a continual refashioning of culture and imagination under the sign of freedom or a quest for it, and to a constant renewal of self and community in local and global contexts.

How, then, do these intellectual debates and positions relate to *Precarious Passages*? First, although pointedly a study of the black literary imagination in the diaspora, not an examination of the African continent or its literature, this book is attentive to narrative moments—fleeting as they in many cases are—that depict encounters with Africa and Africanity. I use "Africanity" synonymously with "Africanness," which, like any other continental "-ness," is an open and capacious signifier that can be filled with a variety of contents. In the spirit of "Keeping Africanity Open" (the title of an 2002 article by Souleymane Bachir Diagne),[111] I refrain from imposing on my sources any preconceived, prescriptive definitions of Africanity; my focus is, instead, on how the *novels* discussed in this book depict the significance of the African dimension of their characters' hyphenated diasporic identities.[112] With the exception of *The Book of Negroes*, Africa in these texts mostly signifies a distant and abstract "homeland," not a specific location to which New World–born protagonists attempt to "return" physically. Except for *Middle Passage* and *The Book of Negroes*, the novels I examine only allude to Africa(nity) very briefly, yet its presence matters. Africa occupies a place in the protagonists' black Atlantic imaginary as an object of those "bitter yearnings" (Hughes)[113] that reveal a need to determine Africa(nity)'s significance for black diasporic memory, identity, and solidarity. Second, I fully acknowledge the continuing importance of black diasporic cultures' African dimensions and reject any antiquated denial of the existence or significance of African survivalisms. However, rather than systematically tracing specific survivalisms (such as particular forms of music, dance, or spirituality) in the Americas or Europe, my analysis—being concerned with the diasporic longing to belong and with the ambivalences characterizing black diasporic identities—explores literary representations of both rupture and continuity, both isolation and connection.

Third, the complexities accompanying diasporans' "returns" to Africa receive attention in chapters 1 and 2, which discuss *Middle Passage* and *The Book of Negroes*, respectively. (Chapter 5, in turn, examines literary representations of African Caribbeans' returns from Britain or North America to the Caribbean.) Both *Middle Passage* and *The Book of Negroes* emphasize the crucial importance of Africa for black diasporic identities, but neither novel portrays physical returns to Africa as resulting in easy, spontaneously occurring reconnections with "roots." Rather, each text depicts attempts at such reconnection not only as existentially important and even imperative, but also as laborious and necessarily open-ended. The main character of *The Book of Negroes* is African-born, yet no simple "return" to cultural Africanity is possible for her when she is finally able to return to West Africa. The protagonist of *Middle*

Passage, in turn—a black American freedman working on a slave ship—physically experiences Africa only once, when waiting for a delivery of a group of slaves at a coastal trading post in West Africa. In his case, "return" to Africanity would mean learning an African worldview and way of life from the captive slaves with whom he communicates as the ship sails back to America. He finds himself yearning for such a spiritual "return," but the realities of the Atlantic slave trade quickly abort his learning process. Nevertheless, his brief encounters with the captive Africans, with whom he temporarily shares the same diasporic in-between space on the slave ship, profoundly transform him and his perceptions of himself, of existential and moral imperatives, and of black diasporic connectivity.

Exile, Migrant, Immigrant, Cosmopolitan

Especially in essays and interviews, many of my selected novelists frequently use the terms "exile," "migrant," "immigrant," "emigrant," or "cosmopolitan," in addition to discussing diaspora and diasporic individuals. Defining these terms has almost become a comparative field of study in its own right. I here limit myself to two clarifying comments.

First, the term "migrant literature" (and "immigrant literature," in particular) usually signifies the migrant writer's deeper involvement with the receiving society than does "exile literature," which tends to highlight the exile's existential isolation. While this distinction is not absolute, the slight differences among the preferred vocabularies of George Lamming, Caryl Phillips, and Edwidge Danticat—black diasporic writers of three generations—are illuminating. Lamming's 1960 essay collection carries the deliberately paradoxical title *The Pleasures of Exile*, and his 1954 novel is entitled *The Emigrants*, rather than *The Migrants* or *The Immigrants*. In other words, Lamming, in his early work, casts his fictional émigrés as individuals who, instead of having arrived at "home," have left behind a place of belonging. Phillips, in turn, frequently speaks of both exile and migrancy (in addition to embodying cosmopolitanism through his transnational life experience),[114] whereas Danticat, rather than employing "exile," refers to herself as an "AHA, African-Haitian-American"[115] and, more recently, as an *immigrant* artist.[116] These slightly different terminological preferences demonstrate a generational development from a diasporic *exile* (Lamming) to a diasporic *exile/migrant* (Phillips) to a diasporic *immigrant* (Danticat). The attribute "diasporic" is warranted in each case, because all three writers reveal their African diasporic consciousness in their oeuvres, although they may not explicitly reference Africa in every single book they have written.

Second, because "cosmopolitan" is a topical concept in current transnational scholarship, I dedicate some space, toward the end of chapter 1, to a discussion of the terminological distinction between "cosmopolitan" and "diasporic," noting that these two terms name two different, albeit partially overlapping, sets of challenges. Otherwise, I will use "diaspora/diasporic" as my key concept, employing such related terms as "exile," "migrant," "immigrant," and "emigrant" (in their most commonplace meanings) as vocabulary supporting my discussion of diaspora and diasporic subjectivity.

A Note on Genre, Form, and Historical Fiction

The roots of the Anglophone novel lie in the colonial era and in the predominantly white-centered worldview of the era's literary production. One of the first major embodiments of the novel was Daniel Defoe's *Robinson Crusoe* (1719), a story about the British owner of a Brazilian plantation who survives a shipwreck in the Caribbean and lives for several years on a desert island, occasionally encountering locals who to him remain Others and "cannibals"—except for Friday, whom he, tellingly, makes his servant. Against the backdrop of this genealogy, the later black adoption and renewal of the genre of the novel serves as one aspect of what James Baldwin in "Autobiographical Notes" (1955) called the black "appropriat[ion]" of "white centuries," the historiographical and artistic process of redefining black diasporic peoples' "special place" in history.[117] My analysis therefore occasionally comments on genre. However, I will not impose any nonexistent formal unity on my primary sources. The body of fiction analyzed here is stylistically so diverse that no programmatic pronouncement on "the" form allegedly characterizing "the" black Anglophone diasporic novel would be credible. My main focus will be on the authors' renderings of diasporic identity formation rather than on form or style.

This said, I *am*, on a secondary level, fascinated by the question of how my selected authors approach the potential of the novel as a genre—that is, how they envision the contributions that long fiction, with its own techniques and devices and with the freedom of imagination available for its creators, can make to the currently fast-expanding body of literary and nonliterary texts on the Middle Passage and later black diasporic predicaments. Terry

Castle's point about the strong presence, from the outset, of orphans (and, by extension, of the trope of the orphan) in Anglophone novels is thought-provoking and compelling:

> [F]or English speakers, it's in classic Anglo-American fiction—in the novel, say, from Daniel Defoe, Aphra Behn, Samuel Richardson, and Henry Fielding to Dickens, Eliot, Twain, James, Woolf, Hemingway, and the rest—that the orphaned, or semi-orphaned, hero or heroine becomes a central, if not inescapable, fixture. Something about the new social and psychic world in which the realistic novel comes into being in the late 17th and early 18th centuries pushes the orphan to the foreground of the mix, makes of him or her a strikingly necessary figure, a kind of exemplary being.... [O]rphanhood—the absence of the parent, the frightening yet galvanizing solitude of the child—may be the defining fixation of the novel as a genre, what one might call its primordial motive or matrix, the conditioning psychic reality out of which the form itself develops.[118]

Castle's observation about orphanhood and the novel is relevant to fictional works that are, overtly or covertly, concerned with black diasporans' loss of "Mother Africa" and with the challenge of a new type of "family formation" in the Western world. Indeed, diasporic fiction often depicts diasporic community formation as family formation in the receiving society. Both "losing your mother" (Hartman) and the subsequent diasporic community formation, metaphorically or microcosmically represented as family formation, are therefore recurring themes in the chapters that follow.

The novelists studied in this book may not share a common literary style, but they do share an interest in intersections of literature, history, and society; yet they are not primarily academic theorists. Writers of fiction, they exercise the power of imagination in order to unveil or rewrite into being what historians and other scholars, operating under the strict rules of verification guiding academic research, cannot always rescue from invisibility and oblivion. Wendy W. Walters states in *Archives of the Black Atlantic*,[119] a 2013 examination of the nexus of literary and historical studies, that black diasporic historical fiction "opens new perspectives on Atlantic history and culture, generating a dialogue between what was and what might have been."[120] Her remark serves as an inspiration for my analyses of *Middle Passage* and *The Book of Negroes*—works of fiction in which Johnson and Hill explore "what might have been" as they reimagine the past of the black Atlantic in light of current insights into the nature of the African diaspora. More generally, all novelists discussed in this book demonstrate a powerful awareness of the past of the black Atlantic diaspora: they place both the temporally remote and the more recent events that they depict within a broader framework of black diasporic history, thus participating in the mediation of a collective black diasporic cultural memory for future generations. In so doing, they actively contribute to the ongoing black diasporic identity formation in the Anglophone Atlantic world.

Synopsis and Organization

This book is organized as follows: chapter 1, examining Charles Johnson's philosophically based *Middle Passage*, focuses on the existential journey of the protagonist—an African American freedman working on a slave ship—to black diasporic consciousness. Although scholars have analyzed *Middle Passage* from a number of angles, little has been done to clarify the obvious, that is, to articulate how diasporic identity formation plays out in the narrative. As chapter 1 fills this void, it foregrounds what I earlier characterized as the "first" and "second" arguments of this book: Johnson's novel contributes to contemporary black diasporic identity formation by participating in the fictive commemoration of the Middle Passage. However, despite this foundational task, *Middle Passage* is far from static or stationary in approach. Instead, Johnson's postmodernist prose is permeated by a phenomenologically and Buddhistically informed vision of the fluidity of black diasporic identity. As a result, *Middle Passage* covertly critiques such ideologies as Afrocentrism and black cultural nationalism, which Johnson sees as having produced fixed and frozen interpretations of blackness. What *Middle Passage* offers as an alternative to normative definitions of blackness is a strong emphasis on a diasporic self-understanding that is fraught with ambivalence and characterized by process rather than by essence.

Chapter 2, concerned with more conventionally crafted historical fiction, discusses Lawrence Hill's *The Book of Negroes*, in which the diasporic ur-experience is expanded to cover post–Middle Passage migrations as well. Both a neo-slave narrative and a novel about Black Loyalist migrations, *The Book of Negroes* contributes to collective black diasporic memory by depicting the early African diaspora in the Western world from the perspective of an African-born woman. Originally a freeborn Muslim, Hill's fictional protagonist is a black diasporic subject who enters modernity on terms dictated by racializing white Others and must fashion her diasporic self out of various conflicting elements, which have to be reconciled within a single psyche. In keeping with this book's fourth argument, "home" (in any imaginable sense) remains perpetually elusive for Hill's racially and sexually subjugated female character once her diasporic predicament has been propelled into being. The hope embedded in *The Book of Negroes* lies in the protagonist's capacity to repeatedly assert her agency against the forces that oppress her and in the connection (familiar to readers of antebellum slave narratives) between literacy, freedom, and the "autobiographical" abolitionist enterprise that Hill inscribes in the novel's frame—an endeavor that metafictionally highlights the link between black diasporic memory and identity.

Chapter 3 is an examination of Toni Morrison's and Caryl Phillips's portraits of African American troops in World War I, World War II, and Vietnam. These authors' stories of African American soldiers and veterans bring together two topic areas that may, at first glance, seem to have little to do with each other, namely, war and diaspora. Military service is typically construed as a sign of loyalty to one's nation, and this chapter indeed interrogates the complex relationship between diasporic subjectivity and national citizenship. Most importantly, utilizing Caruthian trauma theory and tapping into what I have characterized as this book's third argument, this chapter reveals how Morrison, in *Sula* and *Tar Baby*, and Phillips, in *Crossing the River*, subtly link their narratives of *temporary traumatic displacement* on foreign battlefields with *the historical ur-trauma of diasporic dislocation*. In these novels, the wounds that the Middle Passage and slavery inflicted on black diasporic bodies and psyches metaphorically "bleed" into, and coalesce with, traumas and posttraumatic conditions resulting from black participation in modern warfare—participation that both Morrison and Phillips depict in terms of young black men being sent abroad to fight destructive and traumatizing wars that are not theirs to fight. The literal and metaphorical connections that Morrison and Phillips forge between war and diaspora call attention to the greed and large-scale violence that have all too often accompanied the Western project of modernity.

Chapter 4, an analysis of *The Emigrants*, *The Final Passage*, and *Small Island*, brings together this book's arguments by exploring the relationship between diasporic, imperial, and national identity formations in George Lamming's, Caryl Phillips's, and Andrea Levy's novels about West Indian immigrants (who are both African Caribbean diasporans and subjects of the British Empire) settling in Britain after World War II. The chapter also examines how each of these three authors—who represent three different generations of writers in relation to the *Windrush* moment and its aftermath—portrays the gendered aspects of the postwar Caribbean migration to Britain. Chapter 5, in turn, examines Phillips's, Cecil Foster's, and Edwidge Danticat's depictions of contemporary African Caribbean encounters with the United States and Canada, with a particular focus on the complexities of "return"—a theme that facilitates discussions about "origins" and "home" and about formations of both diasporic and national identities and solidarities. Rather than focusing on journeys back to Africa (a topic discussed in chapters 1 and 2), *A State of Independence, Sleep On, Beloved,* and *Breath, Eyes, Memory* all depict black Caribbean-born diasporans' return trips back to the Caribbean. In all their complexity, these visits and their existential consequences play a pivotal role in how Phillips's, Foster's, and Danticat's protagonists interpret their pasts and envision their future identities as members of two or more nations, the Caribbean diaspora, and the African diaspora.

This book's narrative for the most part proceeds chronologically, with respect to the eras that the novels portray, with concessions made for some movement back and forth in time within and among my sources. The most significant departure from this chronology is my decision to discuss Johnson's *Middle Passage*, set in 1830, before *The Book of Negroes*, which recounts events beginning in 1756 and ending in the early nineteenth century. My analysis of *Middle Passage*—a philosophical novel that allows me to elaborate on methodological issues that are relevant for this book as a whole, such as the relationship between history, philosophy/theory, and fiction—in a way serves as an immediate methodological sequel to this introduction; hence my choice to discuss *Middle Passage* first.

In addition to being structured chronologically, my narrative is organized around national and continental categories relevant to Atlantic scholarship. At the same time, however, I acknowledge the limitations of such categories and point beyond them toward what Gilroy in *Against Race* terms "planetary [i.e., global] humanism"[121]—a scholarly and activist mindset that, within the Gilroyan paradigm, draws much of its interpretive potential from diaspora: the concept and empirical phenomenon of diaspora "makes the spatialization of identity problematic," "interrupts the ontologization of place,"[122] and thus continuously calls attention to passages, border crossings, and transnational identity formation.

1

An African American Journey to Black Diasporic Consciousness

Charles Johnson's *Middle Passage*

"An African American concept of space had its beginnings in the holds of the slave ships during the Middle Passage,"[1] Maria Diedrich, Henry Louis Gates Jr., and Carl Pedersen argued in their introduction to *Black Imagination and the Middle Passage* in 1999. The stated aim of their co-edited essay collection was to participate in constructing "a transatlantic imagination" by "reconceptualizing the meaning of the Middle Passage for African American history and fiction";[2] the adjective "transatlantic" has since been broadened, by others, to "circum-Atlantic"[3] or just "Atlantic" in order to ensure that it covers the entire Atlantic rim. Rather than "looking at the Middle Passage as a phenomenon of constricted space and limited time," Diedrich, Gates, and Pedersen sought to "extend its meaning in time and space . . . to the syncretic notion of a space in-between that links geographical and cultural regions."[4] Their historically grounded and interpretively expanded understanding of the Middle Passage as a transitional and connective process/space—which, I must add, *both* links *and* separates—is extremely relevant to my project, because it establishes a foundation for a black diasporic sensibility (the three scholars' chosen term was "a Middle Passage sensibility")[5] that affiliates itself with Cliffordian/Gilroyan routes instead of requiring a geographically and ethnically specific self-identification with "roots."

In the introduction, I highlighted the close connection between black diasporic memory and identity. The African American author Charles Johnson's 1990 Middle Passage novel,[6] which focuses on a slave ship experience and is pithily titled *Middle Passage*, commemorates the foundational historical experience of the African diaspora (the crossing of the Atlantic on slave ships) and depicts the Middle Passage as a transitional process/space that both connects and denotes rupture. The novel also contains, I argue, a hermeneutically significant thematic narrative of the formation of a black diasporic identity. Although much has already been written about *Middle Passage*, its narrative of the emergence of black diasporic subjectivity and identity has mostly been treated as a sine qua non rather than studied in itself. Seeking to fill this void, this chapter maps out the African American protagonist's journey to a black diasporic consciousness and demonstrates that the entire novel can be read as a story about the formation of his diasporic self-understanding.

A few words on Johnson, memory, history, and philosophy are needed to situate *Middle Passage* both within diasporic perspectives and in the context of Johnson's recurring intellectual interests. In 1989, he published an essay titled "Novelists of Memory," a brief survey of the history of the African American novel. When he decided to write *Middle Passage*, he himself assumed the task of being a "novelist of memory." The way in which Johnson (an academically trained philosopher and a philosophically oriented literary author)[7] carried out this historically informed task in relation to hermeneutics/philosophy can be usefully likened to Gilroy's project in *The Black Atlantic*. In *The Black Atlantic*, the sea—as fluid a space as anything can be, characterized by powerful cross-currents whose combined impacts have the potential to surprise even the most experienced traveler—defies the neat, fixed boundaries of modern nation-states and highlights the importance of passages and routes for the evolution of post-Columbian modernity. The trope of the slave ship, too, occupies a special place in Gilroy's theorizing because the ship, "a living, micro-cultural, micro-political system in motion,"[8] embodies the "rhizomorphic, fractal structure of the transcultural, international formation" of the African diaspora.[9] Like *The Black Atlantic*, *Middle Passage* also highlights the importance of the forced Atlantic crossing on a slaver for the emergence of black diasporic consciousness. Moreover, just as Gilroy's academic book *both* examines specific geopolitical contexts and historical figures *and* uses such tropes as the slave ship as hermeneutically valuable chronotopes, Johnson's novel likewise interrogates the nexus of the historical and the hermeneutical/philosophical.

Pairing *Middle Passage* with *The Black Atlantic* requires the parenthetical acknowledgement that although much of the prolific scholarly commentary offered on Gilroy's book has been laudatory, multiple critical voices have also been raised.[10] Simon Gikandi, for example, has articulated the following questions (which, in part, quote and paraphrase Joan Dayan's concerns):

"What ... are the implications of transforming the terror of the middle passage into the metaphorical terror of modernity and rationality? What is the conceptual meaning of the slave ship once it has been re-presented as ... a 'vessel of transit and means to a knowledge'?"[11] These questions—arising from the worry that Gilroy's approach might privilege "culture over experience and hermeneutics over history," as Gikandi puts it[12]—are important, but *The Black Atlantic* hardly fails to consider actual human experience or history. In Gilroy's treatment, even the heavily theoretical term "chronotope" calls attention to time and space in their specific manifestations, rather than seducing the critic into an ahistorical vacuum. In *The Black Atlantic*, the slave ship serves as a chronotope,[13] as noted. In Gilroy's usage of Bakhtinian lexicon, this term refers to a unit of analysis that, in the study of texts, necessitates and facilitates the consideration of both time and space "as x-rays of the forces at work in the culture system from which they spring,"[14] to quote Bakhtin. Through this emphasis on the temporal and the spatial (or, on the historical and the geopolitical), Gilroy affirms that his hermeneutical work is anchored in the lived experience of the peoples of the African diaspora.

In a parallel manner, Johnson's *Middle Passage* is, as the late Rudolph P. Byrd accurately observed, "a philosophical novel rooted in the past."[15] That is, on the one hand Johnson writes fiction that is *primarily* interested in the philosophical. As a result, Johnson's fictional commemoration of the Atlantic ur-crossing in *Middle Passage* does not chiefly aim for a realistic representation of historically verifiable details; even the African ethnic group depicted in the novel is Johnson's invention. Because *Middle Passage* is a highly interpretive enterprise that focuses on the formation of black diasporic identity, the slave ship here indeed becomes an existential and epistemological unit that functions as a "vessel of transit and means to a knowledge" (to summon again Dayan and Gikandi's phrase).[16] On the other hand, Johnson does also address the Middle Passage's historicity, including its physical terror;[17] neither his abundant philosophizing nor his postmodernist experimentation with the genre of the neo-slave narrative negates this fact. For him, as for Gilroy, the philosophical and the historical are intimately intertwined. Creating fiction that is informed by both of these realms is how Johnson chooses to be "a novelist of memory." In *Middle Passage*, his approach results in a fictional representation of the formation of a diasporic self-understanding, a processual identity born from the memory of the Middle Passage as an in-between "space" that both denotes rupture and connects the black diasporic subject with Africanity.

Despite the questions raised by Gilroy's critics, a powerful emphasis on the origins of the African diaspora in trauma and terror is a nonnegotiable aspect of his diasporic hermeneutics, as discussed in the introduction. Given this emphasis, Middle Passage—a highly atypical rendering of the Atlantic slave trade—may at first glance seem to fit poorly within the Gilroyan framework of diasporic theory, because Johnson's postmodernist text addresses the trade's unspeakable horrors by resorting to such seemingly inappropriate devices as comical anachronisms and parody.[18] With its funny quirks and adventurous twists, the novel follows, as Marc C. Conner remarks, "the form and language of the adventure tale, the sea voyage, even of the Roman Comedy whereby the tricky servant schemes and connives his way to freedom."[19] However, despite the elements that may seem unexpected in light of Johnson's grave topic, what ultimately emerges from his unique admixture of historical inspiration, phenomenology, Buddhism, literary intertextuality, and dark humor is not only a good yarn spun by the seaman-narrator but also a lamentation over the suffering that the Atlantic slave trade inflicted on its victims—and, finally, the story of an African American journey toward a black diasporic self-understanding.

Throughout the novel, Johnson highlights the "in-between" and processual aspects of diasporic identity by overlaying the historical concept of the Middle Passage with the more metaphorical connotation of "transformation"—a passage from one state of being to another, or a fundamental change in perception that leads to existential reevaluation. In addition to "transformation," "perception" is, indeed, another key word in my analysis of Johnson's novel. In Middle Passage, transformed/liberated perception is required for a transformed/liberated consciousness, specifically for the narrator-protagonist Rutherford Calhoun's gradual awakening to the existential and moral significance of his identity position as a member of the African diaspora. This chapter, therefore, as its first task identifies three seemingly unrelated influences that inspired Johnson to probe into the nature of perception in Middle Passage. First, Johnson's narrative conducts an intertextual dialogue with Herman Melville's treatment of perception in Benito Cereno (1855/1856),[20] a novella about a black rebellion on a Spanish slaver. In addition to its thematic focus on slave mutiny, it was Benito Cereno's pervasive attention to socially conditioned perception, I argue, that prompted Johnson to see this novella as an apt source for allusion and appropriation or as a suitable foundation for an "American palimpsest," to quote Byrd's preferred idiom.[21] The narrative of Rutherford's perceptual-cum-existential transformation also draws, second, on phenomenology and, third, on Buddhism, both of which Johnson is intimately familiar with. Despite their vastly different genealogies, both phenomenology and Buddhism in their own ways study the role of human perception in individuals' existential processes. They examine the existential significance of how we perceive the world and ourselves and how we might free ourselves of our preconceived judgments based on fixed, frozen perception.

Benito Cereno, phenomenology, and Buddhism share, I repeat, an interest in transformed/liberated perception as a requirement for a transformed/liberated consciousness. It is for this reason, I contend, that Johnson throws these three seemingly unconnected ingredients into his literary melting pot in order to create a story about a journey to black diasporic awareness. Below, my more detailed discussion of these influences serves as a threefold contextualization, within Johnson's intellectual milieu, of the argument that *Middle Passage* can be legitimately read as a literary representation of black diasporic identity formation. This contextualization is followed by a close reading of the novel, with a focus on the narrative of the protagonist's journey to African diasporic subjectivity.

Perceptual Change, *Benito Cereno*, and *Middle Passage*

The events of *Middle Passage* are set in motion when the young African American freedman Rutherford Calhoun escapes personal trouble in New Orleans by, rather dimwittedly, sneaking onto a slaver that is about to depart for the west coast of Africa. Once discovered, he is assigned the lowly position of an assistant to the ship's cook. In this capacity of a semiaccidental black intermediary in the slave trade, he witnesses the Middle Passage of forty captive Africans as the ship eventually sails back from West Africa toward Louisiana with the human cargo in its hold. This forced Atlantic crossing of Johnson's fictional Allmuseri, his countermaterialistic and spiritual "ur-people,"[22] takes place in the summer of 1830, more than twenty years after the importation of slaves to the United States was rendered illegal. Unlawful and clandestine as the enterprise is, the forty African captives are nevertheless being shipped to New Orleans, a major port serving the legal US interstate slave trade at the time.

During the ocean voyage, the narrative spotlight is all along on the gradual existential transformation of Rutherford, the only black crewman on the slaver. Torn between his status as one of the crew and his sympathies with the suffering Africans, he witnesses the horrors that take place on the poorly managed and decaying *Republic*. (The significance of the ship's name has not been lost on scholars.)[23] As the *Republic's* crew and cargo together cross the sea—the vast "living void"[24] or "emptiness"[25] (to echo relevant Buddhist concepts) that Rutherford calls a "theater of transformations"[26]—the presence of the Allmuseri gradually and irreversibly alters the young man's perception of life, reality, and morality. When he first boarded the *Republic*, a vessel that Johnson's existentially laden narrative explicitly characterizes as a "process,"[27] Rutherford was a drifter and a self-absorbed player, a Melvillean/Ellisonian "confidence man."[28] However, during the journey from New Orleans to West Africa and back, he arrives at a completely transfigured understanding of both himself and the world: his transformative experience as a participant-observer on the slaver forcefully brings him to a moral, cultural, spiritual, and political awareness of his diasporic existence.

In *Middle Passage*, Johnson's treatment of perception, a motif vital to his account of Rutherford's journey to an aware existence as a diasporic subject, is in intriguing conversation with Melville's strategic deployment of the same motif in *Benito Cereno*. Perception, which is characterized by unreliability and malleability, is no neutral cognitive event; the beholder's proverbial eye always has a complex relationship with what it has and has not perceived before. Scholars interrogating the malleable social construct of "race" know this very well, as do fiction writers whose work deliberately challenges habitual patterns of thought that contribute to conservative social perception. The first of the two epigraphs that Ralph Ellison, Johnson's deeply admired literary ancestor,[29] chose for *Invisible Man*—a 1952 masterpiece about black identity, socially conditioned perception, and the perils of racialized modes of seeing—was a quotation from the famous closing dialogue of *Benito Cereno*, which Ellison evoked to emphasize the invisibility of "the Negro."[30] The Melvillean epigraph sets the stage for *Invisible Man* quite effectively because the discourse of perception, or of sight and insight, occupies an important role in Ellison's novel, as it does in *Benito Cereno*. Johnson has always been explicit about his profound appreciation of *Invisible Man*,[31] and in *Middle Passage* he engages in a conversation with the same source of inspiration that Ellison highlighted via said epigraph, that is, with *Benito Cereno*. Johnson alerts the reader to his dialogue with *Benito Cereno* by adopting names for several of his fictive Africans (Babo, Diamelo, Francesco, Atufal, Ghofan, and Akim) from the semifictional deposition appended to Melville's novella.[32] Moreover, one of Johnson's minor characters explicitly laments "how some writers such as Amasa Delano have slandered black rebels in their tales."[33] Most importantly, both *Benito Cereno* and *Middle Passage*, resonating at what Ellison would term "the lower frequencies,"[34] explore the relationship between individuals' socioculturally conditioned perceptions and their social and political values.

As a novelist of memory, Johnson indeed used not only black-authored but also white-authored intertextual sources,[35] including *Benito Cereno*, while crafting a fictional representation of the formation of black diasporic subjectivity. This choice both points to the inevitably intertwined fates of black and white Americans (one of Ralph Ellison's favorite topics) and speaks to Johnson's acknowledgment that the diasporic condition is an existence marked by cultural hybridity. Although Johnson's re-formed, postmodernist narrative of a slave mutiny is, on one level, a capricious mix of varied cultural influences, his intertextual dialogue with *Benito Cereno* does not merely represent fashionable stylistic playfulness for its own sake. Rather, in *Middle Passage* Johnson converses with Melville's novella—a revered part of the "white" American literary canon—in order to write about black resistance, black diasporic identity formation, and hybrid New World subjectivity. Perception is a key motif in this intertextual conversation.

Benito Cereno is, as Harold H. Scudder established in 1928, a fictional rendering of chapter 18 of Captain Amasa Delano's 1817 *Narrative of Voyages and Travels*.[36] According to *Voyages and Travels*, Captain Delano from Duxbury, Massachusetts, commanding the American sealer *Perseverance* (in *Benito Cereno*, the *Bachelor's Delight*), sighted a ship without colors while anchored off the coast of Chile on a February morning in 1805 (in *Benito Cereno*, in August 1799). After concluding that the ship, the Spanish *Tryal* (in *Benito Cereno*, the *San Dominick*), was in distress, Delano boarded the vessel to offer assistance and spent several hours on board. He discovered that the ship carried captive Africans, but he initially failed to perceive that the Africans were in revolt. Once this reality dawned on him, he and his men violently suppressed the mutiny, and the Spanish captain Cereno (the owner of the *Tryal* and its cargo, except for the slaves) regained control of his property. Melville wrote his fictionalized version of this dramatic historical event more than five decades after the Haitian Revolution—which he evoked not only by changing the date of the *Tryal* insurrection, but also by renaming the *Tryal* the *San Dominick*—and a few years before the outbreak of the American Civil War. Melville's 1855/1856 rewriting of Delano's 1817 text reflects, if not an actual prophetic understanding of the Americas being in transition from an economic model largely based on slavery toward a legal recognition of black humanity and agency, at least a powerful awareness of the societal crisis in which the United States found itself at the time.[37] *Middle Passage*, in turn rewriting aspects of Melville's story, notes that the "Republic" (the United States) and its racial politics were not in perfect shape in 1830 either; the ship *Republic* was, as Rutherford complains, "perpetually flying apart and re-forming during the voyage, falling to pieces beneath us."[38] Indeed, racial slavery was still part of the Republic's business, and 1830 was also the year when Andrew Jackson signed the notorious Indian Removal Act into law. (Tellingly, the last names of both President Jackson and Vice President Calhoun are embedded in the texture of *Middle Passage*.)[39]

Benito Cereno unfolds as a drama of suspense, focusing on Delano's perceptions of the Spanish ship,[40] its captain, its crew, and the African slaves. Delano is the focalized character, but he is by no means a reliable focalizer. Instead, the text conveys much of its message by gradually revealing the unreliability of the American captain's obscured vision: Delano is unable to interpret what he perceives in ways that might exceed or contradict his original assumptions, and he therefore only sees what he expects to see. Michel-Rolph Trouillot writes that the Haitian Revolution "entered history with the peculiar characteristic of being unthinkable even as it happened"[41]—"unthinkable" because Europeans and white Americans were unaccustomed to even considering the possibility of black agency, initiative, and intelligence. Hermeneutically, Melville's rewriting of the historical Delano's 1817 depiction of his *Tryal* experience makes a similar point: *Benito Cereno* implies that its American protagonist's notorious blindness to the altered power balance on the Spanish slaver stems from his acquired worldview and politics (which, though philanthropic, ignore black agency and intelligence), rather than from any culturally or politically "neutral" perception. It was this aspect of *Benito Cereno*, I argue—its powerful focus on perception and politics, combined with the theme of slave revolt—that provided Johnson with a usable literary antecedent as he wrote his 1990 story about a personal transformation prompted by a change in his protagonist's moral and political perception. Different as they are stylistically, both *Benito Cereno* and *Middle Passage* examine the dynamics of influence among perception, culture, politics, and individual integrity, and both invite the reader to reflect further on the nature and consequences of such dynamics.

By *Benito Cereno*'s end, Delano has allegedly achieved clarity of vision. However, his continuing de facto blindness to his political positionality points, in Melville's treatment, to the antebellum North's insufficient understanding of its complicity in the economic and societal structuring of American life that was still perpetuating slavery at the time of *Benito Cereno*'s publication.

Once Delano's adventure is over, the "good captain"[42] symbolizing American democracy is unwilling to dwell on any political implications of his encounter with an intelligently orchestrated black revolt. Although Delano, a northerner, believes himself to be racially progressive, he refuses to let his life be impacted by this potentially transformative encounter. Instead, he remains an uncommitted individual on the *Bachelor's Delight*, a carefree sea wanderer whose whaleboat is aptly named *Rover*. Delano is Melville's subtly but sharply ironized personification of the ideal of noncommittal liberty. Fittingly, he is an excessive pragmatist who wants to stay narrowly focused on present tasks: convinced that troubles that are out of sight should also be kept out of mind, he cheerfully urges the severely traumatized Cereno to simply forget "it all" and follow the blissfully amnesiac example of the sun, the sea, and the sky, which do not wallow in past events.[43]

Cereno, however, does remember: he cannot rid himself of the "shadow"[44] of Babo, the leader of the slave rebellion, whose human force and complexity the Spaniard encountered at a much more personal level than Delano ever did. Cereno's private struggle with this experience confuses and exhausts him so thoroughly that he dies soon afterward.[45] The novella's final sentence seems to suggest that his death results, at least indirectly, from what we now term posttraumatic stress. In *Middle Passage*, rather similarly, the Spanish explorer Rafael García loses his sanity after encountering the novel's Africans, the Allmuseri.[46] A Cereno refashioned, Johnson's García is unable to forget the encounter that, by placing him in contact with black humanity and intelligence, challenged his profoundly Eurocentric worldview, his cherished lens into reality. Neither Cereno nor García can ignore the cognitive dissonance between his received Weltanschauung and his later personal experience that conflicts with his acquired notions of white superiority and of "civilization" as an exclusively white achievement. In a sense, these two characters' shared psychological refusal to continue to function as before after their worldview has proved to be incompatible with reality is a more logical reaction than their white peers' "sane" behavior in the two stories. However, Cereno's and García's shared tragedy is that neither of them knows how to transform himself—that is, where to go, or with whom to ally himself, in order to embrace a radically egalitarian approach to humanity and adopt a relevant course of action. Both of them therefore reach an impasse and perish.

By contrast, Johnson's Rutherford—a drastically modified and thoroughly reformed black Delano, as it were—eventually orients himself toward a new understanding of (non)self, family, and human community. At the end of

Middle Passage, he no longer pursues a "bachelor's delight," a carefree and uncommitted existence, but instead commits himself to a new mode of daily living as a result of his comprehensive spiritual and moral transformation. Also, rather than amnesiacally forgetting his ordeal at sea, Rutherford acknowledges that his future will always be in dialogue with his newly aquired diasporic memory and identity. At the novel's close, he and his fiancée, though finally at what they envision as their "home,"[47] in their sleep continue to cross "countless seas of suffering";[48] they are still on a journey.

The final scene of *Benito Cereno* highlights aspects of Babo's character that remained invisible to Delano, namely, the African leader's intelligence and his unwavering commitment to black freedom. Furthermore, when Melville tells us that in Lima the killed and decapitated Babo's head, "that hive of subtlety, fixed on a pole in the plaza, met, unabashed, the gazes of the whites,"[49] he brings his novella's treatment of seeing and perception to a new level: he not only highlights the black leader's courage but also reminds us that we never learned what Babo really thought and felt on the *San Dominick*, because there we only saw the events through Delano's eyes. Against this backdrop, it is all the more significant that in *Middle Passage* Babo and his people speak—not as valets to a Benito Cereno, but as proud African Allmuseri who see themselves as followers of ancient traditions that coexist harmoniously with nature and facilitate the participation of the Allmuseri in the Unity of all Being.[50] Moreover, in *Middle Passage* the viewer through whose eyes we see the events is neither a white sea captain nor a white member of the crew, but an African American individual—a black subject familiar with the white world who takes over the task of (re)writing a white sea captain's log after the captain dies. Rutherford's position as narrator and protagonist is an admixture of a black Ishmael, a black Huckleberry Finn, and an Invisible Man: following an established pattern in the American novelistic tradition, Rutherford, or Call Me Illinois, is a partly unreliable first-person narrator who survives an ordeal (one deriving from racial hierarchies and racialized perception, as is largely the case in *Huckleberry Finn* and, surely, in *Invisible Man*), undergoes moral transformation and growth, and writes down his story after the trial is over. In the process, he narrates a profound perceptual change—in this case, one that is brought about by a Middle Passage experience and results in the formation of diasporic subjectivity.

Perception, Phenomenology, Buddhism, and the Middle Path

In *Middle Passage*, Rutherford's existential transformation on the slave ship occurs under extreme duress that shatters any illusion of stability or any fantasy suggesting that the world consists of fixed beings and static entities. In this respect, Rutherford is not alone among the characters who people Johnson's fiction. Johnson has repeatedly created protagonists for whom the "progression from ignorance to knowledge, or from a lack of understanding to some greater understanding"[51] means an insight into the processual nature of reality. In developing characters who move from a "noun" to a "verb," as his favored phrase goes (that is, from a worldview based on the illusion of fixity to a comprehensive vision of continuous process, change, and fluidity), Johnson has drawn inspiration from Husserlian phenomenology—a school of philosophy to which he professes adherence in *Being and Race* (1988) and in various essays and interviews.

Phenomenology, focusing on what goes on in the human consciousness rather than in the external world, is the philosophical study of "phenomena," the study of the *appearances* of objects and events as humans *perceive* them (as opposed to the study of "noumena," the objective and unmediated reality that, according to Kantians and neo-Kantians, may or may not exist but nevertheless remains inaccessible to humans).[52] Phenomenologists, together with cognitive psychologists, argue that perception always involves interpretation, an attribution of meaning that is in dialogue with—and often rather uncritically stems from—the information, values, and categories of thought that already inhabit the perceiver's mind prior to a given instance of perception. Perception, in other words, is no unmediated transmission of external reality to the individual human mind. On the contrary, much lies in the eye of the beholder. Understanding this fundamental aspect of the human condition results in humility, notes Johnson, because it prompts us to recognize that not everyone sees the world in the same way and that any individual's perception is, inevitably, mediated in a way that is not completely obvious to him or her. In a 1993 interview with Jonathan Little, Johnson explicitly described Rutherford's process of becoming "much more humble in terms of making assumptions about objects and others" as an arrival at "a very phenomenological position in the world."[53] Johnson further clarified that by *Middle Passage*'s conclusion "[t]here have been so many profiles disclosed and revealed for the meaning of the world that one has a very humble attitude about making existential claims about it."[54] Such a "humble attitude" characterizes both

Johnson's self-proclaimed approach to the world and the identity position of his protagonist at the novel's end.

In the same interview with Little in which Johnson discussed his interest in phenomenology, he also highlighted his other vital source of inspiration for both writing and personal devotion, another mode of thought that studies perception/illusion and emphasizes process—that is, Buddhism, which Johnson considers fully compatible with both phenomenology and Christianity. Johnson has never shied away from discussing either his original AME background or the Buddhist convictions at which he arrived as a young adult, or the harmonious coexistence of both strands of spirituality in his adult life. For example, in a 2003 interview with Jim McWilliams he said, "I've always been a sincere Christian *and* a Buddhist, just as Thich Nhat Hahn has a portrait of Jesus right beside his Theravada Buddhist shrine."[55] Similarly, in the preface to his 2003 essay collection, *Turning the Wheel: Essays on Buddhism and Writing*, he wrote about having, since young adulthood, "embrac[ed] the Buddhist Dharma as the most revolutionary and civilized of possible human choices, as the logical extension of King's dream of the 'beloved community,' and Du Bois's 'vision of what the world could be if it was really a beautiful world.'"[56] By evoking the forward-looking dreams and visions of Du Bois and King, Johnson here deliberately links his immersion in Buddhism—including its seminal teachings of transience, dependent origination, and the interconnectedness and relationality of all things[57]—with his commitment to an ever-deeper understanding of the African American past, present, and future. Buddhism has, indeed, informed Johnson's writing on African American topics from early on, and *Middle Passage* is no exception.

The Buddhist storyline of *Middle Passage* can be summarized as follows: At the novel's beginning, Rutherford, a self-involved player, supports himself as a small-time crook in New Orleans. However, as he becomes a reluctant crew member on the *Republic*, his process of observing the Middle Passage of the forty violently uprooted Africans becomes for him a passage from a self-centered way of life to a new understanding of (non)self and humanity—a journey toward what Buddhists call a "Middle Path" or a "Middle Way." These concepts, obviously, resonate with the novel's title. In Buddhism, the notion of middle ground has two different meanings, in both cases denoting a position that lies between, or rises above, two extremes. First, a middle path can signify avoiding both indulgence and extreme varieties of asceticism.[58] Second, a middle way can mean transcending both eternalism (the view that an eternal, essential self exists) and nihilism (the complete denial of anything eternal).[59] The first of these two "middle" ideals manifests itself in *Middle Passage*'s dénouement: after surviving the horrendously eventful ocean voyage, Rutherford chooses neither to return to his earlier materialistic and hedonistic way of life nor to pursue enlightenment in isolation. Instead, in a conventional—yet, for him, radical—move, he decides to marry, raise a family, and lead the kind of quiet life that he had previously loathed but by the novel's end considers virtuous and worth pursuing. In a sense *Middle Passage* is, indeed, a classic (some would say conservative) moral tale. The second "middle" ideal, in turn, finds (partial) expression in Rutherford's gradual recognition of the necessity of abandoning the notion of an essential, immutable self and in his decision to focus on the needs of others.[60]

From a slightly different angle, *Middle Passage* can also be read as a Buddhist-influenced meditation on the greed-stricken disposition of human nature in general—that is, on the plight of humanity in the realm of desire, which, according to Buddhism, is the lowest plane of human existence, dominated by the illusory need to own and possess, a need arising from false or obscured perception. In Johnson's novel, this Eastern philosophical perspective on possessions effectively displaces the slaveholding United States' understanding of the alleged prestige of ownership, including the ownership of humans. It also reveals the meaninglessness of Rutherford's pretransformation life as a hedonistic "petty thief"[61] who craves material things and fleeting sensations. With its deliberate postmodern anachronisms, Johnson's narrative invites its readers to creatively apply these reflections to our own (postslavery, but hardly postownership, postmaterialistic, or posthedonistic) condition.

In *Middle Passage*, the Buddhist and phenomenological influences coalesce in the way in which Johnson links his portrayal of perception to the existential and moral process of his protagonist. For Rutherford, his "Buddhist-phenomenological" transformation means, first, gaining insight into the impermanence of reality and of humans' perceptions of it; second, realizing that the desires of the supposed self are as fleeting as the self; third, shifting focus from the cravings of the self to the needs of others in the spirit of interbeing,[62] interdependence, mutual respect, and voluntary sacrifice; and fourth, understanding that his encounter with the Allmuseri, transformative as it was, only was a "middle passage" for him, not the attainment of the final goal of his journey: he remains a work in progress. In "Philosophy and Black Fiction" (1980), Johnson argues that "the final concern of serious fiction is the liberation of perception."[63] In *Middle Passage*, he seeks to liberate the perception of the reader by telling the story of the liberation of the perceptual and existential faculties of his protagonist.

I have above contextualized *Middle Passage*'s treatment of perception within the intertextual dialogues that the novel conducts with *Benito Cereno*, phenomenology, and Buddhism. I now offer a close reading of *Middle Passage* that demonstrates *how* exactly Johnson (drawing on these three influences as well as on the genre of the conversion narrative) unfolds the tale of Rutherford's perceptual and existential transformation, and how this heavily modified "pilgrim's progress" results in the emergence of Rutherford's processual diasporic subjectivity. The chapter concludes with a brief comparison of diasporic and cosmopolitan self-identifications.

The "Pilgrim's" Unawakened Existence before His "Progress"

Before his journey, Rutherford is first a slave under relatively benign conditions in rural Makanda, Illinois, and then, after manumission, a freedman-cum-con-man enjoying the pleasures of New Orleans. He lives out what Friedrich Engels would have called "false consciousness": he is unaware, in any truly informed or consequential sense, of the racialized ideological formations that surround him and affect the conditions (material and beyond) of his and his fellow African Americans' lives. Removed from contact with first-generation slaves and having only experienced a relatively mild form of slavery, Rutherford is barely cognizant of the larger historical and political developments that have generated the Peculiar Institution, nor does he consciously identify with the African diaspora. He is, of course, aware of the most concrete socioeconomic consequences of his "blackness" for his daily existence in a racially ordered society, but he does not draw existential, communal, or political conclusions from this identity position.

Prior to his ocean voyage, Rutherford, moreover, embodies what Johnson in *Turning the Wheel* (in discussing Buddhism's Four Noble Truths, which address the existence of suffering, the origin of suffering, and the possibility of being rid of suffering, and then point to the Eightfold Path as the way of abandoning suffering)[64] identifies as a "thirst (*trishna*) or selfish desire."[65] Tellingly, on the day of their manumission Rutherford and his older brother, Jackson, have a major disagreement triggered by Rutherford's craving for money and possessions—that is, by a materialistic desire to fulfill the supposed needs of the supposed self, as Johnson would say; according to Buddhism, the desire that leads to suffering arises from attachment and from an illusory belief in a separate self whose needs are to be pitted against the needs and alleged selves of others. The rift between the Calhoun brothers opens up when their master, Reverend Peleg Chandler, on his deathbed frees them both in order to reward the selflessness and admirable work ethic that Jackson, a saintly character with "twice the patience of St. Francis,"[66] has consistently demonstrated throughout his years in bondage. Chandler's decision to manumit the exemplary slave and his less praiseworthy younger brother is accompanied by an unexpected offer that the dying man makes in the two men's presence: "I [Chandler] am in your [Jackson's] debt. Whatever you want for you and Rutherford is yours."[67] Jackson, however, responds by demonstrating not only a Franciscan/Buddhist lack of interest in property but also a truly egalitarian spirit: "[T]he property and profits of this farm should be divided equally among all your servants and hired hands, presently and formerly employed . . .—the fixed capital spread among bondmen throughout the county . . .—and whatever remains donated to that college in Oberlin what helps Negroes on their way north."[68] Greedier and more opportunistic than Jackson, a stunned Rutherford feels betrayed by his brother, although later, on the *Republic*, he humbly acknowledges that Jackson could have easily been an Allmuseri priest[69]—so profoundly does the countermaterialistic elder brother's worldview resonate with that of the "Ur-tribe of humanity."[70]

After Rutherford receives his meager share of Chandler's inheritance, he abandons his life in Illinois, lights out for Louisiana, and ends up in New Orleans, where he supports himself through thievery and happily immerses himself in the world of gambling houses and brothels. The one individual in the Crescent City who tries to push Rutherford in the direction of ethical living is Isadora Bailey, "a frugal, quiet, devoutly Christian girl, . . . the fourth daughter of a large Boston family free since the Revolutionary War."[71] Courtship is vaguely in the air, but Rutherford shuns commitment,[72] whereas Isadora is convinced that marital bliss would give them both a sense of purpose. Her last resort in pressuring Rutherford into marriage is blackmail. She enlists the assistance of Philippe "Papa" Zeringue, the man behind all of Rutherford's creditors, an underworld financier whom Johnson has compared to a present-day "drug lord . . . who feeds his own people poison."[73] The naive Isadora strikes a deal with Papa: he will force the reluctant bridegroom to marry her, and she, in return, will pay Rutherford's debts in full. Rutherford, however, is determined to escape this extortion and boards the *Republic* as a stowaway to flee New Orleans. Discovered an hour after the slaver has left the port, he is allowed to stay on board as an unpaid assistant to the ship's cook.

As these turns of events indicate, the alteration of Rutherford's legal status from property to a freedman does not, in itself, emancipate him existentially or spiritually. From a Buddhist perspective, Rutherford's pleasure-seeking existence in New Orleans is governed by samsaric illusions and his dependence on them—that is, by one type of mental slavery. As he later recalls, "I hungered—literally *hungered*—for life in all its shades and hues: I was hooked on sensation, you might say, a lecher for perception and the nerve-knocking thrill, like a shot of opium, of new 'experiences.'"[74] Rutherford's drug-associated lexicon here underscores the nature of his youthful hunger for experiences as an addiction. A later scene on the *Republic*, in which Rutherford breaks into the captain's cabin mainly for the sake of another "nerve-knocking thrill" triggered by the excitement of stealing, reinforces this undertone of helpless dependence: although aware that he is putting himself at risk, Rutherford craves the "familiar, sensual tingle that came whenever [he] broke into someone's home."[75] In *Turning the Wheel*, Johnson lists the eight "steps" on Buddhism's Eightfold Path (Perfect View, Perfect Thought, Perfect Speech, Perfect Conduct, Perfect Livelihood, Perfect Effort, Perfect Mindfulness, and Perfect Concentration)[76] and adds, "for a practitioner, the first realized steps on the Path are stages 3–5 (ethical living)."[77] In Rutherford's pretransformation existence, "[t]heft," as he later admits, "was the closest thing I knew to transcendence."[78] At this point, he has yet to take his very first steps on the Path.

A Journey to Black Diasporic Consciousness

From a Buddhist perspective, Rutherford's eagerness to board a slaver is yet another sign that focused moral contemplation is absent from his life. As he sneaks onto the ship, he is aware of its mission: the *Republic* "would up-anchor and sail eastward against the prevailing winds to the barracoon, or slave factory, at Bangalang on the Guinea coast, take on a cargo of Africans, and then, God willing, return in three months."[79] Obsessed with the need to get away, Rutherford initially suppresses the political and emotional significance of what he has learned about the vessel and its destination. However, despite his psychological defenses, he cannot help being struck by the ship's ominous gloom, suggestive of Ishmael's first sighting of the *Pequod* ("a thing of trophies," a "cannibal of a craft, tricking herself forth in the chased bones of her enemies") in *Moby-Dick*.[80] In Melville's novel about Ahab's fierce fixation, the fate of the *Pequod*, whose name serves as a reference to vanished Indian warriors, can be read as symbolizing the deadly consequences of monomaniacal colonialist/imperialist drive. In *Middle Passage*, a similar dynamic is set in motion in the context of the Atlantic slave trade:[81] "I [Rutherford] had an odd sensation, difficult to explain, that I'd boarded not a ship but a kind of fantastic, floating Black Maria, a wooden sepulcher whose timbers moaned with the memory of too many runs of black gold between the New World and the Old."[82]

On board the *Republic*, Rutherford's strategy of psychological repression—the tactic of limiting and adjusting one's perceptions to fit one's goals—is initially effective. In the first stages of the voyage, he is fully preoccupied with the tasks of securing a position for himself on the ship, discovering the basic rules of life at sea, and learning how to interact with Captain Ebenezer Falcon (an Ahab figure, as several critics have pointed out), the (Starbuck-like) first mate Peter Cringle, and the rest of the crew. It soon becomes apparent, however, that Rutherford's life on the *Republic* is going to consist of one wake-up call after another (including his conversation on his first day on the *Republic* with the ship's cook, the physically ruined alcoholic Josiah Squibb, an embodiment of what Rutherford might himself become if he fails to change his ways)[83]—a series of challenges to his subconscious effort to manipulate his perceptions.

Yet, although Rutherford's perceptions of self and reality begin to change, his transformation takes time. During the initial phases of the sea voyage, when Rutherford has not yet encountered the Allmuseri or adopted what Vincent A. O'Keefe calls their "holistic ideals of humility, process, and reciprocity,"[84] his perception is marred by an objectifying attitude toward his fellow humans. This disposition resembles that of Captain Falcon, despite the obvious differences in Rutherford's and Falcon's respective achievements. Falcon may be dwarfish and deformed physically, but as an imperialist he is quite distinguished.[85] Rutherford, though neither accomplished nor famous, knows craving, greed, and desire as intimately as the potent captain does, and he indirectly admits as much to himself: "I saw something—or thought I did—of myself in him [Falcon] and hated that."[86] O'Keefe, drawing on the nuptial images evoked by the novel's ring symbolism, observes that Rutherford's psychological progress during his tenure on the *Republic* "parallels the evolution of his symbolic marriage to and divorce from Captain Falcon."[87] Indeed, as the ship lies anchored off the West African coast, Falcon makes

Rutherford a spy who is to report to him any "sea changes," or alterations of mood, among either the crew or the Allmuseri. At this point, it seems that Rutherford may have escaped one marriage only to become, both mentally and sexually, the "shipboard bride"[88] (Rutherford's term) of Falcon, who even gives the younger man a magnetic ring similar to his own (a gift that one minor character calls a "queer ring"),[89] hence sealing their "union." For the reader, the identical rings symbolize the initial similarities between the two men's perceptions of the world. However, after two separate mutinies break out on the ship almost simultaneously and Falcon is severely injured in the resulting chaos, Rutherford gives Falcon back his ring, which is, in fact, a gun-ring, a circle-shaped ring trigger. The captain uses it to shoot himself, committing suicide with the help of this symbol of lost loyalty.[90] Rutherford's narrative, written after Falcon's death, is not only a "continuation" but also a "revision"[91] of the captain's log: it reveals Rutherford's eventual need to overwrite Falcon's text, free himself from the captain's influence, and inscribe in the log his own perspective on the fate of the *Republic*.

While Rutherford's existential transformation is, paradoxically, in part facilitated by his philosophical conversations with the slave-trading Falcon (an erudite man who is highly capable of integrative and synthetic thinking),[92] it is his role as a terrified eyewitness to the white captain's brutal treatment of the African captives that most powerfully challenges Rutherford's previously unreflective worldview and opens his eyes to the true horrors of the Atlantic slave trade and its accompanying racialization. When, at Bangalang, forty Allmuseri are loaded into the *Republic*'s hold that is "darker than the belly of Jonah's whale,"[93] the shame of participating in the slave trade—a sentiment indicative of the young freedman's awakening to the moral and existential implications of his African diasporic identity position—begins to overwhelm Rutherford. He witnesses, from the sidelines, how fiercely and desperately the captives resist the fate of becoming slaves: a mother commits infanticide by throwing her baby into the ocean to protect the child from enslavement, and at least two male captives attempt "to follow, [suicidally] straining against their chains."[94] While much of Johnson's narrative includes comic details and abstract philosophical ruminations, his solemn account of Falcon's violent suppression of slave resistance serves to realistically represent the terror that, historically, characterized the Middle Passage. The cruel dehumanization of the Africans by the captain and his crew shocks Rutherford's conscience, and the young freedman is faced with the challenge of black solidarity more acutely than ever before.

Johnson's rendering of Rutherford's emerging moral aversion to the mission of the *Republic* implicitly converses with *The Interesting Narrative* of Olaudah Equiano, who earned the price of his freedom by working as a sailor—not infrequently on vessels whose holds contained human cargo.[95] Equiano's prose, though laconic, reveals his deep distress about participating in the slave trade. He admits, for example, that he knew about white crewmen raping African women and girls during the voyages[96]—a disclosure demonstrating the profound anguish, frustration, and emasculating guilt that he must have experienced while trying to navigate the impossible circumstances in which he found himself as a young slave.[97] Although the fictional Rutherford's predicament is not completely identical with that of the historical Equiano, Johnson's protagonist, too, begins to question the very fundamentals of his ethics and morality when the physical presence of the captured Africans on the *Republic* breaks down his earlier defense mechanism, repression, and compels him to acknowledge his own complicity in perpetuating the slave trade: "It was then my hair started going white.... [I]t behooves me for the sake of my own character, shabby as this is, to explain how murderous my thoughts became after taking part in the captivity of the Allmuseri."[98] Rutherford's self-identification with early black travelers who, like himself, had found themselves on ocean voyages on ships manned by whites, reveals that he now pointedly views himself as an African diasporic subject: "I wondered if the blacks who'd traveled with Balboa and Cortez hated their leaders as much as I did Ebenezer Falcon, if Estéban, the legendary explorer from Morocco, felt as cool toward his companions, three Spanish officers, as I sometimes did toward Cringle, who would never in this life see himself, his own blighted history, in the slaves we intended to sell."[99]

A pivotal question in *Middle Passage* is who perceives what in whom—in particular, who sees himself in whom, as Rutherford's above comment on Cringle indicates. While Falcon's brutality causes Rutherford to distance himself from the crew, his exposure to the Allmuseri and their beliefs makes him long to belong with the Africans. During the journey back to Louisiana, Rutherford increasingly begins to "see himself, his own blighted history"[100] in the Allmuseri. He develops a strong desire to understand them and their philosophy of life more fully—and to be one of them, if possible. The information Rutherford had initially received about the tribe (before having met any Allmuseri, except for the fallen tribe member Santos, Papa Zeringue's right hand back in New Orleans) had been filtered through the perspective of Cringle, who, in turn, had accepted the Spanish explorer Rafael García's characterization of the Allmuseri as "[s]orcerers" and "devil-worshiping, spell-casting wizards"[101] as objective truth. However, Rutherford's perception of the Allmuseri begins to change when he befriends Ngonyama (finally, an actual Allmuseri), whose name William Nash takes to mean "interpreter."[102] Regardless of how exactly one reads the name's etymology, Nash's main point is inarguable: Ngonyama acts as Rutherford's linguistic and cultural interpreter on the *Republic*, teaching the American "his tribe's official history, the story of themselves they stuck by,"[103] as well as key elements of their language, belief system, and aesthetics. The more Rutherford listens to Ngonyama, the more impressed he is by what he learns, and he finds himself yearning to be like the Allmuseri. He realizes that the Allmuseri are "less a biological tribe than a clan held together by values"[104]—values that he used to belittle but now begins to admire.

However, in this novel, in which the transformation of perception is everything, even Rutherford's view of the Allmuseri changes more than once. That is, his perception of the Africans is altered again after two separate mutinies, one by the Allmuseri and another by the crew, coincide on the *Republic*. The Allmuseri triumph over their captors, prompting Falcon to admit, briefly before his suicide, that his scheming had been marred by one fundamental flaw (a miscalculation very familiar to readers of *Benito Cereno*): "Then we underestimated the blacks? They're smarter than I thought?"[105] However, Falcon's belated recognition means little to the Allmuseri. Their victory is bitter because resorting to violence required them to abandon their holistic faith in the Unity of all Being and to enter the corrupt state of "multiplicity, of *me* versus *thee*,"[106] that is, to adopt a dualistic worldview and the accompanying concept of the "enemy." As Rutherford starts to realize, Falcon's death does not erase the fact that the slave-trading captain, in addition to uprooting the Allmuseri geographically, brought them into contact with forces that violently altered their ancient way of life and their perception of themselves.[107] Rutherford begins to see that imperialist "exploration" drastically changes the "explored" or, rather, the exploited.

During the voyage, the Allmuseri go in Rutherford's mind "from being exotic, romanticized avatars of a perfect, timeless age," as Daniel Scott III observes, to being mortals in an in-between stage, diasporic individuals transformed by their Middle Passage.[108] "Stupidly," muses Rutherford, "I had seen their lives and culture as timeless product, . . . when the truth was that they were process and Heraclitean change, like any men, not fixed but evolving."[109] Rutherford's revised perception of the Allmuseri and his eventual encounter with their god on board the *Republic*[110]—ultimately, his encounter with himself and with what he has most passionately loved and hated—open his eyes to see that all humans, including himself, are multifaceted and constantly changing. Rutherford gradually understands that respect for process (again, for the "verb" rather than the static "noun," as Johnson puts it while describing the language of the Allmuseri) is the key to living in harmony with oneself (or one's nonself) and with the world. Rutherford's arrival at this insight is a vitally important phase in his passage from ignorance to knowledge, from mental slavery to freedom.

After the mutiny, the Africans' forced violation of the sacred morality that has upheld them for centuries casts a shadow of doom over the ship, and the *Republic* eventually sinks in a fierce storm. Everyone on board dies except for Rutherford, Squibb, and three Allmuseri children. Most of Johnson's Allmuseri perish en route to the New World, taking with them countless mentally stored individual and communal memories. However, despite this tragic climax of the novel, Johnson does not hold to any antiquated notion of all Africanisms having died in the New World or of all memory of Africa having vanished. On the contrary, the novel's ending resonates with the current scholarly consensus (addressed in my introduction) concerning the inarguable survival of Africanisms in the New World. In "Philosophy and Black Fiction," Johnson briefly discusses "African survivalisms,"[111] and in *Middle Passage* the survival of the three Allmuseri minors calls attention to the fragile, yet very real, continuity that exists between traditional African and black diasporic cultural practices. It is symbolically significant that all Allmuseri survivors are children, embodiments not only of the past but also of the present and the future. They epitomize both loss and hope, both the unspeakable suffering caused by the Atlantic slave trade and the possibility of an individual, communal, and societal transformation. In all their fragility, they personify continuity with the old continent as well as a powerful potential for becoming new creations in the New World—on terms, however, that remain undefined.

Diasporic Existence as a Continuing Journey

As indicated, *Middle Passage* addresses head-on the difficult questions, foundational to the study of diasporas, of "return" and "origins." Rutherford (re)connects with Africa but poignantly realizes that a direct cultural return to some real or imagined ur-Africanity is impossible. His contact with the captive Africans whom he encounters on the slave ship is a profoundly transformative experience for him; yet he, a diasporic subject, does not have an insider's intimate knowledge of their customs and beliefs, nor does he learn to speak their language with native accent or fluency during their brief time together on the *Republic*. His desire to belong with the Allmuseri does not result in any simplistic, formulaic answer to the question of what exactly such a belonging might mean in practice. He poignantly admits to himself that he is largely separated from the Africans' way of life, having always lived in an epistemological and spiritual realm very different from theirs;[112] the shared racial affiliation does not, per se, bring with it any mystical knowledge about how to live out any allegedly "universal" blackness. Rutherford's dialogic and transformative encounters on the slave ship bring him to a powerful awareness of his diasporic identity position, but this consciousness does not come with a set of instructions on how to live out this newly discovered self-understanding.

Yet, Johnson's antihero, lost and blind as he initially seems, does learn a new way of seeing from the Allmuseri, and he carries this wisdom (a transformed perception of being), with its Africanity and universality, back to the United States. The final scenes of *Middle Passage*, filled as they are with parody and comic excess, portray a protagonist who begins to apply his new vision of the nature of human existence to his daily life, although this vision is, inevitably, evolving rather than complete. Rutherford and Isadora find each other again, and they decide to marry and together raise one of the Allmuseri survivors in the United States, possibly back in Makanda, Illinois.[113] As this decision indicates, Johnson's diasporic protagonist—a free black man without full civil rights in antebellum America—has arrived at an understanding of his national belonging that is ambivalent, yet cautiously affirmative: "[I]f this land of refugees and former indentured servants, religious heretics and half-breeds, whoresons and fugitives—this cauldron of mongrels from all points of compass—was all I could rightly call *home*, then aye: I was of it."[114]

In other words, the hope permeating the novel's open-ended conclusion resides in Rutherford's explicit acknowledgment of his diasporic transformation ("The voyage had irreversibly changed my seeing, made of me a cultural mongrel")[115] and in his and Isadora's mutual commitment to partnership, parenthood, and voluntary interdependence/interbeing—including a commitment to a long process of learning to let go of the alleged ego and its alleged needs, to summon Buddhist vocabulary again. However, before the two can reach this ideal state of being, they, as the transformed protagonist intuits, still have to cross "countless seas of suffering"[116] generated by the temptation to adhere to samsaric illusions concerning "selfhood" and the "*me* versus *thee*."[117]

Still on a journey, Rutherford realizes that his transatlantic crossings to West Africa and back—transformative as they were—indeed were only a "middle passage" for him, rather than the attainment of ultimate enlightenment.

The ending of *Middle Passage*, in sum, brings together the motifs of spiritual and geographical destination, safe and intimate domesticity, and national belonging. However, as befits this narrative of a passage to (be)longing, the transformed narrator-protagonist's "home," in all the senses described above, is in the end left at a stage of initial formation. Any mode of belonging remains a work in progress in this complex tale about the emergence of black diasporic subjectivity. For Johnson, the black diasporic existence, defined by its processual character, is more about journeying and routes than it is about any fixed identity that can be locked in by pointing to a precisely definable African "origin" or to a known destination of the voyage.

Johnson, Diaspora, and Racial Antiessentialism

Toward the end of *Middle Passage*, Rutherford acknowledges that he cannot allow oppressive Others, be they "white rascals like Ebenezer Falcon" or "black ones like Zeringue,"[118] to mandate the direction of his journey through life. While the novel exhibits a profound interest in the Buddhist annihilation of selfhood, it also, somewhat paradoxically, at the same time highlights black agency—the right of individuals of African descent to be subjects rather than objects, definers rather than the defined.

In addition to pointing to the paradox that informs "agency" and "*self*-understanding" in the context of Buddhistically informed fiction, the concept of black diasporic identity here also raises the question of how Johnson understands "race." In 2003, Johnson discussed the inadequacies of race-thinking as follows:

> For me, "race" is the grandest of illusions, a perfect example of what Buddhists (and I am a Buddhist) call samsara. Yet I do believe that, as in any age, a respectable percentage of the population will slough off thinking in terms of racial essences or "natures." Just abandon it as excess baggage they realize they no longer need. As a creator, I want to be on the side of those who help encourage that next step in human evolution, however small my contribution might be.[119]

In other words, Johnson sees race as a samsaric illusion and hopes that humanity will eventually transcend it. In *Middle Passage*, he therefore devotes serious attention to the history and consequences of race-thinking and antiblack racism; for example, the novel's critique of Cartesian and other dualisms reflects this perspective.[120] In "Becoming Modern Racialized Subjects" (2009), Hazel Carby examines fictional and nonfictional narratives that depict how "the racialized self is invented in the process of an encounter, produced, in other words, as a subject dialogically constituted in and through its relation to an other or others."[121] *Middle Passage* portrays "racializing encounters" in the sense suggested by Carby (that is, encounters through which the production of racialized selfhood occurs) and, in the process, sternly critiques racialization. As Marcus Rediker writes in *The Slave Ship* (2007), "In producing workers for the plantation, the ship-factory also produced 'race.' . . . At the beginning of the Middle Passage, captains loaded on board the vessel a multiethnic collection of Africans, who would, in the American port, become 'black people' or a 'negro race.'"[122] Johnson's narrative, representing an antiessentialist critique of "race," offers a fictional representation of the historical process described by Rediker and, in so doing, attacks oppression and discrimination based on racialized perception. Although *Middle Passage* is about the formation of black diasporic identity/consciousness, neither "blackness" nor "whiteness" receives any fixed ontological or epistemological definition in Johnson's treatment. Race does, to a degree, operate as an indicator of "kith and kin" for Rutherford in Illinois, in New Orleans, and on the *Republic*, but its *meaning* is continually contested and relativized in each of these contexts.

In keeping with his refusal to essentialize race, in his essays Johnson levels criticisms against the Black Power and Black Arts movements—at the same time, in effect, critiquing Afrocentrism as well. For example, in "Novelists of Memory" Johnson comments on the Black Arts movement as follows: "[T]his astonishing phase of Afro-American literary history would develop its own limitations, the first and foremost of these being a tendency toward separatism that ran counter to the push for integration by the majority of blacks. Secondly, it teetered often toward 'essentialism,' or the belief in an inherent racial nature."[123] Indeed, it befits not only Johnson's postmodernism but also his distaste for all forms of black cultural nationalism (all of which he sees as having produced overly singular, essentialist, and rigid notions of blackness)[124] that *Middle Passage* depicts the emergence of a black *diasporic* identity—that is, the formation of a cultural, political, and existential awareness that is inherently fraught with ambivalences and characterized by processual properties. Johnson is highly suspicious of any approach that denies the diversity and complexity of black life and of any interpretation of blackness that "has become rigid, forced into formulaes."[125] He writes in "Philosophy and Black Fiction" that "Black life is ambiguous, and a kaleidoscope of meanings rich, multisided."[126] For him, the truly productive prompt for serious black fiction (which he sees as necessarily portraying "the quest for identity and liberty")[127] is an interest in hybridity, multiplicity, ambiguity, and ambivalence, all of which are defining characteristics of the diasporic predicament.

Diasporic Consciousness and Cosmopolitanism

Because *Middle Passage* facilitates reflections on the processual formation of a transnational identity, it invites a brief clarification of the difference between diasporic and cosmopolitan orientations. In *Charles Johnson in Context* (2009), Linda Furgerson Selzer deftly contextualizes *Middle Passage* within what she calls "the rise of the new black intellectual" in the United States.[128] She demonstrates the emergence of "a new generation of black intellectuals"[129] since the early 1990s by listing an impressive number of book-length studies that explicitly focus on the genealogy and present status of black intellectualism, from bell hooks and Cornel West's *Breaking Bread* (1991) to Houston Baker's *Betrayal* (2008).[130] In the process, Selzer observes that Johnson's fictional writing "has been increasingly identified with the cosmopolitan wing of black intellectualism"[131] and adds that those critiquing black cosmopolitan orientations in the United States tend to ignore "the degree to which black American intellectual and social culture has historically 'always already' been a cosmopolitan culture."[132] Using "cosmopolitanism" as the key term in her sophisticated analysis of *Middle Passage*, Selzer argues that the novel presents "on a single ship multiple forms of cosmopolitanism that interrogate one another"[133] and that it can therefore be read as participating in the larger conversations whereby such intellectuals as Kwame Anthony Appiah and Henry Louis Gates Jr. have recently sought to "expand the conceptual borders of cosmopolitan thought" by distinguishing among various types of cosmopolitanism (for example, "situated," "patriotic," and "rooted" or "partial").[134]

What changes, then, conceptually and intellectually, when "cosmopolitan" is substituted with "diasporic" as the discussion's key term? In practice, much of the outcome of the scholarly attention remains the same—especially in this case, because Selzer determinedly dissociates her nuanced analysis of *Middle Passage* from any elitist connotations for which the lexicon of cosmopolitanism has often been criticized. While she freely admits that "cosmopolitanism has been frequently identified with the privileged mobility of the elite,"[135] she adds that one of the most important aspects of the recent theoretical work on cosmopolitanism has been the drive to "rethink its relation to non-elites, including the poor and the enslaved"[136]—an effort with which she allies herself. Overall, it would make little sense to pit cosmopolitan and diasporic identities against each other; their overlap is, after all, often significant or even complete in lived experience. Nonetheless, the question of what differentiates the two is worth asking, not only for the sake of fruitful conceptual cross-pollination, but also for the purpose of articulating what is at stake in the use of the term "diaspora."

In *Cosmopolitanism* (2006), Appiah, an English-born Ghanaian American philosopher, introduces a position that he previously called "rooted cosmopolitanism"[137] but here terms "partial cosmopolitanism."[138] While the stereotypical notion of the cosmopolitan as an aloof, disenchanted, and culturally elitist border-crosser who cherishes critical distance and cultivates emotional detachment is well known,[139] Appiah approaches and envisions cosmopolitanism differently. He opens *Cosmopolitanism* with a personal memory that references an anticolonial struggle and thus points to intense engagement rather than to indifferent detachment: "In the final message my father left for me and my sisters, he wrote, 'Remember you are citizens of the world.' But as a leader of the independence movement in what was then the Gold Coast, he never saw a conflict between local partialities and a universal morality—between being part of the place you were and a part of a broader human community."[140] Appiah's "partial cosmopolitanism"—representing what Eric Brown, in his discussion of Stoic cosmopolitanisms, terms "moderate cosmopolitanism" (which, in the Stoic context, allowed for "special consideration for compatriots")[141]—navigates the terrain between two extreme positions: "strict cosmopolitanism,"[142] on the one hand, and anticosmopolitanism, on the other. Strict cosmopolitanism sets the moral bar extremely high by arguing that one's moral responsibilities to any member of the human community are the same. This model rejects the notion that one's moral responsibilities to members of one's nation/state, locality, or community should take priority over one's responsibilities to strangers. According to the strictest version of cosmopolitanism, there is no difference between the needs of an alien living overseas and the needs of one's neighbor, in terms of one's moral obligation to respond to those needs. Anticosmopolitanism, by contrast (according to Richard Shapcott's definition), involves highlighting "contextual origins of community and ethics," denouncing "cosmopolitan universalism," and arguing "that actual particularistic community, such as nationality, overrides any abstract or imagined bonds between members of the human species."[143]

Appiah, in turn—accepting neither the strict version nor anticosmopolitanism—promotes the kind of cosmopolitanism that *both* recognizes the existence of a global human community that creates universal moral obligations *and* acknowledges that we have special responsibilities to those closest to us; hence his term "partial cosmopolitanism." Appiah admits that these two principles at times clash and that cosmopolitanism therefore is, in a sense, "the name not of the solution but of the challenge."[144] Nevertheless, he advocates partial cosmopolitanism as the ideal that we should strive for:

> A citizen of the world: how far can we take that idea? Are you really supposed to abjure all local allegiances and partialities in the name of this vast abstraction, humanity? ... Fortunately, we need take sides neither with the nationalist who abandons all foreigners nor with the hardcore cosmopolitan who regards her friends and fellow citizens with icy impartiality. The position worth defending might be called (in both senses) a partial cosmopolitanism.[145]

On the one hand, nothing in Appiah's definition of partial cosmopolitanism clashes with what has emerged from my reading of the narrative of diasporic subjectivity embedded in *Middle Passage*; in fact, the resonances are obvious. Diasporic consciousness and cosmopolitan awareness have much in common: both embody and articulate a transnational identity, neither is an absolute, and it is true of both that they are the names "not of the solution but of the challenge." On the other hand, cosmopolitanism and diaspora do name two different, even if partially overlapping, sets of challenges. Cosmopolitanism addresses the possibilities and limitations of global citizenship, the condition of being a citizen of the world. Black diasporic interrogations, in turn, are concerned with uprootedness and dislocation, the various ambivalences of (be)longing, and the complex questions of why, how, and to what extent "blackness" might still create a bond and a sense of commonality and solidarity among people of African descent in today's world. As noted in the introduction, it is easy to see that what Brent Hayes Edwards terms the "quagmire of origins"[146] indeed is a quagmire; yet routes, at least (if not necessarily roots), yearn to be addressed in diasporic interrogations.

Conclusion

This chapter has demonstrated, first, that Johnson's 1990 "novel of memory," *Middle Passage*—which, despite its postmodernistically comic quirks, deeply laments the suffering that the Atlantic slave trade inflicted on its victims—contributes to the cultural mediation of the diasporic ur-experience of the forced Atlantic crossing for future generations. Second, this chapter has also shown that *Middle Passage* participates in the ongoing construction of black diasporic identity or consciousness by offering a philosophically and spiritually informed thematic narrative of the formation of a black diasporic subject. By the novel's end, Rutherford has arrived at an analytically and emotionally processed awareness of his identity position as a member of the African diaspora, recognizes that both rupture and connection characterize his relationship with Africanity, and acknowledges the necessity of an ever-continuing existential journey. Third, this chapter has revealed that transformed/liberated perception and transformed/liberated consciousness are inextricably intertwined in *Middle Passage*. Owing to this connection, Johnson bolsters his narrative of the formation of diasporic subjectivity (a narrative of the formation of one type of transformed/liberated consciousness) by conversing with the role of perception in Melville's *Benito Cereno*, in phenomenology, and in Buddhism. Fourth, this chapter has stressed that Johnson's phenomenologically and Buddhistically informed emphasis on the malleability of black diasporic identity offers a counterargument to black cultural nationalistic positions, which he sees as propagating fixed, static notions of blackness.

For some readers, the eponymous theme of *Middle Passage* perhaps evokes Michelle M. Wright's concern, addressed in my introduction, that the "Middle Passage epistemology" may view people(s) of African descent only as victims of antiblack racism and may, due to this narrow focus, be unable to recognize and appreciate black agency. In contemporary black diasporic fiction, however, both black suffering and black agency are usually integral aspects of Middle Passage narratives—and, as this chapter has made clear, both of these emphases are present in *Middle Passage*. But, rather than just giving expression to the dialectic of victimhood and agency, Johnson adds something else to the mix: heavily invested in fluidity and process, *Middle Passage* implicitly critiques black cultural nationalism and Afrocentrism—including their often ahistorical dismissal of how much both Africa, in all its multiplicity, and the diasporic people(s) of African descent have changed over the centuries. Concerned with history and memory, Johnson does emphasize the importance of Africa for black diasporic identity. However, instead of romantically imagining some easy or direct reconnection with "roots" (which would, in Afrocentric constellations, guarantee black cultural "authenticity"), he highlights an awareness of rupture, an ambivalent longing for roots, the complexity (though not a total impossibility) of reconnection, the condition of being perpetually *en route*, and the resulting processual and hybrid nature of black diasporic identity formation.

Having launched my examination of contemporary novelistic renderings of black diasporic identity formation with an analysis of *Middle Passage*, I next discuss Lawrence Hill's *The Book of Negroes*, which takes a more historical approach to the formation of diasporic subjectivity than does the more philosophically based *Middle Passage*. However, rather than presenting Hill's "historical" approach as diametrically opposed to Johnson's more "philosophical" one, I ultimately suggest that each author is heavily invested in both the historical and the existential as he depicts the complexities of the past. Hill may be more interested in historical detail than Johnson, but in *The Book of Negroes* he also strongly focuses on the existential aspects of his protagonist's diasporic identity formation (although he approaches questions of existence and self-understanding from a more psychological perspective than does the philosophically oriented Johnson). And while Johnson may primarily be invested in the existential and epistemological dimensions of the Middle Passage, his novel at the same time affirms that the experience of crossing "the ocean of constant middle passage" (Leon Forrest's term)[147] was historically extremely real, as were the unreasonably costly lessons of resistance, protest, adaptation, and renewed resistance learned first at sea and then on land.

2

Early Black Atlantic Crossings

Lawrence Hill's *The Book of Negroes*

The formation of black diasporic subjectivity is a pivotal theme both in Johnson's *Middle Passage* and in the Canadian author Lawrence Hill's[1] *The Book of Negroes* (the first US edition of which was entitled *Someone Knows My Name*),[2] and both novels forge a deep connection between black diasporic memory and identity. One major difference between these two works is that Hill's accounts of African diasporic history and geography are much more detailed than Johnson's. "Detailed" does not here mean "narrow"; *The Book of Negroes* is a novel with a broad diasporic scope. In *Archives of the Black Atlantic*, Wendy W. Walters examines how historically oriented black diasporic fiction "exposes the nation-state as an insufficient boundary for both reading the archive and reading comparative literature" and "unmoors the concept of archive from its stubborn attachment to national narratives."[3] The category of "national narrative" would, indeed, be an insufficient tool for analyzing *The Book of Negroes*, which is both a neo-slave narrative and a historical novel about black movement and migration in various locations on the Atlantic rim during the latter half of the eighteenth century—mainly in regions linked with the reach and boundaries of the British Empire, with the exception of the protagonist's birthplace in present-day Mali.[4] In a 2013 interview with Winfried Siemerling, Hill elaborated on the purpose of his novel's circum-Atlantic perspective as follows:

> *The Book of Negroes* . . . seeks to unite the black experience because I think it is unhelpful, and it is at odds with my own perceptions of the world, to describe black experiences as being discrete. The black American experience is of course not the black Canadian experience, which is not the Caribbean experience, which is not the African experience,

which is not the experience of, say, blacks in London, England, in the early nineteenth and late-eighteenth centuries. But these are all people of the African Diaspora and they are connected in all sorts of ways. In *The Book of Negroes*, ... I am trying to unite the experiences, the travels, and the voyages of the African peoples in the eighteenth century. They are on the move.[5]

The emergence of Black Loyalism was a major manifestation of people of African descent being "on the move" on the Atlantic Seaboard in the late eighteenth century. During the American Revolutionary War, tens of thousands of enslaved blacks (some of them first generation, others American-born) escaped from southern farms and plantations to serve the British, who, in return, promised to liberate these fugitives at the war's end. Of those Black Loyalists who were in New York City as the war drew to its close, three thousand were evacuated to Nova Scotia in 1783. Nine years later, many of these evacuees were among the approximately 1,200 black migrants who in 1792 sailed from Halifax to Sierra Leone, where they founded the colony of Freetown. Hill's fictional narrator-protagonist, Aminata Diallo, is one of these migrants. This chapter, focusing on Hill's rendering of the formation of Aminata's diasporic subjectivity, teases out of the fabric of *The Book of Negroes* its historically saturated thread of Aminata's long and complex process of becoming who she is by the novel's close—a strong-willed, even if physically frail, survivor of the Middle Passage, slavery, and a hard life in Nova Scotia and Sierra Leone; a Loyalist skeptical of all political affiliations, including her own; a London-based abolitionist; and, most importantly, a diasporic subject with a processual identity.

In writing about the loyalty of many blacks to the British during the Revolutionary War,[6] Hill depicts a phenomenon that some, though not all that many, historians have studied in detail. Hill states in the acknowledgments that he discovered this topic while reading James W. St. G. Walker's 1976 monograph, *The Black Loyalists*,[7] which Ira Berlin in 1978 acclaimed as "a singularly important book" for American historians.[8] The year 1976 also saw the publication of Ellen Gibson Wilson's *The Loyal Blacks*, another groundbreaking and thorough study on the subject.[9] Sylvia R. Frey's *Water from the Rock* (1991) and Simon Schama's *Rough Crossings*, a 2005 work of popular narrative history, have more recently given Black Loyalism new visibility,[10] as have Cassandra Pybus's *Epic Journeys of Freedom* (2006) and Maya Jasanoff's *Liberty's Exiles* (2011), the latter of which includes blacks in its more comprehensive discussion of Loyalism. Each of these scholarly works in its own way underscores that the history of Black Loyalism debunks the myth that black people were "passive, credulous pawns of American or British strategy"[11] in the Revolutionary era's North America. Both Walker and Wilson emphasized black agency,[12] and the later studies fully agree with their position. Hill's literary rendering of Black Loyalism does the same: Hill portrays his itinerant protagonist and her peers as active subjects who are deeply invested in legal freedom and powerfully aware of the complexities of their personal decision making in the midst of major shifts in public life, whether such shifts occur in the emerging United States, Canada, Sierra Leone, or Britain.

By choosing a more historical approach to black diasporic identity formation than *Middle Passage* does,[13] *The Book of Negroes* both uses and reimagines what can be found in archival data. Archives, broadly understood, are sites of knowledge production, as Michel Foucault emphasized; knowledge production, in turn, both draws on and (re)produces power relations. In *Lose Your Mother*, Saidiya Hartman writes about the silence of the archives, about how the lives and fates of countless individual slaves will, biographically, always remain unknown to us. Both Hartman's book and Michel-Rolph Trouillot's similarly oriented study of Haitian history, *Silencing the Past*, offer tragic examples of archives reproducing what Hazel Carby, referencing both Foucault and Stuart Hall, aptly terms relations of dominance and subjugation.[14] However, rather than resigning to the muteness of the "official" archives, historical novels by black diasporic authors—including *The Book of Negroes*—take it on themselves to transform this silence and its implied power relations into what Walters calls "alternate narratives of agency, humanity, and empowerment, as a supplement to the meager traces recorded in the archives of the slave trader, colonizer, or court room."[15]

It befits Walters's dual reference to black agency and the courtroom that while *The Book of Negroes* focuses on the protagonist's personal "emotional survival"[16] during the formation of her diasporic subjectivity (which Hill depicts as a lifelong process), the novel at the same time narrates, and participates in, the public and the political. Hill's rendering of the late-eighteenth-century Atlantic world and British Empire was—as a result of what he calls a "happy coincidence"[17]—published in 2007, the year Britain and the Commonwealth commemorated the bicentennial of the British ban on the slave trade. *The Book of Negroes* offers a counternarrative to what has long been the dominant British mode of such commemorations. In post-1807 Britain, the memory of the slave trade and its closing has typically been transformed into a story of white abolitionist heroism; there has been very little room for the black slave (or the black abolitionist, for that matter) in that celebratory narrative.[18] *The Book of Negroes*, by contrast, foregrounds the black experience by highlighting both black suffering and black resourcefulness as it traces the birth of modern African diasporic subjectivity back to the early African Atlantic experience.

Because this chapter outlines the diasporic identity formation of the protagonist of a relatively recently published novel that has yet to be thoroughly analyzed by scholars,[19] my analysis follows the chronology of the narrative rather closely. In *The Book of Negroes*, the order of narration mostly coincides with the chronological order of events. True, the story has a frame: the novel's present casts Aminata as an elderly woman who, having found asylum among white abolitionists in early-nineteenth-century London, writes down her life story (the book we read, as it were—a maneuver familiar to readers of Ellison's *Invisible Man*, for example). Otherwise, however, the text refrains from self-referentially drawing attention to its own narrative strategies the way postmodern metafiction would. Hill's post-postmodern novel is neither stylistically experimental after the fashion of modernist or postmodernist writing nor laden with allusions to academic philosophy à la *Middle Passage*. Instead, *The Book of Negroes* takes its cues from the realistic style and social criticism (including, albeit in muted form, the sentimental social criticism) typical of classic slave narratives and of such mid- and late-nineteenth-century American and British novels as Harriet Beecher Stowe's *Uncle Tom's Cabin* and much of Charles Dickens's oeuvre.

In brief, *The Book of Negroes* examines the designation "Africa" and explores the formation of the African diaspora. In the process, it depicts the inadequacies of eighteenth-century white cartographies of the African interior (and, metaphorically, of the black psychological and cultural interior); the religious isolation of a literate Islamic slave who in America finds herself separated from her fellow believers; the gender-specific suffering of black girls and women in slavery; Black Loyalism; black displacement, migrancy, and itinerancy; and the complicated, elusive concept of home. All along, *The Book of Negroes* portrays the Revolutionary era from a perspective thoroughly informed by late-twentieth-century and early-twenty-first-century insights into the nature of the African diaspora: in addition to having an extensive geopolitical scope, the novel firmly focuses on black agency and on the complexity and malleability of black diasporic identity.

The Narrative of Aminata Diallo, "Written by Herself"

The Book of Negroes tells the story of Aminata Diallo, narrated and written by herself in the first person, as the novel's frame would have it. According to the text's inner logic, Aminata is the scribe of her own story, the one in control of her identity formation on the page (although Hill is, of course, the ultimate author of the novel). In one of the appendices to *The Book of Negroes*, Hill singles out the autobiographies of Olaudah Equiano, Frederick Douglass, Harriet Jacobs, and Mary Prince as the classic slave narratives that influenced his writing the most.[20] Like Equiano, Douglass, and Jacobs, Hill's protagonist is able to read and write; she therefore does not have to give her project over to an abolitionist scribe, as the historical Mary Prince, for example, had to do. Determined not to let anyone else do the telling of her story, the elderly Aminata instructs John Clarkson, the one abolitionist whom she unconditionally trusts, "to change nothing" should she die before finishing the manuscript.[21] Whatever compromises her illiterate and literate historical predecessors may have had to make in order to get their life stories published, Hill's Aminata, resolute in her desire to define herself on her own terms, does not accept any.

William L. Andrews sums up the significance of the expressive power of the word (here, especially the written word) for African American ex-slave memoirists as follows:

> Literacy is considered the ultimate form of power in the antebellum slave narrative, for at least two reasons. First, language is assumed to signify the subject and hence to ratify the slave narrator's humanity as well as his authority. Second, white bigotry and fear presumably cannot withstand the onslaught of the truth feelingly represented in the simple personal history of a former slave. This romantic trust in the power of language did not go unchallenged in the antebellum black autobiography.... Still, given the paucity of alternative weapons for blacks in the antislavery struggle, the idea that the word could make them free remained an article of faith in Afro-American literature of the antebellum era.[22]

While Hill's thematic treatment of the written word in *The Book of Negroes* resonates with this "romantic trust in the power of language," his narrative links literacy and writing not only with legal and political freedom, but also with identity formation. The latter impulse is, of course, present in classic slave narratives as well. For example, when Douglass revised his 1845 *Narrative* into his second and third autobiographies, he became increasingly articulate and vocal about identity, subjectivity, and agency. However, a twenty-first-century novelist can write about these issues much more explicitly, being free from any immediate strategic concerns and constraints that a black abolitionist had to consider. Indeed, the theme of individual and communal self-understanding—the formation of diasporic subjectivity, in particular—permeates *The Book of Negroes*.

Although the novel's first US heading, *Someone Knows My Name*—which Hill suggested to Norton when the American publisher would not accept the original Canadian title[23]—may be read as the author's metafictional joke satirizing the cross-cultural titling dilemma, it also, more importantly, points to the intimate connection between identity and name. As Nancy Kline observes in her review of the novel, "To have a name is to have an identity."[24] Readers of US African American oral and written texts are very familiar with this equation. It was made famous in negative form (marking an absence) by Malcolm Little's insistence on the last name "X," a signifier of black Americans' lost knowledge of their African family histories, and in positive form (denoting a presence) by such works of fiction as Toni Morrison's *Song of Solomon*, in which the protagonist's embrace of his African American identity is inextricably bound up with his discovery of the names of his ancestors. In *The Book of Negroes*, a teenager named Chekura (later Aminata's husband) utters the words "Someone knows my name" to Aminata during their shared Middle Passage,[25] thereby articulating the vast relief that he feels upon encountering someone familiar on the ship that has cut him off from everything he has ever known. This phrase, when functioning as the novel's title, also indicates that as Aminata—no longer the "Mary"[26] of the Middle Passage or the "Meena Dee"[27] of the New World—writes her memoir, she teaches us her real name and shares with us her true identity. She breaks away from what John Paul Eakin terms "discursive bondage" (in his definition, "what the white reader was prepared to accept as a fact"),[28] offers us herself as seen through her own eyes rather than through those of enslaving others, sheds any simplified or false identities imposed on her from the outside, and proudly narrates her name, genealogy, and selfhood on her own terms: "I am Aminata Diallo, daughter of Mamadu Diallo and Sira Kulibali, born in the village of Bayo, three moons by foot from the Grain Coast in West Africa. I am a Bamana. And a Fula. I am both."[29]

Hill's choice of the last name "Diallo" for his protagonist can be read as commemorating Ayuba Suleiman Diallo (1701–73), also known as Job ben

Solomon (Jallo). He was an African Muslim who was emancipated after less than three years of slavery in Maryland and subsequently became something of a celebrity in the Atlantic world of his era. William Hoare of Bath, England, painted his now-famous portrait of Diallo in 1733, and Diallo's memoir, written down by Thomas Bluett, was published in 1734.[30] By having a freeborn African Muslim as its protagonist, *The Book of Negroes* (written during the post-9/11 backlash against Islam in North America) references the early black Muslim presence in North America, just as Alex Haley's 1976 neo-slave narrative, *Roots*, did by emphasizing Kunta Kinte's Islamic heritage.[31] Through this gesture, Hill covertly critiques current political discourses that cast Muslims as newcomers or "new strangers" in the United States and Canada.[32] In addition, Hill places female subjectivity at the novel's center: his "Kunta Kinte" is an adolescent girl who matures into womanhood in America.

It is also significant that Hill named both Aminata Diallo's father and her son (who both perish because of the slave trade and, by extension, because of racism) "Mamadu." The name evokes the infamous death of the real-life Amadou Diallo (Mamadu, Mamadou, Amadou, and Amadu all being versions of the name Muhammad), the twenty-two-year-old Guinean immigrant to New York City who died, unarmed and with no criminal record, on the stoop of his apartment building in the Bronx on February 4, 1999, with nineteen bullets in his body.[33] Hill chooses to pay homage to the memory of Amadou Diallo in a book that is a neo-slave narrative. This choice serves as a subtle yet powerful reminder that the ever-present ethnoracial mistrust and violence in North America is, in no small part, a legacy of slavery. Ashraf H. A. Rushdy remarks in *Neo-Slave Narratives* (1999), the first book-length study of the genre, that in the 1960s and 1970s the first African American writers of neo-slave narratives "wished to return to the literary form in which African American subjects had first expressed their political subjectivity in order to mark the moment of a newly emergent black political subject."[34] Rushdy here both emphasizes black political agency and observes that connections between past and present, however implicit, have always been part of the motivation to write works in this genre. Hill, for his part, contributes to both of these aspects of the neo-slave narrative tradition.

Finally, the initial US title of Hill's novel also alludes to James Baldwin's "Nobody Knows My Name" (1959), the title piece of his 1961 essay collection. One of the most charged passages of the essay reads, "in exactly the same way that the South imagines that it 'knows' the Negro, the North imagines that it has set him free. Both camps are deluded."[35] Like Baldwin, Hill, too, emphasizes that black people are known by themselves. Those who wish to understand their experience have to listen to them—in *The Book of Negroes*, to Aminata. As she inscribes various allegedly forgotten names and stories on the pages of her "autobiography," the elderly Aminata not only writes her own individual identity into being but, like the authors of such historical pre-1807 slave narratives as Equiano's *Interesting Narrative*, also highlights the plight of all black people in an Atlantic world that accepts the "abomination" of the slave trade.[36] A writer powerfully aware of her mission, Aminata muses, "There must be a reason why I have lived in all these lands, survived all those water crossings, while others fell from bullets or shut their eyes and simply willed their lives to end."[37] During her final years, she finds this "reason," her purpose in life, in abolitionism.

Hill's Dialogue with Equiano's Autobiographical Self-Fashioning as a Diasporic Subject

Once the novel's abolitionist frame—with its recognition of the written word having "the power of the sleeping lion"[38]—is in place, Aminata's story begins in Bayo, her (fictional) home village in present-day Mali. A freeborn African Muslim, Aminata is kidnapped by African slave captors in the immediate vicinity of Bayo in 1756. As the captors raid the village, both Aminata's father (a Fula by ethnic origin and a jeweler by profession) and her mother (a Bamana and a midwife) are killed. The eleven-year-old girl's last glimpse of her home is Bayo burning. After an exhausting three-month march through the West African interior, the slave coffle that temporarily becomes Aminata's community arrives at what is today known as Freetown Harbor in Sierra Leone. The captured Africans' Middle Passage takes them to Sullivan's Island in the port area of Charleston (or, in the era's spelling used in the novel, Charles Town), South Carolina, at the time a major entry point for Africans arriving in America.

The narrative of these events, contained in book 1, lays the groundwork for the rest of *The Book of Negroes*. Hill had Olaudah Equiano's memoir in the back of his mind as he wrote the novel,[39] and his dialogue with Equiano is particularly audible in this section. In the (now-contested)[40] first pages of *The Interesting Narrative*, Equiano offers a wealth of anthropological information about the manners and customs of his people, the Igbo of present-day Nigeria, in effect making the argument that he is writing about a civilization. Hill's Aminata engages in a very similar project as she portrays the people and culture of Bayo and openly displays her pride in her origins. Even Aminata's year of birth is the same as Equiano's: "I was born in 1745, or close to it."[41] According to their narratives, both Aminata and Equiano were kidnapped from their respective home villages by African captors, endured a long journey from the African interior to a western seashore, underwent the Middle Passage, served more masters than one, gained their freedom, experienced firsthand the fragility of black liberty on the Atlantic rim, lived itinerant lives, and eventually wrote down their life stories while living among white abolitionists in London. *The Book of Negroes* mentions Equiano several times, and it is part of the novel's frame that Aminata, who first arrives in London several years after Equiano's death, is familiar with his example as a black abolitionist autobiographer.[42]

As Robert Folkenflik notes, autobiography is not about "a completed life, a telos," but about "a life in process."[43] The genre's processual nature permeates *The Interesting Narrative*, a memoir written by an African (American?),[44] an Englishman, an Anglo-Methodist Christian, an ex-slave, a retired seaman, a former colonial settler/missionary among the Miskito Indians, an abolitionist, a speaker, and a writer. A complex, multilayered, and unresolved text, Equiano's autobiography embodies the various ambivalences of (be)longing that characterize diasporic existence. Regardless of one's position in the ongoing debate over Equiano's birthplace, there can be no doubt about his autobiographical self-construction as an individual with a diasporic consciousness. Both Johnson, in *Middle Passage*,[45] and Hill, in *The Book of Negroes*, tap into this aspect of *The Interesting Narrative* (Hill much more explicitly so than Johnson): they reference Equiano not only because of his status as a major historical figure of the early Black Atlantic, but also because of his deliberate autobiographical self-fashioning as a diasporic subject.

Gender and Religion in Aminata's Early Environment

Hill's Aminata can, to an extent, be read as a female Equiano.[46] In addition to the similarities in the arcs of their lives, Aminata, like Equiano, is a black diasporic subject who enters modernity on terms dictated by Others and who, even while writing, is in the process of fashioning her diasporic self out of various conflicting elements that have to be reconciled within a single psyche/text. However, even though *The Book of Negroes* in many ways echoes *The Interesting Narrative*, it is also true that Aminata is no exact replica of Equiano. During the time that she spends in the New World, she is a triply vulnerable

Other: not only is she black, but, unlike Equiano, she is also female and Muslim.

While Hill fully acknowledges the lamentable denigration of black womanhood in the eighteenth-century British Atlantic world, he refrains from simplistically representing Aminata's gender as a mere vulnerability. Instead, his genealogy of Aminata's exceptional strength and resilience (even while highlighting the energy and confidence that she draws from her ethnic, communal, and familial background) foregrounds gender. The narrative emphasizes that Aminata has, from early on, a clearly defined identity not only as a member of her original community, but also as her mother's daughter. Even as an aged woman writing her memoir, Aminata vividly remembers her early physical bond with her mother that literally tied her to female strength: "As an infant, I travelled on my mother's back. . . . I was swathed in red and orange cloth and rode low down on her back when she walked to market, pounded millet into flour, fetched water from the spring."[47] She also recalls how her early years seemed to further confirm the relevance of her gendered understanding of black strength: "I remember wondering, within a year or two of taking my first steps, why only men sat to drink tea and converse, and why women were always busy. I reasoned that men were weak and needed rest."[48] Hill casts Aminata as a daughter who deeply admires her mother's role in the women's community of Bayo. Sira Kulibali is a respected midwife, and Aminata, too, learns to "catch babies" (the novel's colloquial phrase for tending to births). She uses this skill throughout her life, beginning when at age eleven she delivers the baby of a fellow captive in the slave coffle during her long trek from Bayo to Sierra Leone's largest harbor. The skills in midwifery that Aminata has on arrival in the New World, combined with those that she acquires through practice, in more ways than one put her in the midst of black women's labor in slavery and make her an expert on women's life within the Peculiar Institution.

Despite this emphasis on the self-confidence and strength of Bayo's women, Hill does not envision Aminata's native environment as free from gender bias. In fact, life in Bayo is based on a clear-cut division of labor between men and women. When Aminata mentions her future plans to her father ("I will travel, and cultivate my mind"),[49] he, faithful to what his community has taught him about gender roles, replies, "We will not speak of that. . . . Your task is to become a woman."[50] Nevertheless, he relents on one matter of crucial importance. Aminata yearns to learn how to read and write, and he grants her this wish: "[I]n the privacy of our home, with nobody but my mother as a witness,

I was shown how to use a reed, dyed water and parchment. I learned to write phrases in Arabic, such as *Allaahu Akbar* (God is great) and *Laa ilaaha illa-Lah* (There is none worthy of worship except God)."[51]

Difficult as it is to gather information about the earliest African Muslims in the New World, Hill is, at least in part, on the mark here. In *African Muslims in Antebellum America* (1997), Allan D. Austin discusses seventy-five African-born Muslims who were brought to North America between 1730 and 1860.[52] Several of them were literate in Arabic, he says, specifically mentioning that the Fula (Fulbe), the tribe of Aminata's father, "were proud of their Quranic schools and their ability to read and write" and that "[t]heir literacy included writing Arabic and their own language using the phonetic Arabic letters."[53] At least six of the Fula whom Austin studied "wrote in Arabic in America—and they usually wrote what they chose to write: assertions of their faith in the words of Allah."[54] Austin does not, however, identify any literate Fula women; as he points out, the stories that he draws on "were gathered by men in an era when women were only beginning to be writers who could follow their own agendas."[55] Hill's Aminata, in any case, in Bayo secretly fantasizes about eventually becoming "the only woman, and one of the only people in my entire village, to be able to read the Qur'an and to write in the gorgeous, flowing Arabic script."[56] This hope is dashed by her capture: the Middle Passage permanently removes her from Bayo, its people, and its culture. Her encounter with the prevalent European and American habit of writing from left to right—"Had they all learned to write backwards?"[57]—is one of the lesser shocks that she experiences on the slave ship and in the New World.

The Middle Passage Narrative

As with Hill's rendering of Aminata's early environment, his depiction of her Middle Passage is in close dialogue with the corresponding section of Equiano's memoir. Like Equiano, Hill describes the inhumane conditions, disease, violence, and ever-present threat of death on the slave ship, as well as the Africans' fear of being cannibalized by the white savages (the crew), an unfamiliar breed of humans. However, Hill's focus on the gendered and sexualized dimensions of the slave-ship experience constitutes a significant difference between these two Middle Passage narratives. Free from the multiple constraints under which Equiano wrote in the late 1780s, Hill makes his protagonist depict sexual violence on the slaver much more explicitly than was possible for Equiano. Aminata, though not raped herself, repeatedly sees a white crew member sexually exploit African women. She thus becomes an eleven-year-old eyewitness to the sexual violation and violent sexualization of black women's bodies during the Middle Passage.

Equiano, too, employed the perspective of a recently captured child in the Middle Passage section of *The Interesting Narrative*. This strategy was advantageous for the abolitionist autobiographer because the young Olaudah's uncorrupted point of view gave the mature Equiano license to be "innocently" candid when he, adopting the perspective of a scared and bewildered little boy, applied the racially charged concept of "savage" to the slave ship's white crew.[58] The child's instinctive vantage point allowed the black abolitionist to "turn the tables" by revealing to white British readers an aspect of their civilization that they were not accustomed to seeing. However, this strategic perspective of youthful innocence also meant that Equiano could not make the young Olaudah seem too knowledgeable about rape. (Equiano's text does, however, mention the sexual exploitation of African women on slave ships in a later, post–Middle Passage section of the memoir, in which the narrative point of view is no longer that of a child undergoing his own Middle Passage.)[59] Hill works around the same dilemma by casting adolescent Aminata as a midwife's daughter, who, because of her mother's vocation, is familiar with the realities of sex and reproduction and is therefore able to understand and describe rape.

Unlike in *The Interesting Narrative*, in *The Book of Negroes* the African captives on the ship eventually rebel. Aminata, who witnesses the violent aggression that characterizes both the revolt and its suppression, sees so much death within a short period of time that the losses, combined with the sight of the African dead being treated without due respect,[60] challenge her Islamic convictions and prompt her to create a poignant theodicy applicable to the new situation: "Maybe Allah lived only in my land."[61] Because Aminata draws on traditional African spirituality as well, she also fears that those who die on the ship and have their lifeless bodies thrown into the ocean may have difficulty finding their proper place in the ancestors' spirit world and may be forgotten by all.[62] Her instinctive response to these foreign calamities is to cling to a particularly foundational element of individual and communal identity formation—the importance of names. One day, when the slaves are brought to the deck to dance (that is, to get some fresh air, exercise, and, in the process, entertain the crew), Aminata finds a way to inspire the disheartened group by evoking everybody's name, one by one, in order to keep alive their sense of individuality, community, and humanity: "I began to sing a song while we danced, naming all the people I saw. I tried to name every single face, and give the name of the person's home village."⁶³ Soon the Africans extend this newly established habit (another prompt for the novel's first US title) to their farewells to their dead: "Each rising sun saw more people die. We called their names as they were pulled from the hold."⁶⁴ As Geneviève Fabre has noted, African dancing during the Middle Passage, however coerced, served purposes that the whites failed to recognize—not only coded resistance but also assertion of kinship, affiliation, and loyalties.⁶⁵ Through the simple gesture of naming, initiated in the context of dance, the novel's African captives engage in community formation, fight fear and disorientation, and resist the ostensible power of the slave trade to doom the African dead to oblivion.

Despite these occasional glimmers of hope, the ocean voyage severely traumatizes the Africans, and their distress triggers reactions that contribute to their already heightened sense of alienation. For example, Hill depicts Fomba, a gentle and physically powerful *woloso* (a second-generation captive/slave) who has belonged to Bayo's village chief since birth,⁶⁶ as being so severely affected by the violent uprooting that he loses his ability to speak. Despite his formidable physical size, he is reduced to silently symbolizing the estranged condition of the traumatized. Moreover, a feisty woman named Fanta, the village chief's youngest wife, gives birth to a baby boy and then immediately throws him overboard to prevent his enslavement. This act of resistance (evocative of a similar scene in *Middle Passage* and of Sethe's infanticide in Morrison's *Beloved*) stuns and emotionally overwhelms Aminata, who had just assisted with the birth. As the slaver reaches Sullivan's Island off Charleston in South Carolina, the adolescent Aminata, having witnessed horrifying depths of adult despair, is not only physically ill, but also emotionally devastated and in a state of spiritual anguish. Yet her underlying personal strength, bolstered by the encouragement that she receives from her fellow survivors, helps her to survive the first phase of her new life in the New World. Biton, a man whom Aminata during the Atlantic crossing learned to regard as her new chief, gently exhorts the exhausted and sick child not to give up: "You crossed the big river, child. Don't die now."⁶⁷ And she does not; displaced and dispossessed, yet equipped with a resilient human spirit required for survival and adaptation, she lives on to enter the next stage in her process of "modern encounters" (Hazel Carby's term)⁶⁸ and diasporic identity formation.

Arrival and Acclimatization

One of the distinctive contributions of *The Book of Negroes* to the genre of the neo-slave narrative is its careful attention to the first days and weeks following a first-generation slave's arrival in the New World—a memorable phase in the formation of a new self-understanding. While Hill's rendering of Aminata's first days offers tropes familiar to readers of classic and more recent narratives of involuntary and voluntary black migrations (the bleak sun, the cold weather, and the breath that looks like smoke in the morning),[69] the more original aspects of this part of the story concern, among other things, religion. Aminata immediately learns that her Islamic faith is at odds with New World traditions: both Biton and the first African American slave with whom Aminata is able to communicate forbid her to pray publicly "in [her] manner" because they are convinced that local whites would punish her severely for Islamic worship.[70] The absence of a Muslim community from Aminata's life soon impacts her motivation and ability to pray in private as well.[71] Moreover, during their captivity on Sullivan's Island, the Africans quietly abandon—for the sake of survival—various manners and customs that Aminata's native culture links with piety and morality. For example, several men and women sleep huddled up together in order to keep warm. Although in Aminata's eyes this arrangement is taboo, she before long recognizes its necessity and joins the group.[72] She also finds herself eating rice that has been boiled with pork, this dish being the only food available to the new arrivals.[73]

In addition to these religious compromises, another particularly vivid aspect of Hill's narrative of Aminata's arrival concerns her first impressions of the port area of Charleston. After a brief stay on Sullivan's Island, she and the other African captives are transported to the mainland to be sold on the slave market. In the city, Aminata observes both white and black people and is surprised by the behavior of both. In particular, the sight of Africans and African Americans on the streets of Charleston leaves her bewildered because none of them, it seems to her, is trying to escape: "In their voices I sometimes heard notes of joy and play. No shackles bound their wrists or ankles, but not one of them fought or tried to run away."[74] A few months earlier, during the long march through the West African interior, Aminata had realized that escape from the slave coffle would have been futile even if she had found an apt moment to flee: "To where could a naked person run?"[75] Stripped of clothes and human dignity alike, she had resigned herself to her fate. In her new life, she quickly comes to understand that black South Carolinians, even when not literally in chains, are shackled by a peculiar institution whose reach is so wide as to make flight virtually impossible.

En route to the slave market, Aminata for the first time sees the hustle and bustle of a mid-eighteenth-century American urban port, with its "[s]acks of grain, stacks of corn, hay for horses, piles of nails, cows and pigs being led across streets" and its "streets and gutters . . . filled with waste."[76] She realizes that this market town deals in commodities: "Everywhere I looked, I saw goods."[77] Even though it is not yet quite clear to Aminata that she and her fellow Africans are also viewed as "goods," the raucous reactions of white passersby to the sight of the new arrivals being led to the market make her divine that the world has indeed "gone mad."[78] The New World status of black people as chattel becomes apparent to her when she sees her fellow survivors of the Middle Passage being put on the auction block. She herself is visibly ill and is therefore kept on the sidelines and classified as a refuse captive, a flawed product that someone looking for a cheap bargain might purchase after the first-rate goods have been sold.[79]

While the black community formation that had begun on the slave ship had continued on Sullivan's Island, the slave market experience, in addition to exposing Aminata to capitalism at its worst, permanently separates her from almost everyone she has ever known, including her adopted chief Biton. When he, standing on the auction block, sees her from a distance, he offers her a final gesture of support and solidarity: in what is yet another echo of the novel's first US title, Biton solemnly says Aminata's name out loud,[80] thereby urging her never to forget who she is and where she comes from. He thus implicitly repeats his earlier exhortation that she should draw strength from the memory of her deceased parents, who gave Aminata her name and values.[81] Here, too, Hill explicitly connects diasporic identity formation with diasporic memory, communal as well as familial. Equipped with this final encouragement from Biton, Aminata enters a new world inhabited by whites, whose ways bear little resemblance to any human habits she has known before, and by unfamiliar "homelanders," whose customs also seem confusingly foreign to her.

In the New World, Aminata indeed initially refers to her fellow Africans, of various ethnic origins, as "homelanders." "Africa" and "African" are not concepts for her until they are taught to her in South Carolina. Hill touched on this issue in a 2008 interview with Jessie Sagawa: "[Aminata] is from Bayo, born in 1745; she is not walking around there with Africa in her self-concept.

She is . . . of various ethnic origins, she knows who her parents are and who the people around her are, but 'African' is a foreign concept. It's a white man's word, really, and it's a word that other people use to define the people of Africa."[82] Hill's nuanced awareness of the multiplicity of Africa renders him attentive to the wealth and variety of African languages. In the novel's Charleston, the African arrivals—brought to the port by ships that are constantly coming and going—speak a number of languages, many or most of which are mutually unintelligible. As the newcomers get separated from their fellow survivors of the Middle Passage, many find themselves in complete linguistic isolation in this unfamiliar and frightening Babel. Hill thematizes this aspect of Aminata's arrival with particular sensitivity while portraying her trek from the slave market back to the seashore, from which she will be rowed to Saint Helena Island, the location of her new owner's farm. As Aminata marches with other sold refuse captives in a coffle, she and a fellow captive try to find out whether any African passerby might speak a language that they know.[83] This desperate attempt to communicate reveals the new arrivals' profound sense of loss and displacement.

On Saint Helena Island, Aminata learns that she is now the property of Robinson Appleby, an indigo farmer. She lives for four years as one of his slaves, undergoing the first phase of her North American acclimatization in a unique cultural environment among the Gullah, who, in real life as in the novel, have preserved many elements of African languages and cultures because of their community's relative geographical isolation on the Sea Islands. Gifted linguistically, Aminata quickly learns how to speak both Gullah and standard English. In addition, she continues to master her native Fulfude and Bamanankan and retains some of the Arabic of her religious heritage.[84] She also secretly learns how to read English from the literate African American overseer Mamed, the son of a Fula chief's daughter and a white plantation owner. Moved by Aminata's intelligence and her affinity with his late mother's religious heritage, Mamed clandestinely introduces her to the Latin alphabet and English books. This plot development not only echoes the classic slave narrative tradition's emphasis on the connection between literacy/education and freedom, but also subtly complicates our Anglocentric understanding of it, because in Hill's neo-slave narrative Aminata is already literate (in Arabic) when she arrives in America. This important detail serves as a reminder that Western civilization is not the only cultural influence that has inspired the cultivation of the written word in Africa and among people(s) of African descent in the diaspora.

The narrative of Aminata's years on Appleby's farm describes sexual violations of black women in slavery, including the rape of Aminata by Appleby, and highlights slave owners' indifference to black family ties. On a happier note, Aminata is temporarily reunited with Chekura, the young African who rejoiced in someone knowing his name when he crossed the Atlantic on the same slave ship with her. They marry (spiritually though not legally, slave marriages being invalid in the eyes of the law), and in the spring of 1761 sixteen-year-old Aminata gives birth to their first child, Mamadu. However, ten months later two tragedies strike simultaneously: Appleby sells little Mamadu, and Chekura is also taken permanently away from Saint Helena Island. Separated from both her husband and their baby boy, Aminata sinks into a deep depression. Appleby, fed up with her initially active and now passive resistance, sells her to the indigo inspector Solomon Lindo, a Sephardic Jew from London living in Charleston.[85] Lindo had once visited Appleby to inspect the product of his farm and had, in that connection, observed Aminata. Intrigued, he had recognized her intellectual potential and had deemed her capable of proving correct his philanthropic "hunch that an African can learn anything, if given the opportunity."[86] Lindo's purchase of Aminata results in her transformation into an urban, modern slave and initiates a new phase in her life and identity formation.

Literacy, Scriptures, Slavery, Freedom

Hill portrays Aminata's stay with the Lindos as an atypically benign variety of slavery that is ameliorated not only by the urban environment of Charleston, a very different locale from Appleby's rural and isolated farm,[87] but also by the Jewish family's relative distaste for the Peculiar Institution.[88] Aminata finds the physical conditions of her bondage significantly upgraded.[89] Moreover, reading now becomes an important aspect of her life. In this respect, Hill's characterization of the Lindos can be read as alluding to the Bostonian Wheatley household to which the young African later known as the poet Phillis Wheatley arrived in 1761.[90] With Mamed, Aminata had devoured the Bible, the *Planter's Medicine Guide*, and volumes of *Poor Richard's Almanac*.[91] At the Lindos' home, she also reads the local newspaper, William Falconer's *The Shipwreck*, Voltaire, and Swift—including *Gulliver's Travels*, with its famous passage about the protagonist's "arms and legs [being] strongly fastened on each side to the ground"[92] resonating with Aminata's own condition. Reading allows Aminata to expand her worldview, study connections between monotheistic religions' understandings of captivity and freedom, and mentally critique whites' geographical and mental maps of Africa. She also acquires more language with which to articulate her diasporic predicament and its ramifications for her self-understanding. Against the backdrop of the standards of the era, Aminata becomes an exceptionally well-read black woman. Yet, as with classic slave narratives, the fact of bondage is an ever-present reality in Hill's novel. Even with the privileges that she enjoys, Aminata never forgets that she is a slave who yearns to be free.[93]

As Hill depicts Aminata's stay with the Jewish family, he discusses the im/morality of slaveholding—including the paradox of "benevolent" slaveholding—together with religion. Looking at these two issues together is another gesture evocative of the strategies of classic slave narratives. Douglass, for example, in his 1845 *Narrative* famously attacked southern Christianity's support of slavery by arguing that religious slaveholders were the worst masters of all[94] and by making a categorical distinction between the "pure, peaceable, and impartial Christianity of Christ" and the "corrupt, slaveholding, women-whipping, cradle-plundering, partial and hypocritical Christianity of this land."[95] In Hill's modified neo-slave narrative, reflections on the relationship of slaveholding to the slaveholder's religious and ethnoracial affiliation take the form of Lindo's and Aminata's respective musings on the relationship between Judaism and Islam, and on the place of (white) Jews and (black) Muslims in Christian yet slaveholding British North America. Lindo is powerfully aware of the confluence of religion and "race" in the cultural imagination of Western civilization. He does not want Aminata to regard him as unproblematically white or white in the same way as the Applebys of the Thirteen Colonies—"true" members of Empire (despite their "second-rate" status as colonials) according to Empire's dominant raciology—are white. In Aminata's presence, he cultivates the kind of "minority discourse" that Abdul R. JanMohamed and David Lloyd have termed an "articulation of the political and cultural structures that connect different minority cultures in their subjugation and opposition to the dominant culture."[96] In his slave's company, Lindo accentuates his identity as someone who is in, but not of, Western civilization, in order to separate himself from the racially oppressive practices of the West: "I am not a white man. I am a Jew, and that is very different. You and I are both outsiders."[97] However, as Aminata for the first time listens to Lindo's discourse about his and her shared marginality, she is walking with him on the streets of Charleston as his newly acquired slave. She understandably finds the situation ironic: "I hoped that he could not see disbelief in my eyes."[98]

Hill here walks a fine line. On the one hand, he recognizes the long and cruel history of European anti-Semitism and its continuation in the Colonies. He offers glimpses of anti-Jewish attitudes in the novel's Charleston through such details as Lindo's frustrated comment to his wife about how he "had to grovel just to be let into the [Charles Town Library] Society."[99] Hill also draws a largely sympathetic portrait of the Lindos (Mrs. Lindo, in particular), characterizing them as educated and philanthropic. On the other hand, his narrative emphasizes that Jews had more opportunities to create themselves anew in the New World than did Africans and their descendants, who were doomed—by the fiercely antiblack thrust of the ascendant ideology of "race"—to the most inferior status of all in the eyes of their white contemporaries. At first glance, Hill's representation of black-Jewish relations seems rather different from the approach of Caryl Phillips, who in *The European Tribe* and in the novels *Higher Ground* (1989) and *The Nature of Blood* (1997) casts the Jewish and African diasporas as "connective diasporas," as explained in chapter 3.[100] (Emphasizing such interdiasporic connectivity is, admittedly, the very objective of Lindo's "minority discourse" in *The Book of Negroes*, but his status as a slave owner undermines his words.) However, Phillips's relevant works, especially *Higher Ground* and *The Nature of Blood*, operate on an approach transcending time and place that allows for sweeping connections to be made between different eras and locations, whereas Hill's narrative of Aminata's life in Charleston reimagines racial hierarchies in a single setting in one historical moment. This difference may in part explain the two authors' different perspectives.

Hill's protagonist, in brief, wavers on how she is to think about the Lindos and their benevolence. She learns about the persecution of Jews, including the expulsion of Lindo's ancestors from Spain, and sympathizes with their suffering; she is moved upon learning that pious Jews, like Muslims, refuse to eat pork; she is amazed at parallels that exist between the Hebrew Bible and the Qur'an; she develops a genuinely warm relationship with Mrs. Lindo; and, absorbing knowledge like a sponge, she appreciates the education that she receives from both spouses. Yet, none of these developments abolishes the master-slave relationship, its power dynamics, or the slave's legally unfree status, as Aminata divines while listening to her owner tell her about Hebrew slavery in Egypt: "The discovery was fascinating, yet confusing. Perhaps Lindo could explain why Christians and Jews kept Muslims as slaves if we all had the same God and if we all celebrated the flight of the Hebrews from Egypt."[101] As time goes by and her reading gives her more food for thought, Aminata's questions become more critical and center increasingly on economic status and, in particular, on legal freedom. She is powerfully aware that the Lindo whom she knows "had a big house in town," "did business throughout the lowcountry," "wore fine clothes and came and went as he pleased," and "could sail to London on the next ship if he so desired," whereas she remains his slave.[102] Aminata respects many aspects of the Lindos' way of life, knows that they treat her better than most Christian Charlestonians treat their slaves, and develops a personal attachment to them—to Mrs. Lindo, in particular. However, her attitude toward them (especially to him, her legal owner) remains conflicted. She has not forgotten that she is freeborn. More than anything, she wants to be free.

Imperialistic Nomenclatures and Cartographies of Africa

For most of her youth and adulthood, Aminata defines her diasporic existence as an exile from Bayo, firmly identifying the village of her birth as her true home. At this stage of her life, returning to Bayo is what "freedom" means for her. She knows that white geography locates Bayo in "Africa," and the more she learns, the more preoccupied she becomes with Africa and its absence from her life. This preoccupation is both intellectual and emotional: "*Where was Africa, exactly* . . . ? Sometimes I felt ashamed to have no answer. How could I come from a place, but not know where it was?"[103]

At the Lindos,' Aminata finds out more about Europeans' and colonists' perceptions of Africa, if not about Africa itself. She encounters, for example, the instability of European and American nomenclatures regarding Africa. When Lindo teaches Aminata about the monetary system in Charleston, he mentions that the gold coins of a certain denomination are called "guineas" because they are "made from gold taken from Ethiopia."[104] When Aminata exclaims, surprised, "That's the same word you used for my homeland,"[105] Lindo casually elaborates: "'We call it [Africa] many things,' he said. 'Guinea, Ethiopia, Negritia, Africa—they all mean the same.'"[106] Not only do the alleged synonyms constitute a problem for a stunned Aminata, but for her the fact that the British have named a gold coin after Africa also symbolizes the white exploitation of "Guinea," aptly capturing the capitalist essence of the imperialist project of "exploration": "From my homeland the buckra were taking both gold and people, and using one to buy and sell the other."[107]

Between the lines, the term "guinea" here takes on yet another meaning: as Aminata learns about the world order according to Empire, she gradually realizes that she herself serves as a guinea-pig in a semiscientific experiment conducted by a simultaneously philanthropic and coldly curious Lindo: "[L]et's have an experiment and see how much you [Aminata, an African] learn."[108] Aminata's unspoken response contains a germ of rebellion, a decision to benefit from the owner who benefits from her and her labor: "My eyes drifted to the ring on his finger. *Guinea*, I thought to myself. *Guinea gold. Use me if you must, but I will use you too.*"[109]

Aminata activates her plan to "use" Lindo after she safely delivers the couple's first and only baby: she asks, in return, to see a map of the world,[110] hoping that such visualization might help her to understand how she could find her way back to Bayo. However, the experience that Lindo offers Aminata in the local library is a disappointment. Not surprisingly, she cannot find the small village on any of the maps. More strikingly, she also notices that on each map the African interior is either blank or completely imaginary. Hill opens his novel with two epigraphs, one of which comes from Swift's 1733 poem "On Poetry: A Rhapsody": "So geographers, in Afric-maps, / With savage-pictures fill their gaps; / And o'er unhabitable downs / Place elephants for want of towns." As Aminata learns about the cartographies of exploration, conquest, and imperialism, she realizes that the interiors of both Africa and its people are still almost completely unknown to whites: "[I]nland was mostly sketchings of elephants, lions and bare-breasted women. . . . This 'Mapp of Africa' was not my homeland. It was a white man's fantasy."[111]

Aminata knows, however, that she herself cannot remain ignorant of the ways of whites if she is to gain her freedom. Mindful as ever of classic slave narratives' linkage of literacy with liberty, Hill closely connects his protagonist's English literacy to her yearning to return to Africa: Aminata concludes that constant learning is her only potential route back to Bayo.[112] At the same time, though, Hill indicates that Aminata's reading also significantly contributes to the development of her diasporic double consciousness as an African living in the Western world: "Books were all about the ways of the buckra [the whites], but soon I felt that I could not do without them."[113]

Despite these inner tensions within Aminata's psyche and despite the anti-Semitism to which the Lindos are subjected in Christian Charleston, the Lindo household thrives until the fall of 1774. That autumn, a smallpox epidemic takes the lives of Mrs. Lindo and the couple's young son, leaving both the widower and the good-hearted Aminata grief-stricken and withdrawn. Soon afterward, in early 1775, Chekura unexpectedly finds his wife again after what has been an involuntary separation of thirteen years. He comes bearing the shocking news that the broker of the sale of the couple's baby boy back in 1762 had been none other than Lindo. The child had died of pox a few months later. Before learning about Mamadu's fate, Aminata, though fully cognizant of the evil of slavery, had to a degree considered Lindo her benefactor. The well-read and mild-mannered professional had, after all, been a major improvement over her previous owner, the vulgar and violent Appleby. But when Aminata hears Chekura's news, her trust in Lindo suffers a fatal blow. When she travels with Lindo to New York City on what proves to be the eve of the Revolutionary War, she is, unbeknownst to him, in mourning, rebellious, and in search of freedom.

The British in New York City during the Revolutionary War

When news of the battles of Lexington and Concord reaches New York City in late April 1775, Aminata takes advantage of the general chaos that ensues: she escapes from Lindo and finds shelter in Canvas Town, a poverty-ridden urban shantytown in the southern part of the city.[114] Hill, in fact, here uses creative license; historical sources indicate that the designation "Canvas Town" was not in use until after the Great New York City Fire of September 21–22, 1776.[115] William Dunlap, a historical pioneer of American theater, was a ten-year old boy at the time of the 1776 fire, after which an improvised "Canvass-town"[116]—built out of whatever was available, including old sailcloth from the docks—quickly emerged to replace some of what had burned down. When Dunlap shortly before his death reminisced about the city after the fire, he did not fail to highlight the British influence in this poverty-ridden and ill-reputed district:

> The ruins on the south-east side of the town were converted into dwelling places by using the chimneys and parts of walls which were firm, and adding pieces of spars, with old canvass from the ships, forming hovels—part hut and part tent. This was called 'Canvass-town;' and was the receptacle and resort of the vilest dregs *brought by the army and navy of Britain*, with the filthiest of those who fled to them for refuge.[117]

Hill, whose approach to the life of the indigent is considerably more sympathetic than Dunlap's, is similarly aware that the British-minded poor could find refuge in Canvas Town. Indeed, the main thrust of Hill's Canvas Town storyline is to connect Aminata with the British. Because the story of Aminata's stay in Canvas Town narrates the formation of her loyalty to the British, it paves the way for the next major turn of the plot, namely, her journey to Nova Scotia, which in turn eventually results in her voyages to Sierra Leone and London. Aminata's pro-British stance is a choice that affects the course of the rest of her life.

Aminata ends up staying in Canvas Town for several years, earning her living as a midwife. In addition to delivering babies, she now performs abortions as well (not an entirely new skill for her)[118] at the request of British officers and the destitute black women whom they visit in Canvas Town. She also treats members of the British army and navy who have contracted sexually transmitted diseases. In the past, Aminata had involuntarily contributed to the wealth of slave owners by, in effect, bringing new slaves into the world. Now the political implications of her work change because her services—some of which, particularly the abortions, she performs with profoundly mixed feelings—prove invaluable to the British, and she becomes personally acquainted with British officers of high rank.

Initially, Aminata's allegiance to the British is forged in haste and dictated by necessity, rather than resulting from thorough political reflection. When she is first asked if she is a Tory, she does not even understand the question.[119] Yet, ignorant as she may initially be of the war's lexicon, she knows all along what she values over anything else—her legal freedom. For this reason, her position is perfectly clear by the time she leaves New York City for Nova Scotia at the end of November 1783: "I knew that it [the Thirteen Colonies] would be called the United States. But I refused to speak that name. There was nothing united about a nation that said all men were created equal, but that kept my people in chains."[120]

The time that Aminata spends living and working inside British lines is crucial to the plot as a whole. However, *The Book of Negroes* is no anti-Americanist pamphlet that simplistically glorifies the British.[121] Rather, when taken as a whole, the novel highlights the extremely vulnerable position of black people under either banner, British or American, and demonstrates that in the Revolutionary era black liberty remained elusive at practically any location on the Atlantic rim that had been touched by the slave trade. Hill's protagonist, nonetheless, has to choose sides, and she decides to cast her lot with the British as she pursues her legal freedom during and after the war.

Dunmore's Proclamation and the Original "Book of Negroes"

Historians of Black Loyalism emphasize that looking at the Revolutionary War through the eyes of slaves "turns its meaning upside down," as Simon Schama says.[122] That is, what was a war for freedom for the patriots seemed a war for the perpetuation of bondage for many of those who were toiling away under the yoke of patriot masters.[123] Tens of thousands of black slaves in British North America therefore, in Schama's words, paradoxically "clung to the sentimental notion of a British freedom."[124]

The notion of a black freedom within the British Empire was, indeed, in many ways a "sentimental" or utopian idea because, as Vincent Carretta reminds us, by the 1780s Britain had become the most important participant in the Atlantic slave trade.[125] Also, the reputation of the British Isles as a safe haven (or even "the promised land of freedom")[126] for black people was highly paradoxical because the legal status of racial slavery on British soil, as distinct from Britain's overseas colonies, was ambiguous, to say the least.[127] Nevertheless, a few months after the outbreak of the Revolutionary War, an unexpected development contributed to the idea of a black British freedom and temporarily shook the foundations of bondage in Virginia (and, soon after, beyond): on November 7, 1775, John Murray, the Fourth Earl of Dunmore and the last colonial governor of Virginia, declared that all slaves and indentured servants who would flee from their rebel masters, reach the British lines, and serve with the British army would be granted freedom after the war.[128] (This proclamation, motivated by the military needs of the British, prompted George Washington to label Dunmore—in a phrase that now seems extremely ironic—an "arch traitor to the rights of humanity.")[129] An "Ethiopian Regiment" was indeed established, but the military consequences of Dunmore's proclamation remained more modest than he had hoped.[130] However, the overall ramifications of the "Dunmore effect"[131] reached far beyond the Ethiopian Regiment and Virginia. Dunmore's promise was not only affirmed by the British authorities but was also repeated by the generals Sir William Howe and Sir Henry Clinton.[132]

Enslaved blacks learned about these promises and took them seriously. Estimates of the number of the slaves in the Thirteen Colonies who voted with their feet and took refuge within British lines range, as Walker notes, from tens of thousands to up to one hundred thousand.[133] In 1976 Wilson wrote, "There is no way of knowing how many slaves were lost to the colonies by the Revolution, but it could be as many as 80,000 to 100,000."[134] In 2011 Jasanoff, in turn, cited the figure of 20,000 (initially offered by Pybus in a 2005 article, as acknowledged by Jasanoff) as authoritative and "supportable."[135] Even this more conservative estimate amounts to a significant number of fugitives, considering that at the beginning of the Revolutionary War there were about half a million slaves in British North America.[136] As the war drew to its close, there were three major enclaves of Loyalists (black and white) in the emerging United States: New York, Savannah, and Charleston.[137] *The Book of Negroes* focuses on New York, from which the British eventually evacuated some 27,000 Loyalists to Nova Scotia,[138] including approximately 3,000 blacks.

Hill's Aminata does learn about Dunmore's proclamation (the core passage of which is reprinted in the novel),[139] but by the time of its issuance she has already been with the British for several months. She is, moreover, quick to note that Dunmore's words would not have helped her anyhow. Here, as throughout the novel, Hill is attentive to gender: "The proclamation spoke about people bearing arms. It looked like that meant only men. Surely they wouldn't let a Negro woman bear arms."[140] However, Aminata is truly elated when General Clinton, in his 1779 Philipsburgh Proclamation, promises "*[t]o every Negro who shall desert the Rebel Standard, full security to follow within these lines, any occupation which he shall think proper.*"[141] Aminata, who teaches her fellow blacks how to read in the little free time that she has, strategically exposes all her students to these words. Clinton's promise that *all* blacks within the British lines working in *any* capacity for the British would be granted freedom at the end of the war generates a whirlwind of action in the novel's black New York: "Every Negro who was capable took a job working for the British. This time, it wasn't just soldiers they wanted. They needed cooks, laundresses, blacksmiths and labourers. They needed coopers, robe makers, carpenters and night-soil men."[142]

A few years later, however, this happy burst of activity among Hill's characters is replaced by a bitter sense of betrayal as word spreads about Article Seven of the 1782 provisional Peace Treaty of Paris (preceding the definitive treaty of 1783), according to which "his Britannic Majesty shall, with all convenient speed, & without causing any Destruction *or carrying away any Negroes, or other Property of the American Inhabitants* withdraw all his Armies Garrisons and Fleets from the said United States."[143] As a frustrated Aminata puts it, "[b]y agreeing not to take with them 'Negroes or other Property,' the British had betrayed us and condemned us to fall into the hands of American slaveholders.... Everyone seemed to share my disappointment and anger."[144]

Eventually, however, the British did, historically as well as in the novel, honor the promise that they had made to those in bondage: they decided to interpret the status of blacks behind the British lines in a way that enabled them to evacuate about 3,000 persons of African origin from New York City.[145] The destination, though, was Nova Scotia—a much more difficult environment to live in and glean a livelihood from than the evacuees realized at the time.[146]

In the novel, a British officer explains to Aminata the logic of the British interpretation: "The coloured element is not the 'property' of the Americans. If you have served the British for one year at the minimum, you have already been liberated. You are no man's property. . . . When we remove you to Nova Scotia, . . . we will not be violating any terms of the Peace Treaty."[147] Historically, those deemed eligible for evacuation even included some who had been with the British for less than twelve months: when the British inspected blacks for eligibility between April 26 and November 30, 1783, they ultimately decided to think of the date of the provisional Peace Treaty of Paris as a cut-off date. As Walker writes, "Blacks who were already with the British before 30 November 1782 and who claimed freedom by the proclamations [of Dunmore, Howe, and Clinton] were technically free and therefore could not be considered as American property on that date."[148] By the time George Washington learned about this interpretation (in his eyes, an abomination), it was too late for him to interfere.[149]

When the evacuation of Black Loyalists from New York City was set in motion, all black New Yorkers who wished to sail to Nova Scotia—and there were many of them, in part because more slave catchers were coming to the city as the war's end drew near—were individually interviewed by British officers who determined their eligibility for evacuation. The names of those reckoned eligible were recorded in a military ledger called the "Book of Negroes," a handwritten document of about 150 pages.[150] Hill makes his protagonist the main scribe working on the ledger: in the novel, it is Aminata who records most of the names of the eligible blacks in the "Book of Negroes." Hill freely admits in "A word about history" appended to the novel that this turn of the plot is a departure from history—not only for the obvious reason that Aminata is a fictional character, but also because the British "simply used officers from within their ranks" as scribes for the "Book of Negroes" rather than hiring private individuals for this purpose.[151] The ledger, in any case, loomed so large in Hill's imagination during his writing process that he drew the title of his novel from it.

Black Loyalists' Disappointment in the Promised Land of Nova Scotia

Because of the existence of the "Book of Negroes," the numbers of the individuals of African descent who sailed from New York to Nova Scotia between April and November 1783 are known. Frey writes, "As a reward for their wartime services, 1,336 men, 914 women, and 740 children were given British certificates of manumission and were transported as free men and women to the cold, bleak land of Nova Scotia."[152] Hill clarifies in a 2007 magazine article that these figures do, in fact, include individuals who could not present a General Birch's Certificate or other proof of their status as free blacks but were nevertheless entered into the "Book of Negroes" and allowed to travel.[153] Schama confirms that the British took a "liberal view of black eligibility for departure."[154]

However, not all blacks who sailed to Nova Scotia were free; some of them were white Loyalists' slaves or indentured servants and were recorded in the "Book of Negroes" as such.[155] Nova Scotia, as Schama reminds us, did not decisively declare slavery to be illegal until 1800.[156] Hill's Aminata, accordingly, witnesses many white Loyalists leave New York for Canada with their slaves in tow: "[T]he British were indeed sending some fugitives to freedom, but were also allowing white Loyalists to bring along slaves."[157] Aminata's husband, Chekura, reunited with his wife after another long separation (this time, of nine years), is openly outraged upon realizing that Nova Scotia permits slavery: "'Slaves and free Negroes together in Nova Scotia?' he said, sucking his teeth. 'Some promised land.'"[158] Hill, indeed, included the historical fact of slavery in Canada in *The Book of Negroes* in order to raise Canadians' awareness of this aspect of their nation's past, as he indicated in a 2008 interview:

> [S]lavery was thriving in New Brunswick and Nova Scotia when the Loyalists arrived in large numbers in 1783, so if I had a novel set there with no people enslaved, then that would be a little ridiculous.... Most Canadians know extraordinarily little or nothing about Black history in Canada.... Some of them do not even know that slavery existed here in Canada.[159]

Hill's narrative emphasizes, throughout, that black people's lives in North America were uncertain and vulnerable, regardless of whether they were politically subject to the British or to the newly formed United States, as the inclusion of Nova Scotian slavery in *The Book of Negroes* demonstrates. However, having to make *a* decision, Hill's protagonist and her husband conclude that leaving New York City on a British ship is their best chance for achieving legal freedom.

Expecting their second child, Aminata and Chekura head for Nova Scotia but are forced to take separate ships. The vessel carrying Chekura goes down. Aminata does not learn about his tragic fate until several years later, but she does realize upon arrival in Nova Scotia that she once again needs to create a new life for herself by herself. Reaching the "promised land" on the very last ship carrying evacuees, Aminata sees no other free blacks disembarking the vessel, just white Loyalists with their slaves and servants. As she wanders about in the town of Shelburne, she is told, in no uncertain terms, that she needs to find her way to Birchtown, a newly founded black settlement where others of "her kind" live.

This cold reception foreshadows what is to follow. Life in Nova Scotia proves to be extremely hard for the Black Loyalists; Hill again portrays a known historical development.[160] Only some of the black settlers receive a plot of land, although such a provision had been promised to them all.[161] In the winter, the harsh climate makes mere survival a harrowing struggle in the destitute conditions of Birchtown. Although the black migrants came to Nova Scotia to be free, many of those without a trade end up indenturing themselves or their children to avoid starvation. Not surprisingly, they feel that the British, after all, broke their promise by relocating the New York evacuees to a place where many of them—in effect, even if not legally—have to give up their newly acquired freedom to secure survival.

The Black Loyalists find comfort in each other in the midst of these difficulties. In the novel, black community formation in the Nova Scotia of the 1780s and early 1790s revolves around evangelical Christianity, as was also the case historically.[162] Most of the black settlers are, unlike Aminata, American-born and Christians—Wesleyan Methodists, Baptists, or Huntingdonians. Hill's storyline focuses on the Methodists. When Aminata arrives in Shelburne, she first finds her way to Birchtown in the tow of "Daddy Moses" (Moses Wilkinson), a black Wesleyan Methodist preacher and a strong leader, historically as in the novel, despite his blindness and severely limited mobility.[163] Aminata—who again finds herself negotiating her identity as an insider and an outsider, as someone who does and yet does not quite belong—joins Daddy Moses's flock in Birchtown because she needs a community. She is honest with the preacher about her existential stance and never fakes a conversion.[164] Daddy Moses does not judge her. Hill not only portrays Moses Wilkinson as the fiery preacher that he historically was[165] but also depicts him as having a gentle side. When Daddy Moses offers his and his wife's simple home as the first shelter for Aminata, he provides one of the novel's most touching characterizations of her ever-itinerant condition: "We are travelling peoples, as you [Aminata] say so well, and you are one of the travellest of them all. . . . Even travelling peoples need homes, and failing that they need hosts."[166] Aminata develops a warm relationship with the preacher and befriends many who come to his gatherings. She also considers the church pew to be the one safe space where she can "let [her] sadness erupt."[167] When the black Methodists "s[i]ng out to Jesus" and are "in the throes of ecstasy," Aminata participates in the emotionally charged atmosphere in her own way, mourning her private losses and drawing "from [her] own well of tears."[168]

Aminata preserves her freedom even in the midst of Nova Scotian hardship. Thanks to her literacy, she gets a job at a local printing press, where she agrees to work in exchange for necessities and reading privileges. Soon the Witherspoons, a white family, hire her to be their maid and housekeeper. This job, however, results in a tragedy: in the aftermath of Nova Scotia's first race riot (initiated by disbanded white soldiers aggravated by a competing workforce, the free blacks, taking "their" jobs),[169] the Witherspoons abruptly leave Shelburne County and, without Aminata's knowledge or permission, take her second child, the baby girl May, with them. From 1787 to 1791, a disconsolate Aminata does everything she can to find her, without success.

In 1791, one of the black settlers in Nova Scotia, Thomas Peters—a former Black Pioneer, a wartime member of a black regiment established in 1776 out of Dunmore's Ethiopian Regiment—travels to London in order to bring his fellow black Nova Scotians' misery to the attention of British abolitionists.[170] Soon after Peters returns from his trip, abolitionist Thomas Clarkson's younger brother John arrives in Nova Scotia, authorized by the newly formed Sierra Leone Company to respond to Peters's plea.[171] John Clarkson urges those discontented black Nova Scotians who feel betrayed by the Crown to migrate once more—this time to a new colony in Sierra Leone, to be established under the auspices of the Sierra Leone Company.

This storyline within *The Book of Negroes* draws directly from the historical record, and Thomas Peters and the Clarkson brothers are three of the novel's many semifictional characters based on real-life individuals. Historically, the London-based British abolitionists behind the Sierra Leone Company regarded their mission as a revival of the less resourceful St. George's Bay Company's 1787 attempt to establish a colony of the "Black Poor" in Sierra Leone—a project which Equiano was initially involved in but soon dismissed from because of a major disagreement with the settlement's future superintendent.[172] The Sierra Leone Company decided that the second group, the black Nova Scotians, should found the new colony—Freetown—at the location of the first, unsuccessful Granville Town (so named after the abolitionist Granville Sharp), the capital of the short-lived Province of Freedom. This is what the new settlers indeed did under John Clarkson's leadership. Historical sources are sketchy on how much exactly the black Nova Scotians knew about the first, ill-fated experiment before they headed for their West African destination—probably very little, as far as any details were concerned. In *The Book of Negroes*, they do not learn about it at all until after their arrival in Sierra Leone.

One piece of historical information that Hill does not include in his novel (and his main source, Walker, does not mention) is that Peters, according to both Gibson and Schama, had heard about the Sierra Leone resettlement project before his 1791 trip to London and was therefore much more than just a passive recipient of a suggestion dropped in his lap by the white abolitionists.[173] It is even possible that the historical Peters was sent to London by Nova Scotia's black community rather than having acted as a lone wolf. Hill, in any case, highlights Peters's courage and initiative, seeking to raise readers' awareness of this early black leader whose name is unfamiliar to many or most students of black history in North America.

In Hill's admixture of fact and fiction, John Clarkson quickly befriends Aminata and realizes how valuable a literate black woman would be for his mission. Aminata, however—tempted but torn—wants to stay in Nova Scotia and wait for May and Chekura.[174] In response, Clarkson, a lieutenant in the Royal Navy, finds out about the fate of the ship that Chekura had boarded back in 1783 and informs Aminata of the shipwreck and Chekura's death. While processing the news, she also resigns herself to the fate of never seeing her daughter again, inferring that she had been too optimistic on both counts. Now there is nothing left to hold her back, and so Aminata, searching for home as intensely as ever, agrees to yet another migration: "There was nothing left for me in Nova Scotia. . . . On January 15, 1792, our fifteen ships lifted anchor and set sail for Sierra Leone."[175]

An Ambivalent Return to Africa

While *The Book of Negroes* is 470 pages long (afterwords excluded), only seventy-three of those pages are dedicated to Aminata's experience in Sierra

Leone,[176] even though Hill's interest in the historical founding of Freetown was one of the major motivators prompting his decision to write the novel in the first place. The realities of the era's Sierra Leonian life may have been even more difficult to reimagine than those of black life in the emerging United States and Canada, due to a smaller number of sources. More importantly, at the center of Hill's narrative is ambivalence about all of the diasporic subject's attempts to belong, including her attempts to belong to Africa, once her diasporic condition has been ushered into existence. Although Hill's Aminata, unlike Johnson's Rutherford, is African-born, no existentially simple "homecoming" or "return" to Africanity is possible for her, either; this difficulty or impossibility is an important similarity between *Middle Passage* and *The Book of Negroes*.

Hill is, again, particularly strong in depicting an arrival. As he portrays the Nova Scotians' flotilla reaching St. George's Bay (Freetown Harbor) in Sierra Leone, he dramatizes the moment by having a slave ship pass by the settlers' *Lucretia* before they even disembark.[177] The scene memorably illustrates the fragility of black freedom at any location touched by the Atlantic slave trade, including West African shores. Upon seeing the slave ship, the Nova Scotians learn that they, according to the Sierra Leone Company's reasoning, need to be in the vicinity of a British community in order to successfully establish a new colony in a region in which they have no expertise (since all of the settlers were either born in the New World or had left Africa very young, and since Clarkson, too, is a first-timer in Africa). The company, with few options to choose from, has therefore brought them to a spot that is less than twenty miles from the nearest British slave factory, on Bance Island.[178] Shocked and fearful of being reenslaved, the Nova Scotians wonder whether they have arrived in Africa just to find themselves betrayed by the British again. Clarkson, however, repeats his earlier promise that there will never be slavery in Freetown.[179] With mixed feelings, the settlers disembark. In Hill's rendering of the events, they find themselves being rowed from the ship to the shore by black locals who are Temne—members of the dominant African ethnic group in the region who cooperate with the British slavers on Bance Island, supplying them with African captives. All are eventually brought to the shore safely, without incident.

While this dramatic encounter with the slave ship stems from Hill's literary imagination, the gist of what he describes (the Nova Scotians' initial dependence on help from the London-based Sierra Leone Company and their tension-ridden relationship with the Temne) is historically based. The same is true of the extreme hardship that the settlers experience at the beginning of their project. Historians tell us, as does Hill, that the whites whom the company had sent to the location in advance to start the work of establishing the new colony had done nothing. It became the newcomers' job to build everything from scratch. Unaccustomed to the climate (the rainy season, in particular) and living in an era preceding the late-nineteenth-century scientific breakthroughs in the study of malaria, the Nova Scotians found their numbers drastically reduced in the first months of their stay; the shipboard deaths during the ocean voyage had been only the beginning. Anna Maria Falconbridge, the wife of Alexander Falconbridge (a former slave-ship surgeon turned abolitionist, who worked in Granville Town/Freetown as a Sierra Leone Company representative in 1791–92), was, historically, the first white Englishwoman to write a firsthand account about the resettlement project. In her *Narrative of Two Voyages to the River Sierra Leone during the Years 1791-1792-1793*, she famously crystallized the settlers' plight in the following sentence: "It is quite customary of a morning to ask, 'how many died last night?'"[180] In *The Book of Negroes*, it is the fictive Aminata, rather than Anna Maria Falconbridge, who utters these now well-known words,[181] but the Falconbridges are included in the historically based characters whom Aminata meets. Aminata, in fact, first hears about Olaudah Equiano and his memoir from Mrs. Falconbridge and receives a copy of *The Interesting Narrative* from her.[182]

Throughout the Sierra Leone narrative, Aminata describes the strong will of the settlers, who, against the odds, create a town out of nothing. However, she also records the settlement's growing pains, including the historically based schism between John Clarkson and Thomas Peters, as well as the quickly established competition between the churches and the taverns for the settlers' souls: "[D]rink and religion shot up side by side in our colony."[183] Aminata herself has no interest in the solace offered by alcohol, and her participation in religious life continues to be primarily motivated by her need for community. Having lived her entire adult life without any organic connection to Islam, she has become an independent thinker who does not identify with any organized religion, although she does recognize in 1802, upon finding herself in the company of West African Muslims, that some aspects of Islam still appeal to her.[184] In 1804, while laboring on her memoir in London, she quietly professes to a nondenominational and undogmatic form of personal spirituality, thinking of God as a "gentle voice" who each morning gives her the strength to carry on with her abolitionist activities.[185]

One important aspect of Aminata's narrative of her life in Sierra Leone concerns her relationship to the Temne. The novel's Nova Scotians do not initially know that the fate of the 1787 Black Poor resettlement project was sealed in December 1789 when the Temne leader King Jimmy and his men destroyed the remnants of the seriously ailing Providence of Freedom in what seems to have been a misguided act of retaliation.[186] However, the settlers learn about this history soon enough,[187] and Aminata realizes that bonding with the Temne will be extremely difficult even for her, a native West African, both because of the political position of the Temne as intermediaries in the slave trade and because of her unfamiliarity with the local language and customs. This situation, a major disappointment for Aminata, prompts another identity crisis in her life: "In South Carolina, I had been an African. In Nova Scotia, I had become known as a Loyalist, or a Negro, or both. And now, finally back in Africa, I was seen as a Nova Scotian, and in some respects thought of myself that way too."[188] Over time, Aminata learns to speak the language of the Temne, but they never truly embrace her as a fellow West African. As a woman named Fatima bluntly tells her, "You have the face of someone born in this land, but you come with the toubabu [white men]. You are a toubab with a black face."[189] This reaction reflects the historical fate of the settlers (the first-generation arrivals and beyond), who indeed found themselves to be "Nova Scotians" in Sierra Leone—a distinct group of cultural hybrids.

After Aminata realizes that she will not be accepted by the Temne, her belief that she needs to find her way to Bayo is reconfirmed. What follows is perhaps the most fantastic episode in the novel. Aminata joins Alexander Falconbridge on a trip to Bance Island and forms connections that, after much planning and years of waiting, result in a new journey. In September 1800, six years after her first visit to Bance Island, she risks everything, including her life and freedom, in a desperate attempt to return home: she makes an inland excursion toward where she believes Bayo or its remnants should be. Plagued with homesickness, she abandons her usual caution and travels with Temne slave traders, the sole experts on the route—only to discover that her deceitful guides intend to sell her.[190] Aminata escapes but falls seriously ill while wandering about in the heat. A local Fula community comes to her rescue and saves her life.

While recovering among the Fula, Aminata thoroughly rethinks her concept of home. In an hour of self-reflection that, in all its simplicity, is perhaps the most dramatic moment of the entire novel, she lets go of her dream of returning to Bayo and concludes that freedom is more valuable to her than finding her place of birth: "I felt no more longing for Bayo—only a determination to stay free.... Bayo, I could live without. But for freedom, I would die."[191] While some aspects of this episode stretch credibility, Aminata's desperate and unsuccessful attempt to reach the village of her birth gives expression to a pivotal theme in black diasporic fiction, the difficulty of defining and finding "home." After being stolen from what, indeed, was her home at the time of her capture, Aminata remains perpetually in transit and "in between." However, although home/Bayo remains out of her reach, one of Aminata's lifelong dreams comes true for her among the Fula who nurse her back to health: in this community, she is able to temporarily assume the role of a *djeli*, a storyteller. She shares her life story with the villagers, a receptive audience, before returning to Freetown.

From this experience, the mental, even if not the physical, journey to the next phase in Aminata's life is short. She accepts John Clarkson's offer to move to the capital of the British Empire and, once there, assumes the role of a *djeli* in abolitionist circles. The elderly Aminata becomes a black abolitionist celebrity in London and is even received by the king and queen. During the royal audience, the queen (in a profoundly ironic move on Hill's part) gives Aminata a copy of Swift's "On Poetry: A Rhapsody"—an important subtext, as noted before, for the novel's discussion of the cartographies of colonialism and imperialism.

In England, Aminata wants to publicly criticize both the Atlantic slave trade and slavery rather than accept the white abolitionists' pragmatic stance, which is dictated by their understanding of *realpolitik*, that the movement must first focus on abolishing the slave trade and only then attack the institution of slavery. Aminata views the two causes as inseparable and is offended by the suggestion that she should, for political reasons, refrain from criticizing the Peculiar Institution.[192] This aspect of the narrative implicitly references Douglass's struggles with those white abolitionists who wanted him to tell audiences his story ("Give us the facts") but cautioned him against drawing political conclusions from his own narrative: "[W]e will take care of the philosophy."[193] As Douglass wryly notes in *My Bondage, My Freedom* (1855), "I could not always obey, for I was now reading and thinking."[194] Hill portrays the development of the activist dimension of Aminata's diasporic identity in a similar light, casting the elderly African-born woman as a reader and thinker who—rather than wishing "to adorn the abolitionist movement,"[195] as she notes sarcastically—is fully capable of articulating to others the poignant political and existential significance of the formation of her diasporic subjectivity in a world in which she is "African" in the West and a cultural stranger in West Africa.

The Book of Negroes closes on a positive note: in a surprise happy ending (another rather fantastic turn of the plot), Aminata is reunited with her daughter. May is indeed alive and has ended up in London. She learns about Aminata's fame and realizes that the celebrated woman must be her mother. Aminata and May are finally able to live as mother and daughter. The novel ends with a quiet scene set in a London apartment that the two women share, with the frail Aminata awaiting word about the passage of the Abolitionist Bill. She drifts into sleep (possibly, death) while waiting for her daughter to come home with good news about the bill—"home" being, fittingly and poignantly, the novel's last word.

Conclusion

This chapter has discussed *The Book of Negroes* as a literary representation of black diasporic identity formation that is concerned both with historical detail and, to quote Houston A. Baker Jr., with "the symbolic and psychosocial conditions of modernity's dynamics of race and displacement."[196] While the formation of black diasporic subjectivity is a central theme both in *Middle Passage* and in *The Book of Negroes*, Hill's contextualization of this theme within African diasporic (particularly Black Loyalist) history and geography draws much more extensively on historical research than Johnson's more philosophically oriented novel does.

Soon after the publication of *The Book of Negroes*, Hill answered an interviewer's question about a fiction writer's "responsibility to the past" by stating that his novel "purports to represent history faithfully."[197] One way of getting an initial handle on the complex issue of any novel's historical accuracy is to ask whether the physical settings are of the correct vintage. In *The Book of Negroes*, they in many ways are: Hill's representations of both natural landscapes and human habitats are credible. Then again, Hill openly admits that he has "taken several liberties with dates and places and so forth."[198] While all novelists take liberties with their historical material to create works of fiction, Hill has taken some that seem rather generous, both with the "dates and places and so forth"[199] and beyond.[200] Ultimately, it is Hill's focus on black agency and intelligence that serves as key to his diplomatic statement that in *The Book of Negroes* he wanted to "project [history] honestly, meaning to project it in a way that's faithful to [his] *intellectual* understanding of the time, places, and conditions in which African people were living."[201] That is, through his creation of Aminata, a composite character who embodies various aspects of the early African diasporic experience,[202] Hill reimagined enslaved and free black people's initiative and skill in negotiating the terms of their daily lives in the slavery era as well as the extent to which such negotiations were possible in each context that he portrays. This focus on agency and negotiation constitutes the most important continuum within Hill's representation of the range of forms that the black diasporic existence took in the late eighteenth century.

While creating his late-eighteenth-century diasporic protagonist, Hill—in addition to reading historical scholarship—examined classic slave narratives, including Olaudah Equiano's memoir. In all its constructedness, inner tensions, and hybridity,[203] Equiano's *Interesting Narrative* is testimony to the poignant and laborious nature of African diasporic identity formation. At the same time, it offers powerful evidence of black diasporic modernity as a "cultural bricolage" (Vincent L. Wimbush's term)[204] characterized by a survivalist, radically innovative, and successful combination of adaptation, resistance, and resilience. Like Equiano's autobiography, Hill's neo-slave narrative portrays a diasporic individual who, upon entering modernity, goes through a process heavily laden with physical and emotional suffering, is racialized by the "white" society's gaze as "black," mentally reconstitutes herself as an African diasporic subject, and finds her activist writerly voice as the author of her memoir.

Arlene Keizer has justifiably remarked, in discussing Johnson's male-focused *Middle Passage*, that Johnson's writing "presents formidable complications for a black feminist critic."[205] Hill's novel, in turn, is actively attuned to gender politics throughout: it depicts *both* the oppression to which Aminata, surrounded by sexual and racial ideologies denigrating black womanhood,[206] is subjected in the Western world *and* her active self-fashioning as a woman living out her diasporic predicament. That is, *The Book of Negroes* on the one hand describes sexual violations, forced abortions of Aminata's family formation, and various forms of sexually and racially inflected condescension that she has to endure. On the other hand, Aminata's first-person narration gives expression to her identities as a daughter, wife, and mother; as a competent midwife; and eventually as a woman who speaks to white power, using her public voice both on the abolitionist platform and through her "memoir" (the novel we read). Intellectual and political activism remains an important part of Aminata's life even when she is finally allowed to resume her motherhood. Her eventual "home," established very shortly before her looming death, consists of two dimensions: first, her partially renewed family formation (as a single mother who has tragically lost her husband and one of her two children), and, second, her writing project, which enables and empowers her to tell the story of her enslavement, her fragile freedom in the Atlantic world, and her diasporic subjectivity.

Brian Cheyette notes in *Diasporas of the Mind* (2013) that "diaspora" can be understood either in ways that are "deeply conservative and imbricated in historical narratives concerning a timeless exile from an autochthonous 'homeland'" or "as a state of creatively disruptive impurity which imagines emergent transnational and postethnic identities and cultures."[207] He argues that the writers discussed in his book "work through and between" these two "versions of diaspora."[208] Hill's narrative, too, can be situated in an in-between terrain vis-à-vis the polarity of the "victim" and "celebratory" diasporas.[209] Hill depicts Aminata's perpetual "homelessness" as a tragedy rather than simplistically praising the "creatively disruptive impurity" produced by diaspora. He highlights the ambivalences of all attempts of a diasporic individual to belong once her diasporic predicament has been propelled into being. It is highly paradoxical, in Hill's treatment, that Aminata is *compelled* to reinvent herself multiple times under duress and that she is required to live out the dialectic of continuity and rupture in relation to her Africanity even upon returning, as a mature woman, to West Africa. What Hill celebrates is not the diasporic *condition* per se but the diasporic individual's capacity to respond to it: his protagonist simultaneously resists, adapts, and innovates and finally assumes the role of an autobiographical speaker/writer who deliberately and purposefully narrates her black diasporic subjectivity into being.

3

War, Trauma, Displacement, Diaspora

Toni Morrison's and Caryl Phillips's African American Soldiers

A portion of *The Book of Negroes* is devoted to the 1792 migration of black Nova Scotians to Sierra Leone, but the founding of Liberia—another unique episode in the history of the early Black Atlantic—has received little attention from novelists of the African diaspora, with the notable exception of one section of Caryl Phillips's *Crossing the River* (1993). What frames Phillips's modified, expanded Middle Passage novel[1] is the history of the Atlantic slave trade, embodied by a devastated African father who sells his three children into slavery after his crops fail. The rest of the text consists of four sections or narratives. The first offers excerpts from the log of the white sea captain who is in charge of transporting the three children and a shipload of other captive Africans over the Atlantic. The second depicts the transformation of an African American missionary, who in 1834 travels to Liberia in order to convert local "heathens" to Christianity but, instead, gradually finds himself transformed by the very culture that he, at the beginning of his enterprise, so fervently attempts to "civilize." The third section unfolds the fate of an African American woman who tries to reach California in the era of the US western expansion, and the fourth relates the story of a black American soldier who wishes to establish an interracial family in England during World War II. As the organization of the novel suggests, the protagonists of the second, third, and fourth sections are meant to be interpreted, in a time-transcending manner, as the African father's three children.

Crossing the River, in other words, *both* participates in the cultural transmission of the memory of the African diaspora's ur-trauma (the Middle Passage and enslavement) *and* explicitly connects this originary event/process to more recent African American experiences of traumatic displacement, viewing the latter through the interpretive prism of the former. Maria Diedrich,

Henry Louis Gates Jr., and Carl Pedersen—inspired by Edward Brathwaite's notion of "nation language"—have theorized what they term the "Middle Passage sensibility" as a discursive reality that, "[s]ubmerged beneath the surface of the dominant language, ... constantly seeps through and inevitably affects it."[2] *Crossing the River*, an active participant in the construction of the African diasporic imaginary, is a prime example of such "seepage." By hermeneutically linking post–Middle Passage generations' varied experiences of traumatic displacement with the trauma of the Atlantic slave trade, the novel treats the African diaspora's ur-trauma as a usable past for the purpose of contemporary black diasporic identity formation.

Invested in this hermeneutical linkage, this chapter, which leaves behind the late-eighteenth-/early-nineteenth-century Atlantic world of *The Book of Negroes* and moves on to the twentieth century, takes its cue from the fourth section of *Crossing the River*: Phillips's story of an African American GI in England examines war and diaspora in conjunction with each other. This chapter does the same. War and diaspora can be read as being linked by traumatic displacement, which not only is an inherent aspect of diaspora but also characterizes, albeit in a more temporary manner, the experiences of those who participate in modern warfare abroad and carry out what US military lexicon loftily terms "missions," "operations," and "campaigns." While warfare, most obviously, frequently turns civilians into refugees, the experiences of troops overseas, which may leave indelible wounds or scars on soldiers' bodies and psyches, often form another variety of traumatic displacement caused by war. Even though overseas deployments are not physically permanent dis-/relocations for those who survive and return, such assignments nevertheless can, as is well known, make troops experience a powerful sense of existential displacement both during and after combat.

As historical and sociological phenomena, the temporary wartime displacement of African American soldiers and the historically more permanent African diasporic condition of dispersal share such similarities as the pivotal role of large-scale violence in the genealogy of both types of uprooting. Of course, war and diaspora also have a number of obvious qualitative differences. Nevertheless, several black diasporic authors have placed these two phenomena in dialogue with each other in their fiction, in order to illuminate the nature of one or the other or both, or to explore the often complicated and tension-ridden relationship between national citizenship and black diasporic loyalty. An exploration of this interpretive gesture is warranted in this book, which examines black novelists' diasporic *imagination*, including any unconventional hermeneutical connections that the authors make between diaspora and other historical events/processes involving persons of African descent.

In addition to *Crossing the River*, another example of an interpretive linkage between an African American soldier's temporary displacement and the more permanent condition of the African diaspora can be found in *There Is a Tree More Ancient Than Eden* (1973), the first novel of the late Chicagoan/Evanstonian writer Leon Forrest. The "Lives" section of this novel includes a sketch of the life of a minor character called Jamestown, an artist-turned-soldier whose very name, synonymous with the location in Virginia that in 1619 witnessed the arrival of the allegedly first group of Africans as indentured servants in America, points to the African diasporic predicament. After serving in Korea and thus fulfilling a citizenship duty for the pre–civil rights United States, Jamestown returns to America, embraces militant revolutionary politics, and ends up being pursued by US authorities. He is eventually wounded, probably fatally (Forrest does not disclose this detail), in Mozambique in 1971 while fighting on the side of the Front for the Liberation of Mozambique against the Portuguese rule and thus demonstrating his loyalty to an African anticolonial and anti-imperialistic cause. *There Is a Tree* includes a highly symbolic scene, set in an unnamed location, that depicts Jamestown's physical struggle with an unidentified enemy combatant who attempts to drown him. This complex scene evokes death as well as resurrection, the possibility of both destruction and of a new beginning, by alluding simultaneously to baptismal water and to the Middle Passage.[3] The references to the Middle Passage place Jamestown's fierce fight against his enemy within the context of his public and private war against the long-lasting legacies of colonial modernity.

Delving deeper into the literary potential of this type of time-transcending linkage, this chapter explores the connection between war and diaspora in two novels by Toni Morrison—*Sula* (1973), which features a veteran of World War I, and *Tar Baby* (1981), whose male protagonist fought in Vietnam—and in the World War II section of *Crossing the River*. As befits Morrison's and Phillips's shared avoidance of lengthy, detailed depictions of actual warfare, my analysis is not primarily concerned with military history.[4] Instead, I examine "frames of war," to quote the title of Judith Butler's 2009 book:[5] I investigate how and to what extent these novels allude to the Middle Passage and/or depict black transnational connectivity (that is, lateral diasporic connections) while portraying black soldiers and veterans. As my discussion will show, such allusions and connections, which speak to diasporic sensibilities, are the least obvious, yet present, in *Sula* and the most overt, through the novel's explicitly diasporic frame, in *Crossing the River*.

One of the key concepts of this chapter will be "trauma," which means "wound" in the original Greek. Trauma theory, which has to a considerable degree evolved in conjunction with Holocaust studies and humanistic memory studies, is now such a vast and rich field that it cannot be surveyed in detail here.[6] My more limited remarks on trauma—primarily inspired by the insights of the psychoanalytically oriented trauma theorist Cathy Caruth—will serve to illuminate my argument that as Morrison and Phillips portray African American veterans, they forge connections between the historical diasporic ur-trauma of dispersal/dislocation and more (con)temporary experiences of traumatic displacement on foreign battlefields. In *Sula*, *Tar Baby*, and *Crossing the River*, literary representations of physical and psychic wounds acquired in twentieth-century wars coalesce with the cultural memory of the death and damage that Africans' and their descendants' forced initiation into Western modernity inflicted on black bodies and psyches during slavery. Caruth has conceptualized posttraumatic stress disorder, a condition depicted in both *Sula* and *Tar Baby*, as follows: "If PTSD must be understood as a pathological symptom, then it is not so much a symptom of the unconscious, as it is a symptom of history. The traumatized ... carry an impossible history within them, or they become themselves the symptom of a history that they cannot entirely possess."[7] In Morrison's and Phillips's narratives of war and African American veterans, two kinds of "impossible histories" intersect and converse with each other: references to captive, traumatized, injured, and dead black bodies as "collateral damage"[8] of the slave trade *and* to the physically and emotionally traumatizing black participation in twentieth-century warfare merge in these two authors' representations of the large-scale violence that has typically accompanied the Western project of modernity.

To rephrase, the Middle Passage, the Atlantic slave trade, and slavery together embodied a phenomenon of post-Columbian modernity whereby violence served, Eurocentrically speaking, a societally "justified" goal—namely, the white beneficiaries' economic interests. In modern warfare, too, "efficient" mass violence serves socially sanctioned purposes, although the exact reasons why modern nation-states enter into wars vary. Morrison and Phillips allow wounds (traumas) caused by the Atlantic slave trade and wounds (including PTSD) caused by modern warfare to bleed into each other in their fiction. In so doing, they problematize aspects of modernity by calling attention to connections between slavery, the rise of modern capitalism and industrialism, the emergence and racialization of the nation-state, and modern wars fought between nation-states or between their easy or uneasy alliances. Such critical interrogations highlight the African diaspora as a phenomenon that emerged as a "by-product" of post-Columbian modernity, continues to fit poorly into current modernity's dominant categories (such as the nation-state), and critiques modernity from an identity position that, while often seen as marginal, offers a unique vantage point precisely because of its "between-camps" (Gilroy's term) positionality.[9]

This chapter first discusses the diasporic qualities of *Sula*, demonstrating that Morrison links the trope of "crossing the river" to the most significant events in the life of the World War I soldier/veteran Shadrack. These events include his crossing over into mental illness when, after crossing a small river, he breaks down on a foreign battlefield where he is physically and existentially so far from home as to be hopelessly lost. As indicated by the title of Phillips's *Crossing the River* and by Biton's consolation of Aminata in *The Book of Negroes* ("You crossed the big river, child"),[10] black authors occasionally use the trope of crossing the river to refer to the Middle Passage because many captive Africans from the continent's interior, who had no word for the sea, compared the Atlantic Ocean to a vast river.[11] The repetition of this trope in *Sula* reveals, as my discussion will elaborate, that a diasporic awareness of the Middle Passage and its ramifications is an important, albeit covert, presence in this novel.

In black diasporic fiction more generally, the trope of crossing the river can allude to captivity or to freedom, or simultaneously to both. It refers back to the Middle Passage, but it also points to liberty—in US contexts, to crossing the Ohio River in particular, to fleeing from bondage to freedom.[12] In *Sula*, the connotations of "crossing the river" are primarily traumatic,[13] as my analysis will demonstrate: they refer to disenchantments or catastrophes following brief illusions of freedom and empowerment.

After analyzing the diasporic overtones of *Sula*, I will point to the importance of Middle Passage references in the opening of *Tar Baby*—a novel featuring Son, an African American Vietnam veteran who suffers from a subtler form of postcombat stress than does Shadrack in *Sula*. I will then underscore, by discussing aspects of *Tar Baby* that anticipate its ambiguous ending (which depicts Son's pursuit of communion with mythical black warriors allegedly inhabiting a remote location on a Caribbean island), that in this novel Morrison places a strong emphasis on black transnational connectivity. This emphasis has been overlooked by readings that focus solely on Son's interactions with his Baltimore-born lover and with the novel's white cast, at the expense of its

Caribbean characters. At the chapter's end, my brief remarks on *Crossing the River*'s narrative of the experiences of an African American GI who temporarily finds himself in Yorkshire, England, pave the way for chapter 4 by bringing black diasporic interrogations to bear on World War II Britain.

A World War I Veteran's Traumatic Displacement in *Sula*

Even though the African American freedom struggle is an ongoing process that neither began during the Civil War nor ended with the civil rights movement's legal victories in the mid-1960s, some episodes in its centuries-long history have nevertheless been "particularly formative, or even transformative," as Adriane Lentz-Smith observes in *Freedom Struggles* (2009).[14] World War I, as she and others have argued, undoubtedly was one such episode. Prior to the Great War, comments Lentz-Smith, African Americans—as slaves, as free men and women, and as soldiers in the American wars of the eighteenth and nineteenth centuries—"had performed the bitter, often crushing, work of helping to build American nation and empire."[15] Their work (a paradoxical effort, considering their status as an oppressed minority) had been motivated by an imaginary "trade-off," as Lentz-Smith notes: African Americans had believed that, in exchange for "join[ing] themselves to the American national project in all its light and shadows,"[16] they would be granted full citizenship and its benefits. However, as the new century dawned, it became increasingly obvious that the alleged "trade" was not working out the way African Americans had hoped it would. Full national belonging still remained beyond their reach because even the brave new era was bogged down by what W.E.B. Du Bois in *The Souls of Black Folk* famously called "the problem of the color-line."[17]

Under these circumstances, the declaration of war on the Central Powers by the US Congress on April 6, 1917, seemed to many African Americans an important opportunity to demonstrate their loyalty to their country of citizenship. Du Bois appealed to African Americans in his "Close Ranks" editorial in *The Crisis* magazine of July 16, 1918: "Let us, while this war lasts, forget our special grievances and close our ranks shoulder to shoulder with our own white fellow citizens and the allied nations that are fighting for democracy."[18] (Then again, in his equally well-known "Returning Soldiers" editorial in *The Crisis* of May 18, 1919, a disillusioned Du Bois angrily chastised the United States for failing to receive the returning African American soldiers as citizens with full civil rights.)[19] Not every black intellectual, however, was as enthusiastic about the opportunities that the war allegedly provided for African

Americans as Du Bois was at the time he wrote "Close Ranks." In November 1917, the young radicals Asa Philip Randolph (who later became a tireless civil rights leader and the first president of the Brotherhood of Sleeping Car Porters) and Chandler Owen wrote in their then newly founded *Messenger* that "every man and woman called upon to fight" should ask themselves the critical question of "[w]ho shall pay for the war."[20] The stance of these two young socialists was clear:

> [O]bviously, those who profit from the war ought to pay for it.... How can profits be made out of the war? The answer to this question is: by selling to the government those things which are needed to keep the war going; for instance, food and clothing for soldiers, steel for battleships, submarines, aeroplanes, coal for transports, etc., money to lend to the government. Now, Mr. Common-man, do you own any of these things? If you don't then you cannot profit from the war.[21]

As if taking her cue from Randolph and Owen, Toni Morrison, in "Unspeakable Things Unspoken" (1989), calls World War I a "most wasteful capitalist war."[22] Moreover, in discussing the war's cost to America's black communities she specifically mentions that the Great War meant a "traumatic displacement" for African American troops.[23] This carefully chosen term has diasporic overtones: it hermeneutically aligns itself with the cultural memory of the black diaspora's origins in the traumatic uprooting from Africa (that is, in the ultimate "unspeakable") under the sign of preindustrial capitalism.

This diasporically informed emphasis on the Great War as a traumatic displacement for African American soldiers permeates Morrison's second novel, *Sula*. The post–World War I years in the United States witnessed the rise of a proud New Negro militancy,[24] including active black resistance during the Red Summer of 1919 and the publication of such racially self-assertive Harlem Renaissance poems as Jamaican-born Claude McKay's "If We Must Die" and Langston Hughes's "I, Too [Sing America]."[25] However, *Sula* addresses the other side of the (hi)story, namely, the breaking rather than the "making" of African American men in the war. Instead of introducing a triumphant black-veteran-turned-New-Negro, *Sula* features a permanently shaken Shadrack, whose defining encounter with modernity takes place in the context of modern warfare on a French battlefield.[26] Like the biblical Shadrach in the Book of Daniel (3:13–29), Morrison's Shadrack survives a trial in a fiery furnace—here, an ordeal on the western front of World War I. However, unlike his Old Testament predecessor,[27] who emerges from his trial by fire miraculously unscathed, Morrison's humbled veteran returns home in a lowly condition, so severely "shell-shocked" that his inadequately treated PTSD[28] ossifies into chronic mental illness. Caruth's above-quoted description of PTSD as a "symptom of history"[29] offers a fitting interpretive key to Morrison's narrative of Shadrack as a PTSD sufferer: centuries ago, the geopolitics of slavery (one type of "impossible history")[30] disconnected Shadrack's ancestors from Africa, and the geopolitics of war, in turn (another kind of "impossible history"), disconnects him first from his hometown in Ohio and then, as a result of his traumatic combat experience in France, from his selfhood and from his ability to connect with others. Service in the war does not become a passport to full national belonging for Shadrack. For him, it instead results in a lifelong alienation from self and society, an irreversible psychic exile and vagrancy.

After Shadrack is discharged from military service and from the midwestern hospital where he recuperates for more than a year, he has no idea how to find his way back to his hometown, Medallion[31]—more specifically, to its African American neighborhood, which is jokingly called the Bottom.[32] After leaving the hospital grounds, Shadrack desperately tries to figure out a route to "his window, his river, and his soft voices just outside the door,"[33] but he is in no condition to do so. At the scene's ironic anticlimax, he is arrested for vagrancy. In 1919, Frederick Walker Mott, a British pioneer in neuropathology and psychiatry, wrote that the "dazed," shell-shocked veterans of the Great War whom he had examined seemed to have lost their sense of "time and place."[34] His clinical description resonates with Morrison's depiction of the mentally and physically disoriented Shadrack who, upon leaving the hospital, "didn't even know who or what he was."[35] The war had literally made him a "private,"[36] a man "with no past, no language, no tribe, no source, no address book."[37] As J. Brooks Bouson points out, Morrison's references to an erased "past," "language," and "tribe" here serve as "a veiled allusion to the horrors of slavery" and cast the veteran's displacement as "the repetition of catastrophic trauma in African-American experience."[38] Indeed, the shadow of the slave ship falls even on *Sula*, whose events are set from the year 1919 (which saw the strengthening of the self-assertive and even militant New Negro but also witnessed the quiet homecomings of many shell-shocked Shadracks) through the year 1965, which marked the passage of the Voting Rights Act (a major victory for the civil rights movement) but which, in *Sula*, disappointingly sees Shadrack having been demoted from an independent fisherman to a worker hauling trash to earn his keep.[39] Awareness of African Americans' diasporic displacement and its aftereffects permeates even this twentieth-century setting and storyline, as Morrison evokes the vanished "past," "language," and "tribe" in depicting the life's arc of the traumatically dislocated and permanently affected soldier.

Sula, in other words, *subtly* links early-twentieth-century African American war trauma, depicted in the novel as Shadrack's combat-induced PTSD, with the African diaspora's ur-trauma (the Middle Passage and New World slavery). Notably, what my earlier chapters say about the "silent archives" of slavery is also largely applicable to the "archives" documenting—or, rather, failing to document—the war traumas of real-life Shadracks. In *Literature in the Ashes of History* (2013), Caruth writes that "the disasters that mark the end of the millennium" (a phrase she borrows from Jacques Derrida) "are not simply the objects of archives, or objects that call out for archiving; they are also, themselves, unique events whose archives have been repressed or erased, and whose singularity, as events, can be defined by that erasure."[40] World War I qualifies as one such disaster, particularly given how many "archives" of individual soldiers' experiences have been lost. This is emphatically true of the experiences of African American troops. In *Sula*, Morrison uses the trope (or chronotope) of "crossing the river" to cast the silent archives of slavery and those of World War I as two types of what Caruth, again summoning a concept of Derrida's, terms "*archives du mal*'—archives of evil (or suffering)."[41] Caruth argues that such archives "not only leave an impression"[42] but also "hide or prohibit their own memory."[43] However, fiction can spotlight forgotten aspects of history by doing what Roger Luckhurst in *The Trauma Question* (2008) calls bending history's rules.[44] Luckhurst, examining what Anne Whitehead in 2004 termed "the emerging genre of trauma fiction,"[45] specifically focuses on the "trauma novel."[46] The gist of what he says about Morrison's *Beloved* (1987) being a highly developed trauma novel also applies, albeit to a lesser extent, to *Sula*: as Luckhurst points out, Morrison's writing reveals "how important the role of fictional narrative can be in the trauma paradigm, for it demonstrates the novel form's capacity to *bend the rules of history, causation and representation* in order to bring into presence an *occluded traumatic violence*."[47] In *Sula*, Morrison's employment of the trope of crossing the river, while transcending "the rules of history, causation and representation," helps to highlight "occluded" African American suffering during two historical processes of epochal violence—colonial modernity (particularly the Atlantic slave trade and racial slavery) and World War I.

Because *Sula*'s subtle linkage of early-twentieth-century African American war trauma with the African diaspora's ur-trauma is primarily accomplished through the trope of crossing the river, it is only logical that, on the level of plot, this trope is central to several narrative moments that are, one way or another, about Shadrack, death, and change. First, it is immediately after crossing a river in France that Shadrack's existence changes permanently as a result of his first (and last) exposure to combat: "For several days they had been marching, keeping close to a stream that was frozen at its edges. At one point they crossed it, and no sooner had he stepped foot on the other side than the day was adangle with shouts and explosions."[48] Just a few moments later, Shadrack, "[a] young man of hardly twenty, his head full of nothing,"[49] witnesses the violent death of a fellow soldier and crosses over from sanity to PTSD—and to permanent mental illness, as it later becomes clear.

Second, when Shadrack eventually returns to the Bottom as a PTSD sufferer, he settles on the bank of the river that runs through Medallion, "happily fishing" there and isolating himself to his little cabin,[50] but not without the presence of a "little blank bridge that crossed the river to [his] house."[51] After a local child, Chicken Little, drowns while playing with Sula and Nel by the river, the young Sula crosses this very bridge—that is, crosses the river—as she runs to Shadrack's house in the immediate aftermath of the tragedy, still shocked by the dramatic, traumatic moment when the river's "water darkened and closed quickly"[52] after taking in a black life. On the level of plot, Sula visits Shadrack to ascertain that he, a potential eyewitness to what the community might interpret as a criminal act, had not seen the accident to which she had inadvertently contributed. On the level of the text's psychodynamics, however, the narrative here briefly pushes Sula into the company of another individual familiar with posttraumatic stress and guilt. Most importantly, the text's emphatic repetition of the "[dark,] closed place in the water"[53] in the description of the little boy's disappearance into his watery grave evokes images of unceremonious burials of black bodies in the sea during the ur-crossing of the Atlantic (burials that rarely left behind "archives") and conjures up the stunning emptiness that black witnesses felt in the aftermath of such impromptu funerals: "There was nothing but the baking sun and something newly missing."[54]

Third, *Sula* again links "crossing the river" with death when Shadrack, a few hours after the dawn of the fateful National Suicide Day of 1941,[55] "walk[s] over the rickety bridge and on into the Bottom,"[56] horrifyingly correct in his "certain[ty] that this would be the last time he would invite them to end their lives neatly and sweetly."[57] That is, the most significant phase in the series of events terminating the existence of Medallion's African American neighborhood begins when the black veteran—shattered, more than two decades earlier, by his violent encounter with early-twentieth-century forces of modernity in a foreign location across the Atlantic—again "crosses the river." It is after this "crossing" that the isolated veteran once more appears on the street with a cowbell and a hangman's rope on National Suicide Day, proclaiming his annual gospel that "this was their only chance to kill themselves or each other."[58] This time a catching, childlike euphoria spreads even among those who have never before participated in his morbid celebration, and a sizable crowd joins the surprised prophet, forming a joyous parade behind him. However, when the celebrants pass by a "tunnel they were forbidden to build"[59]—in Patricia McKee's words, a reminder of "the loss of hope, promise, repair, credit, attention, occupation"[60]—their mood suddenly changes. Outraged by what they perceive as a symbol of the politics, policies, and social structures causing their unemployment and poverty, they fight a brief but dramatic war against all that the Valley and its inhabitants represent to them by "kill[ing]" the tunnel.[61] While they are inside, the tunnel collapses and the cave fills with water. In what becomes, in Grewal's phrase, a "literal enactment" of National Suicide Day,[62] most of the "killers" themselves die by drowning. After this catastrophic communal trauma and loss, Medallion's black neighborhood loses its vitality and yields to the forces of capitalism and urban renewal. Shadrack, in other words—by unintentionally becoming a subverted Pied Piper of Hamelin who leads his "followers" to death[63]—significantly contributes to the events that end the collective life of the only community that accepted him upon his return from World War I.[64]

To recapitulate, Morrison scholars have previously recognized the associations that exist between *Sula*'s eponymous female protagonist and water/fluidity. However, what has not been fully acknowledged is that through the trope of crossing the river the narrative also associates Shadrack with water (despite the obvious rigidity of his psychological coping mechanisms) and that *one* of this trope's functions in *Sula* is to allude to the traumatic origin of the African diaspora in the Middle Passage. It must be understood, though, that *Sula*'s veiled references to the diasporic ur-crossing eschew neat one-to-one equivalences or exactly definable cause-effect relations. Morrison's allusive and metaphorical writing invites the reader to make connections and leaves room for interpretation.

Morrison's use of the African American veteran's "crossing the river" as an allusion to the ur-trauma of the African diaspora invites a further remark on "trauma fiction" and the relationship of *Sula* to it. Luckhurst argues that "[e]xemplars of the trauma novel cluster in the late 1980s and 1990s, after the clinical elaboration of PTSD."[65] He emphasizes that the thematic scope of such "exemplars" is not limited to narratives of war,[66] despite the prominent role of the Vietnam War in the process that led to PTSD being listed in the *DSM* (*Diagnostic and Statistical Manual of Mental Disorders*). In Luckhurst's view, *Beloved* was chronologically the first item in this "cluster of trauma fictions."[67] Although Luckhurst's general point about the "cluster" is well taken, it is important to note that even Morrison's first novel can be read as a "trauma novel": *The Bluest Eye* (1970) not only thematically focuses on the dual trauma of interracial and intraracial victimization but is also aesthetically similar to two of the three aspects of *Beloved* that, in Luckhurst's eyes, make the latter a paradigmatic trauma novel. These two aspects are the "disarticulation of linear narrative"[68] (consider *The Bluest Eye*'s narrative frame and the adult Claudia's narrative intrusions) and the "closing reflections on the transgenerational transmission [of trauma] and the complex accommodations communities need to make with such traumatic history"[69] (consider the hope embedded in the adult Claudia's decision to save Pecola from oblivion by passing on a story that, to quote from *Beloved*'s much-discussed ending, "was not a story to pass on"). Luckhurst's discussion of *Beloved* also highlights the importance of the novel's "figuration of trauma in the ghost"[70] and makes insightful observations about the role of ghosts and haunting in trauma fiction.[71] In my view, the absence of ghosts from *The Bluest Eye* hardly disqualifies it from being a trauma novel, but my aim is not to engage in a debate over prescriptive criteria for the aesthetics of the genre here. Rather, I foreground Morrison's foundational preoccupation with trauma, which is clearly evident even in her first novel, simply to reemphasize that *Sula*, too, is a complex trauma narrative in which the traumatic displacement of a black soldier/veteran points beyond itself to another "forgotten wound."[72] If there is a "ghost" in *Sula*, as is the case with *Beloved* (a repressed, haunting presence that returns intrusively as a sign of "a hurt that has not been honoured by a memorializing narrative"),[73] it is the origin of the African diaspora in trauma and terror that serves as such a specter, and this "ghost" does its "haunting" through the text's repetition of the motif of crossing the river.

Finally, yet another question to consider in discussing the diasporic qualities of *Sula* is how Morrison treats "blackness" in her narrative. On the one hand, she does thematize it. For example, after Shadrack is arrested for vagrancy, he in jail manages to locate a point of connection with his earlier self. What provides this continuity of identity is his "blackness,"[74] which he sees reflected in his substitute for a mirror, the water in the toilet bowl in his cell. (Given *Sula*'s other subtle allusions to Virginia Woolf's work, it is fair to say that this scene subversively alludes to *Mrs. Dalloway*, in which mirrors play a significant role.)[75] While staring at the water—the element that in *Sula* evokes both black history and, in conjunction with the female protagonist, the fluidity of black identities—Shadrack recognizes and reclaims his blackness and is soothed and comforted by it: "There in the toilet water he saw a grave black face. A black so definite, so unequivocal, it astonished him. He had been harboring a skittish apprehension that he was not real.... But when the blackness greeted him with its indisputable presence, he wanted nothing more."[76] This discovery serves as a stabilizing moment of reconnection with the self for the PTSD sufferer whose identity has been disrupted by trauma, which, as Luckhurst observes, "disrupts memory, and therefore identity, in peculiar ways."[77] It is as a result of this turning point that the traumatized veteran is able to start the process of resituating himself in the world, however imperfectly.

On the other hand, even though *Sula*—an early, second novel of Morrison—thematizes blackness, it does not focus on *transnationally* conceived blackness. For example, the Senegalese units that fought under the French in World War I are never mentioned in the narrative. Shell-shocked Shadrack's recognition of his blackness reconnects him with his place of birth, the Bottom of Medallion, rather than linking him with black diasporic communities beyond the borders of the United States. Morrison's fourth novel, however, takes a different approach: *Tar Baby* gives metaphorical expression to the diasporic condition of an African American war veteran not only by depicting his transnational wanderings, but also by portraying the final stage of his search for selfhood and wholeness as a yearning to be included in an African Caribbean community that for him represents black communion transcending the constraints of time and place, of history and geopolitics.

A Vietnam Veteran's Search for Transnational Black Communion in *Tar Baby*

Tar Baby is usually overlooked in scholarly discussions about American novelists' renderings of the Vietnam War (a war fought by a disproportionate number of African American soldiers, a fact reflecting racial and socioeconomic disparities in the US draft at the time)[78] and its aftereffects.[79] The novel features a male protagonist, William "Son" Green, a Florida-born African American Vietnam veteran whose life, like Shadrack's, has been profoundly altered by his war experience and his subsequent postcombat stress.

Engaging in intertextual play within her own oeuvre, Morrison covertly alludes to Shadrack in *Tar Baby*'s very opening. Son starts what will be his new life with a *plunge* when he, a young seaman, out of mental restlessness jumps ship in the Caribbean in order to start his life anew. When, in *Sula*, the PTSD sufferer Shadrack "t[akes] the plunge" by leaving the hospital,[80] his temporary safe haven, he immediately finds himself in a state of total helplessness where even untying his own shoelaces is an insurmountable challenge and where his struggle with the laces' knots reflects the condition of his psyche.[81] Son, by contrast, displays a much higher degree of functionality when preparing for his dramatic dive.[82] However, despite its casually successful beginning, Son's plunge soon becomes an intensive encounter with both death and his fear of it—that is, a real and symbolic repetition of the panic that he had previously experienced first in Vietnam and then during the "war" on his home front that had culminated in his wife's accidental death.[83] Eventually, however, after having gone "down, down, and found himself not at the bottom of the sea, as he expected, but whirling in a vortex,"[84] Son finds his way back to the realm of the living, drawing air with the intensity of a newborn baby when he, upon emerging from the sea's watery womb, can again breathe, cough, and spit.[85]

This opening of *Tar Baby*, set in 1979, casts Son as an anonymous, undocumented black fugitive without any possessions or connections, who "had no things to gather—no book of postage stamps, no razor blade or key to any door."[86] Besides utilizing fugitive imagery, the beginning of the narrative—with its heavy focus on the sea, the ship, and the Caribbean waters "bloodtinted" by the sun[87]—also alludes to forced maritime transportations of slaves, as is evident in the passage in which Son gets his first glimpse of the (fictional) island of Isle des Chevaliers, where he will experience some of the most transformative encounters of his post-Vietnam existence: "[H]e could see very little of the land, which was just as well because he was gazing at the shore of an island that, three hundred years ago, had struck slaves blind the moment they saw it."[88] As she does in *Sula*,[89] Morrison here provides the story's fictional setting with an etiological myth that describes the origin of black settlement in the area. While in both novels the myth of origin refers back to the days of slavery, in *Tar Baby* the founding mythology of Isle des Chevaliers specifically depicts a forced voyage of a group of slaves within French Caribbean waters—a Middle Passage reference that gives the novel an emphatically diasporic frame and focus. Jenny Sharpe remarks on a group of black diasporic writers and artists that they "not only resurrect middle passage images in order to let the dead bear witness to the past, they also transform those images so that they can speak to the more recent migration.... Time, for a transatlantic black diaspora, is broken; the past can, and does, coexist with the present."[90] While Sharpe here specifically discusses the creative work of a group of black Britons, the coexistence of the past and present that she mentions (in particular, a powerful awareness of the Middle Passage and all that it synecdochically signifies) also permeates *Tar Baby*, in its opening and beyond.

Tar Baby discloses Son's status as a Vietnam veteran to the reader relatively late, although this delay is shorter than the corresponding deferral in *Beloved*, in which the reader does not learn until the penultimate chapter that the male protagonist Paul D had "worked both sides of the [Civil] War."[91] In both novels, the narrative delay suggests a return of the repressed. In *Tar Baby*, Son's traumatic war memories form, metaphorically speaking, a specter that haunts him, even though this specter, unlike the ghost or memory of slavery in *Beloved*, is not personified in the narrative. Through fleeting but significant allusions to Son's service in Vietnam, *Tar Baby* gradually paints a portrait of him as a relatively functional yet profoundly affected war veteran with untreated PTSD. As the *DSM* indicates, unwelcome flashbacks, which fall into the category of "intrusion" symptoms ("recurrent, involuntary, and intrusive recollections of the event"), are typical of PTSD.[92] Morrison inserts several such flashbacks into her narrative of Son's struggle with his traumatized condition.[93]

The passage of *Tar Baby* that eventually provides the keyword "war"[94] evokes *Sula*'s Shadrack while alluding to the origins of Son's PTSD in warfare. When Morrison depicts the two young soldiers' respective experiences, she utilizes the same minor motif, that of hands. The body parts that the eighteen-year-old Son most wanted to remain uninjured in Vietnam were his hands, because he would need them back home to materialize the daydream that was his lifeline in the forests of Southeast Asia—the dream of earning a living as a jazz pianist in his small hometown of Eloe, Florida, after repatriation.[95] This dream reveals his longing for a condition where "[h]is *hands* would be doing something nice and *human* for a change."[96] This phrase, in turn, serves as implicit intertextual commentary on Shadrack's pathological need, in *Sula*, to get rid of his "monstrous" hands, which had been trained to do inhuman deeds.[97]

Morrison's representation of these two traumatized soldiers' guilt and shame, as well as of their desire for redemption, echoes the 1970s debate, conducted in the medical community and beyond, over the inclusion of PTSD in the *DSM*. Somewhat paradoxically, one challenge that Robert Jay Lifton and other psychiatrists faced in developing PTSD as a diagnostic label in the aftermath of the Vietnam War was its broad applicability—that is, its applicability to traumatized soldiers, too, not only to the affected victims of their deeds.[98] As Didier Fassin and Richard Rechtman claim, "By applying the same psychological classification to the person who suffers violence, the person who commits it, and the person who witnesses it, the concept of trauma profoundly transforms the moral framework of what constitutes humanity."[99] Not all audiences were immediately ready for such a "transformation." The subtitle of Lifton's 1973 book, *Home from the War*, was, tellingly, *Vietnam Veterans: Neither Victims nor Executioners*. Morrison's depictions of the two veterans' guilt—expressed, in particular, through the motif of Shadrack's and Son's conflicted attitudes toward their hands—in part allude to the complex cultural negotiation that accompanied the creation of PTSD as a *DSM*-sanctioned diagnosis.

The intrusive flashbacks that Son has to his war experience, which started the chain of events leading to his life as an exilic "undocumented m[a]n"[100] and an uprooted outlaw, resonate with Luckhurst's above-quoted argument that trauma disrupts identity.[101] The ability of trauma to threaten the continuity of personal identity is, indeed, a pervasive theme in *Tar Baby*. However, even after being disconnected from various aspects of his selfhood during and after the war, Son in the novel's opening manages to "rise and burst from the waves."[102] He is, in other words, symbolically reborn. After his dramatic dive that sets the plot in motion, Son arrives on Isle des Chevaliers, his new "single hard surface"[103] with "the immediate plans of a newborn baby"[104] who has just emerged from the life-giving womb of the sea. Or, to use a metaphor that references the historical trauma of black enslavement and captivity, after his "Middle Passage" Son reaches the shore of a new world and is ready to embrace the opportunity to become a new creation. However, as Evelyn Jaffe Schreiber points out in discussing *Tar Baby* and Morrison's sixth novel, *Jazz*, "physical relocation does not erase trauma."[105] The return of the repressed (the involuntary resurfacing of intrusive recollections of Vietnam) that occurs immediately after Son's arrival on the island reveals that his new beginning is not, after all, quite the fresh start that he had hoped for; his past is still part of his present.[106]

At *Tar Baby*'s conclusion, Son is again at a loss. His attempt to create a new, lasting identity by sharing his life with the Paris-educated, light-skinned, cosmopolitan Jadine (who, in the Caribbean minor character Thérèse's view, "has forgotten her ancient properties")[107] has failed. Things are once more "all mixed up, like when he ran out of laughter ammunition and kicked an M.P. in the groin [in Vietnam]."[108] In the midst of this confusion, Son experiences another rebirth. The novel's mythical structure—in which, as in Forrest's *There Is a Tree*, Middle Passage references evoke the possibility of both destruction/death and a new beginning/resurrection—comes full circle in the last chapter, where Son once again arises from the sea and "grab[s] with both hands the surface of the rock and heave[s] himself onto it," at first "crawl[ing] the rocks one by one," until "the nursing sound of the sea [is] behind him" and he realizes he can stand up.[109] In the final scene, which is imbued with what Rachel Lee aptly terms Morrison's "aesthetic of ambiguity,"[110] Son disappears from the reader's sight into the hills of Isle des Chevaliers in order to join the "chevaliers," the black warriors who do not fight wars but, instead, "ride those horses all over hills" and happily "race each other."[111]

Morrison inserts one version of the etiological myth of Isle des Chevaliers into a passage depicting a conversation between Son and a black local named Gideon.[112] According to this legend, the blind slaves who "hid" in the remote parts of the island became the mythical "chevaliers," the one hundred blind and naked black men "rac[ing] those horses like angels all over the hills where the rain forest is, where the champion daisy trees still grow."[113] These are the black horsemen whom Son, at the novel's ambiguous conclusion, yearns to join. Son is possessed by the need to believe in an Edenic black paradise beyond the island's swamp, and he yearns to see and share the secret inner visions of the legend's sightless slaves. He therefore responds to a call whose ultimate character—deception or redemption?—remains ambiguous. The reader can only hear Son's "lickety-split" (the sound associated with the running of Brer Rabbit, the cunning trickster of the traditional Tar Baby story) as the confused war veteran in search of self heads toward a mythical African Caribbean past, hoping that it will bring peace to his present and his future.

The narrative prepares the ground for Son's eventual decision to search for the meaning of diasporic blackness and black communion in the Caribbean, rather than in the United States, by offering the reader brief glimpses of Son's life during his eight exilic years as an outlaw. During those years, he viewed the United States from a distance and developed a profound discomfort with its politics:

> Since 1971 Son had been seeing the United States through the international edition of *Time*, by way of shortwave radio and the views of other crewmen. It seemed sticky. Loud, red and sticky. Its fields spongy, its pavements slick with the blood of all the best people. As soon as a man

or woman did something generous or said something bold, pictures of their funeral lines appeared in the foreign press. It repelled him and made him suspicious of all knowledge he could not witness or feel in his bones.[114]

Paradoxically, however, Son's desertion of the royally named HMS *Stor Konigsgaarten* at the novel's opening is prompted by nothing less than a surge of homesickness for the United States—or rather, for Eloe, which he nostalgically imagines as a place completely separate from any power plays or violent evildoing in which his home country, as a political entity, might be involved: "[I]t was time to go home. Not to the sticky-red place, but to his home in it. That separate place that was presided over by wide black women in snowy dresses and was ever dry, green and quiet."[115] As Schreiber notes, the concept of home may offer "protection from trauma."[116] Son's idealized memories of the gentle Floridian matriarchs, who for him represent safety and maternal nurture, reveal that he indeed seeks a buffer against trauma and its aftereffects. Moreover, Son thinks of the bond between himself and his male friends from Eloe, who all fought in Vietnam together, as a "fraternity"[117] based on race, gender, nationality, and regional belonging as well as on the shared war experience. Son yearns to relive this brotherhood in actuality, not just in and through his memories.

A seemingly insignificant incident sets in motion the process that results in Son dramatically jumping ship in the Caribbean in hopes of finding a route back home to the United States: during a relaxed moment of fishing in Argentinian waters, his shipmates notice a violent impulse in him when he suddenly loses his temper in a less-than-Hemingwayesque struggle with a fish that refuses to die.[118] This incident quickly gains symbolic significance because, soon afterward, a Mexican seaman offers a blistering critique of the violent and neo-imperialist aspects of American foreign policy by giving Son a drawing, "a map of the U.S. as an ill-shaped tongue ringed by teeth and crammed with the corpses of children."[119] Referring back to Son's violent suppression of the resistance of a creature at his mercy, the Mexican calls him "*Americano. Cierto Americano.*"[120] This scene touches on the complex intersectionality of neo-empire and diaspora in the Western Hemisphere.[121] Although Son is a member of a discriminated-against minority and of the African diaspora within the United States, the Mexican sees him as being more American, more of a citizen of a nation with neo-imperial aspirations, than the black veteran himself is willing to admit. In the Mexican's eyes, neo-empire overrides diaspora, as far as Son's affiliations and political loyalties are concerned. Having dealt death in Vietnam firsthand, Son cannot easily shrug off this accusation—not within his own traumatized and guilt-ridden psyche, regardless of whether his shipmates know about his service in Vietnam (Morrison does not disclose this detail).

The experience of being labeled a participant in US expansionist imperialism and capitalism alienates Son from his fellow seamen. This estrangement, in turn, makes his long-repressed longing for "fraternity" with his childhood friends and fellow Vietnam veterans from Eloe return with an intensity that temporarily suppresses any doubts about his American belonging that have been building in his psyche during his eight years of vagabondage. When Son and Jadine become lovers, they indeed return to the United States together. However, they cannot reconcile "his" Eloe with "her" New York City, as several critics have noted.[122] That is, they cannot reconcile their differences, which these two locations come to epitomize. Son and Jadine's trip to Eloe finally opens up an unbridgeable chasm between them, as it painfully emphasizes for each the sense of displacement and in-betweenness with which they both, in their own ways, still struggle intensely—having failed to become, as Philip Page accurately observes, a "place" (or a home) for each other.[123]

Some critics analyzing black identity and "authenticity" in *Tar Baby* view Son categorically as Jadine's binary opposite, a black nationalist/separatist whose romantic and essentialist attitude toward blackness serves as a foil for her cultural assimilationism.[124] Other scholars emphasize the novel's deliberately ambiguous treatment of blackness, which does not simplistically demand that readers "choose" between the perceived dispositions of Jadine and Son.[125] Linda Krumholz argues in the latter vein (and, in my view, convincingly) that in *Tar Baby* Morrison "immerses readers in competing concepts of blackness to show the pitfalls in constructing meanings of blackness, while at the same time asserting the urgent need to engage with those meanings."[126] Moreover, the complexities of "race" in *Tar Baby* can usefully be read in conjunction with the novel's depiction of black transnational/diasporic identity formation—a topic that has received less scholarly attention than it deserves. Critics examining Son's relationship to his blackness have, in effect, largely focused on *whiteness* by discussing, in detail, Margaret Street's repulsed and openly racist initial reaction to Son (an encounter reducing him to a racialized and sexualized object under the white gaze), Valerian Street's patriarchal patronage of Jadine and Son, and Son's mental processing of his blackness vis-à-vis Jadine's culturally "whitened" worldview. However, Sandra Pouchet

Paquet's 1990 observation that much of Son's psychological and political processing of his blackness takes place through his encounters with *black* characters throughout the novel's *Caribbean* sections warrants further emphasis.[127] I here expand on this observation, which provides the necessary foundation for recognizing and appreciating the diasporic qualities of *Tar Baby*.

The scene in which Son, who has always identified whiteness with privileged Otherness that has not been his to share, takes a long and luxurious shower after becoming an acknowledged guest at L'Arbe de la Croix—the Caribbean mansion of the Streets,[128] a wealthy, retired, white couple whose primary residence is in Philadelphia—serves as a preface to the storyline that focuses on black diasporic contacts beyond the US border. Morrison ironically casts Son's project of thoroughly washing himself squeaky clean as a rite of purification whereby he metaphorically cleanses himself of his blackness.[129] When Son accidentally gets some bath gel into his mouth, he swallows the lather, discovers that it "taste[s] like milk," and then "squirt[s] it all around in his mouth."[130] This reference to milk not only reinforces the imagery of rebirth and Son's metaphorical status as a newborn, but it also suggests that he wishes to become white inside out as he subconsciously readies himself for a new life with Jadine and her white patrons.

Immediately after this cleansing ritual, however, Son glances out the window and happens to see the back of Gideon, the Streets' local landscaper-cum-handyman, who is working in the yard. The black worker's weary back is exposed, in all its sun-beaten bareness, to Son's scrutinizing gaze while he himself is wrapped up in a dazzling white towel after his indulgent shower. Son is suddenly overcome with a feeling of intense solidarity with the older black man who is immersed in working-class labor that benefits whites—the kind of work that has defined Son during much of his adult life. Moved to tears as he quietly studies the history of black labor inscribed on Gideon's back and the curve of his spine (a more gentle variation on the motif that Morrison later, in *Beloved*, transformed into the heavily scarred back of the female slave Sethe), Son realizes that he had, just a few moments earlier, launched his project of social upward mobility by symbolically attempting to rid himself of his "blackness" and distance himself from his own affiliation with black labor in order to participate, however marginally, in the privilege awarded by "whiteness."[131] After this influential moment of accidental voyeurism, Son—concerned that "something [i.e., his blackness] was leaving him and all he could see was its back"[132]—begins to seek contact with the black people (besides

Jadine) whom he can reach at or through L'Arbe de la Croix: Sydney and Ondine Childs, and Gideon and Thérèse.

The Baltimore-born "Philadelphia Negro" Sydney (who is familiar with Du Bois's 1899 book and extremely proud of his acquired class status as an industrious black Philadelphian)[133] and his wife, Ondine, are servants of the Streets. While the Childses excel at their work, they at the same time quietly resent the fixed race- and class-based arrangements in their social environments and have profoundly mixed feelings about their dependence on the Streets. However, they themselves look down on local black Caribbeans—including Gideon, whom they impersonally call "Yardman" (and who is, unbeknownst to the Americans, a former immigrant to Canada and the United States), and his aunt Thérèse, the Streets' near-blind laundress and the novel's embodiment of local cultural knowledge. Sydney and Ondine indifferently think of Thérèse as one of the island's many "Marys," barely bothering to distinguish her from Alma Estée, a young cleaning woman working at the nearest airport who occasionally shares in some of Gideon and Thérèse's work and private life. When Sydney and Ondine first encounter Son, they view him, too, through the lens of class difference and therefore initially feel no affiliation or sympathy with the southern working-class wanderer. No "Phil-a-delphia Negro" (Sydney's overly prim articulation),[134] Son fails to measure up to their standards.

Ondine, however, eventually recognizes "the orphan in [Son]"[135] and empathizes with his predicament. Sydney, too, finally relents. The three exiles briefly share a sense of camaraderie and fellowship,[136] but these fleeting sentiments do not form a basis for a permanent alliance. Son quickly becomes uncomfortable with the Childses' servitude and loyalty to the Streets because he comes to see Valerian as an archetypal white capitalist who in his candy business (his life's work) benefited greatly from cheaply imported Caribbean sugar and cocoa and then, during his retirement, exploited Gideon and Thérèse's labor, only to fire them unexpectedly.[137] During the heated dinner table discussion that ensues once the Street household learns about the sudden firing of "Yardman" and his "Mary," the Childses' astonishment and anger over Valerian's hasty decision only arises out of concern for the smooth operation of L'Arbe de la Croix. What is at stake for Son, by contrast, is racial and class-based solidarity: "The man who respected industry [Sydney] looked over a gulf at the man who prized fraternity [Son]."[138]

Unlike the Childses, Gideon and Thérèse (and, with them, Alma Estée) embrace Son from the outset. When he is still hiding at L'Arbe de la Croix, they mentally ally themselves with him and are concerned about his well-being before he is even aware of their existence.[139] Later, they are proud of his company, entertain him, and help him with matters big and small. From the moment Thérèse senses Son's presence at Valerian's house, she thinks of him as a lost member of the mythical horsemen's tribe.[140] At the novel's end, she becomes the guide/"pilot" (not unlike Pilate, the male protagonist Milkman's "pilot" in *Song of Solomon*) who leads Son to where black geography and black mythology meet, in hopes that he might there be able to reconnect with black history and with his own diasporic, transnational blackness. How to assess Thérèse's contribution to Son's self-discovery is one of the dilemmas that *Tar Baby* poses for its readers. On the one hand, Thérèse, a former wet nurse and a traditional "mother earth" figure, epitomizes local folk wisdom. K. Zauditu-Selassie, in particular, reads her "as the female healer who demonstrates the power of interacting with the natural, non-human world and the necessity of spiritual return."[141] On the other hand, Thérèse is, as Paquet observes, an "ambiguous figure"[142] precisely because her knowledge is so local: "[Thérèse] speaks authoritatively in a 'national-historical' context, but her authority beyond this time-space mode is limited."[143] Morrison's narrative implies that Thérèse is "one of the "blind race,"[144] a descendant of the "chevaliers." This is, of course, a vastly ambiguous and ambivalent characterization because of the status of the black horsemen as mythical figures. Given this ambivalence, Thérèse's poor eyesight may symbolize either a heightened spiritual understanding, as emphasized by Zauditu-Selassie, or a fundamental inability to guide Son in any meaningful direction. (In fact, as Paquet notes, Thérèse in the novel's final scene suddenly seems a rather "menacing, devouring figure.")[145] Rather than resolving this dilemma, the novel—as part of its larger project of giving expression to the complexities and ambiguities of diasporic self-identification—leaves the reader to wrestle with it.

Just before the novel culminates in Thérèse ferrying Son (now a visitor from New York) from the larger island housing the local airport to Isle des Chevaliers, the exhausted and confused traveler—in mental turmoil over his loss of Jadine—runs into Alma Estée. The young woman is wearing a poorly fitting red-brown American wig that, in her mind, provides her with the kind of beauty that television has taught her to admire. In Son's eyes, the wig is an absurd embodiment both of American consumerism and of the power of the media to miseducate black people, particularly women, to conform to white standards of beauty without regard to the potential emotional and cultural cost (a theme also found in *The Bluest Eye* and in *Song of Solomon*'s depiction of Hagar's final, tragic shopping spree). The sight of Alma Estée's "sweet face, her midnight skin mocked and destroyed by the pile of synthetic dried blood on her head"[146] is the final shock that completely throws Son off balance. Notably, the narrative here repeats the phrase "It was all mixed up" four times within two pages, deliberately using this phrase to connect Son's emotional upheaval caused by various distortions and disparagements of diasporic blackness with his resurfacing memories of Vietnam[147]—that is, with his memories of another profoundly confusing experience of displacement and unbelonging.

Another, related meaning of the phrase "It was all mixed up" is that when Son looks at Alma Estée in the hideous wig, he recognizes in her body and psyche the same complex problematics of racial belonging that both he and Jadine have struggled with. Notably, Jadine also happens to see the wig-wearing Alma Estée at the airport just before heading for Europe during the novel's dénouement. For Jadine, however, the encounter does not signify a "mirror image" moment. She does not see herself or her own questions in this "Mary," whom she does not even remember from L'Arbe de la Croix.[148] Son, by contrast, reacts very strongly: "So he had changed, given up fraternity" (that is, had abandoned a real or imagined brotherhood with his fellow Vietnam veterans, with Eloe, and by extension, with an ancestrally based definition of blackness) in order to be with Jadine and share her values, "or believed he had, until he saw Alma Estée in a wig the color of dried blood."[149] The tragic, grotesque sight of the young black woman trapped in unrecognized racial self-loathing triggers in Son a powerful desire to be part of a black community, or of brotherly communion, where diasporic blackness is perceived as a source of pride, strength, and dignity.

It is, indeed, such "fraternity" that Son is after as he runs toward the peace-loving blind warriors who allegedly still inhabit a secluded territory on Isle des Chevaliers. After his complex and painful encounters with cultural and class-based divisions within the African diaspora, he now pursues community and communion with black figures whom he longs to claim as his brothers or ancestors and whom he thinks of as male embodiments of an uncorrupted ur-blackness and warrior spirit. Both Jadine and Son confront questions about blackness and black "authenticity" throughout the novel, but they arrive at very different solutions to their respective dilemmas of belonging. Having experienced the highlights of her career as a fashion model in a privileged French environment, Jadine, a graduate of the Sorbonne, returns to Europe.

Son, by contrast, ends up seeking the company of the self-emancipated slaves who, according to Thérèse, will embrace him as one of their own.[150] He intuitively envisions the company of the mythical black "chevaliers" as a transnational black diasporic fellowship for which he, too—an undocumented US African American—is eligible because he is of African descent.

The variety of black communion that Son here pursues is, tragically, imaginary, grounded as it is in local folklore and mythical figures rather than in empirical reality (a community of actual living human beings). Yet, at what is simultaneously both Son's hour of ultimate despair and his climactic moment of self-discovery, the idea of a black transnational community based on an ancestral past genuinely represents a site of belonging for him. Whether his ambiguous pursuit of a paradise lost, a historical connection lost, and a selfhood lost represents self-destruction or hope is open to debate. Either way, Morrison's narrative of Son's quest invites a discussion about black transnational interconnectedness in a way seldom seen in African American fiction prior to *Tar Baby*. Also, as Morrison's exasperated Vietnam veteran at the novel's end opts for running away from reality toward the promise of an allegedly peaceful and harmonious future based on the mythical black warriors' glorious past, the reader is left to ask complex questions about the current political significance of the original and subsequent traumatic displacements of the Sons and daughters of the African diaspora—African American war veterans included.

Finally, the dual subject matter of war and diaspora in *Sula* and *Tar Baby* calls for a brief elaboration of Caruthian trauma theory, history, and fiction. In *Unclaimed Experience* (1996), Caruth links her psychoanalytically based understanding of trauma with literary narratives' potential to converse with history in a way that, while not always strictly referential, may significantly deepen our understanding of the past: "Through the notion of trauma, ... we can understand that a rethinking of reference is aimed not at eliminating history but at resituating it in our understanding, that is, at precisely permitting *history* to arise where *immediate understanding* may not."[151] Caruth also acknowledges that the literary trauma narrative encompasses a "dimension that cannot be reduced to the thematic content of the text or to what the theory encodes," a dimension that "stubbornly persists in bearing witness to some forgotten wound."[152] As Morrison, in *Sula* and *Tar Baby*, allows such "forgotten wounds" as black soldiers' traumatic displacement on foreign battlefields, combat-induced PTSD, long-term war trauma, and the historical ur-trauma of black diasporic displacement to bleed into each other, she utilizes the power of the literary narrative to "attempt to tell us of a reality or truth that is not otherwise available,"[153] as Caruth puts it. In other words, the unconventional trauma "narratives" embedded in *Sula* and *Tar Baby* (consisting, in effect, of brief references to war traumas and of even more fleeting allusions to the Middle Passage) participate in processing that which is too much for the human mind to comprehend. The incomprehensible/unspeakable must be processed over and over again, so that it will not be erased or repressed but instead will, in Caruth's terms, be "resituate[d] in our understanding"—not as a watered-down, palatable version of reality but as something that will always at some level remain impossible to understand, yet needs to be faced. These narratives, in other words, help to "resituate" trauma (here, particularly the Middle Passage and New World slavery, as well as black soldiers' war experiences) "in our understanding" in a way that allows "history to arise."

An African American GI in England during World War II: A Reach toward Interracial Communion in Phillips's *Crossing the River*

The question of the relationship between trauma, history, and fiction touched on above invites a note on "memory." Like trauma studies, humanistically oriented memory studies now constitute a veritable industry, and books dealing with cultural memory and its transmission (particularly in connection with the Holocaust) are legion.[154] One observation that emerges from reading scholarship in memory studies is that the key concepts "trauma," "identity," "history," and "memory" frequently appear in conjunction with each other, although the way in which their connections are articulated varies, depending on the theoretical orientation of each scholar.[155] Regardless of how exactly these concepts are tied together within different intellectual frameworks, the question of *cultural mediation* usually occupies a pivotal place in articulations of such connectivity. In *At Memory's Edge* (2000), James E. Young—in discussing representations of the Holocaust by artists of the second and third generations rather than by Holocaust survivors themselves—writes about the "hypermediated" nature of such works of cultural memory: "Coming of age after—but indelibly shaped by—the Holocaust, this generation of artists, writers, architects, and even composers does not attempt to represent events it never knew immediately but instead portrays its own, necessarily hypermediated experiences of memory. It is a generation no longer willing, or able, to recall the Holocaust separately from the ways it has been passed down."[156] In *The Generation of Postmemory* (2012), Marianne Hirsch makes a similar point when she elaborates on second-generation writers' and artists' "postmemory," noting that "[p]ostmemory's connection to the past is . . . mediated not by recall but by imaginative investment, projection, and creation."[157]

The gist of Young's and Hirsch's shared argument also applies to black diasporic writers' representations of slavery, of twentieth-century historical events that the writers are too young to have experienced themselves, and of any events in between. However, the extent to which works of black diasporic fiction explicitly exhibit awareness of the "hypermediated" nature of their representations of history and cultural memory varies. Caryl Phillips's writing is situated at the highly aware end of that spectrum. Phillips has given literary expression to diaspora in a number of ways. He has written about the old African diaspora—including, by extension, the West Indian migration to Britain after World War II, which is the topic of his first novel, *The Final Passage* (1985). He has also depicted new African diasporas. For example, in his 2003 novel, *A Distant Shore*, the fictional protagonist encountering Britain is a black refugee fleeing the civil war that has devastated his West African home country—an unnamed former British colony largely modeled on Sierra Leone. In *Foreigners* (2007), Phillips recounts the fate of the historical David Oluwale, a Nigerian who settled in Leeds in 1949 and died there twenty years later at the hands of the police. In these two works, as in his 2015 novel, *The Lost Child*, Phillips explores the intersectionality of (post)colonialism, Empire, and diaspora. Moreover, in his early travelogue, *The European Tribe*, and in two of his novels, *Higher Ground* and *The Nature of Blood*, he places the African and Jewish diasporas in conversation with each other as "connective diasporas" (to modify Hirsch's concept of "connective histories").[158]

These examples not only attest to Phillips's strong focus on "diaspora" per se, but also speak to his high awareness of the culturally mediated and reconstructed nature of collective memory. While *Crossing the River*—a work of multivoiced black diasporic fiction, with characters who traverse temporal, geographical, and racial boundaries—may not go quite so far as to thematize its own role in the process of transmitting and constructing black diasporic memory, its frame nevertheless makes its hermeneutical work clear and transparent: *Crossing the River* connects various postslavery black experiences of displacement to the Middle Passage and the original formation of the African diaspora. The novel's discrete yet interconnected narratives—including an African American GI's courtship of, and marriage to, a white Englishwoman during World War II—cast black dislocation as the disintegration of an African family whose members find themselves scattered across the globe and across historical eras. The voice of the guilt-ridden father who sold his daughter and two sons into slavery frames the novel, serving as a prophetic voice that addresses the African diaspora across time and space. In each setting, World War II Britain included, Phillips's storytelling overtly or covertly links the Middle Passage motif to a poignant interrogation of home and belonging.

Phillips opens his 1993 essay "Water," in which he discusses the design of *Crossing the River*, by explaining the significance of the essay's title: "Water. To a large extent my life has been determined by a journey across water. An actual journey. Across the Atlantic Ocean. I cannot remember the journey that I am speaking of."[159] Readers familiar with Phillips's biography may initially assume that the "journey" he references is his migration from the Caribbean to England as an infant; he moved with his parents from St. Kitts to Leeds when he was only a few weeks old. However, it soon becomes clear that he is referring to something else, namely, the Middle Passage: "In all likelihood it [the journey] occurred some time in the eighteenth century. Seventeen hundred and something. I was captured and sold into the custody of the Englishman."[160] It befits the time-transcending paradigm revealed by Phillips's self-identification with Middle Passage survivors in "Water" that *Crossing the River*, through its frame, links the dislocation of an African American soldier with the diasporic ur-displacement much more explicitly than either *Sula* or *Tar Baby* does. In addition, as Alan Rice observes, the World War II section of *Crossing the River* (although it subtly calls attention to Phillips's own Yorkshire background and to his "hybrid identity as both regional Englishman and black Englishman")[161] destabilizes "generalisations about Phillips as simply a black British writer" and points to his more universal black diasporic "loyalties and allegiances, including those towards African Americans."[162]

Phillips reveals, in "Water," that the very first two characters he had in mind when he started to write *Crossing the River* were the protagonists of what eventually became the novel's last section, "Somewhere in England," which tells the story of Travis, an African American GI stationed in a village in Yorkshire.[163] The reader's only access to Travis's life and death is through the temporally disjointed memories and journal entries of Joyce, a white working-class Englishwoman. Although the reader cannot access Travis's thoughts, he is a central presence in the story. Given the novel's overall structure, "Somewhere in England" *is* about him, about his experience of dislocation within the diasporic predicament. Prior to *Crossing the River*, Phillips had written another heavily modified Middle Passage novel,[164] *Cambridge* (1991), in which, as in "Somewhere in England," the core (a black man's own perspective on his life) mostly remains behind the veil but is, ultimately, defined by a black diasporic experience and black suffering caused by white oppression. Just as in *Benito Cereno* and Johnson's *Middle Passage*, a change in perception occupies an important position in *Cambridge*—in this case, as a rapidly progressing blindness: during her stay on her father's Caribbean plantation, the fictional white upper-class Englishwoman Emily Cartwright, originally rather critical of slavery, gradually begins to see the world in the way a representative of the slaveholding class is expected to perceive it (although her fall from grace at the novel's end finally reveals the hollowness of her newly acquired "wisdom"). In "Somewhere in England," by contrast, the white focalizer's journey moves in the opposite direction: Joyce, although initially accustomed to race-thinking and rather ignorant of the alleged Other, soon allies herself with Travis.

In September 1939, prior to meeting Travis, Joyce, who is in her twenties, marries Len Kitson, a thirty-year-old white shopkeeper. Len has black lung disease, also known as (coal) miner's asthma, and is classified as unfit to fight in the war. He is eventually arrested and goes to prison—not, however, for "working off the embarrassment of not having a uniform"[165] by beating Joyce (no one seems to consider this transgression significant enough to warrant any legal consequences), but for having taken advantage of the war by trading illegally obtained foodstuffs in the black market for significant profit. Because of her husband's crime, Joyce is treated as an outcast in their home village. Her pariah status in part facilitates her alliance with and allegiance to another who, in the villagers' eyes, does not belong either, namely, an African American GI. Travis's African American unit (of the still-segregated US army) arrives in the village in June 1942. Even though Travis and Joyce do not initially quite know how to approach each other, they soon start an affair. Joyce's community disapproves of the interracial romance,[166] but she nevertheless divorces her abusive husband and—pregnant with a son who will look "like coffee,"[167] as a nurse puts it—marries Travis, who receives his commanding officer's permission to wed, as long as he understands that he must not attempt to live in an interracial union in the United States. Travis is, in effect, barred from returning with his new family to his home country, where, as Graham Smith reminds us, interracial marriages were at the time still "forbidden in about twenty states ... whether such marriages were contracted abroad or not."[168] Despite these trying circumstances, what is a simple but deeply felt "GI bride's wedding"[169] signifies hope and a fresh start for both Joyce and Travis. However, a few months before the war's end, Travis—stationed in Italy following the fall of Mussolini—is hit by a bullet and dies "[i]n a strange country," "[a]mong people he hardly knew,"[170] without ever seeing his and Joyce's newborn son.

Because Joyce is penniless, she reluctantly gives up the infant, Greer, to the County Council's care, to be put up for adoption.

Although most of Joyce's diary entries date back to the war years, two entries, both dated "1963," describe her thoughts on the day when eighteen-year-old Greer, having sought out his mother, unexpectedly visits her. Joyce, now remarried and with children, avoids sentimentalizing her encounter with the diasporic orphan, but her diary nevertheless reveals the reunion's vast significance for her: "My God, I wanted to hug him.... He was my son. Our son."[171] At the same time, her self-deprecating comment about "home" poignantly reveals her guilt for having decided to give Greer up: "I almost said make yourself at home, but I didn't. At least I avoided that."[172] Rather than judging Joyce, Phillips's narrative focuses on the genealogy of the choice that she made back in 1945. Social services, instead of offering options, recommended adoption (or, in fact, brusquely took the baby away), not only because Joyce was a single parent, but also because of Greer's mixed-race status.[173] The social services representative evaluating the situation racistly and patronizingly assumed, without further discussion, that the biracial baby had to be an unwanted child—or, at the very least, too much of a challenge for a young woman to handle.[174] Looking for a safe haven in, or financial assistance from, the United States was not an option for Joyce, as the preemptive decree from Travis's commanding officer had made clear. The era's racial ideologies left the single mother of a biracial child in limbo on both sides of the Atlantic, even though she was the widow of a GI who had given his life for the Allied cause in the war.

The ultimate "crossing" that *Crossing the River* at times narrates and at other times implies is, as Travis's fate indicates, death. However, the novel also offers a significant undertone of hope through its postulation of a black diasporic connectedness that comes alive in the "chorus of a common memory"[175]— a collective "many-tongued,"[176] polyvocal, heteroglossic black remembrance that yearns to outperform any white noise promoting historical amnesia. Moreover, as Farah Griffin observes, Phillips's text makes the voices comprising this chorus bear witness not only "to the disruption, displacement, and loss of Diaspora," but also "to the common humanity of the enslaved, the enslavers, and their common descendants."[177] In "Water," Phillips emphasizes that identifying with those who experienced the Middle Passage is a process that concerns not only blacks but also whites, because the history of the slave trade and slavery is not only "black" history (that is, not only a past "somehow assigned to blacks," as Paul Gilroy notes sardonically in *The Black Atlantic*, not only black peoples' "special property"),[178] but part of the history of modernity as a whole:

> It was the people of the west coast of Africa who, looking out at the vastness of the ocean, first thought of it as a mighty river. Their journey—my journey—*our journey, for if some were below, then others were on deck*—our journey, back then in seventeen hundred and something, has changed for ever [sic] the nature of both British and American society. If I learned anything writing this novel, I certainly learned that.... The fact is the journey is rooted deeply in my soul. And in your soul too. Water. Ribbons of water which ineluctably bind us together, one to the other.[179]

Crossing the River shares this ethos by exploring the inevitable interdependence of people(s) who cannot escape their post-Columbian interconnectedness. In so doing, the novel looks for signs of hope, however tentative and fragile, for a new culture of interracial peace and reconciliation.

Joyce's feelings of guilt, evident in the two 1963 entries, parallel those of the African father of the novel's frame, because both characters regret having given their (black) child/ren away. In an interview, Phillips also offers another (related, but less guilt-oriented) reason why the African father in the novel's final pages embraces Joyce as one of his children:[180] "It seemed emotionally correct. She grew up without a dad, and what binds her to the others is that lack."[181] A number of US African American novels—including Morrison's *Tar Baby* and *Jazz* (1992) and Leon Forrest's *The Bloodworth Orphans* (1977)—treat orphanhood as one of the prominent characteristics of, and metaphors for, the diasporic condition. Phillips here does something similar, albeit with a twist: Joyce is a white orphan (her mother died in a bombing during the war) who allies herself with the African diaspora, consequently gives birth to yet another orphan, and is eventually adopted into the diaspora by the African father's time-transcending narrative voice.[182] Phillips does not, of course, here attempt to offer any fixed definition of the African diaspora by trying to determine, once and for all, who "qualifies" as a member and who does not. Rather, *Crossing the River* contains narratives that, while fleshing out the concept of diaspora, at the same time remind us how fluid and porous the boundaries of the African diaspora can be. Rather than being geographically drawn demarcation lines, such boundaries or factors of definition move with black bodies into realms where interracial encounters take place, countering prevailing sociocultural expectations and creating new alliances.

Conclusion

This chapter has shown that as Morrison and Phillips write about traumatized, invisible, forgotten, or fallen African American war veterans, they link the veterans' experiences of traumatic displacement on foreign battlefields to the ur-trauma ("wound") of diasporic dislocation (the original violent uprooting and slavery)—not to forge simplistic cause-effect relations, but to critique the large-scale violence that has typically accompanied the project of modernity. References to the Middle Passage in *Sula* and *Tar Baby* may be covert and fleeting, but they are nevertheless unmistakably significant. *Crossing the River*, in turn, is quite explicit about its cultural memory/identity project from the outset: through its frame, the novel overtly links an African American GI's experience of wartime displacement to the original formation of the African diaspora, metafictionally treating the diaspora's collective originary trauma as a usable past for the purpose of contemporary black diasporic identity formation. As Fassin and Rechtman write, in a context originally unrelated to either literary studies or the African diaspora, "The psychoanalytic understanding of trauma facilitates this return to the collective through the individual, from the intimate wound to the wounded memory."[183] This claim, which speaks to the legitimacy of creating time-transcending interpretive connections between individual and collective memories, has a great deal of relevance at the intersection of literary and trauma studies, and it resonates powerfully with Morrison's and Phillips's shared strategy of linking "connective histories" (Hirsch) of black displacement with each other.

It is true that Dominick LaCapra, in *Writing History, Writing Trauma* (2001), famously calls for "historical specificity" in accounts of trauma and sternly criticizes the "insistently theoretical orientations relying on a more transhistorical notion of trauma which is structural or in some sense originary."[184] However, although LaCapra here uses the terms "transhistorical," "structural," and "originary" to point to an unsound neglect of the historical, he primarily applies his criticism to the work of historians, not to the liberties that creative writers inevitably take with historical detail. Singling out *Beloved* as an example, LaCapra specifically concedes that literary narratives may "involve truth claims on a structural or general level by providing insight into phenomena such as slavery or the Holocaust."[185] *Sula*, *Tar Baby*, and *Crossing the River* all provide insight into traumatic wartime experiences of African American soldiers, casting them as one type of black dislocation. Even more importantly, these novels associatively connect such experiences with the Middle Passage. In so doing, they participate in a large-scale cultural memory project—namely, the cultural (re)construction of African diasporic memory—that facilitates black diasporic identity formation.

Finally, the commentary that Phillips provides in his essay "Water" on the ideas and historical facts that led him to write *Crossing the River* is relevant both to this chapter and the next. In "Water" (whose very title embodies this book's focus on precarious passages, Middle Passage sensibilities, and the fluidity of diasporic identities), Phillips, in addition to reflecting on the ur-crossing, muses on the presence of African American troops in Britain during World War II: "[I]t struck me that many English people's attitudes to race had, in all probability, been conditioned by this first encounter with black people during [World War II]."[186] Although much of my chapter 4 analyzes fictional renderings of the *Windrush* era rather than of the war years preceding it, Phillips's important genealogical statement inspires my discussion of Andrea Levy's *Small Island*, in particular, as I next delve deeper into literary representations of black diasporic experiences in England.

4

Journeys to the Heart of Empire after World War II

George Lamming's, Caryl Phillips's, and Andrea Levy's Caribbean Migrants

In his first monograph, *There Ain't No Black in the Union Jack* (1987), Paul Gilroy critiqued the racialization of the nation-state—in particular, any reductive and racially exclusivist identification of "Britishness" with white Britishness or, even more narrowly, with white Englishness. He argued that such "a morbid celebration of England and Englishness from which blacks are systematically excluded" had, in British academia, resulted in a silence about "race" (or racialized thought) that implicitly supported a fallacious understanding of race "as an eternal, essential factor of division in society."[1] While launching these criticisms, Gilroy at the same time highlighted the creative potential of the cultures of the African diaspora to act as counterforces to the discontents of Western modernity in Britain and beyond. He claimed—as early as *There Ain't No Black*, six years before the publication of the "paradigmatic" *Black Atlantic*—that the development of black Britain's expressive culture was a living process characterized by "complex, dynamic patterns" of transnational "syncretism" that were producing novel understandings of blackness through an intermixture of "raw materials" provided by other peoples of the African diaspora.[2] In other words, even Gilroy's first book underscored that nations, with their clearly defined borders, cannot constitute an adequate or sufficient basis for examining black histories and analyzing black cultures.[3]

As an empire and post-empire, Britain, the subject of *There Ain't No Black*, has long been a site of contestation for the meaning of "race." Peter Fryer's *Staying Power* (1984), chronicling the history of people of African descent in Britain since the arrival of the Roman imperial army on the British Isles, offers myriad examples of such contestations—which, however, are seldom about "race" alone, about "race" in a vacuum. Questions about where a diasporic and colonial subject is to locate home, mentally and physically, factor in as well. Taking its cue from such questions of home and belonging, this chapter examines how postwar and contemporary diasporic novelists of African Caribbean descent have depicted the tension-ridden dialogue between black diasporic existence and the mother country's dominant understanding of Englishness/Britishness in World War II and postwar Britain. I here refer to Englishness/Britishness as defined, at the time, by the white English/British on the basis of the colonial and imperial "greatness" of Britain—a "greatness" that, though already waning, was still an important sociocultural imaginary for many white Britons and their collective identity formation. True, at the end of the 1990s, Simon Gikandi's *Maps of Englishness* (1996) and Ian Baucom's *Out of Place* (1999) did groundbreaking work in showing "how notions of Englishness had already been unsettled by imperial activity abroad," as John Clement Ball reminds us in *Imagining London* (2004).[4] These scholars' shared premise was, as Ball sums it up, that "the national cultural identities of colonizing peoples are as unsettled and altered by imperialism as those of the colonized."[5] However, this chapter, interested in a different angle, investigates novels that do not primarily focus on the internal instability and critical self-evaluation of the imperial gaze, but instead tell the story of what it was like for diasporic and colonial subjects to find themselves to be racial and cultural Others "under English eyes,"[6] despite their legally acknowledged British subjecthood and membership in Empire.

The large-scale post–World War II immigration from the West Indies to Britain began when the troopship SS *Empire Windrush* arrived at Tilbury Docks, near London, on June 21, 1948, with 492 Caribbeans (mainly Jamaicans) on board. This "*Windrush* moment," as it is routinely called, has become the starting point for most narratives, literary and nonliterary, of how post-1945 Britain became a "modern racialized state," to quote Hazel Carby.[7] Even today, the "story" (if we wish to use the singular) of the postwar black Caribbean exodus to Britain is worth listening to, although it may by now sound familiar. On the one hand, it is true that Britain's 1998 celebration of the fiftieth anniversary of the *Windrush* moment in many ways helped to inscribe this historical moment and its aftermath in Britain's national memory.[8] Books highlighting the importance of the *Windrush* era for understanding modern black Britishness include *Windrush: The Irresistible Rise of Multi-Racial Britain* (1998), by Mike Phillips and Trevor Phillips, *Empire Windrush: Fifty Years of*

Writing about Black Britain (1998) edited by Onyekachi Wambu, and *Writing Black Britain, 1948–1998: An Interdisciplinary Anthology* (2000) edited by James Procter. In 1998, the airing of the four-episode BBC2 television documentary *Windrush*, part of the same project that resulted in Mike and Trevor Phillips's book, also contributed significantly to raising the British public's awareness of the postwar black Caribbean diasporic experience in Britain. This development, which has increased white Britons' familiarity with black British history, has had numerous positive ramifications. On the other hand, however, what has by now become mainstream commemoration of the *Windrush* moment and its aftermath has, to a degree, resulted in the kind of remembrance culture that celebrates "black success stories" while glossing over hardships caused by racism in the mid- and late twentieth century and beyond, as Eva Ulrike Pirker points out in *Narrative Projections of a Black British History* (2011).[9] As Pirker argues, it is imperative that such hardships be remembered as well because "there is not only a history of black people making it in Britain, but also one of survival, of having to live with traumatic experiences and loss that are hardly acknowledged as trauma in the collective British narrative; and there is a history of racism in Britain that is still very much an unfinished book."[10]

To elaborate, post–World War II West Indian immigrants to Britain, who were aware and proud of their RAF volunteers' contributions to the war effort, assumed that the mother country would receive them—her loyal colonial "children"—with open arms, as the 1948 British Nationality Act (discussed below) seemed to promise. However, the "mother"[11] envisioned by the West Indian arrivals was, of course, the same Empire that had enslaved their African-born and African-descended diasporic ancestors in the Caribbean. During their migratory experience, the colonial-cum-diasporic admirers of the culture of "Old England" (the title of an early poem by Claude McKay) quickly came to understand that the racist legacy of the era of racial slavery in the Caribbean was still much more powerfully alive in Britain than they had imagined when envisioning themselves as the mother country's beloved, even if geographically distant, sons and daughters. All three novels that constitute this chapter's main sources—*The Emigrants* (1954) by Barbadian-born George Lamming, *The Final Passage* (1985) by Caryl Phillips, and *Small Island* (2004) by London-born Andrea Levy, of Jamaican parentage—portray this disparity between the optimistic pre-emigration expectations and the disillusioned post-immigration existence of black Caribbean colonial and diasporic subjects. In the process, these novels emphasize the disappointing continuity between Empire's Anglocentric and imperialist past and its allegedly newly configured political and socioeconomic present.[12]

Given these novels' emphasis on the continuity between Empire's past and present, and given that Claude McKay (one of the most accomplished black diasporic authors of the early twentieth century and thus a literary "ancestor" of several Caribbean novelists studied in this book) encountered the intersectionality of "race," diaspora, citizenship, and Empire briefly before the *Windrush* era, it is useful, even at the risk of digression, to briefly reflect on McKay's development into an individual with an explicitly articulated diasporic identity. It is well known that British imperialism, as Deborah A. Thomas emphasizes, "was not merely a system of economic exploitation and political domination but also one of cultural control that attempted to socialize colonial populations into accepting the moral and cultural superiority of Englishness."[13] In 1912, the young Jamaican writer McKay—at the time, an emerging diasporic writer whose poetic voice was to gain its true stylistic and political force in the late 1910s and the 1920s—published a poem titled "Old England," which reads like a demonstration of the efficacy of the imperial cultural control mentioned by Thomas. The poem's interlocutor, expressing his wish to "view Westminster Abbey, where de great of England sleep, / An' de solemn marble statues o'er deir ashes vigil keep,"[14] humbly articulates his longing "Just to view de homeland England, in de streets of London walk, / An' to see de famous sights dem'bouten which dere's so much talk."[15] The poet's approach to his subject matter may well include a touch of irony. Nevertheless, as a result of the colonial education that he had received in Jamaica, McKay himself too,[16] not just the poem's "I," had learned to admiringly think of the heart of Empire (represented in the poem by London's monumental embodiments of imperial power) as the core of what he at the time considered his national belonging; hence this poem about a colonial subject's marvel at his "homeland England" (where the young poet had never been)—a praisesong to Englishness here envisioned, optimistically, as a transracial realm of imperial and cultural belonging that all colonial subjects shared with white Britons.

The same year "Old England" appeared in print, McKay left his native island for the United States. In 1918, he published a short essay[17] that contrasted US antiblack racism, which had turned out to be much more blatant than he had expected, with its more benign counterpart in Jamaica (where whites were, numerically, a small minority). Notably, McKay's positive remarks about Jamaica, a British colony, revealed something about his understanding of race relations in the mother country, too, by disclosing his romantic notion that the "prejudice of the English sort" was "subtle and dignified, rooted in class distinction—color and race being hardly taken into account."[18] This acquired vision of "dignified" social prejudice (to which his later exposure to racism on English soil, on the one hand, and to Marxist theories of social class, on the other, offered correctives) indicates that in 1918 he was still under the spell of Empire, which distorted his perception of the intensity of both racism and class-based discrimination (and of the nature of their intersectionality, for that matter) in his adored "homeland England."[19]

McKay eventually traveled to London in 1919 and stayed there for over a year and a half. English antiblack racism, contrasting sharply with the notion of the gentle and genteel mother country that he had cherished in his colonial imagination, shocked him profoundly. In his 1937 travelogue, *A Long Way from Home*, McKay reminisced about having "felt entirely out of sympathy with the English environment."[20] From 1919 onward, he distanced himself from the idealized notion of Englishness that his early education had inculcated in him. This process was a major precipitator of his transnational and diasporic identity formation, the outcome of which—his fluid self-understanding as a border-crosser—he articulated while recalling his response to a Moroccan doorman's inquiry about his national identity: "I said I was born in the West Indies and lived in the United States and that I was an American, even though I was a British subject, but I preferred to think of myself as an internationalist. The *chaoush* said he didn't understand what was an internationalist. I laughed and said that an internationalist was a bad nationalist."[21] McKay's transformation from a loyal colonial subject into a "bad nationalist" and an "internationalist" was, in no small way, prompted by his disappointment in having been viewed in England as a racial Other rather than as someone who, on the basis of his colonial affiliation, belonged. The disillusionment that McKay experienced in post–World War I England resonates, I contend, with later, post-*Windrush* accounts of African Caribbean diasporans' encounters with Englishness/Britishness in the heart of Empire—including Lamming's rendering of this historical experience in *The Emigrants*, Phillips's representation of it in *The Final Passage*, and Levy's thematically similar but in many ways more optimistic narrative in *Small Island*.

The Emigrants, a groundbreaking text, launched the literary tradition that conveys and interprets the black Caribbean experience in postwar Britain through the medium of the novel.[22] This chapter will, however, first briefly call attention to references to Anglocentric imperialism and colonialism in *Natives of My Person* (1972), a later novel by Lamming, in order to highlight the dialogue between (post-)Empire's past and present that informs his representation of black diasporic identity formation in *The Emigrants* as well. Most importantly, the powerful presence of the Middle Passage trope in *Natives of My Person* both underscores the significant role of the African diasporic imaginary in Lamming's intellectual framework and spotlights the intersectionality of diaspora and Empire—a crucial nexus in *The Emigrants*, too—in his oeuvre. Phillips's similar emphases were discussed in the previous chapter.[23] Levy's *Small Island*, in turn, may initially seem to be carved out of rather different materials, given that direct references to early black Atlantic history are absent from this novel. However, *Small Island*'s powerful interrogation of Britain's post–World War II status as an empire, albeit one in decline, implicitly speaks to the text's awareness of the past activities of the British Empire in the Atlantic slave trade and in West Indian slavery. Although the pre-1833 activities of Empire are not explicitly thematized in *Small Island*, the novel is grounded in a postslavery, postimperial, and postcolonial awareness. Moreover, Levy's oeuvre, when taken as a whole, reveals the historical depth of her diasporic consciousness, especially because *Small Island* (which focuses tightly on the 1940s, with some flashbacks to the preceding decades) was followed by *The Long Song*, Levy's 2010 novel set in the tempestuous times surrounding the end of chattel slavery in Jamaica.

Six years after the publication of *The Emigrants*, Lamming offered his writerly manifesto in *The Pleasures of Exile*. In the first, *Tempest*-inspired pages of this 1960 essay collection, he referred to himself as a twentieth-century descendant of both Caliban and Prospero: "I am a direct descendant of slaves, too near to the actual enterprise to believe that its echoes are over with the reign of emancipation. Moreover, I am a direct descendant of Prospero worshipping in the same temple of endeavour, using his language—not to curse our meeting—but to push it further."[24] Prompted by this articulation of a dual genealogy, scholars have since keenly analyzed Lamming's reflective, subversive, and innovative appropriation of "Prospero's language" (the language of Shakespeare and Empire) in *The Emigrants* and beyond.[25] Sandra Pouchet Paquet's *The Novels of George Lamming* (1982) was the first comprehensive study of Lamming's fiction—offering, among other things, a foundational introduction to *The Emigrants'* main themes, characters, and narrative techniques.[26] Simon Gikandi, Supriya Nair, A. J. Simoes da Silva, James Procter, J. Dillon Brown, Celeste Wheat, David Ellis, and others have since contextualized *The Emigrants* within Lamming's treatment of colonialism, anticolonialism, exile, and migration,[27] often situating this dense and stylistically experimental novel within the contexts of both modernity and modernism.[28]

Rather than duplicating previous research, my analysis of *The Emigrants* will address this diasporic novel's largely, though not completely, overlooked dialogue with a French influence, namely, existentialism[29]—which, in addition to being inspired by the West's existential agony after World War II, also developed in dialogue with the crisis of French imperialism. I will show that Lamming borrowed idioms and tropes from this school of thought and used them to enhance the political and societal dimensions of his narrative in *The Emigrants*. In the early 1950s, Lamming viewed French existentialism as having the potential to inspire political action rather than just being theory for theory's sake. He therefore saw the existentialist lexicon as a suitable language for expressing the predicament of first-generation black Caribbean diasporans in Britain. As this "French" act of appropriation for its part demonstrates, Mary Louise Pratt's notion of "contact zones"—which refer to "social spaces where disparate cultures meet, clash, and grapple with each other, often in highly asymmetrical relations of domination and subordination"[30]—aptly illuminates Lamming's multifaceted experience and identity position at the time he wrote *The Emigrants*: he was a black diasporic colonial literary artist living in London—a European metro-/cosmopolis and the heart of the British Empire—who conversed with a variety of cultural and political influences, Anglophone and beyond.

Following my commentary on *The Emigrants*, this chapter examines the new layers of the black Caribbean migration story that Phillips's *The Final Passage* and Levy's *Small Island* add to the tradition founded by Lamming. That is, my analysis of *The Emigrants*—including a discussion of gender—paves the way for my argument that, even as Phillips and Levy align themselves with the tradition initiated by Lamming (and by Trinidadian-born, Indo-Caribbean Sam[uel] Selvon), they at the same time critically revisit and reform it: both *The Final Passage* and *Small Island* offer more nuanced representations of women than do Lamming's (and Selvon's) more male-focused renderings of the *Windrush* era. Instead of utilizing a masculinist lens and patriarchally privileging male mobility, *The Final Passage* offers a sensitively drawn portrait of a marginalized and indigent West Indian woman in London at the end of the 1950s and the beginning of the 1960s. *Small Island*, in turn, envisions a stronger and more confident Caribbean diasporic female agency lived out by a Jamaican ex-RAF volunteer's wife in the same metropolis in 1948.

Another aspect of *Small Island*'s historical and sociopolitical significance is that in this novel Levy not only reimagines the black Caribbean presence in the mother country *after* the *Windrush* moment, but also calls attention to Jamaican airmen and ground crewmen's contributions to Britain's war effort *during* World War II. In discussing the presence of both African American and black Caribbean troops in Britain during the war, Hazel Carby argues that "it is not the *Windrush* alone which initiated a new phase in the formation of a Caribbean diaspora in the UK and ushered in a new racial state"; in addition to the *Windrush* era, "the presence of black civilian and military personnel during World War II" also needs to be considered.[31] In *Small Island*, Levy—in addition to including African American GIs in the novel's spectrum of characters—similarly highlights black Caribbean subjects' affirmative response to the wartime call of the mother country. Like Carby, she, too, reminds us that contacts between the African Caribbean diaspora and white Britain were already taking place during World War II, not just afterward.

All along, my analyses of *The Emigrants*, *The Final Passage*, and *Small Island* demonstrate that Lamming and Phillips—members, respectively, of the first and second generations of post-*Windrush* writers—convey a "Middle Passage sensibility"[32] more powerfully than does Levy, who, in the generational classification of post-*Windrush* novelists, belongs to the "third" generation. (In depictions of Levy's *family*, however, the generational discourse operates differently because it was her father, not her grandfather, who arrived in London on the *Empire Windrush*.) Like *The Emigrants* and *Final Passage*, *Small Island* foregrounds the antiblack racism experienced by West Indian migrants to Britain. Yet, exilic melancholy, though a presence, does not dominate *Small Island* in the way it controls Lamming's and Phillips's writing. In Levy's treatment, the story of the postwar black Caribbean diaspora in Britain grows into a narrative of active "diaspora-making," to summon Frank A. Guridy's term that underscores black agency.[33] To a degree, active diaspora-making is thematically present in *The Emigrants* and *Final Passage* as well, but Levy, an author intimately familiar with the kind of confidently multicultural London that Zadie Smith portrays in *White Teeth* (2000), focuses on it much more determinedly. My phrase "confidently multicultural" is not, of course, intended to suggest that Levy (or Smith, for that matter) fails to perceive the serious challenges posed to multiculturalism by xenophobia, nationalism, anti-immigration sentiment, and nostalgia for the past "greatness" of Empire (challenges that Gilroy addresses in his 2005 book, *Postcolonial Melancholia*, strongly emphasizing the need to understand "the political conflicts which characterize multicultural societies" as "exist[ing] firmly in a context supplied by imperial and colonial history").[34] Rather, my point is that, as Ashley Dawson reminds us, "[a]t least three generations of black and Asian Britons have now encountered and fought back against various forms of institutional and popular racism."[35] While clearly aware that the struggle against racism and antimulticulturalism is far from over, Levy and Smith build upon the activist and artistic work done by the previous generations and are therefore able to depict black diasporic agency in Britain much more assertively than was possible for Lamming in the early 1950s or Phillips in the mid-1980s.

Englishness, Then and Now: Anglocentric Imperialism in Lamming's *Natives of My Person*

Scholars apply partly overlapping critical labels—"black British," "Caribbean," and "postcolonial" among them—to the oeuvres of Lamming and Phillips. This book focuses on one such label, namely, "black diasporic" or "African diasporic" (while at the same time fully acknowledging the validity of the other categorizations, which respond to different conceptual, intellectual, and contextual challenges). It resonates with Lamming's and Phillips's strong emphasis on diaspora that they both frequently insert the Middle Passage trope into their critical interrogations of "white" Englishness/Britishness and of the imperial "greatness" of Britain. Their narratives of the black post–World War II migration from the Caribbean to Britain can therefore be legitimately read as representations of what Michelle Ann Stephens, in discussing the connectivity of Empire and diaspora, calls the second "of two acts of displacement"[36]—the first being the Middle Passage and, the second, the journey from the colonies to the heart of Empire[37] (which the title of Phillips's first novel poignantly terms the "final passage").

In *Cambridge*, Phillips, as mentioned previously, brings the notion of the Middle Passage to bear on the literal and metaphorical voyage to the West Indies of a white upper-class Englishwoman, Emily Cartwright. He then places Emily's post–"Middle Passage" existence on her father's Caribbean plantation in dialogue with that of Olumide/Thomas/David Henderson/Cambridge, a first-generation slave on the same plantation. Phillips's critique of Anglocentric imperialism is crystallized in the subjugated and Anglicized African diasporic individual's final name, Cambridge, which is imposed on him at the site of his Caribbean slavery. In this novel, the name Cambridge—which here epitomizes white English civilization generally, rather than just Oxbridge culture—ultimately signifies the silencing and overwriting of black diasporic history by Empire. Phillips's critical interrogation of imperialism in *Cambridge* resonates with his use of the line "History is now and England" (from T. S. Eliot's "Little Gidding")[38] in the epigraph to his first novel, *The Final Passage*. In both novels, Phillips evokes Englishness to refer to the oppressive ramifications of white patriarchal Anglocentrism, the worldview and ideology of Empire. Given that both *Cambridge* and *The Final Passage* are concerned with black diasporic subjectivity and Empire's desire to erase it, Phillips's simultaneously tragic and ironic emphasis on "history" being "now and England" in each novel highlights the disenchanting continuity between the colonial past and the (post)colonial present.[39]

Lamming, another Caribbean-born black author who addresses the continuity between Empire's past and present throughout his oeuvre is, like Phillips, deeply concerned with "history" being "now and England." His oeuvre is a prime example of what Ngũgĩ wa Thiong'o and others have termed "the literature of decolonization."[40] The early 1950s (when Lamming's first two novels were published) was "a time," writes Thiong'o, "pregnant with the tension between what had been ... European imperial ascendancy in the globe, ... and what was about to be—the redrawing of the power map of the world by the forces of decolonization."[41] Lamming embraced the era's anticolonial and anti-imperial developments and made them a powerful presence—indeed, a driving force—in his fiction. Lamming's and Phillips's shared interests and emphases are no coincidence. Phillips, the younger of the two, openly acknowledges his literary and intellectual debt to Lamming. In his 1998 essay "Following On: The Legacy of Lamming and Selvon," he singles out *Natives of My Person* and *The Pleasures of Exile* as particularly significant influences on his own writing and intellectual formation, noting specifically his and Lamming's shared preoccupation with "the Atlantic slave experience":

> The first book of George Lamming's I read was a remarkable novel from 1972 entitled *Natives of My Person*.... Lamming was in a different league from the vast majority of the other Caribbean writers whom I had been attempting to read. And then I came upon his book *The Pleasures of Exile*.... [It] makes links between the Atlantic slave experience and the colonisation of language. It places the migration of Caribbean peoples to Britain into a global political and cultural context, and in this sense the book is—as I later discovered—in the tradition of the work which C.L.R. James had been pursuing for many a decade.[42]

In *Natives of My Person*, Lamming uses and modifies the Middle Passage motif to interrogate the significance of England's colonial and imperial power for the construction of Englishness/Britishness—a strategy later adopted by Phillips. *Natives of My Person*, an allegory of imperialism and colonialism, takes the reader back to an early post-Columbian era as it portrays an ocean voyage from the fictional Kingdom of Lime Stone (England in thin disguise) to the Caribbean via the west coast of Africa. Lamming narrates a modified "Middle Passage" (the title of the novel's second section), namely, the journey of a motley crew of Europeans, each of whom chases a different dream or flees a different private or political predicament. The raison d'être of the voyage is to conquer San Cristobal, located on Lamming's fictional Isles of the Black Rock in the Caribbean,[43] and to establish there a utopian settlement envisioned by the ship's captain, the Commandant, who is eager to leave behind the corruption plaguing Lime Stone. However, the hope of a new beginning is dashed before the ship, the *Reconnaissance*, even reaches San Cristobal: the crew and the officers mutiny, and the insurrection both results in the Commandant's death and symbolically functions as collective suicide. Even though the revolt leaves behind survivors, it in effect terminates the project of building the planned utopia (although the ending is, characteristically of Lamming's modernist writing, left open).

To grasp the purpose of Lamming's project in *Natives of My Person*, it is crucial to understand that while the Commandant's enterprise may be utopian, it is also profoundly imperialist, even though the project is not state-sponsored. The Commandant's goal is to "plant some portion of Lime Stone in the virgin territories of San Cristobal."[44] Two aspects of this phrase aptly illuminate his imperial mindset. First, the territories of San Cristobal—inhabited by local Caribs, or Caribbean Amerindian "Tribes," whose extinction is already imminent—are "virginal" only in the imagination of the imperial colonist. Lamming's postcolonial irony is palpable here. Second, the Commandant's projected utopia is ultimately a replica of what he has left behind. Even though he, a member of Lime Stone's nobility, chooses to operate outside the law of his native kingdom, and even though he has utopian aspirations that are not solely based on greed, his political imagination fails him when he faces the challenge of envisioning a radically new, democratic way of communal existence. During the journey, he falls back on the hierarchical models of community-building that he has learned and internalized in Lime Stone. Lamming's tale of the Commandant's conflicted enterprise (new wine in old wineskins) is a fictionalized account of a significant failure of political and cultural imagination—in the final analysis, a representation of the persistence of colonialism's mindset in the depicted era and beyond.

Chapters 7–11 of the novel are set in an unnamed location on the west coast of Africa. The officers and crew of the *Reconnaissance* make "bold expeditions"[45] inland by traveling along a mighty river in longboats. Like the Congo in Joseph Conrad's *Heart of Darkness* (1899),[46] the unnamed river is formidable and mysterious, practically a living creature in its own right whose "true nature"[47] the white visitors cannot decipher. The mission of the Commandant's men on these expeditions is to capture natives to be taken as slaves to San Cristobal. The first expedition is preceded by a bad omen: while the men are still on the *Reconnaissance*, which lies in anchor at the river's mouth, a vast flock of fowl unexpectedly flies over the ship.[48] The birds suddenly start to fall on the deck, dying en masse.[49] This incident foreshadows the crew's massacre of a group of African locals during the first expedition[50] and the subsequent collective suicide of the African survivors: after being captured, loaded onto the longboats, and eventually forced onto the deck of the *Reconnaissance*, the captive Africans take the Commandant's men by surprise by jumping ship while chained to each other.[51] They end their Middle Passage before it even begins, choosing drowning over slavery, and the *Reconnaissance* eventually heads for the New World without black human cargo in its hold.[52] The captured Africans' demise metaphorically anticipates the fate of the envisioned white San Cristobal community—the crucial difference being, however, that the Africans die together just as they had lived together, whereas the whites on the *Reconnaissance* are divided by regional and class-based differences, which play an important part in precipitating the mutiny, the final rift between the crew and the officers.

The deaths of the Africans, together with the fate of the Carib "Tribes," constitute the novel's silent center, which epitomizes the heart of darkness of the Commandant's colonial/imperial enterprise. Lamming, focalizing his narrative through white characters, leaves the Africans and the "Tribes" of San Cristobal behind the veil, so that they remain as nameless and faceless to the reader as do their real-life counterparts whose biographies are lost to history. However, it is these racially subjugated characters, victims of imperialist and colonialist avarice, whom Lamming invites the reader to sympathize with. Their fates are in direct dialogue with the Commandant's conflicted efforts to both break away from Lime Stone and adhere to its core values—values that Lamming depicts as thinly veiled Englishness, which is inextricably tied to the racially charged ideologies of imperial and colonial power.

Since nonwhite characters do not speak in *Natives of My Person*, the task of envisioning a new future is left to the white women on the *Penalty* (the sister ship of the *Reconnaissance* anchored off San Cristobal), who, locked out of time, wait in vain for their men to arrive. Without their knowledge and contrary to the Commandant's original intention, the ship has become their prison, as its name has ironically suggested all along. Lamming, like Phillips in *Cambridge*, here draws various parallels between racial and sexual oppression, including the "collateral damage"[53] that both forms of oppression frequently bring about. Eventually, one of the women on the *Penalty*, the Lady of the House, utters the novel's final words: "We [the women] are a future they [the white Englishmen] must learn."[54] On the level of plot, she is only speaking for herself and for her white female peers. Yet, her exclamation—regardless of her identity position as a privileged daughter of Empire—acutely points to the need for a utopia/society based on democratic principles of inclusion. Lamming, in other words, uses the novel's final sentence to address the need for a new world order, one no longer based on the racial and sexual subjugation that Anglocentrist imperialism entails.

"Looking for a Better Break": Lamming's Project in *The Emigrants*

Natives of My Person casts an unsuccessful early colonial enterprise as a failure of community formation on a ship headed for the Caribbean. The projected community falls apart as its members, white (English) colonizers from varied regional and class backgrounds, attempt to cross the Atlantic together but remain enslaved to their preexisting hierarchical and undemocratic modes of thought. The first part of Lamming's *The Emigrants*, "A Voyage," also narrates an Atlantic crossing—this time, a passage to the heart of Empire of a shipload of black West Indians following the 1948 British Nationality Act, which guaranteed all British subjects the right to live and work in Britain.

In postwar Britain, the relationship between national citizenship and British subjecthood had to be clarified after the Canadian government announced in September 1945 that legislation on Canadian nationality would be revisited and revised.[55] The process that began in the aftermath of this Canadian announcement resulted in the 1948 Act, the gist of which Kathleen Paul summarizes in *Whitewashing Britain* (1997):

> Under the terms of the act, London recognized the right of dominion governments to create national citizenships, which would then provide

access to the common, imperial status of British subject. The Attlee government even followed this principle itself by creating its own area of citizenship—the United Kingdom and Colonies. Yet at the same time the Labour government chose to ignore all these newly created citizenships by emphasizing that in UK law all British subjects remained equal. The Parliament at Westminster would continue to consider the imperial nationality of British subjecthood the only nationality that mattered. Unlike the Canadian government, *the UK government made no distinction between its own citizens and the larger class of British subjects. This major privilege resulted once again in equality of status and rights throughout the empire: all were equally entitled to live and work in Britain.*[56]

Understandably, this legal development was a major source of hope for those black British subjects who were suffering from postwar unemployment and its socioeconomic ramifications in the Caribbean. However, as Victoria R. Arana and Lauri Ramey observe, "Britain opened the door to the Empire, but certainly did not expect the colonials to come, to stay, and to expect the same life that the Anglo-Saxons themselves enjoyed."[57] Hazel Carby elaborates: "The British Nationality Act created a type of global citizenship, extending British subjecthood to all members of the empire," but in practice "policy makers conceived of separate spheres of nationality: residents of the empire with a white skin and European cultural descent were British stock; residents of the empire with a skin of color and African or Asian heritage were British subjects only."[58]

Eventually, Enoch Powell's now-infamous "Rivers of Blood" speech—in which the Conservative MP dramatized his address with allusions to Virgil's prophecy of war, metaphorically comparing black immigration to conquest and armed conflict—came to represent an extreme example of antiblack and anti-immigration rhetoric in the era's British politics.[59] However, the post-1948 racial tension did not take two decades to develop. Powell delivered his speech in 1968, but the distinction between "British stock" and "British subjects" (Carby), which caught the postwar black Caribbean arrivals off guard, was a powerful presence in their lives from the very beginning of the *Windrush* era. The black migrants' immediate discovery that in the mother country they were primarily viewed as racial Others rather than as fellow Britons, is the historical background of Lamming's subtle utilization of the Middle Passage motif in "A Voyage." Although the narrative depicts a voluntary crossing, it alludes to the days of chattel slavery, as a young female passenger's identification of herself and her fellow black migrants as "a bit o' cargo they puttin' from one place to a next" suggests.[60] Paquet elaborates: "The journey and the exile that follow, repeat in a different key, the 'middle passage' theme of displacement in an alien and hostile environment.... [M]ost of the emigrants are crowded together in a dormitory arrangement that recalls and yet differentiates between the emigrant journey and the circumstances of the slave ship."[61] The emigrant ship's name, *Golden Image*, poignantly alludes to the passengers' high hopes that are about to be dashed by the realities of antiblack racism and Britain's bleak postwar economy.

The references that *The Emigrants* makes to the histories of imperial and colonial subjugation do not end with the novel's manipulation of the diasporic Middle Passage trope. "A Voyage" also educates its readers about empires and Atlantic history through a long soliloquy by a black Jamaican male passenger. After reading a book on the foundational events of the Caribbean's colonial past, the man sarcastically concludes that the "West Indies people is a sort of vomit you vomit up":[62]

> Was a long time back England an' France an' Spain an' all the great nations make a raid on whoever live in them islands. Whatever the book call them me no remember, but most o' them get wipe out. Then de great nations make plans for dese said islands. England, France, Spain, all o' them, them vomit up what them din't want, an' the vomit settle there in that Caribbean Sea. It mix up with the vomit them make Africa vomit, an' the vomit them make India vomit, an' China an' nearly every race under the sun. An' just as vomit never get back in yuh stomach, these people, most o' them, never get back where them vomit them from. Them settle right there in that Caribbean Sea.[63]

The Jamaican's vernacular recapitulation of the role of European empires in the formation of the Caribbean past and present reveals a colonial subject's newly awakened consciousness of his identity position as someone who is not of Empire's "center" but of its "periphery," as the logic of Empire would have it. The novels discussed in this book offer renderings of black diasporic subjects' tension-ridden relationships with national and, even more so, with imperial belonging, including interrogations of the very desirability of belonging in a nation with an imperialist past/present. Here, the politically awakened Jamaican passenger, who is in transit (neither in the colony nor in the mother country), finds himself in an in-between space that for him evokes both the Middle Passage and the promise of a new beginning. Ambivalent about his migration project, he seeks to make sense of his dually diasporic identity position both as Africa's forced "vomit" and as a British subject who is voluntarily on his way to the heart of Empire.

At the same time, the Jamaican's soliloquy challenges imperial interpretations of history. As Kerwin Lee Klein wryly reminds us, "When G.W.F. Hegel spun his epochal story of universal history, he left little doubt that 'History' belonged to some people but not to others."[64] In *Lectures on the Philosophy of World History*, Hegel wrote about sub-Saharan Africans:

> The first [that is, sub-Saharan] part of Africa is ... Africa proper, which we can leave aside since its points of contact [with history][65] are minimal.... The Negroes display great strength of body and a highly sensual nature along with affability but also a shocking and inconceivable ferocity. These peoples have never emerged out of themselves, nor have they gained a foothold in history.... This Africa remains in its placid, unmotivated, self-enclosed sensuality and has not yet entered into history; its only further connection with history is that in darker days its inhabitants have been enslaved.[66]

The gist of Hegel's argument was that the absence of writing among various indigenous peoples (including, but not limited to, sub-Saharan Africans) doomed them to being "peoples without history."[67] In the West Indies, the British Empire's project of socializing colonial subjects into embracing the "superiority" of Englishness was accompanied by the importation of the English education system. However, literacy and writing skills—fundamental to Hegel's understanding to how a people may "enter into history"—did not, in themselves, solve the political problem of West Indians' alleged historylessness because the history taught in the colonies was that of Englishness and Empire. Lamming's semiautobiographical debut novel, *In the Castle of My Skin* (1953), in which Barbadian schoolchildren are taught to think of Barbados as "Little England"[68] and to be proud of that designation, offers a vivid depiction of Empire's approach to educating Caribbean colonial subjects about history. The socialization of children into a gentle and genteel English imaginary goes so far that the historical reality of Barbadian slavery is explicitly denied in the classroom: "[Slavery] had nothing to do with people in Barbados. No one there was ever a slave, the teacher said. It was in another part of the world that those things happened. Not in Little England."[69] Lamming's critique of colonial historiography in his first novel resonates with his rendering of the Jamaican passenger's frustration in *The Emigrants*—a sentiment that, not unlike the experience of the Barbadian schoolchildren, attests to the need for history books in which Caribbean subjects would not be cast either as Empire's Others or as her passive children, but as active agents in the West Indies' past, present, and future.

While critiquing imperial historiography's profoundly flawed vision of black colonial diasporans as historyless, "A Voyage" also contains hopeful dimensions, reflective of what the emigrants on the ship wish to accomplish by moving to Britain. In an interview conducted by Caryl Phillips in 1996,[70] Lamming discussed both his own 1950 migration to England, where he traveled on the same ship with Sam Selvon, and the voyage of the fictional passengers featured in *The Emigrants*. Regardless of what the most important push factor of emigration was for each historical or fictional émigré—be it unemployment, the relatively limited educational opportunities in the postwar Caribbean, or the rather small literary marketplace there (a concern for writers)—all West Indian migrants were, as Lamming pointed out to Phillips, "travelling towards an expectation" and "looking for a better break."[71] They believed that the mother country would welcome them warmly and help each of them to find a niche in British society: "Everybody was in search of an expectation, and because of what they would now call your 'socialization,' because you had lived so much with the idea of England as facilitator, everybody was more or less sure that England would come to their rescue. . . . Whatever was the expectation embryonically in your mind, would get realized in England."[72]

In *The Emigrants*, the optimistic migrants in search of this "better break"[73] come from various Caribbean islands, mainly Trinidad, Barbados, Grenada, and Jamaica. During the voyage, they begin their important, albeit fragile, community formation: they get acquainted, discuss the importance of education and employment, debate interisland differences and the logic of Empire, and gradually articulate to each other their hopes, plans, and dreams. As they get to know each other better, they also cautiously start to disclose and share their insecurities, anxieties, and doubts about the mother country and the migration's projected outcome. Most of them are on a journey into a new, unfamiliar mode of being—although two men, the "Governor" and Tornado, have been to England previously, having served in the RAF during World War II. Indeed, the motif of West Indians' RAF experiences in Britain, later expanded on by Levy, is already present in *The Emigrants*, albeit in nascent form. The novel's second section, "Rooms and Residents," chronicles the initial phase of the migrants' adjustment and acclimatization to England, including their discovery of such safe spaces/meeting places as the hostel, the barbershop, the hairdresser's, and the basement room of a hospitable young Caribbean couple, Tornado and Lilian (who plan to return to Trinidad as soon as financially feasible). The third and final section, "Another Time," reveals the migrants' complex existential predicament a couple of years after their arrival—for most of them, a profoundly disillusioned existence as black Others on the margins of a white-dominated and white-controlled society, an exilic life whose vicissitudes are in part, but only in part, alleviated by their collective West Indian identity formation.

Collective West Indian identity formation was a cause close to Lamming's heart when he wrote *The Emigrants*. In essays and interviews, he has repeatedly stressed that West Indians, somewhat paradoxically, truly became West Indians as a result of their postwar exile from their respective islands: Jamaicans, Trinidadians, Barbadians, and other Anglophone islanders encountered each other in English cities, finding themselves there (particularly in London) in interisland contact and communion in a way that had not occurred in the Caribbean. Lamming articulated this sentiment very clearly in the 1996 interview with Phillips: "[M]y generation's West Indian and Caribbean formation was, to a large extent, if not initiated, directed and reinforced in London, not before. Most of us were not West Indians until the London experience. I had not met a Jamaican until I got to London."[74] In "A Voyage," the Jamaican passenger who uses the metaphor of vomit to refer to Caribbean colonial history is, in fact, an advocate of the sociocultural and political West Indianization of West Indian emigrants abroad. His impromptu speech on the ship almost prophetically anticipates the emergence of the West Indies Federation,[75] which was established in 1958, four years after the publication of *The Emigrants* (but was, to Lamming's deep disappointment, dismantled in 1962):[76]

> [T]hem [the "great nations"] stir an' stir till the vomit start to take on a new life, it was like ammonia, get too strong for those who stirrin' it. Now it explodin' bit by bit. . . . When them [black Caribbean colonial subjects] stay back home in they little island them forget a little an' them remain vomit; just as them wus vomit up, but when them go 'broad, them remember, or them get tol' w'at is w'at, an' them start to prove, an' them give w'at them provin' a name. A good name. Them is West Indians. Not Jamaicans or Trinidadians. Cause the bigger the better. Them is West Indians.[77]

In addition to West Indian alliances, encounters with African colonial subjects based in Britain were also part of Lamming's London experience from the beginning, strengthening the African dimension of his African Caribbean diasporic consciousness.[78] For the sake of comparison, it is noteworthy that when Claude McKay was looking for ways to emotionally survive what he described in *A Long Way from Home* as "the ordeal of more than a year's residence in London,"[79] he began to frequent two clubs with an international membership. One of them, located in a basement in Drury Lane, was a meeting place for "a host of colored soldiers in London, from the West Indies and Africa, with a few colored Americans, East Indians, and Egyptians among them."[80] This club of transnational transients offered the black diasporic poet both a circle of friends and acquaintances and an opportunity to discuss politics with black expatriates and colonial subjects. McKay's experience resonates with Elleke Boehmer's description of "the cosmopolitan London of the 1910s and 1920s"[81] as a place where "elites from different colonial contexts were able to mingle and exchange opinions . . .—in effect to experience different forms of cultural and political self-representation."[82] C.L.R. James too, as is well known, developed a profoundly deepened vision of global black solidarity while living in London.[83]

What intensified Lamming's similar experience was its timing: not only did Lamming travel to England's multiethnic metropolis in the *Windrush* era, but he also arrived there at what Thiong'o has aptly called "the high noon of anti-imperialism."[84] Coming into contact with anticolonial movements of Africa (especially that of the Gold Coast/Ghana) in London played an important role in politicizing his writing at the time. In a 2002 interview with David Scott, Lamming, reminiscing about a London hostel where he and Selvon initially stayed, not only identified the real-life model of Selvon's Nigerian "Captain" ("You would have had West Indians there, Africans, the Nigerian in Sam's *Lonely Londoners* shared a room with the two of us"),[85] but also elaborated on how he in England's cosmopolis became interested in the political realities of Africa, thus experiencing a significant and meaningful deepening of his African diasporic consciousness:

> I am in England in 1950 where I am hearing all the time of the anticolonial struggle in the Gold Coast, which is going to be Ghana. Nkrumah was around there in 1948 and is coming back. And I remember going to a meeting at which Nkrumah is in fact speaking to people in London. Every Sunday I used to go over to a place called WASU in Chelsea—it was the West African Student Union—to listen to the same discussions that went on there as went on in the WISU, the West Indian Student

Union. I got this very great interest in hearing and feeling Africa, the *political* Africa, the anticolonial Africa.[86]

In addition to these "British" experiences of McKay and James, the French exile of Richard Wright, who wrote an introduction to the first edition of *In the Castle of My Skin*,[87] also resonates with Lamming's intellectual development in a European metropolitan "contact zone"—a zone where, it is important to note, influences from *multiple* empires and their colonies come into dialogue with each other through a constant multidirectional flow of people and ideas. (For example, when C.L.R. James in 1933 departed for his six-month research trip to France to research the Haitian Revolution for *The Black Jacobins* there, he was in the midst of his "British" years.[88] He was thus ideally situated to compare the projects of two empires and converse with myriad cultural influences simultaneously in the capacity of a diasporic cosmopolitan.) Like Wright in France, Lamming, while primarily based in Britain, also responded enthusiastically to the call of French existentialism. Wright's and Lamming's shared interest in existentialism is often ignored in comparative analyses of these two writers. For instance, Joyce Ann Joyce's 2009 discussion of Wright and Lamming references Wright's friendship with Sartre and de Beauvoir[89] but does not mention Lamming's fascination with these same intellectuals' work. Yet, even as Lamming portrays the emergence of postwar black Britain, an Anglophone sociocultural formation, he draws on French existentialism— a powerful current in the European intellectual life of the 1950s.

Lamming's Dialogue with French Existentialism in *The Emigrants*

In 1987, Wendy Griswold wrote that Lamming's fictional works "bear traces of both the English writers he read during his formal and informal education and the experiences of the West Indian peasants, workers, and earnest middle-class professionals with whom he had grown up."[90] The sources of inspiration that Griswold identifies are relevant for any thorough analysis of Lamming's novels, but her approach fails—not atypically of Lamming scholarship in the 1980s and even the 1990s—to consider the possibility that in the early 1950s an Anglophone black Caribbean writer might have been actively conversing with influences beyond the British–West Indian axis and placing them in dialogue with his own experience. As noted, however, a cosmopolitan "contact zone" incorporates influences from multiple imperial, colonial, and anticolonial realms. Inspired by Pratt's "contact zones," Karen L. Thornber has coined the closely related term "contact nebulae," which emphasizes the indistinct and porous qualities of contact zones' boundaries and the creolizing and "transculturating" cominglings of influences within such "nebulae."[91] In the above-quoted interview with Scott, Lamming—discussing the keen interest that he, in the early 1950s, developed in French existentialism—demonstrates the hybridity and multidirectionality of intellectual interactions within one such contact nebula, postwar London:

> I'm also reading voraciously. But I'm not reading English writers. They don't interest me very much. I am reading the French. I am interested in Albert Camus and Jean-Paul Sartre and Simone de Beauvoir and André Malraux. And I begin to make no separation between the man of culture and the man of public affairs, the man of letters and the man of action. I am absorbing this now from my reading of the French writers.... I'm reading everything by Sartre, everything by Camus, everything by de Beauvoir, all of the debates going on [among] the French and that is having an influence on me at this time.[92]

Lamming here makes a point about the writers of the African Caribbean diaspora similar to the one that Ralph Ellison, yet another eminent black postwar novelist attracted to existentialism, made about US African American authors when he declared that "one can, as artist, choose one's ancestors."[93] Raising his voice to challenge any stereotypical understanding of what kinds of sources "authentic" African American literature "should" draw from, Ellison emphasized that black novelists, like literary authors of any ethnoracial extraction, were free to choose as many artistic ancestors as they wished and to pick them from any ethnoracial groups—free to choose, as he himself did, Pete Wheatstraw *and* T. S. Eliot, Louis Armstrong *and* Dostoevsky (or, to apply this notion to Lamming, Barbadian rural English vernacular *and* Shakespeare's *The Tempest*, the Haitian Ceremony of Souls *and* Camus's *The Stranger*). As Ellison put it, "[F]or the novelist of any culture or racial identity, his form is his greatest freedom, and his insights are where he finds them."[94] Because Lamming from early on operated with a similarly inclusive and integrative mode of thinking, his commitment to writing about the African Caribbean experience in Britain did not limit him to drawing only on those "white" sources of inspiration that were British. In the early 1950s, he was searching for an intellectual framework that would facilitate a meaningful, intimate relationship to political action, particularly in conjunction with West Indian identity formation. What he perceived as the French existentialists' emphasis on the inseparability of thought and action spoke directly to his concerns.[95] *The Emigrants*, preceding any widespread public debate on whether Camus's solidarity lay with colonizer or colonized,[96] engages in an intertextual dialogue with French existentialism in general and with Camus's *The Stranger* and Sartre's dialectic of recognition in particular, including the latter's concept of "the Look."[97]

Of recent discussions of Camus, one that resonates with Lamming's thinking particularly well (without engaging in dialogue with him) is the 2009 reading of *The Stranger*, *The Plague*, and *The Fall* by Christopher C. Robinson, who sees Camus as "isolat[ing] theorizing as an activity performed not from a transcendental perceptual vantage of perfect light and vision, but from the immanent perspectives achieved in the city, among friends, or by exile."[98] In classical and medieval philosophy, "theory" referred to beholding—that is, to meditatively "seeing" and contemplating "the truth," as if "the truth" were a vista opening up in front of the beholder/philosopher, laid out before the mortal to be gazed and reflected upon by him. The ancients and medievals considered this kind of contemplative seeing, or "theorizing," to be clearly distinct from praxis or action. By contrast, in the writings of Camus, Sartre, and other existentialists (who, for their part, paved the way for postmodernist epistemologies), "beholding" or theorizing is always a *subjective* and *interpretive* activity, and any prompts for such activity (above characterized by Robinson as "immanent perspectives achieved in the city, among friends, or by exile") always represent a call for *action*, too. It is true that in Camus (and, hence, in Robinson's reading of him as well), the relationship between individual self-realization, on the one hand, and any communal organizing possibly included in "action," on the other, remains thinly developed. Nevertheless, Lamming, as noted above, detected in existentialism the gospel of "no separation between the man of culture and the man of public affairs, the man of letters and the man of action,"[99] and in the 1950s he viewed both Camus's and Sartre's writings through this lens.

The Emigrants opens with a scene in which the first-person narrator, Collis[100]—a Barbadian writer who has recently lived for four years in Trinidad—recounts what he observes in the port of Guadeloupe, a stop in the French Caribbean,[101] while waiting for the voyage to England to continue. In so doing, he offers a glimpse into the existential aspects of his in-transit experience. This reflection, of about twenty-two pages, combined with the novel's ending, contains a number of motifs and themes that appear in Camus's *The Stranger* as well: the simultaneously stagnant and pregnant atmosphere of waiting; the role of the "stranger" as a detached observer; the (participant-)

observer's alienated sense that he has made a major decision in life quickly, without much thought, almost by accident; the exhausting heat that contributes to his sense of detached estrangement; the strong presence of both death and religious ceremony in the narrative, seen through the narrator's/protagonist's secular eyes; an impending death sentence in the name of the people of France (a major theme in *The Stranger*'s conclusion and a minor motif in *The Emigrants*);[102] and the trope of obscured vision (written by Camus into Meursault's disorientation by the dazzling glare of the sun as he kills the Arab and by Lamming into the medically inexplicable deterioration of Collis's eyesight as all faces look "grey" and indistinguishable to him toward *The Emigrants*' end).[103] Other shared themes include the influence of colonialism, imperialism, and race-thinking on people's fixed, predetermined perceptions of each other (hence the emphasized anonymity of those characters who are only referred to by their ethnoracial designations, such as "the Arab" in *The Stranger* and "the African" and "the Jugoslav" in *The Emigrants*); the existentially charged opposition of freedom and confinement (examined keenly in *The Stranger*'s prison section and epitomized, in *The Emigrants*, by the ship experience and the limited immigrant existence); and, perhaps most importantly, the challenge and opportunity to give meaning to life and death[104]—that is, the necessity and freedom to interpret and act.[105]

The most conspicuous Sartrean influence in *The Emigrants*, in turn, may for some readers be the concept of nothingness (salient in Sartre's 1943 *L'Être et le néant*, or *Being and Nothingness*), because the term "*no-THING*," challenging any overly enthusiastic immigrant optimism, figures prominently in a pivotal scene that portrays the hopeful Caribbean passengers' arrival in England after their Atlantic crossing.[106] However, Lamming's use of the term *no-THING* in that scene ultimately has more to do with the prevalent and commonsensical usage of the term "nothingness" than with the highly theoretical distinctions that Sartre makes between *l'être* and *le néant* in his magnum opus on human consciousness and existence. A much more pervasive Sartrean (here, Hegelian-Sartrean) influence on *The Emigrants* is perceptible in Lamming's treatment of intersubjectivity, the subject-object relation, and the dialectic of recognition. Lamming's understanding of these intertwined philosophical topics is, at least in part, mediated by Fanon, who in his classic *Black Skin, White Masks* evoked both Sartre and Hegel, displaying a fondness for the Sartrean and existentially laden concepts of shame, self-contempt, and nausea.[107] Drawing especially on Hegel's dialectic of recognition, including his master-slave dialectic, Fanon claimed, "Man is human only to the extent to which he tries to impose his existence on another man in order to be recognized by him. As long as he has not been effectively recognized by the other, that other will remain the theme of his actions."[108]

An early scene in *The Emigrants*, in which Collis and the Barbadian schoolteacher Dickson meet in their shared dormitory on the emigrant ship,[109] reads like a faithful literary rendering of this Hegelian-Sartrean notion mediated by Fanon. Collis openly exhibits a profound need for recognition (of his existence, at the very least), but Dickson withdraws from contact. Collis's anxiety in the face of this rejection is palpable. He does not leave Dickson be; the other indeed remains, to borrow Fanon's phrase, "the theme of his actions." Dickson eventually becomes openly hostile rather than just rudely unresponsive. The crisis escalates, and Dickson attacks Collis physically. After the assault, the experience of having been negatively objectified, as opposed to positively recognized, by the Look of the other overwhelms Collis. He is so preoccupied and paralyzed by confusion, anger, and shame that he never even properly explains to his fellow passengers what happened, even though they have to physically rescue him from Dickson's violent aggression, which Dickson justifies to himself as self-defense.[110]

If in *The Emigrants* even an encounter between two black male equals easily turns into a hellish game in which the two subjects constantly objectify, and thereby undermine, each other, then alienation from self and community/society is inevitably intensified when racialized seeing becomes a key component of the Look. When subjected to the white colonial gaze, the black Caribbean male (here the focus is, indeed, on men) has few opportunities to return the gaze, as the prevalent power relations prohibit such reciprocation. Fanon, describing a different geographical context but a comparable colonial situation, famously wrote about the racialized subject-object relation in the language of vision: "The black man among his own in the twentieth century does not know at what moment his inferiority comes into being through the other.... And then the occasion arose when I had to meet the white man's eyes."[111] Lamming evokes the DuBoisian/Fanonian hell of being seen through the eyes of a racializing Other in the scene in which Collis has dinner with the Pearsons, a white English couple whose understanding of race prevents them from seeing Collis as their equal and from bonding with him in any meaningful way.[112]

The DuBoisian/Fanonian lexicon of the gaze is even more prominently present in the passage depicting Dickson's encounter with his landlady and her sister. In London, Dickson rents a room from a white Englishwoman with whom he became acquainted on the ship during the voyage to England.[113] She soon begins to treat Dickson with an increasing level of familiarity, suggesting that her interest in him is sexual. One evening, after an intimate conversation that Dickson assumes to be intended to seduce him, she slips out of his room and then unexpectedly returns with her sister. The two white women, curious and eager to see the black man in his near-nakedness, simply stare at him, objectifying him through their gaze both sexually and racially.[114] The consequences of this humiliating encounter are devastating for the emotionally volatile and fragile Dickson. The women's objectifying gaze strips the vulnerable immigrant of any sense of identity so completely that he needs the help of a mirror (which enables him to physically see his body through his own eyes again, albeit in mediated fashion) to reconnect with his selfhood and to regain a sense of who he was before being reduced to a sexually potent brute.[115] From this point on, the life of the mentally derailed Dickson is "a perpetual struggle to avoid eyes."[116] In the post-*Windrush* cityscape, many whites regarded black Caribbean men as "inherently" promiscuous (as discussed, for example, by Marcus Collins),[117] but Lamming's account of Dickson's breakdown counters this offensive stereotype, inverting traditional expectations about who might abuse whom in black-white encounters in a London unwilling to face its own prejudices.

Both Dickson and Collis embody aspects of Lamming's own biography: Dickson is a Barbadian-born schoolteacher (the profession of the young Lamming), and Collis is a Barbadian-born writer. *The Emigrants* being a modernist novel that contains various instances of doubling, masquerade, and multiple identities, Dickson and Collis can be read as each other's doubles. As Linda Dryden notes, "The literature of duality is, at its most obvious level, a literature about identity, or even lack of identity."[118] In the Dickson-Collis doubling, the point at issue is the breakdown (Dickson) or instability (Collis) of a previous, long-standing identity in the face of a new, unknown one—a diasporic/immigrant identity in Britain. Toward the novel's conclusion, the narrator/Collis reflects on Dickson's mental breakdown and realizes that he himself is not protected—by anything, really—from the same fate, from a disintegration and loss of self. His thoughts on Dickson's condition develop into a meditation on the profound estrangement and disillusionment of black immigrants in the heart of Empire: "[O]n the ship and even in the hostel, there was a feeling, more conscious in some than others, that England was not only a place, but a heritage.... But all that was now coming to an end. England was simply a world which we had moved about at random, and on occasions encountered by chance. It was just there like nature, drifting vaguely beyond our reach."[119] At the novel's end, most of *The Emigrants*' characters are in limbo: they have yet to establish a meaningful existence in the mother country and the Old World.

Any hope that can be found in the final sections of *The Emigrants* resides in Collis's/Lamming's act of narrating the African Caribbean migrant experience for readers rather than in the events themselves. Through the writerly activities of Collis/the narrator (Lamming's alter ego), *The Emigrants* reveals Lamming's powerful awareness of his vocation as a novelist portraying, in real time, the post-*Windrush* moment and black Caribbean identity formation in Britain. In *The Pleasures of Exile*, Lamming briefly discusses a different but related matter: the role of the novel in Caribbean history. He identifies three major milestones in the history of the Caribbean—namely, Columbus's "discovery," the abolition of slavery and the subsequent arrival of East Indians and Chinese in the area, and the rise of what he calls "the West Indian novel."[120] Critics have frequently commented on Lamming's unexpectedly heavy emphasis on the final item, the local emergence of a literary genre. Supriya Nair insightfully argues that this emphasis should be read against the backdrop of an influential 1493 narrative that was profoundly concerned with the Caribbean: Columbus not only made his first and most famous ocean voyage in 1492 but also wrote about it in the following year, thus laying the groundwork for subsequent political and cultural interpretations of the significance of his "discovery."[121] Indeed, Lamming's awareness of this historical detail invites him to reflect on the power of the written word, which he himself utilizes, some half a millennium later, to advance anticolonialism and to portray and support black community formation in Britain. In light of Lamming's Atlantic thinking (which both *Natives of My Person* and *The Pleasures of Exile* powerfully illuminate), *The Emigrants* can be read as implying that if Columbus's "printed voyage" (Richard Helgerson's term)[122] succeeded in contributing heavily to the European-centered mythology of the "Old World" and the "New World," then fictionalized "printed voyages" by former New World inhabitants pursuing a novel relationship with the Old World (that is, African Caribbean diasporans in Britain) also have the potential to actively influence the course of history rather than just passively reflect it. In *The Emigrants*, any hope for a black future on British soil lies in this metafictional aspect of the narrative.

Gender in *The Emigrants*: It's a Man's World

In *There Ain't No Black in the Union Jack*, Paul Gilroy quotes and paraphrases Stuart Hall's now-classic 1980 definition of race as "'the modality in which class is lived,' the medium in which it is appropriated and 'fought through.'"[123] In *The Black Atlantic* he adds, significantly, that "gender is the modality in which race is lived."[124] This emphasis on the importance of considering gender in diasporic interrogations—an emphasis ignored by those who, on the basis of Gilroy's source material (which, admittedly, is male-focused), criticize *The Black Atlantic* for being single-mindedly masculinist[125]—certainly applies to black diasporic existence, including the black Caribbean experience in Britain in the *Windrush* era. Lamming's approach to gender roles merits discussion because such later writers as Phillips and Levy have critically revisited this particular dimension of *The Emigrants* in their novels set in the same historical era. The definitive study of Lamming's treatment of gender in his oeuvre is Curdella Forbes's *From Nation to Diaspora* (2005). Looking at Lamming and Selvon together, Forbes writes:, "we witness in the work of Selvon and Lamming an intuitive recognition of the role of gender as a shaping force in all social relations. Each in his own way exhibits a groping towards an understanding of this construct as it manifests itself in complex ways in West Indian society."[126] Forbes offers an impressive series of theoretically sophisticated analyses of Lamming's and Selvon's renderings of Caribbean immigrants' cultural performances of gender. Yet her word "groping" (whose innuendo may or may not be intended), with its connotation of a tentative and uncertain search for a direction, is very apt here. No matter how generously one reads Lamming's and Selvon's portrayals of what Forbes, in shorthand, calls "West Indian gender" (and Forbes's readings *are* both generous and nuanced), it is clear that both of these male writers take a rather masculinist approach to gender-related issues. In both *The Emigrants* and *The Lonely Londoners*, black Caribbean immigrants' search for a new identity in a new context—their pursuit of a shared West Indian identity, in particular—primarily takes place on men's terms. In *The Emigrants* women rarely, if ever, play prominent roles in any politically informed collective identity formation. Instead, they mostly remain props who help to move the plot along, shed light on men's motives and actions, or offer men passing relief from their loneliness—mainly through sex and short-lasting romance rather than through long-term companionship.

Lamming spoke to David Scott in 2002 about how his and Selvon's roles as husbands in the West Indies related (or rather, did not relate) to their respective decisions to emigrate in 1950. Lamming mentions his then wife appreciatively but does not emphasize joint spousal decision making as a necessary, or even a very relevant, category of thought or action: "Well, I was married and I left a wife, Nina, behind. The thing was how strongly rooted you were in a kind of marital connection. She came a year later and was very helpful. Sam was married, and the wife, Drusilla, followed. But in each of these cases, I would say that the marital bond didn't have the weight of preventing you from doing what you were going to do."[127] It resonates with the male-centered ambience of these remarks that while *The Emigrants'* male characters do not usually force women to obey their decisions, they do not include them in decision-making processes either. Rather, in this novel the men act as they will and then passively observe whether the women play along or not. Occasionally, a male character uses either physical or psychological force to coerce a woman into submission.[128]

The Guadeloupe section that opens *The Emigrants* sets the tone for the rest of Lamming's treatment of women in the novel. In the port area of Guadeloupe and then again on the ship's deck, Collis/the narrator encounters a Trinidadian fellow passenger named Queenie, a beautiful, optimistic "queenie" from a Caribbean colony on her way to the heart of the king's/queen's Empire. Upon noticing her sensual beauty, Collis mentally reduces the young woman to a mere body/object much in the same way that Camus's Meursault solely views Marie as a source of physical pleasure in *The Stranger*: "This was the limit of my interest . . . : this attraction to the body. I saw it now as an object with its own secret resources that reduced all interest to a sheer delight in the presence of the object."[129] Later, Collis further cherishes the image of this "object" in his mind and retrieves it from his memory in eroticized, naked form.[130] Collis's erotic fantasy, representing the anticipation of an imagined fulfillment, powerfully contrasts with the various tropes of death embedded in the Guadeloupe scene: Good Friday, with its evocation of the crucifixion of Christ; the lifeless stuffed birds at a local museum; two men, accused of high treason, being sent to France for trial and likely execution; and troops being shipped to war. Against the backdrop of these impressionistically narrated reminders of death (symbolic of the emigrant's fear that some grave disappointment might await him at the destination and terminate his projected existence there), Collis's erotic daydream of Queenie makes him feel vigorous and revitalizes his optimism about the new life waiting for him in England. However, he achieves this hopefulness by casually objectifying a female body for his own pleasure—albeit, in this case, in the realm of the imagination only.

At times, *The Emigrants* counters its own male-centeredness and, in so doing, paves the way for the more visible role that the parallelism between racial and sexual objectification plays in *The Natives of My Person*. In particular, Collis eventually recognizes the fundamental similarity between the racializing gaze and the sexualizing gaze.[131] The scene contains a nascent, even if undeveloped, realization by Collis/the narrator that treating women as mere objects under the male gaze will not be beneficial for black Caribbean community formation in Britain in the long term. Moreover, if in *The Emigrants* any mode of immigrant existence equals happiness, the locus of such contentment is Tornado and Lilian's relationship. Their commitment to each other outlasts the challenges of the immigration process. They also actively keep in touch with the rest of the black Caribbean diasporans in London, for whom the couple's apartment functions as a safe space, a friendly and hospitable meeting place. The site of Lilian and Tornado's family formation thus serves as an important site for West Indian community formation as well. Finally, the open ending of *The Emigrants* briefly juxtaposes Lilian and Tornado's happiness with the Governor's failed marriage and with the abortion performed on a minor character named Julie. Both the Governor's physical assault on his wife and the dangerous backroom abortion speak to Lamming's emerging interest in bringing gender to bear on his portrayal of black Caribbean social formations in England.

Nevertheless, the roles of the female characters in *The Emigrants* are mostly passive. The women and their life events mainly serve to contribute to the novel's metaphorical framework. *The Emigrants* opens by portraying the lively radiance of the women of the port of Guadeloupe who collectively serve as an in-transit anticipatory sign of the promise of a new existence for Collis/the narrator, just as his private erotic fantasy of Queenie does. In a similar vein, toward the novel's end, Julie's abortion symbolizes the difficulty that the black Caribbean community experiences in creating and nurturing a new life in London. In contrast with Lamming's treatment of women either as symbolic elements or as supporting actors in a collective drama, Phillips, in *The Final Passage*, places a female migrant at the heart of his narrative of the *Windrush* era and the black Caribbean diasporic experience in Britain.

Gender in *The Final Passage*: The Marginalized Female Migrant in the Mother Country

The Final Passage, as its title indicates, retrospectively casts the postwar Caribbean exodus to Britain as a sequel to the Middle Passage, or as the final arm closing a tragic oceanic triangle. The contrast with the diasporic migrants' expectation of the mother country welcoming them with open arms could not be starker. Attentive to the interplay of race, class, and gender (and to the complex convergence of race, gender, and class oppression) in the formation of the African Caribbean diaspora in Britain, *The Final Passage* narrates the story of the transatlantic migration of a West Indian couple and their little son with a particular emphasis on the genealogy of the tragic marginalization of the young wife and mother—a black diasporic woman and colonial subject—in postwar London. Phillips's focus on a female protagonist is an important addition to the tradition launched by *The Emigrants* and *The Lonely Londoners*, which primarily portrayed single men migrating to England. In 2008, Tina Campt and Deborah A. Thomas expressed their fully justified concern that existing "scholarship on the African Diaspora in both the humanities and social sciences" tends to "privilege the mobility of masculine subjects as the primary agents of diasporic formation, and perpetuate a more general masculinism in the conceptualization of a diasporic community."[132] As early as 1985, *The Final Passage*, through its focus on a woman's migratory experience, offered a critique of such masculinism in the realm of post-*Windrush* fiction—a critique that is credible and powerful despite, or perhaps precisely because of, the novel's quiet and tragic bleakness. As a child and a teenager, Phillips, the eldest son of two St. Kittitian *Windrush*-era migrants to England, witnessed the heavy toll that the migration and its aftermath, including his parents' divorce when he was eight, took on his mother.[133] His first novel uses muted tones, minimalist techniques, and carefully weighed, economical prose to give expression to the profound disillusionment experienced by the fictional female protagonist in an unwelcoming London.

The Final Passage consists of five sections: first, "The End," depicting the day when the protagonist, Leila Preston, her husband, Michael, and their baby boy, Calvin, leave for England; second, "Home," which portrays the young couple's pre-emigration life on their home island (modeled after Phillips's native St. Kitts, though never identified explicitly); third, the fourteen-page "England," which anticipates the emigration's disappointing outcome for Leila; fourth, "The Passage," which describes the final moments of the Prestons' two-week journey across the sea and their first days and months in England; and, fifth, the "Winter" of Leila's discontent. Her mother dies in London, and, even more disastrously, Michael abandons his wife and son. At the novel's end, the twenty-year-old Leila—pregnant with Michael's second child and unable to keep a job due to health problems triggered, in no small part, by her psychological and financial distress—lives with Calvin in a barely habitable London apartment in the winter of 1959–60, dreaming of a return trip to the Caribbean that she cannot afford.

In "A Search for Caribbean Masculinities" (2013), the US-based novelist Patricia Powell describes her entire literary oeuvre as a project focusing on gender, in response to the gender inequality that she witnessed while growing up in Jamaica—that is, sexual politics based on full-blown patriarchy: "In the Jamaica where I grew up, men had all the power. . . . My male cousins, my uncles, my brothers, could do anything they wanted. They could make independent decisions about their lives. . . . The women around me gave everything to their men, they gave their bodies, their love, their support, their loyalty, and oh how they suffered in love."[134] Phillips, likewise, has been outspoken in his criticism of traditional gender roles in Caribbean societies. He commented on the oppressive male dominance characterizing Caribbean public and political life in a 1986 interview with Kay Saunders as follows:

> [I]t seems to me that there are curious kinds of contradictions in the Caribbean. Women seem to have much more of a responsible role in the family—perhaps because men are far more irresponsible. Women have a far more central role in the bringing up of children and being responsible for the running of the place on a day-to-day basis. But their actual access to power—political power, social power—is as limited as it was in prewar Britain. Their role in the larger Caribbean society seems to be pretty . . . minimal. They don't have any access to real power, to making structures in those societies.[135]

Shortly before making these highly critical remarks, Phillips had, befittingly, cast Leila Preston in the role of a woman tragically bound up in a fixed, sexist division of labor. In *The Final Passage*, Leila's sole task is to be a wife, a mother, and a nurturer in the domestic sphere, without a voice in public life. Even her experience of the Atlantic crossing is dominated by her family-centered role as a caregiver,[136] and she therefore misses the opportunity to participate in the kinds of politically and historically inspired conversations about Africa, Empire, and the colonial Caribbean that Lamming's male migrants enjoy en route to England in *The Emigrants*. The only exception, the single "loud, fast, furious," and less than well-informed conversation by four men that Leila overhears on the deck when the ship has already reached its destination and is about to dock, changes little in this respect.[137]

In London, the house that Leila secures for the family is a sad sight that grimly reflects the Prestons' marginal socioeconomic status in the heart of Empire.[138] However, what for Michael offsets this dismal housing situation is his access to London's black Caribbean immigrant community, which is much more readily available to him than it is to Leila, who, in the absence of any arrangements for child care, is tied to the domestic sphere. During their arguments, Michael, ironically enough, cruelly casts Leila as a failed immigrant,[139] due to her single-minded dedication to family and home. Phillips consistently portrays Michael as a demanding and self-centered man who wields patriarchal authority over his wife and, without fail, puts his own needs first.

In the 1986 interview with Saunders, Phillips mentioned Michael's "irresponsibility born of . . . an aimlessness of the life which has been bestowed on him by colonialism."[140] Yet he sternly refused to lay all the blame for what he called "a long tradition of wilful or unwilful neglect or absence on the part of [West Indian] men" on the Caribbean's colonial past.[141] His response to Saunders's mention of "the experience of slavery when family life was unstable"[142] was blunt: "[T]hat's a familiar argument, but I really don't buy it. That was 150 years ago. It is a convenient cop-out for a lot of blokes, 'Well, we've not actually owned our children.'"[143] Phillips, in other words, views the colonial and slavery past as an inevitably influential, but not a predetermining, factor in shaping contemporary Caribbean family life and gender roles—a legacy but not a destiny. In keeping with this vision, in *The Final Passage* the minor character Bradeth, Michael's closest friend and his more caring and responsible peer on their home island, serves as a foil to Michael's patriarchal narcissism.[144] Bradeth's presence in the narrative complicates what would otherwise be a too simplistic causal explanation pointing to the slavery past as a factor exonerating Caribbean men from responsibility for contemporary gender inequality in the region.

The Final Passage also ties its treatment of gender to the gendered motif of the mother country. When the SS *Winston Churchill* starts its journey to England with the Prestons on board, Leila "listened to the useless tune of the sea and thought of her mother."[145] As the narrative progresses, this phrase, with its focus on the "mother," gains both literal and symbolic significance. Phillips juxtaposes the mother country's ideological, colonially based deceptive maternalism with three similarly gendered (her)stories: those of Leila, her mother, and, in between the lines, the island.

Perhaps most importantly, Leila's life in many respects symbolizes the condition of her home island: weakened by the forcefully naturalized rule of others over her, she no longer knows how to take control of herself. Her life therefore primarily consists of passive waiting and reacting both before and after emigration. Leila's disillusioned and harsh mother, in turn (who remains nameless for the reader, as befits her partially symbolic role in the narrative), is a complex composite *both* of the island *and* of various residues or reproductions of the Empire/mother country, the imperial usurper in maternal disguise. She represents the island, a space exploited by colonizers, insofar as she is portrayed as a victim of patriarchally "justified" sexual exploitation. The novel reveals that as a child she was repeatedly victimized by an incestuous great-uncle.[146] As an adult, she is so determined to protect her daughter from exploitative sexual contact that her overly strict parenting often in itself amounts to emotional and physical abuse.[147] The incestuous sex that was forced on her at an early age also rendered her incapable of forming a loving and trusting relationship with any man.[148] In her later sexual encounters, even as a consenting adult she "always felt used."[149] After giving birth to Leila, however, she learns to exploit her exploiters: she successfully blackmails three white men with whom she has had casual sex, accusing each of them of paternity and threatening each with a lawsuit.[150] The money that she receives from the men helps her and her daughter financially, but it cannot prevent her from becoming an emotionally hardened individual who knows little about affectionate and compassionate parenting.

Leila's mother embodies both resistance and accommodation, both a yearning for freedom and a fatal dependence on the imperial parent—the mother country that eventually consumes her. She despises white men and their exploitative behaviors, but she nevertheless seems to harbor a romanticized view of a welcoming Britain where whites are different from the irresponsible and sexually predatory tourists whom she has encountered in the Caribbean. Her actions suggest that she believes in the idealized notion of Britain as a caring "mother" to her colonial "children"—or, at the very least, in the concept of Britain as a safe haven for colonial subjects. When she learns that her chronic respiratory problems are so serious as to be potentially fatal, she clandestinely leaves the island and travels to England to be cured.[151] However, England drains her of what little vitality she still possesses upon entering the country. Contrary to her expectations, she literally cannot breathe properly at the heart of Empire but, instead, ends up producing "high asthmatic whistle[s]" in a hospital bed in London.[152] She dies, within months of arrival, at age forty-one.[153] In *The Final Passage*, the mother country disappoints her colonial "children" and consumes their vital energies instead of fulfilling her parental promise.

On the level of plot, it is Leila's mother's departure for the mother country that prompts Leila, Michael, and Calvin to follow her.[154] Despite all the complexities of the mother-daughter relationship, Leila, symbolically embodying the complex and internally conflicted anxieties and ambiguities of the colonized, does not know how to establish a life for herself on the island once the domineering mother is gone. Unable to let go of her maternal protector/abuser, Leila follows her to England in hopes of establishing a new and fresh relationship with her there. However, when she arrives in London, her mother is already so ill that she is, much of the time, beyond reach.[155] Nor does the mother, in her more lucid moments, express any desire to reconsider the mother-daughter relationship's nature, potential, or power structure.[156] In this respect, in particular, she resembles the mother country. The mother's journey to England turns out to be her final passage, and the narrative's open ending suggests that Leila's fate may, tragically, be the same: Leila, too, seems incapable of either breathing in the heart of Empire or leaving the suffocating environment. A return trip to the home island would require funds, but after her mother's death Leila's only inheritance is the mother country, a society in which she has no place.[157] Although Leila's decision to emigrate initially seemed to suggest active agency, in the final analysis she remains captive, just as her mother did.

The epigraph to *The Final Passage* is, as noted, a quotation from T. S. Eliot's "Little Gidding": "A people without history / Is not redeemed from time.... / History is now and England."[158] In Phillips's treatment, this reference to time and history on the one hand alludes to the condition of colonial subjects, who, in the white imperial imaginary, did not have histories of their own apart from their situatedness within the history of Empire.[159] On the other hand, the heavy and stagnant timelessness conveyed by the high-modernist epigraph anticipates Leila's final predicament in London. Phillips is powerfully aware of his modernist predecessors, white as well as black, Eliot as well as Lamming. His evocation of Eliot, deploying Prospero's language to point to the tragic consequences of British imperialism, for its part affirms Gikandi's claim, in *Writing in Limbo* (1992), that "Caribbean writers and scholars exhibit extreme anxiety and ambivalence toward the beginnings of modernity and modernism."[160] While the circular style of *The Final Passage* may have been influenced by modern*ism*, the content of Phillips's narrative critiques the colonialist projects of post-Columbian modern*ity*,[161] the oppressive legacies of which are very much alive in the daily struggles of his characters, particularly Leila.

In the course of *The Final Passage*, Leila's reflection on leaving her native island, placed early in the novel, takes on a tragic quality that firmly situates her fate within an African diasporic framework: "Against the deep blue-black sky the African breadfruit trees towered, sunburnt in the daylight, charcoal-black at night, proud of their history. They were brought here to feed the slaves."[162] Leila, who is about to board the emigrant ship, here realizes that the breadfruit trees, which in her eyes represent continuity with black Caribbean diasporans' African past, "would not feed Calvin."[163] At the narrative's end, it seems unlikely that they will ever again feed her either, even though she dreams of returning to the Caribbean. She and her Anglophone diasporic peers will have to rethink the meaning and significance of the African dimension of their African Caribbean identities in what for them is both the mother country (that is, the supposedly welcoming and culturally familiar "old England") and an environment where they are treated as racial Others. However, in this novel, whose timeline does not extend beyond 1960, Phillips refrains from depicting cultural processes that anticipate affirmative black British identity-building. Instead, the novel closes by emphasizing that while Leila's move to England may not have been literally forced, her condition both on her home island and in England ultimately reflects the power dynamics of the imperial and patriarchal order that leaves the black woman as a diasporic and colonial subject in a socially and politically undefined liminal space—or rather, in an absolute cul-de-sac.

Black Caribbean Family Formation as Black British Identity Formation in Levy's *Small Island*

The Final Passage, a literary representation of a diasporic formation in England, addresses sexual politics by focusing on disparities between the gendered immigrant experiences of Leila and her husband. For Michael, the new life in London means freedom, particularly freedom from family responsibilities, and a real or perceived opportunity for upward social mobility.[164] For Leila, by contrast, it quickly comes to signify a literal and metaphorical confinement, including a second, unplanned pregnancy and low and stagnant socioeconomic status. Andrea Levy's fourth novel, *Small Island*, also attends to migration as a gendered experience, but its representation of the theme of black Caribbean family formation on British soil—which, in Levy's treatment, grows into a metaphor for black British identity formation—is considerably more optimistic and gender-egalitarian than is the case in *The Final Passage*. *Small Island* features the Jamaican newlyweds Hortense Joseph, a strong female migrant who arrives in England as an educated woman (a licensed schoolteacher in Jamaica), and her husband, Gilbert Joseph, an ex-RAF volunteer. Hortense follows Gilbert to London when he, after a brief postwar stay back in Jamaica—which, after his RAF experience, seems a "small island" to him[165]—returns to England in 1948 to live and work there. Levy's relatively extensive description of Gilbert's time in the RAF adds a new dimension to the novelistic tradition discussed in this chapter, as does her depiction of Hortense: in contrast to Phillips's tragic portrait of Leila in *The Final Passage*, Levy's narrative of Hortense's immigration celebrates black female strength and resourcefulness, even though Levy, too, portrays some of the initial adjustment difficulties rather realistically.

My discussion touches on both of these aspects of *Small Island*, focusing on Gilbert's RAF experience more than on the details of Levy's characterization of Hortense. However, the novel's ultimate emphasis is, I repeat, on Hortense and Gilbert's shared family formation, which comes to symbolize the emergence of a new and self-confident black Britishness and a determined faith in a black future on British soil. Both *The Emigrants* and *The Final Passage* in many ways build on a tragic diasporic Middle Passage sensibility, but in Levy's treatment the story of the postwar black Caribbean diaspora in Britain develops into a narrative of active diaspora-making that highlights black agency. The tragedy of the forced removal from Africa to the New World, the *first* of African Caribbean diasporans' "two acts of displacement" (to summon Michelle Ann Stephens's phrase again),[166] remains in the background in this novel. There is no doubt that Levy's oeuvre, when taken as a whole—including *The Long Song*, a novel about the final phase and aftermath of Jamaican chattel slavery, with its memorable scene in which members of a Jamaican Baptist congregation bury a coffin representing slavery on the midnight of July 31, 1838[167]—demonstrates her sophisticated vision of the African dimension of the African Caribbean diasporic experience. *Small Island*, however, exemplifying Levy's strong interest in the mid- and late-twentieth-century Jamaica-England axis, willfully focuses on the *second* of said "two acts of displacement."

Even though *Small Island* depicts a dislocation, it reinforces Khachig Tölölyan's argument that it would be misguided to assume that, just "because diasporas develop as a result of displacement" (and Tölölyan includes "secondary" migrations in diasporic displacement), "attachment to place does not have and could not have a major role in their contemporary self-conception and practice."[168] In *Small Island*, the "attachment to place" that Tölölyan urges diaspora scholars to examine focuses on the *Windrush* era's black Caribbean migrants' claim to "Englishness." Their claim to national belonging, initially intertwined with imperial belonging, takes center stage in Levy's novel. *Small Island*, in other words, challenges what Claire Alexander and Caroline Knowles aptly (and critically) term "primordialist associations between race and place-as-nation"[169]—here, the racially exclusive identification of Britishness with white Englishness. In a 1997 interview, Levy, a Londoner born and bred, exclaimed to Maya Jaggi: "If Englishness doesn't define me, redefine Englishness."[170] In *Small Island*, this politically decisive and emotionally confident disposition is inscribed in the way in which Hortense and Gilbert, after their initial culture shock, start to build a new life as a family in postwar England. At the same time, Levy's narrative implicitly acknowledges that the situation of the historical Hortenses and Gilberts was very different from that of the black Britons of the early 2000s. The latter, including Levy's generation, are able to build on the demanding and complex processes of diasporic (African Caribbean) and national ([black] British) identity formation that the first-generation West Indian immigrants went through.

Published six years after Britain's celebration of the fiftieth anniversary of the *Windrush* moment, *Small Island*, written in an entertaining mode that appeals to wide audiences, enjoys unprecedented critical and commercial success among the novels belonging to the literary tradition initiated by *The Emigrants*. In its year of publication, *Small Island* won the Orange Prize for Fiction, the Whitbread Novel Award, and the Whitbread Book of the Year Award. In 2005, it received the Commonwealth Writers' Prize and the Orange Prize for Fiction's "Best of the Best" Award. In 2007, when Britain and the Commonwealth celebrated the bicentennial of the closing of the Atlantic slave trade, a yearlong event titled "*Small Island* Read" became the largest community-based reading initiative ever organized in Britain. As Anouk Lang summarizes, during "*Small Island* Read" fifty thousand copies of the novel and eighty thousand readers' guides were distributed across Britain (Liverpool, Bristol, Glasgow, and Hull being the focal points of this initiative), at least a hundred stories about the project were published by the British press, and over a hundred events relating to the initiative took place.[171] The two-episode TV adaptation of the novel, which first aired in the United Kingdom in December 2009, won several British awards and an international Emmy award in the United States in 2010.

In addition to reimagining the immediate aftermath of the *Windrush* moment, Levy's enthusiastically received novel also participates in the inclusion of Jamaican RAF volunteers' stories in the history of World War II and postwar Britain. Her choice to write about West Indian RAF experiences resonates with Carby's previously quoted comment that it is not the *Windrush* moment alone, but also the preceding wartime presence of black civilian and military personnel, that initiated a new phase in the formation of the black Caribbean diaspora in Britain.[172] In the realm of nonfiction, there are two particularly important participants in the cultural project of inscribing the West Indian contribution to the war effort in Britain's national memory. One is E. Martin Noble's 1984 autobiography, *Jamaica Airman: A Black Airman in Britain, 1943 and After*, which succinctly expresses its gist in its opening sentence: "This is the story of my life as an airman, and the rejection I met as a civilian once the war was over."[173] The other is Robert N. Murray's 1996 *Lest We Forget: The Experiences of World War II Westindian Ex-Service Personnel*, based on oral histories. More recently, general interest books have also been written on the topic, including chapters 11–15 of Humphrey Metzgen and John Graham's *Caribbean Wars Untold: A Salute to the British West Indies* (2007). In novels depicting the West Indian experience in Britain in the 1940s and beyond, the black presence in the RAF in wartime has been acknowledged since this literary tradition's inception in *The Emigrants*, in which two male characters, the Governor and Tornado, are former RAF volunteers. However, while Lamming's references to these two characters' service remain brief (making plain, nonetheless, that after the war neither man any longer views England as a promised land of milk and honey), Levy's narrative, alternating between 1948 and "Before," describes Gilbert's wartime service extensively. Levy's characters, in fact, include both ground personnel and an airman: Gilbert signs up for the RAF in the hopes of becoming an air crewman but ends up serving as ground crew in England,[174] whereas Michael Roberts, Hortense's remote cousin and the object of her unrequited love back in Jamaica, indeed becomes an airman, a rear gunner. Michael is shot down in France and listed as missing, but, unbeknownst to the authorities and his family, he survives.

After the war, he spends some time in England and then heads for Canada in 1948, in order to start a new life there.

Even though Levy's characters are fictional, *Small Island*—largely focusing on a black Jamaican couple settling in England after World War II—is, nevertheless, loosely based on the lives of her mother and father. In a 2004 interview conducted by Bonnie Greer, Levy discussed the role that "race" played in her parents' lives after their migration:

> My parents came from a class in Jamaica called "the coloured class." There are white Jamaicans, black Jamaicans and coloured Jamaicans. My parents' skin was light. They were mixed race, effectively. They came to Britain with a kind of notion that pigmentation represented class. They didn't necessarily have more money or education, but because they were somehow closer to being white, this was seen as a badge of pride. . . . My parents arrived here and were surprised to discover that they were considered black. They thought that people would look at them as white. That sounds very funny now. . . . I was growing up knowing that things were so completely different. I didn't have any subtleties of shade. If someone didn't want to be my friend because I was black, that was it.[175]

Similarly, Hortense and Gilbert are forced to rethink the meaning and significance of both "race" and their British subjecthood/Englishness once they leave Jamaica. Gilbert begins the process of consciously considering the intersectionality of the two while serving in the RAF. In fact, his service initially leads him to encounter race and racism in a US context, because he is transported to England via a military camp in Virginia.[176] Such positive aspects of the American holding-camp experience as the comfortable facilities and the excellent food are, as Alan Rice notes, quickly overshadowed by "Gilbert's first encounter with Jim Crow."[177] That is, Gilbert initially envisions the United States as a land of plenty but soon comes to associate it with blatant antiblack racism and legally sanctioned segregation. An American officer makes the West Indian trainees aware of the realities of segregation by crudely pointing out to them their extraordinary status, grounded in British military law: "You will mix with white service personnel. Have you boys any idea how lucky you are? You will not be treated as negroes!"[178] Reflecting back on this experience, Gilbert thinks to himself sarcastically, "I soon realised we were lucky the American military authorities did not let us off the camp in Virginia. We

West Indians, thinking ourselves as good as any man, would have wandered unaware, greeting white people who would have swung us from the nearest tree for merely passing the time of day with them."[179]

Gilbert is relieved to leave the United States for England. However, his encounter with "Mother," whose embrace he is eager to experience and whom he expects to be like "a beautiful woman—refined, mannerly and cultured,"[180] results in one disillusionment after another. Gilbert and his peers are completely unprepared for what they encounter, namely, a country ravaged and impoverished by war:

> Let me ask you to imagine this. Living far from you is a beloved relation whom you have never met. Yet this relation is so dear a kin she is known as Mother.... Your daddy tells you, "Mother thinks of you as her children; like the Lord above she takes care of you from afar."... Then one day you hear Mother calling—she is troubled, she need your help. Your mummy, your daddy say go. Leave home, leave familiar, leave love.... The filthy tramp that eventually greets you is she. Ragged, old and dusty as the long dead. Mother has a blackened eye, bad breath and one lone tooth that waves in her head when she speaks. Can this be that fabled relation you heard so much of?[181]

What for Gilbert represents the ultimate affront is "Mother's" failure to recognize her colonial sons: "She offers you no comfort after your journey. No smile. No welcome. Yet she looks down at you through lordly eyes and says, 'Who the bloody hell are you?'"[182] Gilbert, indeed, discovers that imperial cartography looks very different when viewed from the "center" instead of from the "periphery." In England, he finds himself having to repeatedly explain where Jamaica is located on the world map, although he and the other "colony troops" seem to know everything that there is to know about Britain's geography and political infrastructure.[183] For him and the novel's other black Caribbean RAF volunteers, the general wartime hardship on British soil is exacerbated by white Britons' ignorance about Empire's colonies and colonial subjects and by the racism accompanying this ignorance.

Perhaps most offensively, the white Englishmen whom Gilbert encounters are unaware, and reluctant to believe, that West Indians could identify strongly with the mother country, feel an intense loyalty to her, and voluntarily rush to "Mother's" assistance in a time of war—indeed, be willing to sacrifice their lives for her. When a middle-aged white man asks Gilbert, "Why would you leave a nice sunny place to come here if you didn't have to?"[184]

Gilbert's response, "To fight for my country, sir," prompts his interlocutor to scoff at the black volunteer's belief that he is someone who belongs: "Humph. Your country?"[185] Although this scene is set in wartime, the white Englishman's reply points to what Carby, as noted, has termed the "separate spheres of nationality" that emerged in the aftermath of the 1948 British Nationality Act.[186] The Act did not, in daily life, alter the prevailing notion that the Britishness of a colonial subject of color was something considerably less full, true, and authentic than the Britishness of a white Briton—of a white Englishman, in particular. In *Small Island*, few of the novel's white Britons believe that they have anything significant in common with colonial subjects of color. Because this absence of a sense of global community based on shared British subjecthood challenges everything that Gilbert has ever learned about "Mother," Jamaica is not the only island that seems small in this novel. In Levy's treatment, the British Isles, too—desperately clinging to white Britishness as the cornerstone of British identity—fall short of their purported greatness.[187]

Having witnessed this "smallness" of Great Britain during the war, Gilbert is already a seasoned cultural negotiator when he returns to England in 1948, and even more so by the time Hortense first sets foot there later that year. She comes from a modest rural background and has suffered both romantic and professional disappointments during her young life, but has had just enough support to stay determinedly forward-looking, goal-oriented, and upwardly mobile. When she arrives in England, she eagerly anticipates the mother country's warm embrace, just as Gilbert had done during the war. However, she finds herself in a London where both the economy and the people are still struggling to recover from the devastation caused by the war and where black immigrants encounter racial prejudice on a daily basis. Hortense experiences her initial acclimatization to the British environment primarily in a domestic setting, through her interactions with Queenie Bligh, her and Gilbert's white landlady.

Levy, indeed, weaves her narrative of Gilbert and Hortense together with the story of a white couple based in London—namely, Bernard Bligh, a bank clerk who volunteers for the RAF and does not return from the war's Asian theater until 1948, and, more centrally to the novel's plot, his wife, Queenie, a butcher's daughter from Yorkshire turned Londoner who, during her husband's prolonged absence, supports herself by taking in West Indian tenants. Queenie's name can, as Cynthia James notes, be read as an intertextual nod to Lamming's black Queenie in *The Emigrants*.[188] Moreover, as James also observes, the name is part of Levy's pervasive project of parodying Empire.[189]

Levy launches her parodic project as early as the prologue, which includes a flashback to the young Queenie's excitement at the British Empire Exhibition at Wembley, where her working-class father tells his little white daughter of Empire that she has "the whole world at [her] feet."[190] In the novel's present, the narrative accomplishes much of its parody of Empire through comic scenes in which black and white characters (Hortense and Queenie, in particular) fail to understand each other for reasons related to either language use or cultural differences, or both.[191] However, this comedy has somber undertones: what is ultimately at stake is how Levy's black and white characters respond to ideologies supporting Empire and its views on race, class, and gender.

By joining the fates of the Josephs and the Blighs, *Small Island*, while exploring the possibilities of interracial friendships and romantic liaisons, points to the severely limited scope of such relationships in late 1940s Britain.[192] Toward the novel's end, Queenie gives birth to a biracial baby boy. The baby's father is a former Jamaican airman who has left England for Canada, namely, Michael Roberts, Hortense's distant relative and first love, believed by his family and the authorities to have died in the war. (Levy's readers discover this connection, but her characters do not.)[193] After the infant is born, Queenie, in a stunning turn of the plot, asks the Josephs to adopt him.[194] Though initially too shocked to respond, Hortense and Gilbert, reluctant to leave the black child where he is not wanted, ultimately agree to become the baby's parents.[195] However, Queenie's request seems to sever any friendship that has formed between the white woman and the black couple. Although she admits that she does not have the "guts" or the "spine" to raise a "coloured" child,[196] she cannot bring herself to acknowledge that this failure of nerve is, at least in part, grounded in prejudice. This evasion demonstrates that although Queenie is much more open-minded than most of her white peers, she has nevertheless internalized the race-thinking of Empire's "center" to a greater extent than she is willing to admit.

Small Island reveals Queenie's shortcomings, but it also makes an effort to understand the genealogy of her choice. (The 2009 television adaptation of the book goes further in the latter direction than the novel does.) In 2004, Levy usefully summarized her rationale for writing the book: "In the end, the whole process is about trying to understand. For instance, I just wanted to understand Bernard and Queenie. I want to understand why my parents came to this country, and who they were back in that country. I'm still on that quest."[197] Reflective of Levy's effort to "understand" Queenie as part of this "quest" for a comprehensive understanding of race relations in postwar Britain, the narrative indicates that Queenie is genuinely afraid that the white environment's racist pressure might gradually wear her and Bernard down and make them inadequate parents of a biracial child. Queenie has also read a newspaper article suggesting that all mixed-raced babies born in Britain after the war might be sent to live in America.[198] This suggestion seems absurd now, but at the time such a program was indeed publicly debated, particularly with respect to babies fathered by African American GIs.[199] Queenie has learned to like and trust the Josephs, and she wants her child to be raised by a reliable couple who will take good care of him. Even so, the sociocultural implications of her request are profoundly disturbing. The young white mother's choice to give her biracial baby up for adoption reveals her complete lack of faith both in the capacity of her community to become more accepting of diversity and in her own capacity to act as a catalyst for such change.

However, what matters most in the open-ended conclusion of *Small Island* is that Hortense and Gilbert's decision to adopt Queenie's baby represents their willingness to work for a new black life—or, more metaphorically, for a new black way of life on British soil. While Sofía Muños-Valdivieso acknowledges that Levy uses "metaphors of belonging" (the house as a nation, the mother country as the alleged protector of her colonial children, and the Wordsworthian daffodils as a symbol of "imperial control"),[200] she argues that "Levy does not resort to [them] frequently" in this novel.[201] What she fails to mention is that in Levy's celebratory treatment, the Josephs' family formation serves as a metaphor for an early postwar stage of black British identity formation—that is, for the emergence of a new, simultaneously national and diasporic identity that is neither identical with nor completely separate from the Josephs' British-cum-Jamaican self-understanding during their life in the Caribbean.

In Jamaica, Hortense and Gilbert's union was one of convenience, based on utilitarian considerations. They married in haste because the marriage made the migration to England possible for both. Hortense, who had more savings than Gilbert, financed his transatlantic passage on the *Windrush*. She received, in return, the respectable status of married woman that she considered necessary for her success as an immigrant. Levy depicts neither the marriage nor either spouse as picture-perfect. At first, the newlyweds do not, in fact, seem compatible. While the spontaneous and carefree Gilbert is hardly a paragon of responsibility, the overly prim Hortense is a class-conscious twentieth-century Victorian woman preoccupied with manners and mores. She initially seems a caricature of exaggerated propriety who lacks the creative flexibility and adaptability that any immigrant needs. However, after a difficult start, Hortense and Gilbert bond and find a way forward. During the brief time span that constitutes the novel's present, their marriage of convenience develops into a solid union, and their family formation culminates in their adoption of Queenie's biracial baby. At the novel's end, the Josephs begin to establish a life as a British family of Caribbean descent in postwar London, representing a transition that has, in real life, made it possible for the next generations of black Britons to lay claim to Englishness/Britishness explicitly and without hesitation.

Conclusion

The previous chapter demonstrated that as Morrison and Phillips depict war and veterans, they at the same time address the complex relationship between diasporic subjectivity and national citizenship by debunking the myth that fighting in one's nation's wars automatically earns the fighter a "passport" to full national belonging. Another way in which literary authors often metaphorically depict the relationship between diasporic and national self-identifications is by portraying black diasporans' family formation in the host country, as this chapter has shown.

John McLeod makes a similar point in observing that "recent postcolonial fiction about diasporic Britain has often focused on the fortunes of children such as Galahad's son [a British-born black infant in Selvon's *The Lonely Londoners*], who find their lives caught up in, and often produced by, the conflicted social terrain of an allegedly multicultural Britain."[202] He also notes that "the figure of the adopted child—born to one set of parents but raised by another—has begun to emerge as a significant personage in such writing."[203] In light of McLeod's observation, the following trajectory, which emerges from the British-based narratives discussed in this and the previous chapter, is noteworthy: at the end of *The Emigrants*, the West Indian woman Julie, who is pregnant with another black immigrant's child, chooses to have an abortion. Her decision symbolizes the novel's Caribbean characters' doubts about whether it is beneficial to continue to live as black diasporans in postwar England, let alone bring a new black generation into existence there. At the conclusion of *The Final Passage*, it seems that Leila's young son and his unborn sibling are likely to face a bleak future as children of an impoverished West Indian immigrant mother whose life is an upward struggle after her husband has abandoned her. However, the ending is left open, and we do not learn anything conclusive (tragic or hopeful) about the two children's future or fate. Toward the end of *Crossing the River*, a white woman, Joyce, is pressured to give up her "brown baby" to the County Council's care, to be put up for adoption by strangers. Yet, despite the tragedy of the severed mother-child connection, we discover that Joyce's son lives and grows up to be a young man. Finally, at the end of *Small Island*, a black Jamaican couple adopts a white woman's biracial baby, planning to raise the child proudly as their own and live as a black family in London. The generational trajectory marked by these novels is, in other words, from the elimination of a new black generation toward an established black Britishness.

True, this trajectory should not be read too simplistically. Adding, for example, Caryl Phillips's *In the Falling Snow* (2009) to the mix complicates matters. In this novel, Keith Gordon, an English-born, middle-aged male protagonist of black Caribbean descent, struggles to understand his elderly father, a first-generation West Indian immigrant, and his own biracial teenage child, a second-generation native son of London. Though actively seeking reconnection, Keith feels profoundly alienated both from the generation of his parents and from that of his son. As if anticipating the rioting of disaffected youth in several English cities and towns in August 2011, *In the Falling Snow* points to a complex cluster of socioeconomic and sociocultural issues that Britain, a former empire still suffering from what Gilroy terms "postcolonial melancholia," has not been able to resolve. Overall, contemporary black Britishness, including the experiences of those new African diasporans who have come to Britain directly from Africa, is a complex, evolving process, not a monolithic whole. Nevertheless, the arc that emerges from the fictional treatment of black or "brown" babies from *The Emigrants* to *Small Island* speaks of a black Britishness that is gradually becoming more settled and recognized in the United Kingdom, while simultaneously remaining powerfully aware of its African and African Caribbean diasporic origins.

While the next chapter includes some references to Britain, the novels discussed in it are mainly set in the Caribbean, the United States, and Canada. My focus will be on ambivalences accompanying black Caribbean diasporans' "returns" to what they have envisioned as their Caribbean "home." As the references to the concept of "return" in my analyses of *Middle Passage* and *The Book of Negroes* in chapters 1 and 2 demonstrated, this concept activates a plethora of complex questions about origins, home, and belonging that are extremely relevant to diaspora studies. The late-twentieth-century settings of the novels examined in the next chapter will further illuminate the ways in which the notion of return invites discussions about the formations of both diasporic and national self-understandings and solidarities. Also, as with the British context addressed in this chapter, the Caribbean diasporic novels discussed in the next chapter depict major differences in the ways in which different generations (Caribbean-born versus Canadian- or US-born) view the diasporic and national aspects of their identities.

5

Roots, Routes, and Returns

Caryl Phillips's, Cecil Foster's,
and Edwidge Danticat's Caribbean Returnees

As Derek Walcott remarks in *Midsummer* (1984), "exiles must make their own maps."[1] One aspect of such exilic mapmaking is the psychological cartography of "return." In diasporic contexts, the concept of return mobilizes a plethora of dilemmas about "origins" and "home," including the question of where each diasporic subject mentally locates his or her home and belonging. Mark Stein has noted that "[r]eturning is related to seeking an earlier state or position, to giving into nostalgia and yearning for home."[2] Even this minimalistic attempt at a definition makes clear that there is nothing simple about "return." My discussions of historical and fictional black diasporans' "returns" to Africa have already reinforced this point. This chapter, in turn, examines three black diasporic novels in which the pivotal points of departure and return are located in the Caribbean: Caryl Phillips's *A State of Independence* (1986), Barbadian Canadian Cecil Foster's *Sleep On, Beloved* (1995), and Haitian American Edwidge Danticat's *Breath, Eyes, Memory* (1994). At first, however, a brief introduction, in the form of an impressionistic vignette into topics addressed by assorted Caribbean diasporic return narratives, is warranted.

When Claude McKay, a literary ancestor to several novelists studied in this book, entered the initial phase of his peripatetic existence by leaving Jamaica for the United States in 1912, he wrote in a farewell poem, "The boy you knew / Will come back home a man: / He means to make you proud of him, / He'll breast the waves and strongly swim / And conquer,—for he can."[3] He renewed this promise in a later poem, written in London in 1920: "I shall return, I shall return again, / To ease my mind of long, long years of pain."[4] Despite these sentiments, McKay never physically traveled back to Jamaica. He returned there only through his writings, particularly through his 1933 novel,

Banana Bottom, and the memoir of his boyhood, *My Green of Hills of Jamaica*, published posthumously in 1979. However, the island that he nostalgically reminisced about in these works was, in Sandra Pouchet Paquet's phrase, "the mythicized Jamaica of his vanished childhood,"[5] a point of departure rather than a place of return.

Adopting a different approach, *Praisesong for the Widow* (1983) by US novelist Paule Marshall, of Barbadian parentage, focuses on a "return" to a place the fictional female protagonist has not previously inhabited or even visited but which, through an unexpected turn of events, nevertheless facilitates her reconnection with her African heritage. In this novel, Avey Johnson—a sixty-four-year-old African American widow whose comfortable middle-class lifestyle has distanced her from her materially humble Harlem origins—visits the Caribbean for the first time and experiences there a semimythical "return" to what the narrative casts as Africanist, communal, and nurturing ur-blackness in which diasporans can participate fully and meaningfully. The events are set in motion when Avey leaves her hometown of White Plains, New York (this place-name being one of the novel's myriad references to the US-imposed "whiteness" of which Avey needs to be "purified"), to board a cruiser heading for the Caribbean. What is intended to be a carefree vacation does not go as planned. As the text's explicit allusion to the Middle Passage suggests,[6] Avey's body seems to "remember" the troubled history of the waters through which the ship is passing. At the symbolic level of the narrative, Avey's physical discomfort in the Caribbean functions as a metaphor for the suppressed existential and spiritual unease of an individual out of touch with her diasporic history and identity. Avey collapses completely in Carriacou, brought to her knees by a severe episode of gastrointestinal distress, vomiting, and diarrhea. The locals unselfishly help the tourist who needs to be cared for like an infant. While convalescing, Avey is symbolically born again: surrounded by African Caribbean culture and community, she spiritually returns to the vision of blackness as communion and caring that her adult life has obscured for her.[7]

A considerably less idealized concept of return is embedded in Marshall's first novel, *Brown Girl, Brownstones* (1959), in which the young female protagonist's father, Deighton, an illegal immigrant to the United States, harbors the dream of an eventual return to Barbados. This initially vague fantasy begins to turn into a plan of action when Deighton inherits a small piece of land on the island. His wife, however, sells the lot in order to channel funds into the family's new life in Brooklyn. The marriage never recovers from this deception. Deighton turns away from his family to another community, the "kingdom" of the Harlem-based black Messiah Father Peace (a character modeled on the historical Father Divine). Ever restless, Deighton eventually boards a ship heading for the island of his birth, but he "either jump[s] or fall[s]"[8] overboard just as the ship is about to reach its destination. Tragically, the distressed returnee drowns just off the Barbadian coast. His lonely death serves as a chilling metaphor for what the novel portrays as the first-generation immigrant's perpetual in-betweenness.[9]

A fundamental sense of in-betweenness is also inscribed in Trinidadian Canadian Dionne Brand's debut novel, *In Another Place, Not Here* (1996), as the book's title indicates. The novel tells the story of the lives and sensual love of two African Caribbean women, Elizete and Verlia. They meet on the unnamed island of their origin (modeled on Grenada) when Verlia returns there after a thirteen-year exile in Toronto, in order to organize the local rural sugar-cane workers and to participate in the island's bourgeoning political revolution. Verlia left the island at age seventeen in search of new tools for self-definition, and immersed herself in the Black Power movement in Toronto. At age thirty, however, she sees the movement gradually wane and travels back to the Caribbean to renew her political vision in her original environment. Elizete, one of the sugarcane workers whom Verlia meets, is a strong and deeply rooted woman, whose life is irreversibly changed by her encounter with the urbanized and educated "[s]ister" who "dream[s] of things we don't dream."[10] The women enter into a passionate relationship, but their love is cut short: Verlia dies in an armed conflict as the United States and its allies from nearby islands violently suppress the revolution that has become central to Verlia's freedom dreams. The novel's final scene poignantly brings together the deep and troubled waters of the Middle Passage, Verlia's relentless search for both autonomy and connection, and an image drawn from the folktale of flying Africans: Verlia runs out of options while fleeing gunfire and is last seen leaping off a cliff into the sea, which becomes her grave. Even before we see Verlia jump, the narrative—structured around a nonlinear, cyclical concept of time—has already allowed us to witness a vicarious "return" to Toronto: after Verlia's disappearance, the disconsolate Elizete travels to the Canadian metropolis in order to gain deeper insight into Verlia's life and her diasporic existence. This aspect of the narrative reveals the newly configured geographies in the landscape of Elizete's soul: while mourning, she begins to search for a more profound understanding of black diasporic connectivity and communion. Through the story of Elizete and Verlia, Brand presents the African diaspora as a historical and empirical reality that must be explored in depth (as Elizete does while living in poverty in Toronto) in examinations of black psychological and political identities.[11]

As even this brief sampling suggests, African Caribbean return narratives tell stories as varied and diverse as the migrant populations and individual migrants they portray. This chapter offers more examples, gleaned from three novels written by Caribbean-born authors. *A State of Independence, Sleep On, Beloved,* and *Breath, Eyes, Memory* all depict the geographical movement of persons and influences between the Caribbean and North America. In *A State of Independence,* the returnee is, admittedly, a Caribbean-born male who has spent most of his adulthood in England. However, although the shadow of the British Empire hovers in the background, neither the novel's present nor any flashbacks that are rendered in detail are set in the British Isles; instead, the United States is a powerful (neo)imperialist presence in the narrative. *Sleep On, Beloved* is set in Jamaica and in Toronto. The events of *Breath, Eyes, Memory,* in turn, take place in Haiti and in the United States, the US locations being Brooklyn, New York, and Providence, Rhode Island. Testing the boundaries of "Anglophone," this chapter indeed includes a discussion of *Breath, Eyes, Memory* because this debut novel of Danticat's—though partly concerned with Haiti, a former colony of France—was written in English and converses with US immigration and socioeconomics.

Although this final chapter is, to some extent, a collage organized around the theme of return, it pursues two threads of analysis and argumentation. First, this chapter examines how these three novels, all of which feature African Caribbean diasporic subjects whose identities draw on dual or multiple geographical and sociocultural locations, utilize the trope of return to depict the protagonists' complex processes of familial, national, and diasporic identity formation. While each main character struggles with a sense of in-betweenness and uprootedness, what varies from protagonist to protagonist is whether, and to what extent, he or she also experiences diasporic identity as a source of insight and strength. The crux of the matter is that regardless of where the protagonists fall on this spectrum, their return trips back to the Caribbean play a crucial role in how they interpret their personal pasts and envision their futures as members of their families, of two nations, of the Caribbean diaspora, and of the African diaspora.

To elaborate, the protagonist of *A State of Independence* is heavily burdened by the existential weight of his migratory existence, which makes him a semi-outsider everywhere. However, through his eventual return to his home island, he—despite the emotional ambivalence characterizing his return experience—gains new insight into the positive potential of his transnational identity position, which the novel, toward its open-ended conclusion, tentatively outlines in terms of positively understood interdependence. Both *Sleep On, Beloved* and *Breath, Eyes, Memory*, in turn—each being highly attentive to the intersectionality of gender, class, race, and generation in the formation of black diasporic experience and identity—sympathetically portray a working-class immigrant woman who is consumed by the hardships dominating her existence first on her home island and then in North America. In both novels, the mother and her 1.5-generation immigrant daughter (who arrives in the receiving society under age eighteen, as the sociologist Rubén G. Rumbaut's definition of "1.5" would have it)[12] experience a serious conflict and falling-out during the daughter's maturation into adulthood in the host country. However, in each case the daughter's return trip to the Caribbean (in Danticat's novel, two trips, in fact) plays a significant role in how she eventually defines and reconciles her multiple identities as a member of her family, as an immigrant, and as an African diasporic subject. Hope lies in the prospect that the life of the daughter and the lives of the generations to follow may contain fewer struggles and more personal, familial, and communal fulfillment than does the tragic existence of the overworked and exploited first-generation immigrant mother. In both novels, as in Levy's *Small Island*, family formation symbolizes the development of black hyphenated identities (here, Caribbean-Canadian and Haitian-American ones) that are simultaneously both nationally and diasporically focused. The formation of such identities speaks to the importance of national belonging and of "attachment to place" (Tölölyan)[13] while at the same time also reflecting the uprootedness, in-betweenness, and multiple affiliations characteristic of a diasporic self-understanding.

The second thread of my analysis concerns the depicted black diasporans' relationship with Africa. All three novels examined in this chapter acknowledge black Caribbean diasporans' historical connection with Africa, albeit only ephemerally. The original African "homeland"—understood as an abstraction, the generalized "home" from which the African forefathers and foremothers were violently uprooted—remains an important part of the protagonists' black Atlantic imaginary, but they do not dream of physically returning to the continent of their ancestors. Their "Africa" is either an identity-related dilemma that they do not quite know how to approach, as is the case in *A State of Independence* (which briefly raises the complicated question of how to memorialize former sites of African slave labor on a sugar island), or a source of spiritual consolation, as is the case in Foster's *Sleep On, Beloved* and in Danticat's *Breath, Eyes, Memory*. For example, the opening chapter of *Sleep On, Beloved* offers a vivid portrait of a Pocomania community (a Jamaican religious group practicing a syncretic, partly African-derived form of spirituality) evoking "Mother Africa"[14] as a source of maternally understood spiritual nurture and solace during their worship services. In *Breath, Eyes, Memory*, the women of Danticat's Haitian and Haitian American Caco family refer to death and the afterlife as going to "Guinea," which is the name of a cemetery in the novel's rural Haitian setting. Even though this name in today's common parlance designates a West African state, in the colonial era the term was frequently used by Europeans to denote the whole of West Africa. The decision of Danticat's Haitian community to call their cemetery "Guinea" therefore points to the syncretic religious hope that, after passing through the last Door of No Return, New World descendants of Africans may finally be reunited with their African ancestors. As these examples demonstrate, in *A State of Independence, Sleep On, Beloved* and *Breath, Eyes, Memory*, Africa is evoked almost subliminally, but it nevertheless remains an object of diasporic longing, ambivalence, and hope.

Phillips's Returning Male Migrant in *A State of Independence*

In a 2005 article on Caryl Phillips's second novel, *A State of Independence*, Elena Machado Sáez discusses one type of Caribbean return narrative by summarizing the Guyanese author and critic A. J. Seymour's 1967 commentary on the representation of the male exile's/migrant's return to the West Indies in Anglophone Caribbean literature.[15] The trajectory that Seymour had discovered was the "negative depiction of the migrant male" in V. S. Naipaul's, George Lamming's, and John Hearne's pre-1967 works.[16] Seymour had, in Sáez's words, concluded that these authors, still writing to resist colonialism, portrayed men who after exile returned to the West Indies "in order to participate in or incite political change, only to emerge at the end of their struggles as tragic failures."[17] Seymour, who wrote during the shift from the colonial to the postcolonial, hoped to see Anglophone Caribbean writers move on to promote what he envisioned as an optimistic aesthetic of nation-building among the newly independent Caribbean nations.[18] Sáez evokes the trajectory identified by Seymour as background and foil to her nuanced discussion of *A State of Independence*. She points out that Phillips does not fit the paradigm of Caribbean "nation-building novelists"[19] envisioned by Seymour because, "[r]ather than conceiving of the postcolonial moment in terms of full independence, Phillips's postcolonial is defined by neocolonial relations of power."[20] Her observation is on the mark. Moreover, J. Dillon Brown's "A State of Interdependence" (2013) adds another twist to the conversation by expressing deep dissatisfaction with interpretations of *A State of Independence* in which "the U.S. slips smoothly into Britain's place as the imperial oppressor, simply taking up where its predecessor left off."[21] Brown urges critics to contest "the conventional critical equation of contemporary US power with its imperial British forerunner"[22] and calls for detailed analyses of Phillips's approach to "the affective, political, economic *nuances* of global U.S. power."[23] In what follows, I will first offer a close reading of the main aspects of the novel's return narrative and will then bring my reading into dialogue with Brown's and Sáez's analyses of it.

Phillips's fictional protagonist Bertram Francis is a returning migrant who left St. Kitts (or, to be exact, the novel's unnamed, partly fictional island, modeled after St. Kitts)[24] in 1963, at age nineteen, to study law in England. He returns there twenty years later in order to witness the moment when the island gains and celebrates its independence. The story of Bertram's homecoming is narrated within two time frames: Phillips recounts Bertram's first three days on the island and also provides glimpses into his youth through flashbacks. Upon return, Bertram reestablishes contact with the islanders who used to be closest to him (his mother, his former friend Jackson Clayton, and his high school sweetheart Patsy Archibald) and participates in the independence celebration. All along, he finds himself torn between his desire to belong in his native Caribbean context and his ambivalence about the potential of his return. The entire novel is an unfolding of this dilemma. Phillips invites the reader to see the perspectives of both the islanders and the returnee and avoids any simplistic closure. In the process, he portrays—and gently ironizes—the complexities of both personal and national aspirations to what is, at times hastily and lightly, termed "independence."

In an essay on St. Kitts's independence celebration, Phillips writes that those expatriate St. Kittitians who returned to the island for the festivities of September 19, 1983, including himself, "were in danger of being undone by the troubling complexity of the word 'home.'"[25] His fictional narrative of Bertram's emotionally complicated reencounter with "his own island"[26] resonates with this remark. The novel reveals, throughout, both Bertram's deep yearning to belong in his native context and his sense that his long stay in England has made him an outsider, almost a "foreign visitor."[27] Bertram tentatively intends to create a new life for himself on the island, but his plans are still in their infancy, and the depth of his commitment to a long-term or permanent stay is unclear. The time that he spent in England, which is never described in any detail, seems to have been a disappointment. For example, he never finished his law degree. Yet the return is no easy task either, because Bertram has to confront both his own alienation from the island's way of life and the island's altered perception of him.

During the lengthy cab ride from the airport to his mother's house, Bertram's senses are overwhelmed by the contrasts that he perceives everywhere around him. He sees the familiar, stunningly beautiful landscapes of a tourist's paradise, but he also finds himself staring at seemingly endless rows of sugarcane, a reminder of the island's slavery past; his gaze registers cane cutters, "who were now free for the day but still walked like condemned men with neither hope nor desire."[28] Similarly, in the first village that the taxi passes by, Bertram notes the "green vegetation which to [his] eyes seemed almost plastic in its perfection,"[29] but the scene also includes a pack of "snarling dogs" and "a mother furiously beat[ing] a piece of rope across the back of a child's legs."[30] Bertram is struck by what to him seems a major contradiction between "the optimism of this imminent independence" and the primal poverty evident all around him.[31] Bertram's political, cultural, and socioeconomic in-between-ness is apparent in his struggle to determine how reliable his first impressions are and whose perceptions and class position he should identify with: "He wondered if he was suffering from those same feelings of liberal guilt that he had always despised in some English people, or if in fact his thoughts did contain astute insights into the current state of the island."[32]

At the core of such possibly "astute insights" is the returnee's desire to examine the island's present in dialogue with its history. The legacy of slavery and colonialism still affects the emerging nation's socioeconomic and political infrastructure in ways that Bertram can discern clearly, benefiting from the perspective provided by his long absence. In the novel's opening, he literally enjoys a bird's-eye view of his native island from the descending airplane—that is, from a critical, detached, and transnationally informed distance. As the plane flies over a clearing, Bertram sees "the crumbling stones and wild fern clusters of a disused sugar mill and broken-down Great House."[33] The islanders' dilemma of how to make the colonial and slavery past a usable past is epitomized, in Bertram's mind, by these still extant "abandoned and crumbling sugar mills, modest, almost discreet reminders of a troubled and bloody history" that no one quite knows what to do with.[34] In *The Final Passage*, Phillips's islanders are out of touch with their collective past because their history has been systematically rendered absent in the colonial historiography that the novel briefly references.[35] In *A State of Independence*, too, Phillips calls attention to the silent archives: soon after his arrival, Bertram learns that the island's library has burned down, as has, tragicomically, its fire station.[36] This dual disaster symbolically emphasizes the difficulty of salvaging local history as recorded and interpreted by the islanders themselves.[37] With the archives gone, what is left are the decaying sugar mills. Embodying the tragic aspects of the history of African diaspora, these artifacts are pregnant with the history of slavery, colonialism, and imperialism. However, they do not, in and of themselves, offer any guidance about how exactly the islanders should embrace their past, present, and future. What these scenes do indicate, though, is that as he watches the islanders prepare themselves for the independence celebration, the returnee Bertram is acutely aware both of the island's African diasporic history and of the complex question of the "uses" of history.

Bertram's conversations with his mother occupy a pivotal position in the novel and illuminate the complexities of their life situations. The grief caused by her younger son's death has consumed the sick and elderly woman, and her sense of having been abandoned by her older son (who, immersed in his new life in England, never seemed to think of the contact's drying up in such active terms) has rendered her harsh, embittered, and unforgiving. She disowns him, evicts him from her house—and, strikingly, tells him to "go back to wherever it is you come from."[38] Defeated on the familial home front, Bertram turns his attention to the island's independence celebration, which, however, becomes yet another source of disillusionment. On the night of the festivities, many islanders' shared attitude toward the "*English* West Indian"[39] is encapsulated in the inhospitable advice offered by Bertram's childhood friend Jackson Clayton, now the new nation's leading politician. Jackson's hostile monologue echoes the rejection previously articulated by Bertram's mother: "I think you should go back to where you came from. . . . England is where you belong now. Things have changed too much for you to have any chance of fitting back, so why you don't return to the place where you know how the things are?"[40] The irony of this pompously delivered and self-righteous discourse is unmistakable because, in Britain, black Caribbeans have had to listen to the racist exhortation to "go back to where you came from" ad nauseam. Phillips has wryly remarked on his own experience as a black Briton: "If I had a pound for every time I've been told to go back to where I came from, I'd be a rich man."[41]

Another irony, also unintended by Jackson, that Phillips embeds in the words of this opportunistic politician is that even though the island may have changed more than Bertram had expected, it has changed substantively less than its Jackson Claytons assume. Bertram sees everywhere signs of the island's purported "independence" being, in effect, treated as a transition from an openly acknowledged political and economic dependence on Britain to an economically and culturally configured reliance on the United States. The personal connections and materialistic ambitions of the island's leading politicians have led them to conclude that living "under the eagle"[42] is better than any other imaginable alternative. Moreover, young people are seized by fantasies inspired by American popular culture, and many of them think of relocation to the United States as their highest goal. As the teenager named Livingstone enthuses to Bertram, "New York Yankees, Washington Redskins, Michael Jackson, you can't want more than that."[43] The irony in the islanders' symbolic performance of their newly forged neocolonial dependence finds its culmination in the novel's final scene: on the evening of the independence day, the island is connected to an American cable TV network that will, it is hoped, abolish the mental and cultural distance between the island and the United States.[44] However, this connection only works in one direction, because the cable is a conduit by which American influences are brought to the island but not a conduit by which the island is brought to the States.

Brown, as noted, not only justifiably critiques interpretations of *A State of Independence* that overlook the important role of the United States in it, but also seeks to complicate readings that simply see the British Empire as being *replaced* by the United States as an imperialist oppressor in the novel. He calls attention to what he, with deliberate ambiguity, characterizes as "the critique or the ambivalent embrace of American power suggested by Phillips in *A State of Independence*."[45] While Brown's article is nuanced and full of rich detail relevant to an analysis of Phillips's current positions, his powerful focus on Phillips's "ambivalent *embrace* of American power" (italics added) is, in my view, most strongly supported by references to statements that Phillips (who, as Brown acknowledges, was not yet based in the United States in 1986) has made long *after* the publication of *A State of Independence*.[46] In the 1986 interview with Kay Saunders quoted in the previous chapter, Phillips reminisced about how he personally witnessed, in St. Kitts, the moment when St. Kitts and Nevis became independent:

> I was there doing a programme for the BBC and I remember standing there when the British flag came down the pole, I was five yards away when the new flag of the nation went up. I just kept thinking to myself:

"This is nonsense because *already the place is completely infused with an American colonialism*; not just because you can pay for stuff with U.S. dollars, but the TV, the music, the food, the cars, etc." It didn't strike me that there was going to be any intervening period where an indigenous Caribbean cultural form of expression could flourish.... It is inevitable that a country the size of St. Kitts and Nevis is going to be dependent upon colonial masters of some sort.... You cannot be independent if you're a country of 35,000 people ... And given the geographic proximity to America, *the outcome was obvious. It was sad—but inevitable.*[47]

This commentary from 1986 hardly seems "ambivalent." Rather, Phillips here laments the new nation's neocolonial dependence on the Western superpower. I agree with Brown that the ambivalences and nuances in Phillips's attitude toward the United States that he finds in Phillips's oeuvre (and which he eloquently and accurately calls a "sense of agonized engagement with both the pleasures and perils of American affiliation")[48] do exist. However, to what extent they are present in *A State of Independence*, an early novel of Phillips, is debatable. It is true that *A State of Independence* was written at a historical moment when it remained to be seen what exact form St. Kitts's dependence on the United States would take and that Phillips therefore left the novel open-ended. From this point of view, Brown's reference to Phillips's ambivalent "critique" of US power,[49] as distinct from a crushingly "straightforward condemnation,"[50] may make sense. It is also true that colonialism and neocolonialism, though very closely related, are two distinct phenomena that cannot always be analyzed using the same tools, as is suggested by Brown's argument that *A State of Independence* is an "uneasy fit within the conventional modes of postcolonial criticism."[51] Nevertheless, it is noteworthy that in the interview with Saunders, Phillips in no way contested Saunders's reference to "[t]he *changing of masters* from Britain to the United States"[52] that took place during the independence celebration of St. Kitts and Nevis. On the contrary, Phillips opened his response to her by stating affirmatively, "Well, that is something I witnessed in 1983."[53]

An important detail embedded in *A State of Independence* that critics tend to overlook in discussing the novel's attitude toward the United States is that the text actually includes two narratives of returning male migrants: in addition to focusing on Bertram, the novel also relates, through flashbacks, the story of the return of Bertram's father from the United States. Through its brief but significant references to the perpetually absent father (a migrant worker gone over to the States before Bertram's younger brother was born),[54] Phillips's narrative sternly counters the notion of the United States as a promised land for Caribbean migrants and, in the process, critiques the neocolonial influence of the "eagle" on the Caribbean. When Bertram was about eight years old, the father whom he had never known returned to his native island terminally ill. His sons never had the opportunity to meet him during his hospitalization, although Bertram eventually attended his funeral. Whatever the complexities and flaws of his personality ("he was a wild type of man"),[55] the father's failure to be in contact with his young sons both during his years of absence and during his final illness here symbolically renders the United States an all-powerful entity capable of completely consuming the black Caribbean migrant, silencing him, and eventually draining him of all vitality.

In my view, *A State of Independence* reflects less ambivalence toward the United States than Brown suggests, but I join him in questioning Sáez's assertion that "the novel's overtly cynical rendition of a migrant subject has led to a general silence regarding this early work, since its cynicism acts to disrupt celebratory diasporic readings of Phillips's fiction."[56] Even though Sáez's observation that *A State of Independence* has only attracted scant critical attention is valid,[57] her claim about Phillips's pervasive "cynicism" in this particular work is, in my opinion, less persuasive. True, Phillips consistently treats the African diaspora as a condition that originated in terror, and he portrays, time and again, diasporic characters whose lives and fates are bleak at best and outright tragic at worst. However, *if* there is a novel in Phillips's oeuvre that cautiously "celebrates" (to borrow Sáez's term) the in-between identity position of a diasporic subject, then that novel, I would argue, is none other than *A State of Independence*. In this work, Phillips explicitly and openly acknowledges the positive potential of a migrant's perspective on his place of "origin." Phillips casts the migrant's unique vantage point as a mixed blessing, but "mixed" indeed contains both positive and negative elements, not just negative ones. The novel's opening, in which Bertram observes his native island from a bird's-eye perspective while sitting in a descending airplane, represents one form of this acknowledgment. The scene emphasizes the breadth and acuity of the returnee's vision, although this clarity is, ironically, challenged as soon as the plane lands and Bertram actually begins to mix with the islanders. A fuller and much more positively pitched form of the same acknowledgement is embedded in a scene featuring Bertram and Livingstone: after Bertram has tired of navigating through the crowd of international attendees of the independence celebration who have congregated in a hotel lobby, Livingstone leads him to the summit of a high hill—symbolically, to a private "summit" or regrouping. The explorer's youthful namesake there utters words to Bertram that almost seem prophetic: "You have your view so don't spoil it by rushing off. Not many people ever get this vantage point."[58]

Most importantly, despite the various emotional complexities characterizing Bertram's "homecoming," his encounter with his former girlfriend Patsy, who, as Ulla Rahbek observes, "allows Bertram to try and make sense of his return,"[59] introduces an optimistic pitch to the narrative's conclusion. The reconciliation of these former lovers suggests, however tentatively, the possibility of a new beginning. Much is left open-ended. For example, we do not find out with certainty whether Bertram is the father of Livingstone, whom Patsy had had out of wedlock and whom Bertram had not known about prior to returning to the island. Both Bertram and Jackson are possible father candidates, although the narrative's dynamics strongly point to Bertram's paternity.[60] No matter how impatient, Phillips's returnee cannot receive answers to all his questions at once. The gaps that have opened up during twenty years will take time to fill. Phillips's deliberate withholding of information from us, the readers, is designed to make us experience some of the confusion and disorientation of the returnee. Nevertheless, despite all the uncertainty and ambiguity permeating the text, the conciliatory and supportive presence of Bertram's lover (and, very likely, of his son)[61] at the novel's end offers a glimmer of hope by evoking a possibility of genuine bonding—here, of a family formation that is rooted in the past and points to the future.[62] On a more symbolic and political level, this sign of hope suggests the possibility of a positively understood interdependence in human communities including and beyond families. Interdependence, as distinct from independence, is here construed as a life-affirming rather than a corrupting or humiliating force, both socially and politically. Phillips himself uses this important term, "interdependence," in the interview with Saunders,[63] and Brown makes it the key concept of his analysis of *A State of Independence*.

One question raised by the novel's acknowledgement of the positive potential of the returnee's unique perspective on his place of "origin" is whether Phillips here adopts the European American high-modernist notion of exile by romantically privileging exilic in-betweenness over unambiguous belonging in a single context.[64] This line of inquiry is important, but such privileging hardly takes place in *A State of Independence*. The narrative acknowledges that Bertram's exilic in-betweenness has sharpened his cross-cultural perception (a skill usually considered advantageous), but it also emphasizes that his liminality is a heavy burden to bear. Tellingly, even though Bertram is "desperate that he should not appear either lost or rootless on his own island,"[65] he finds himself sweating like a tourist under the Caribbean sun.[66] In other words, "lost," Other, and "rootless" is exactly how he feels while trying to make sense of his ambivalence during the handful of days that the novel depicts—days that mark not only the political transition of a new country but also the intense personal turmoil of a returnee. Nevertheless, *A State of Independence*, rather than being cynical throughout, is more optimistic than *The Final Passage* and Phillips's later novels, albeit hopeful in a cautious and provisional mode. As *A State of Independence* closes, we leave Bertram wondering how he can "help his mother."[67] Although this laconically rendered open ending neither provides a detailed plan of action for Bertram nor cements his future in any predictable mold, it does indicate that a tentative sense of reconnection is emerging in the soul of Phillips's returning migrant.

Foster's Jamaican Canadian Returnees in *Sleep On, Beloved*

Cecil Foster's *Sleep On, Beloved* is set in Jamaica (more specifically, St. Ann's Parish and Kingston) and, primarily, in Toronto. In this novel, Foster (b. 1954)—a Barbadian-born journalist and academic who immigrated to Canada in the late 1970s[68]—narrates the lives of two fictional female protagonists, mother and daughter, who are black Jamaican migrants to the Canadian metropolis.[69] While *A State of Independence* is, in its entirety, about a migrant's return, the return narratives of *Sleep On, Beloved*, which describe the separate return trips of the mother and the adult daughter first to Jamaica and then back to Toronto, only cover a tiny portion of the novel's 325 pages. Nevertheless, these narratives play a significant role in Foster's fictionalized account of generational evolution from an African Caribbean identity on Canadian soil toward a black Canadian identity. As Carol Boyce Davies remarks in *Black Women, Writing, and Identity*, her groundbreaking 1994 book about literary renderings of black women as migratory subjects, "Home can only have meaning once one experiences a level of displacement from it," and even then "home is contradictory, contested space, a locus for misrecognition and alienation."[70] In *Sleep On, Beloved*, the respective return experiences of both the first-generation immigrant mother and her 1.5-generation immigrant daughter resonate with this insightful commentary on "home," but do so very differently from each other. The mother, Ona Nedd, breaks down psychologically after she returns to Jamaica to bury her own mother. After this return trip, which is dominated by grief and mourning, she poignantly loses herself in the diasporic individual's in-betweenness back in Toronto. Her daughter, Suzanne, by contrast, for the first time truly begins to embrace Canada (in particular, Caribbean Canada) as her home after realizing, during her longed-for return to Jamaica as a young adult, that she can no longer find a physical, emotional, or spiritual place of belonging for herself in her country of birth.

In *Sleep On, Beloved*, Foster offers a literary rendering of the complex and emotionally difficult dialectic of diasporic uprootedness and a nationally grounded "attachment to place" (Tölölyan). He accomplishes this task, first, by using diasporic individuals' family formation as a metaphor for their developing sense of belonging to a nation, just as Phillips and Levy do in *A State of Independence* and *Small Island*; second, by depicting the role of religion in this dialectic, as Danticat briefly does in *Breath, Eyes, Memory* (although spirituality does not offer any easy solutions to diasporic dilemmas in either Foster's or Danticat's narratives); and, third, by highlighting a shared and more secular African Caribbean cultural heritage as a basis for diasporic connectivity that can be lived out meaningfully in the new home country. In a 2010 essay on hip-hop in Canada, Rinaldo Walcott writes about "diasporic connectivity as an important way to read the ways in which black Canadian culture elaborates the nation."[71] In explaining his verb of choice, "elaborate"—which he prefers to "contest" or "challenge"—Walcott emphasizes that "there is no contradiction between transnational identification and an insistence on belonging to a national scene"[72] and that diasporic consciousness facilitates acts of "read[ing] expressive culture beyond the narrow confines of the nation."[73] Like Walcott's essay, *Sleep On, Beloved* and its return narratives in the final analysis focus on the nature and potential of a diasporically "elaborated" Canadian nation. Even though the bulk of *Sleep On, Beloved* focuses on melancholically and tragically rendered diasporic uprootedness, the novel includes an important scene set in Toronto's annual Caribana festival.[74] The scene highlights black Caribbean diasporic connectivity as a life-affirming force and depicts it as being grounded in a common, even if internally diverse, cultural heritage that enables African Caribbean diasporans to share a sense of belonging in predominantly white Canada. Together with the novel's ending, the festival scene points to black diasporic connectivity as a future facilitator of Caribbean Canadian "elaborations" of the Canadian nation and of its official policy of multiculturalism. Foster has discussed Canadian multiculturalism extensively in his later nonfiction, particularly in part 2 of *Blackness and Modernity* (2007) and in *Genuine Multiculturalism* (2014). Being an early novel of Foster, *Sleep On, Beloved* concludes by tentatively anticipating, rather than conclusively articulating, such simultaneously critical and productive future "elaborations."

In contrast to *A State of Independence,* which portrays a male protagonist whose adult life approximates a middle-class existence, *Sleep On, Beloved* is emphatically about working-class women. By telling the story of fictional Ona Nedd, this little-researched novel focuses on the plight of black Caribbean female domestic workers in Toronto.[75] The book's desire to give visibility to Caribbean domestic workers, a group of black women migrants whose inner lives are seldom featured in fiction, makes it an important text in the black Canadian literary canon.

In the 1950s, Caribbean women began to migrate to Canada in order to work there as live-in domestics. Especially in the late 1970s and early 1980s, a significant number of Jamaican women moved to Canada as part of this decadeslong Caribbean migration.[76] Foster's Ona emigrates as part of the early 1980s wave. Her decision to leave Jamaica for Toronto is prompted by a newspaper article about a change in Canadian immigration policy[77]—an allusion to the 1981 institution of the Foreign Domestic Movement program (FDM), although the novel does not identify the program by name. Foster's narrative uses the generic term "domestic servants scheme,"[78] which some critics seem to have interpreted as pointing to the "Second Domestic Scheme"[79]—that is, to an earlier program, effective from 1955 through the end of 1967, which specifically allowed for the admission of Caribbean domestic workers to Canada. (Previously, most domestics had been British and white.) Nigel H. Thomas, for example, refers to Ona "emigrat[ing] via the Domestic Scheme."[80] However, the newspaper article from which Ona gleans her information about the relevant immigration program mentions that "Jamaicans and other Caribbean people had claimed their sovereignty and independence *almost two decades earlier.*"[81] Given that Jamaica had achieved independence in 1962, this marker of time indicates that Ona immigrates to Canada through the FDM rather than through an earlier program.[82]

Foster's fictional but realistically told tale of Ona's immigration experience highlights the financial hardships and exploitative working conditions that Caribbean domestics faced in Canada in the latter half of the twentieth century, regardless of which immigrant program they arrived through. Patricia M. Daenzer emphasizes this "neocolonial" continuity and its racially based aspects in an article published in 1997, when the 1981 Foreign Domestic Movement Program had already given way to the Live-in Caregiver Program of 1992: "The current Live-in Caregiver Program (LCP), in place since 1992, and the 1981 Foreign Domestic Movement Program (FDM), its predecessor, are both characterized by neocolonial features. Women from the labour forces of selected poor nations are conscripted to work under conditions that are reminiscent of indenture, in work greatly devalued by Canadians."[83] Daenzer makes an important comparison between domestic workers' rights during the era preceding the Second Domestic Scheme and the era that saw the arrival of domestic workers of color: "Historical analysis of the LCP and FDM shows that the exploitation of immigrant domestic workers increased when non-white women were included in the program. Prior to the 1940s, the British white domestics who predominated in the program enjoyed citizenship and mobility rights upon entering Canada. The post-1940s saw an erosion of these rights during the period when most domestic workers were non-white."[84]

This comparative observation provides crucial historical context for Foster's portrait of Ona, whose life in Toronto *Sleep On, Beloved* follows for about two decades. A relatively detailed overview of the novel's events is critical to understanding the significance of the brief but important return narratives embedded in the text. The plot is set in motion when Ona, a seventeen-year-old Jamaican single mother who finds it extremely difficult to financially support herself and her baby daughter, Suzanne, on her native island, learns that affluent Canadian families are looking for live-in domestics. She leaves Jamaica to accept such a job in Toronto. Unfamiliar with the costs of living in the Canadian metropolis and with the socioeconomic conditions of Caribbean domestic workers there, she is dazzled by the projected wages and is convinced, beyond any doubt, that the emigration will open up an opportunity for a substantially better life for herself and Suzanne.[85] Daiva K. Stasiulis and Abigail B. Bakan's explanation, in *Negotiating Citizenship* (2003), of the benefits offered by the FDM clarify why moving to Canada might have seemed like a solution to all of life's problems for a young mother looking for a long-term improvement in her and her child's standard of living: "Under this programme, a foreign domestic worker was eligible to apply for landed immigrant status after two years of live-in service with a designated employer.... If the worker successfully achieved landed status, all of the restrictions associated with the FDM ceased to apply, providing access to all formal citizenship rights open to permanent residents."[86] As Stasiulis and Bakan note, a path to citizenship was what domestic workers had been demanding, and they embraced this aspect of the FDM as an important victory.[87]

However, what would have been difficult for Ona and her real-life peers to find out was that the FDM, like the preceding legislation, in fact sought "to impede the turnover for foreign workers out of compulsory live-in domestic service."[88] To this end, "[e]mployers could only be changed with the approval of a federal immigration officer" under the FDM.[89] As Stasiulis and Bakan elaborate, this restriction left migrant women with abusive employers in vulnerable situations because it "institutionalized the potential for employer abuse, including the threat of deportation while the worker remained effectively imprisoned by temporary residence, and compulsory live-in, status."[90] Unaware of these problematic aspects of the FDM, Ona moves to Canada and leaves her ten-month-old daughter in the care of her own mother, Mira Nedd, intending to send for the child as soon as her financial situation permits and envisioning a wait of only a few years before the reunion. In Toronto, however, Ona's host family exploits her economically and sexually. Fleeing employer abuse, she leaves her legally acquired position, ends up working in the shadow economy for the sake of financial survival, and soon runs into difficulties with immigration officials. These obstacles keep Ona and her daughter apart for twelve years, despite the hard-working young mother's repeated and persistent attempts to expedite the unification process.

When Ona is finally able to send for Suzanne, she finds her daughter a stranger. Suzanne, who is on the verge of becoming a strong-willed teenager, knows little about Ona's struggles and sacrifices. She unequivocally identifies as Jamaican and is confused and traumatized by what she experiences as a forced relocation. She blames Ona for having torn her from her beloved Grandma Nedd, who has raised her, from the rest of her familiar social and physical environment in rural Jamaica, and from her spiritual home, a tight-knit religious community practicing the traditional Jamaican Pocomania faith. Suzanne feels imprisoned in the urban diaspora in the northern metropolis. Ona, in turn, is puzzled and overwhelmed by what to her seems incomprehensible ingratitude on her daughter's part. With the exception of a short period of a relatively harmonious family life during Suzanne's initial cultural acclimatization, mother and daughter fail to reconnect. In Suzanne's eyes, the separation that has lasted most of her life seems an unbridgeable chasm. Her stepfather, Barbadian-born Joe, initially assumes the role of a steadying influence and a source of emotional support, but he soon betrays Suzanne's trust by repeatedly abusing her sexually, unbeknownst to Ona. Displaced and sexually victimized in her new "home," Suzanne becomes a rebellious teenager and young adult: she starts to earn a living as a table-top dancer, is initiated by friends into petty crime, clashes with the law repeatedly, and eventually has a serious falling-out with an exasperated Ona.

While rebelling against her mother and white Canada, Suzanne copes with her existential in-betweenness by resorting to the defense mechanism of splitting: she conceives of herself as two Suzannes, who are separate and completely different from each other. One Suzanne lives life in the fast lane in Toronto while the other, the "real" one, fantasizes about moving back to Jamaica without Ona. The "real" Suzanne yearns to reembrace her grandmother and their shared spiritual life in St. Ann's parish.[91] However, despite the idealized image that Suzanne cherishes of her "true" (that is, Jamaican and spiritually pure) self, the profound alienation that she experiences during her eventual brief return to Jamaica reveals that life in Canada has changed her more profoundly and irreversibly than she had realized. After this disappointing return to the location that she has in her memory and imagination treasured as her home, Suzanne flies back to Toronto and sinks into a deep depression while dealing with the profound loss that her newly discovered emotional distance from her original environment represents for her. She recovers, however, and gradually embarks on a new phase in building a black diasporic Caribbean Canadian identity. For Ona, by contrast, the emotional turmoil triggered by *her* brief return to Jamaica—where she goes soon after Suzanne's visit, in order to bury Mira—becomes the final straw that makes her burden too heavy to bear. At the novel's end, the completely overwhelmed Ona is a psychiatric patient in acute psychosis, hospitalized in Toronto indefinitely.

Because the scant scholarship that exists on *Sleep On, Beloved* has paid little or no attention to how prominently Ona and Suzanne's religious heritage figures in their visions of "home" and diasporic (be)longing, the significant role that this heritage plays in the narratives of each woman's returns to Jamaica and then back again to Toronto has also been overlooked. The novel uses the idiom of religion—which is extremely well suited to constructing and describing imagined communities—to depict diasporic sensibilities, particularly a sense of connection with Africa (or with what "Mother Africa" signifies in these religious practitioners' collective imagination and discourse) and with spiritual kith and kin in the black diaspora. This is also true of the novel's return narratives: in them, too, Foster utilizes religious idiom to portray a lived experience of, or a longing for, affirmative black identity-building, community, and communion.

Foster's choice to use the language of diasporic theology in the novel's return narratives resonates with his decision to place the early events of the plot in St. Ann's Parish, Jamaica. There, spirituality—represented by traditional Pocomania (also known as Pukumina), a Jamaican blend of Christianity and West African traditions with close ties to the Jamaican Revival tradition that Carol B. Duncan characterizes as "a Caribbean variant of the Sanctified Church"[92]—is the way in which Ona and Suzanne originally construct their identities as members of a black community that both includes and extends beyond Mira Nedd's household. The novel's Pocomania followers, who form a small community in a rural setting, have a strong sense of belonging together, as well as of being part of the African diaspora. They actively cultivate a diasporic awareness of "Africa" being their original spiritual parent, envisioned in maternal terms: "This is the faith of our fathers and mothers that goes back to Mother Africa."[93] A spiritual imaginary here connects a local community to a global one by transcending such demarcation lines as national borders or the division between the living and the dead.

The novel's opening introduces two concepts that are first given religious significance in the context of Pocomania services but which later in the novel take on meanings related to immigration to Canada: "journeying" (that is, attending a special Pocomania celebration outdoors) and "the dream." The novel's treatment of these two concepts can be usefully read in conjunction with Paul C. Johnson's definition of "diasporic religion" in *Diaspora Conversions* (2007): "Diasporic religion is composed on the one hand of memories about space—about places of origins, about the distances traveled from them, and physical or ritual returns imagined, already undertaken, or aspired to. And on the other hand it is about how those memories arise *in* space, out of a given repertoire of the available and the thinkable."[94]

In the opening scene, the links between the religious significance of "journeying" and immigration/diaspora—which reinforce Johnson's above remarks on "space"—are articulated through the young adult Suzanne's nostalgic memories of a fulfilling spiritual and communal life in St. Ann's. Whenever the congregation's minister, Pastor Grant, "took his small flock on a *journey*,"[95] the group "set up the tabernacle at the intersection of two roads that ran through the village" and "journeyed to the intersection ostensibly in search of souls for Christ."[96] The journey was physical (the worshippers walked outdoors), but its main significance, inspired by the spirituality of "Mother Africa" as well as Christianity, was metaphorical: "Grandma Nedd had explained [to the young Suzanne] it was customary for African people to gather at these crossroads, at the place where the paths of communications between the human and spiritual worlds were joined."[97] Practicing a hybrid diasporic spirituality, the worshippers both danced in a circle[98] (a markedly African influence) and engaged in "Bible reading and personal testimony"[99] (practices deriving from Pocomania's Protestant heritage). In an equally syncretic and ecumenical manner, the officiating minister "call[ed] on the Holy Spirit to enlighten those of the true faith who had journeyed to the four corners of the earth, who were exiled in foreign places or even among the dead,"[100] thus evoking the undogmatically interpreted Spirit as the guiding spirit of the living and the dead of the African diaspora. While presented as emotionally supportive in itself, this spiritual discourse here poignantly anticipates Suzanne's discovery, in Canada, of her own identity position as an exile journeying "among foreigners and sinners"[101]—that is, among people whose ways are foreign to her, who classify her as an alien, and who are uninterested in engaging in community formation with her.

The term "dream," in turn—which conceptually and existentially resonates with Johnson's comments on diasporic aspirations—also has both religious and political significance as early as the novel's opening. On the one hand, as the Pocomania congregants journey through their home village, bearing "witness to His [Christ's] name and glory"[102] and reenacting visions and events both sacred and secular, they "belie[ve] that at the end of the painful journey would be a great feast, a remarkable celebration for having the courage to keep their eyes on the prize and their feet on the straight and narrow path. The reward for bringing home the dream."[103] Here, the fulfillment of "the dream" primarily means the "reward" promised to religious believers in the form of an afterlife with God and with the faithful. On the other hand, the crossroads to which the Pocomania congregants journey for their celebration also evokes memories of rebellious slaves "who were forefathers of these latter-day journeyers"[104] and whose rebellion colonial armed forces had suppressed: one of the two roads meeting at this symbolically significant intersection ("called Cross Roads on the maps of the area and Damnation by the residents of the region")[105] leads to a location where "the forefathers, neutered of their rebellious sting, were allowed to set up hamlets" and "where they were permitted to live free of hassles as long as they never incited insurgence," that is, "[a]s long as they let the dream wither and die."[106] "The dream" here signifies an aspiration to political freedom and full civil rights—a dream suppressed, a dream kept alive, and a dream eventually materialized in the political and legal sense, yet socioeconomically deferred. The believers blend the past black generations' experiences of both "journeying" and "dreaming" with their own, as they, in their collective spiritual imagination, reenact the past and envision a better future through their ecstatic celebration at Cross Roads: "They had survived the fiery furnace, had outlasted the crossings. They lived to nourish the dream."[107]

Later in the novel, "the dream" takes on the meaning of the immigrant dream of opportunity and upward mobility—an aspiration that remains a dream deferred for both Ona and Suzanne as they struggle to survive and make sense of their immigrant existence in Canada, the highly ambivalent promised land where their "journeying" has taken them.

While the novel's first scene depicts the young Suzanne happily and ecstatically worshipping with the Pocomania community, the young Ona had, by contrast, experienced the church as an oppressive influence. Mira Nedd, one of the respected elders of this religious group (a community allowing women to have active leadership roles),[108] had "never let Ona forget how she should prepare to eventually take over from her mother."[109] However, the young Ona's dreams of personal and communal fulfillment had focused on a single ambition: she had wanted to be a professional dancer. Around the time she turned fifteen, Ona had, defying Mira's will, moved to Kingston to join a prestigious dance troupe, having successfully passed a demanding audition. However, she soon returned to St. Ann's and to Mira's house, pregnant with Suzanne. The furious Mira harshly labeled Ona as being under the spell of a "family curse"—a term that she used, without hesitation, in both its moral and supernatural senses. Mira believed that the women in the Nedd family were "destined to relive their mothers' lives," namely, to procreate out of wedlock, as Mira's own mother, she herself, and now Ona had done.[110]

Despite this early oppressive encounter with the judgmental aspect of her mother's religiosity, in Toronto the young Ona, detached from her Pocomania heritage, finds her way to the Spiritual Baptist Church, which was founded in St. Vincent and Trinidad and is therefore one manifestation of what Duncan aptly terms "the extension of the Caribbean as a geopolitical-spiritual space into the Canadian landscape."[111] The Spiritual Baptist Church is a syncretic, tradition-blending denomination that, according to Duncan, "developed through long periods of inter-religious and inter-cultural dialogue by black people with Euro-American forms of Christianity, Islam, traditional African religions such as Yoruban Orisha, Hinduism, Buddhism and Kabbalah in the Caribbean."[112] During her first years in the intimidating and hostile Canadian metropolis, Ona seeks solace in this church and discovers there both a community of other African Caribbean female migrants and a familiar variety of religiosity that helps her to stay spiritually connected with her Pocomania background. Foster's choice of denomination for Ona is historically well informed. Duncan, writing about the late 2000s, notes that at that time the "vast majority" of Toronto Spiritual Baptists were black Caribbean women who had immigrated to Canada between 1965 and 1980 and were employed as domestic workers.[113] In other words, the Spiritual Baptist Church had, from the outset, attracted women with cultural and socioeconomic backgrounds similar to Ona's. However, Ona distances herself from the Spiritual Baptists rather quickly. She fears that the rurally raised and spiritually focused African Caribbeans' way of life might hold her back and prevent her from achieving her immigrant dream, or what is left of it after her initial experiences at the hands of exploitative employers: "[T]he religion of her mother and Pastor Grant . . . was simply incompatible with her life in Canada. And she wanted nothing, especially any baggage from home, to hold her back."[114]

Toward the novel's end, however, Ona's relationship to religion changes again. When Mira dies, Pastor Grant calls Ona from St. Ann's, asking her to "come back home" in order to take care of the funeral arrangements and to oversee "the special Pocomania wakes, the fasting and then the celebrations . . . that had been handed down over the centuries from her African forebears."[115] Charged with the responsibility to "perform the age-old rites and duties to her mother" that, according to a Pocomania tradition, only the daughter of a deceased woman can perform, Ona surrenders to the call of the faith of her childhood, travels back to St. Ann's, and dutifully does "a daughter's job."[116] This trip, saturated with grief and mourning, makes the sorrow of Ona's cultural and emotional in-betweenness as a migrating subject surface with a force that she cannot suppress or control, and she experiences a delayed psychological breakdown after returning to Toronto.

While still in St. Ann's, Ona thinks hard about the concept of "home." She tries to formulate a satisfactory definition of it for herself but instead arrives at the conclusion that home is nowhere, neither "here" nor "there." It is not in Jamaica: "Here, this little porous shack with every downpour rotting the wood, was home. And yet it wasn't. She had been away too long."[117] It is not in Toronto, either: "Ona had no illusions as to what she was going back to in Toronto: a life on the periphery, stuck in a no-man's land of never being fully West Indian and yet not Canadian. Toronto would never be home."[118] This intense struggle of the first-generation immigrant with home and belonging becomes, for Ona, intertwined with an issue that returns from the realm of the repressed to haunt her: the calling to be a spiritual leader. As a young girl, Ona had rejected the notion that she would eventually inherit Mira's role as an elder in the Pocomania community. However, while overseeing her mother's wake, Ona strongly feels that the "leadership role" is being "passed on to her" by the community and by the spirit of her departed mother.[119] She leaves

Jamaica bewildered, not knowing how to deal with this burden of responsibility. As she flies back, soaring above the waters of the Atlantic Ocean ("that vast body of water that over the years had separated and drowned so many millions of her people and their dreams"),[120] she reflects intensely on the Middle Passage, the African diaspora, and her own migration to Toronto. On the plane, a new idea hits her with a force that destabilizes her mental balance: "[M]aybe there was a reason for passing the leadership to her. Maybe it wasn't intended for her to journey among the people of St. Ann's, but perhaps among the lost souls in the new Ninevah, that great city Toronto."[121]

Soon after returning to Toronto, Ona retreats from the world into her apartment for three weeks. She emerges from this period of self-examination with a firm conviction that her twenty-one-year attempt to adapt to Canadian culture has been grounded in self-deception: "She had no choice but to strip away all the masks she had packed on top of her real self, on the Ona that in Jamaica had been baptized and chosen. The real Ona that never died despite attempts to smother her, to lock her away, to pretend she no longer existed."[122] Convinced that she has finally found her true calling and returned to an authentic African Caribbeanness, Ona starts to preach the second coming of Christ on the streets of Toronto, believing that she is thereby fulfilling the role assigned to her by her native Pocomania community back in St. Ann's. However, although Ona is certain that she has now achieved a true clarity with respect to her spiritual and ethnic identities, she is, in fact, spiraling downward into mental illness. Completely immersed in Bible study and prayer in her lonely apartment, she is no longer taking care of either herself or Telson, her two-year-old son from her recently failed marriage with Joe (a marriage into which she entered in Toronto in her late twenties in order to facilitate Suzanne's immigration to Canada). She does not notice that her little boy has turned into "a naked, dirty and hungry child running through the apartment building."[123] Tragically and ironically, the Ona who works the streets of Toronto as a frail and exhausted preacher of apocalyptic fire and brimstone has herself already been burned out, consumed by the hardship of having lived her entire adult life as a black immigrant in a society that has, despite its official policy of multiculturalism, proved unwelcoming and hostile. Eventually, an obviously disturbed Ona "preaches" in a local mall in a particularly intrusive mode, "shouting at anyone willing to tolerate her presence" while busy Torontonians are doing their last-minute Christmas shopping.[124] As a result, she is committed to a psychiatric facility, and Telson is placed in the care of the Children's Aid Society.

For Suzanne, in turn, the consequences of the phone call that she receives from Pastor Grant during Mira Nedd's final illness are very different than they are for her mother. Before her return trip to Jamaica, Suzanne not only thinks of herself as a Jamaican in Toronto but also categorically pits her Jamaican identity against Canadianness because she feels "no acceptance in Canada."[125] In her experience, the term "Jamaican" is used in Canada as a "confining label flung, whether deservingly or not, at all black people, unjustly signifying inferiority and backwardness."[126] This exposure to racially based negative attitudes toward African Caribbeans has only strengthened Suzanne's self-identification as Jamaican:

> Fortunately, Jamaica was, and always would be, the country in her blood, the place of friends and family, of the memories that erased any craving to belong elsewhere. In Jamaica, she was not *alien*. She had a strong national pride—imbued by Grandma Nedd's wonderful stories about life in the old days, about how Suzanne should be proud to be Jamaican, West Indian and African, to be part of a small but proud nation and a region where black people were the majority and ruled themselves. Her Jamaican passport was more than her only identification.[127]

However, for Suzanne, her visit to Jamaica at age twenty-two signifies a series of challenges to the nostalgia for "home" that she has cherished for a decade during her exile in Canada. Just like the returning migrant in *A State of Independence*, Suzanne discovers that both her original environment and she herself have changed much more than she had thought possible. When she arrives at the airport, she, like Phillips's Bertram Francis, notices that she had forgotten about the "direct heat [that] actually stung the skin,[128] and she, too, finds herself scoffing at the slow airport routines and impatiently expecting "that the entire world moved at the same faster pace to which she had, evidently, now become accustomed."[129] More significantly, she fails to recognize Pastor Grant—the towering, dignified male authority figure of her childhood—at the airport: "In her mind was the image of this man immaculately dressed in his white and black robes with the bows around his waist.... Instead, standing in front of her was an old man with sunken cheeks."[130]

Seeing Pastor Grant through new eyes is a profoundly confusing experience for Suzanne, but meeting the utterly frail creature that her energetic Grandma Nedd has become shocks her even more. Suzanne had hoped that she and her beloved grandmother might again go "journeying" together and once more joyously meet at Cross Roads. However, Mira is not just confined to her hospital bed. She is also mentally disoriented, and the long and intimate conversations that Suzanne had anticipated are therefore impossible. Suzanne also discerns, for the first time, the vast difference between Mira's and her own life experiences, realizing that even if Mira were healthier, she could not be the kind of mentor that the granddaughter had envisioned:

> Grandma Nedd had never lived in Toronto, never lived outside the Caribbean for that matter. She would never understand some things in Suzanne's life.... [S]he felt the distance between them. Grandma Nedd knew of only one kind of life. She never had to pull up stake and start all over in a strange new country, with the only guiding light blind ambition and a belief that life simply had to get better.... Grandma Nedd had taught them how to nurture the dream. But she never told them how to bury it once it was smothered.... Grandma Nedd hadn't seen the immigrant dream die.[131]

Suzanne gradually realizes that, with her grandmother terminally ill and hospitalized, she herself no longer has a childhood home in her native country, nor does she have any role to fulfill either in her extended family or in Jamaican society. Her short stay in Jamaica turns out to be a disappointing visit rather than a homecoming, and she soon returns to Toronto. In response to the depression triggered by the unsettling trip—a psychological turmoil representing a new stage in her identity crisis as a diasporic migrant in search of self-definition—Suzanne seeks out new, Canadian-based sources of support and advice. She turns to Reverend Lucas, who serves a black congregation within an "established" Christian denomination in Toronto (left unidentified by Foster).[132] However, during the entire conversation that she has with Reverend Lucas, Suzanne is powerfully aware of the differences between his life experience as a Canadian-born black Torontonian and her own experience as a Caribbean-born immigrant. For Suzanne, mere blackness is not enough to create a sufficiently significant connection, and she articulates this sentiment quite directly: "You just don't understand West Indians. We are not like you, black but Canadian born. You don't understand how we have to put up with changes. How we have to square the things they taught us back home with what we know we have to do to get ahead here."[133] Suzanne leaves the church feeling that the Canadian man of the cloth "wouldn't understand the heavy burden of the dream."[134]

After the disappointment with the "established" black Canada that Reverend Lucas represents for her, Suzanne eventually seeks solace in the Caribana festival, where she finds communion and connection with other African Caribbean immigrants. This experience signals both closure and the beginning of a new phase in her identity formation—the gradual emergence of a black Caribbean Canadian identity. Moreover, as Suzanne learns about her mother's breakdown, she gradually gains new insight into the hardship that had been Ona's lot in Toronto all along, and she "finally grasp[s] what her mother had tried to teach her, the strategies Ona had adopted as her own survival techniques."[135] As part of her process of healing and internal integration, the daughter realizes that she does not need to be two Suzannes, one Canadian and the other African Caribbean, but that the two can be reconciled within a single psyche.[136] At the novel's conclusion, Suzanne articulates for herself the beginning of her identity formation as a diasporic black Caribbean Canadian in the idiom of song, music, and dance—a language that in *Sleep On, Beloved* acknowledges both the Caribbean and African aspects of her diasporic heritage: "Now she [Suzanne] understood not only the need to take on a new voice in the hope of integrating, but also the importance of not silencing the old and faithful voice. Of learning to waltz like Canadians but still being able to wind the waist in pleasant outlandishness like West Indians, like Africans. To hear the drums and to dance freely and openly."[137]

However, even as Suzanne makes these discoveries and embarks on her journey of black Caribbean Canadian identity formation, her exhausted mother is psychologically splitting herself into two, just as Suzanne had previously attempted to do. Ona is in the process of abandoning her semi-integrationist immigrant identity in favor of a self-understanding which she sees as a cultural return to her Jamaicanness, but which in her Canadian environment represents an option that, tragically, does not exist. In the midst of this crisis, Suzanne decides to become the guardian of her two-year-old stepbrother, Telson, who has been placed in the care of social services following Ona's hospitalization. Ona, beyond reach because of her psychiatric condition, does not learn of this sign of reconciliation. The narrative here evokes the opening of the hymn "The Christian's Goodnight," with Sarah Doudney's lyrics, which gives the novel its title ("Sleep on, beloved, / Sleep, and take thy rest"), to indicate that it is now Ona's turn to rest and "sleep on."[138] At the novel's end, hope lies in the future of the next generations—here, in the intertwined futures of Suzanne, a 1.5-generation Jamaican immigrant settled in Canada, and little Telson, a first-generation Canadian of Caribbean (Jamaican and Barbadian) parentage. Telson's mother is in a psychiatric facility and his father is in jail for theft and fraud, but his sister is willing to fight for his custody and well-being.

In Levy's *Small Island*, the Jamaican Josephs' family formation in Britain, including their adoption of a baby (who, without the couple's knowledge, is a member of Hortense's extended family, her diasporic blood relative born on British soil) symbolizes a step toward a black British identity formation. Here, similarly, Suzanne and Telson's projected black Caribbean family formation in Canada, facilitated by Suzanne's "adoption" of her half-brother, symbolizes a step toward a black Canadian identity formation—the emergence of a self-understanding that, while acknowledging the possibility of (and even a desire for) national belonging, at the same time retains its diasporic consciousness and sensibility, its diasporic (be)longing.

Land, a Sense of Place, and Diaspora: Danticat's Haitian American Returnees in *Breath, Eyes, Memory*

Because Edwidge Danticat is the pioneering and critically most acclaimed contemporary Haitian American author, her debut novel, *Breath, Eyes, Memory*, a post-Duvalier work set in the Duvalier era, has already been astutely analyzed by myriad scholars. Nevertheless, a brief discussion of this novel—in which, as Martin Munro notes, Danticat's own emigration to New York City "comes back in commuted form"[139]—is warranted here because return narratives play a pivotal role in it, as does land, a motif that is closely related to return, due to the connotative links of land with homeland and a place of belonging. Danticat's narrative connects land (with its various meanings, including earth and soil) with nation, migrancy, up/rootedness, home, diaspora, and return, on the one hand, and with women's bodies and sexualities, on the other. Her prose thereby reinforces Carol Boyce Davies's assertion that "for the Caribbean-American woman writer, cultural politics have to be worked out and articulated along with sexual politics."[140] Both in leaving Haiti and in returning there, Danticat's diasporic Haitian American women struggle with the public and private legacies of the political and gender violence of Duvalierist Haiti, but they also draw strength from other aspects of Haiti's cultural and spiritual landscape.

Because my discussion focuses on the tropes of land and return, I must also mention Danticat's 2010 book, *Create Dangerously: The Immigrant Artist at Work* (a project in part prompted by her Toni Morrison lecture at Princeton in March 2008), which, during the final stages of the writing process, took the form of a simultaneously grief-stricken and reflective response to the 7.0 magnitude earthquake that struck Haiti on January 12, 2010. Alluding to Morrison's dedication of *Beloved* to those who died because of the slave trade and slavery (in Morrison's contested count, "Sixty Million and more"), Danticat dedicated the book to the "two hundred thousand and more" who perished in the quake.¹⁴¹ Even though *Create Dangerously*, named after a similarly titled piece by Albert Camus, largely draws on Danticat's previously published essays, the book in its final form evokes the quake and its ramifications several times. Danticat not only mentions the man-made changes to the Haitian landscape, such as deforestation, that contributed to the severity of the quake's consequences, but also calls attention to the decadeslong centralization of the country's economy in what gradually became an overpopulated Port-au-Prince. As Laurent Dubois reminds us in *Haiti: The Aftershocks of History* (2012), the centralization of Haiti's economy in the capital city began with the US occupation of Haiti (1915–34), during which the Haitian Constitution was rewritten in 1918 to lift the ban on foreign ownership of land.¹⁴² This revision enabled foreign companies to replace small locally owned farms with large corporate-owned plantations.¹⁴³ In *Create Dangerously*, Danticat notes these developments and the accompanying "import-favoring agricultural policies that have driven so many Haitians off their ancestral lands" into Port-au-Prince.¹⁴⁴ She characterizes the capital as a "city built for two hundred thousand that was forced to house nearly three million" and that was therefore particularly vulnerable to the devastation caused by the quake.¹⁴⁵ In chapter 12, titled "Our Guernica," she meditates on the concept of "ground":

> Haitians like to tell each other that Haiti is *tè glise*, slippery ground. Even under the best of circumstances, the country can be stable one moment and crumbling the next. Haiti has never been more slippery ground than after this earthquake, with bodies littering the streets, entire communities buried in rubble, homes pancaked to dust. Now Haitian hearts are also slippery ground, hopeful one moment and filled with despair the next. Has two hundred and six years of existence finally reached its abyss? we wonder. But now even the ground is no more. . . . With thousands hastily and superficially buried or lodged in miles and miles of rubble . . . , Haiti is no longer just slippery ground, but also sacred ground.¹⁴⁶

These reflections—with their slippage between whether Haiti, or the areas hardest hit by the quake, should now be regarded as "slippery ground," or as "sacred ground," or as ground that no longer exists, or as all of these at the same time—seem all the more poignant when read in dialogue with Danticat's

Breath, Eyes, Memory, in which land, home, diaspora, return, and women's struggles against political and gender violence are inextricably intertwined.

While primarily focusing on the story of a 1.5-generation Haitian American immigrant, Sophie Caco (whose last name both denotes a red bird and alludes to the Haitian peasant guerrillas who fought against the US occupation), *Breath, Eyes, Memory* offers glimpses of the lives of four generations of Haitian and Haitian American women/girls. The matriarch of the matrilineally defined Caco family, Grandmè Ifé, lives in La Nouvelle Dame Marie in rural Haiti. Embodying the traditional "storytelling" wisdom of Haitian women, Ifé in many scenes resembles Mother Earth incarnate. However, the Haitian earth or soil takes on a very different role in the life and memories of Martine, one of Ifé's two daughters: at age sixteen, Martine was brutally raped and impregnated by a Tonton Macoute,[147] a member of Haiti's feared Duvalierist paramilitary force who pinned her down in a cane field in La Nouvelle Dame Marie, a location whose name, ironically, points to virginity and idealized motherhood. The rape scene evokes the violence of both the slavery era, referenced by the sugarcane, and of the Duvalierist regime, embodied by the rapist who forcefully misuses sexual and political power. As Donette Francis reminds us, Duvalier's militia's "own brand of *politically motivated rape* was a notorious method of maintaining their power."[148] After giving birth to her daughter, Sophie, Martine emigrated to Brooklyn, New York. Her sister, Atie, raised Sophie in the Haitian town of Croix-des-Rosets until the child turned twelve. In the novel's present, Atie dedicates her life to taking care of Ifé back in La Nouvelle Dame Marie and to loving a local woman, Louise, who does not love her back romantically.[149] While Martine and Atie represent the second of the Caco generations depicted in the novel, the third generation is embodied by the narrator-protagonist, Sophie, whose life the novel follows from age twelve, when Martine summons her to Brooklyn, to approximately age twenty, when she is a young wife and mother living with her African American husband, Joseph, in Providence, Rhode Island. Sophie and Joseph's little daughter, Brigitte, who is about six months old when the novel closes, represents the fourth generation.

Just as in *Sleep On, Beloved*, in *Breath, Eyes, Memory*, too, the hard-working and well-meaning first-generation immigrant mother and her young adult immigrant daughter experience a serious conflict and falling-out, although Sophie is no urban rebel like Foster's Suzanne. Nevertheless, in Danticat's novel, unlike in Foster's, the mother and the daughter are reconciled during their return to their native Caribbean. Martine and Sophie travel to Haiti separately, but they fly back to the United States together and then enter into a new, mutually respectful and loving phase in their mother-daughter relationship. Sadly, this phase is soon cut short by Martine's suicide, triggered by an unplanned pregnancy that overwhelms the chronically exhausted survivor of rape, breast cancer, and two decades of hardship during her life as an immigrant. Despite this tragedy, however, Sophie and Martine's reconciliation in Haiti during their return there plays a crucial part in the narrative of Sophie's process of defining herself as a member of the matrilineally understood Caco family, as a Haitian American immigrant, and as an African Caribbean diasporic subject.

Sophie and Martine's reconciliation in La Nouvelle Dame Marie is facilitated by Grandmè Ifé, a peasant woman whose down-to-earth wisdom the narrative closely associates with her rootedness in her ancestral land in Haiti. In *Sleep On, Beloved*, Suzanne (rightly or wrongly) concludes during her brief return visit to Jamaica that her maternal grandmother, even if she were still healthy and lucid, could never guide her toward a hyphenated Jamaican-Canadian identity, having never been an immigrant herself. Danticat's Ifé, by contrast, encourages intergenerational reconciliation among the Caco women, including herself, in a way that acknowledges the importance of process and change, which are necessary to facilitate cultural hybridity. The encounter with the elder's spiritual generosity helps the adult Sophie to believe that Haitian American creolity/*métissage*—or cultural syncretism, vital to Voudou—is possible. *Breath, Eyes, Memory* is the story of Sophie's search for an identity position where the African, Haitian, and American aspects of her diasporic and migratory self-understanding can be in constructive and dynamic dialogue with one another. Her return visit to Haiti crucially aids her in this quest, because the reconciliation that the trip facilitates helps her to again perceive her African Haitian heritage as a source of strength in her life in the United States.

At the novel's beginning, twelve-year-old Sophie lives with her deeply beloved guardian Atie (a selfless practitioner of "othermothering," to quote a term coined by African American feminists)[150] in Croix-des-Rosets, Haiti, where "most of the people were city workers who labored in baseball or clothing factories and lived in small cramped houses to support their families back in the provinces."[151] The day-to-day realities of urban working-class life have not destroyed the familial atmosphere of this community, where potlucks, "open to everybody who wanted to come,"[152] are a frequent occurrence because "the workers used their friendships in the factories or their grouping in the common yards as a reason to get together, eat, and celebrate life."[153] These communal events even have a myth of origin:

> Tantie Atie said that the way these potlucks started was really a long time ago in the hills. Back then, a whole village would get together and clear a field for planting. The group would take turns clearing each person's land, until all the land in the village was cleared and planted. The women would cook large amounts of food while the men worked. Then at sunset, when the work was done, everyone would gather together and enjoy a fest of eating, dancing, and laughter.[154]

As Dubois reminds us, the 1804 creation of Haiti resulted in what the Haitian sociologist Jean Casimir calls a "counter-plantation" system.[155] That is, when rural Haitians established their own modest-sized farms, they at the same time founded a system of "self-sufficient agriculture."[156] In fact, Dubois and Deborah Jenson have argued that this system not only "forestalled any possibility of a return to the large plantations" that had been the hallmark of the slavery era, but also "provided a better quality of life than that of African descendants anywhere else in the Americas."[157] Similarly, Danticat's story of communal gatherings in the hills of Croix-des-Rosets at the time when the town was still a rural village is highly celebratory. It applauds the villagers' close relationship both with the land and with each other by depicting their cooperation in cultivating the land as having been crucial for the first flourishing of their community.

It is worth mentioning that the role that food has in this story of origin sharply contrasts with the role that food plays for Sophie (and, to a lesser degree, for Martine before her) in her life as an uprooted diasporic subject in the United States. The story that Atie tells little Sophie about how the villagers used to joyously "enjoy a fest of eating" on the evenings of the planting season is a piece of fictionalized oral history that respectfully salutes the Haitian peasants' "counter-plantation" system as well as emphasizes that the shared suppers helped the agricultural workers to cherish a sense of community and local rootedness. In her lonely and guilt-ridden bulimic sessions with prepackaged and frozen foods in America,[158] the young diasporic adult Sophie, by contrast, uses food to fill what Meg Wesling aptly terms "the geographical and emotional gaps that comprise the experience of diaspora."[159]

When the adolescent Sophie arrives in New York City and the United States for the first time, she brings a tangible reminder of Haiti and its soil with her—namely, a Mother's Day card, which she had originally prepared for Atie and to which she had attached a pressed daffodil that had bloomed in Croix-des-Rosets. When Martine finds the rumpled card in Sophie's dress pocket in Brooklyn, the flower is no longer there, but the text that the child had penciled on the card is still legible.[160] It praises Caco women's strength in an idiom that stirs up memories of the Haitian landscape in Martine's mind: "My mother is a daffodil, / limber and strong as one."[161] In Jamaica Kincaid's *Lucy* (1991), daffodils represent the culture of the colonizer, a foreign influence to which the novel's eponymous Caribbean female protagonist responds angrily: while working as an au pair in the United States, Lucy, upon seeing a field of daffodils for the first time, bitterly recalls how she at school had to learn by heart William Wordsworth's "I wandered lonely as a Cloud," even though she had never seen a single daffodil during her entire Caribbean childhood.[162] In *Small Island* Levy, in portraying Hortense's childhood and schooling in rural Jamaica, also alludes to the same poem about daffodils as epitomizing Englishness and the colonizer's imperial culture.[163] In *Breath, Eyes, Memory*, by contrast, daffodils symbolize Haitians' bold cultural and political resistance that, from early on, enabled them not only to adopt and appropriate French influences, but also to domesticate such cultural imports and innovatively transform them into their own likeness.[164] It is through Atie's oral storytelling (which, together with Ifé's stories, plays a vital role in Sophie's psychosocial development and cultural learning)[165] that Sophie is exposed to this symbolic significance attached to daffodils by the Caco family, including Martine:

> Tante Atie told me that my mother loved daffodils because they grew in a place that they were not supposed to. They were really European flowers, French buds and stems, meant for colder climates. A long time ago, a French woman had brought them to Croix-des-Rosets and planted them there. A strain of daffodils had grown that could withstand the heat, but they were the color of pumpkins and golden summer squash, as though they had acquired a bronze tinge from the skin of the natives who had adopted them.[166]

Simone A. James Alexander's analysis of *Breath, Eyes, Memory* associates daffodils with the rape of Martine.[167] However, the rape, as noted, took place in a cane field,[168] a setting reminding the reader of slavery's violent exploitation and objectification of black bodies. Throughout the novel, the memory of the cane field alludes to the exploitation of Haitians, especially women, by various patriarchal institutions—empire, nation, army, militia, and communally sanctioned public and private sexism. The novel's vegetative imagery thus links sugarcane with violation and captivity, whereas most of the time it connects daffodils with the political and cultural agency and autonomy of Haiti.

When Sophie leaves Croix-des-Rosets for Port-au-Prince in her daffodil-embroidered dress to board her plane and fly to the United States,[169] the landscape providing context to "the only life that [she] had ever known"[170] suddenly seems empty and vacant, as if it were an external expression of Sophie's internal landscape, that is, of the grief and alienation that she feels while trying to come to terms with the reality of emigration: "There were no children playing, no leaves flying about. No daffodils."[171] In New York, her mother's modest Brooklyn home initially seems less than welcoming.[172] However, Martine's hard work results in a material reward some six years later, when she and Sophie are able to move to "a one-family house in a tree-lined neighborhood,"[173] a symbol of Martine's immigrant upward mobility. For Martine, daffodils have, by this time, become a generalized metaphor for the Haitian homeland and for everything that it represents to her personally, the painful memories and the material poverty included. She therefore decides to grow hibiscus, rather than daffodils, in her new backyard once she reaches a relatively stable phase in her US existence.[174] Alexander interprets hibiscus as a symbol of Haiti and of Martine's longing for the Haitian homeland.[175] This reading, however, overlooks the fact that species of hibiscus are found throughout the world, not just in Haiti. An umbrella term for a myriad of related species of flowers and shrubs, hibiscus is a plant that can be easily hybridized and that thrives in both tropical and warm temperate climates. Given Danticat's strong and positive linkage of the imported (and consciously "adopted") daffodil with Haiti, Martine's desire to cultivate hibiscus symbolizes a diasporic individual's effort to embrace and represent cultural hybridity in her new home country, the United States. At this point of her life, Martine seeks to distance herself from being *solely* defined by the Haitian dimensions of her identity.

However, even though the hybrid and transnational flowers that Martine grows in her backyard represent her yearning for a fresh start, she continues to carry her past—in particular, the experience of having been violently raped—with her in the form of nightmares, which haunt her throughout her adult life. The cane field of Dame Marie never lets go of its oppressive hold on her. The theme of Caco women's bondage, subjugation, resistance, and search for freedom permeates the novel. Danticat all along brings this dialectic of captivity and liberty in complex dialogue with "home" in the sense of the Haitian homeland, a home that she profoundly appreciates but does not blindly idealize. Davies insightfully observes that for Caribbean American women writers "the rewriting of home," which she identifies as "a critical link in the articulation of identity," not only is "a play of resistance to domination" (for example, resistance to the kind of US cultural domination that seeks to erase black immigrants' memories of their cultural specificity) but also "locates home in its many transgressive and disjunctive experiences."[176] Resonating with Davies's observation, Danticat's "rewriting of home" is fraught with ambivalences. While most of the Haitian homeland's "transgressive and disjunctive" qualities that Danticat critiques in *Breath, Eyes, Memory* concern the legacies of slavery, French imperialism, US neo-imperialism, and the dictatorships of the two Duvaliers, she also reveals the tragic consequences of Haitian women having, in some respects, internalized the patriarchal values surrounding them.

Martine's tragic internalization of the patriarchal norms by which she was victimized during her Haitian youth is epitomized by the hurtful and oppressive family custom of "testing" (which plays such a pivotal role in the novel that practically every critic analyzing the book has discussed it), the alleged maternal duty of each Caco woman to regularly ascertain that her unwed daughter's hymen is still intact. As a teenager, Martine, who was frequently "tested" by Ifé, fiercely resisted this crude ritual of the "virginity cult."[177] As a struggling immigrant mother, however, she finds herself mentally bound by this inherited custom and conforms to it in order to protect Sophie's "honor" and guard her marriage prospects. A traumatized Sophie eventually liberates herself from being tested by taking her own virginity: desperate to free herself from Martine's control and to achieve sexual autonomy, she violently penetrates herself with the same pestle that she had used in the past to prepare Martine's favorite foods.[178] In the process, Sophie in effect rapes herself. She thus inadvertently creates a new form of physical and emotional bondage for herself and fails to break the cycle of Caco women's suffering caused by gender violence.

After this dramatic incident, which leaves the mother-daughter relationship in a state of profound crisis, Sophie moves out of Martine's house, marries Joseph, and moves to his place in Providence, a town whose name she sees as promising redemption and protection from all evil.[179] The early history of Providence, especially the founder Roger Williams's pursuit of freedom and tolerance, embodies several principles later inscribed in the founding documents of the United States. Nevertheless, residing in Providence does not, in or by itself, give Sophie the kind of life, liberty, and happiness that she had pursued by moving there. "[T]rauma travels," notes Donette Francis in discussing how the raped Martine inevitably brings her posttraumatic stress with her from Dame Marie's cane field to Brooklyn.[180] Sophie, similarly, carries her physically and emotionally traumatized condition from Brooklyn to Providence, where she attempts to create a new life for herself and for her new family. Because of this "traveling trauma," her project of self-liberation remains incomplete: due to her emotional burdens and her self-inflicted vaginal injury, she has severe difficulties with her self-image and with sexual intimacy, and she develops bulimia. However, belonging to a different generation than Martine, Sophie knows how to seek help from various sources—Western, African diasporic, and transnational alike. In addition to seeing a doctor who practices Western medicine, she sees a black female therapist, Rena, "an initiated Santeria priestess" with two years of service experience "in the Peace Corps in the Dominican Republic."[181] Rena embodies both traditional African Caribbean spiritually grounded wisdom and Western psychotherapy's emphasis on listening and empathy. Sophie also belongs to a women's "sexual phobia group"[182] whose other members are a circumcised Ethiopian student and an incestuously abused Chicana. These three sexually victimized women support each other on their journeys toward emotional and sexual healing. In all these therapeutic settings, Sophie actively processes her identity in relation to her family as well as to her African diasporic, Haitian, and US affiliations.

When her daughter Brigitte is almost six months old, Sophie takes the baby and extemporaneously travels to Haiti, returning there for the first time. She goes to La Nouvelle Dame Marie, where she was born and where Ifé and Atie now live together in the family house, a dwelling well maintained with the help of the remittances that Martine regularly sends from the States.[183] On her way to the family home, Sophie observes female street vendors by the road: "When one merchant dropped her heavy basket, another called out of concern, '*Ou libéré?*' Are you free from your heavy load?"[184] She discerns in this friendly salutation a reflection of her own yearning to liberate herself. Her return trip indeed becomes an important part of her journey toward self-liberation and healing, not least because of her grandmother's intervention and contribution. Refusing to accept any permanent breach of a mother-daughter relationship within the family, Ifé alerts Martine to Sophie and Brigitte's presence in Dame Marie, and so Martine, too, returns from New York to the family's ancestral land for three days. Martine and Sophie, who have not seen each other since their falling-out and Sophie's move to Providence, reconcile. They finally discuss the "testing," which they both now recognize as a form of gender violence. Martine now makes a connection between the "testing" and such obviously damaging forms of the sexual abuse of women as rape, discerning that both are grounded in the same ideology, the patriarchal control and denigration of women: "I realize standing here that the two greatest pains of my life are very much related.... The testing and the rape. I live both every day."[185] During the same discussion, Martine remorsefully references family tradition as her rationale for having adopted the harsh practice of testing and for having thought it beneficial: "I did it... because my mother had done it to me. I have no greater excuse."[186]

Indeed, although Danticat deeply loves and respects traditional Haitian culture, her refusal to uncritically idealize all of its aspects comes across in her treatment of gender and sexual politics. These dynamics play an important role in her portrait of Ifé, an elder. Danticat primarily casts Ifé as a wise matriarch and celebrates her deep rootedness in rural Haiti, but she also portrays Ifé as a product of her environment, who, having had little opportunity to critically interrogate her culture's patriarchal values, has accepted them unquestioningly. Not only did Ifé "test" Martine and Atie, but in the novel's present she also condemns Atie's attraction to Louise, having, the narrative implies, been taught to abhor gay/lesbian desire. However, although Danticat makes plain Ifé's role as a mediator of what Carine Mardorossian terms "patriarchal scripts of femininity,"[187] the narrative highlights the matriarch's personal depth in a pivotal scene in which Sophie directly confronts her about "testing."[188] Though initially skeptical of Sophie's claim that the "testing" produces long-lasting traumatic effects, Ifé chooses to give more weight to her granddaughter's testimony than to her own cultural pride or to her status as Sophie's elder. She apologizes to Sophie in a way that both honors and transcends their roles as elder and granddaughter: "She [Ifé] walked into her room, took her statue of Erzulie, and pressed it into my hand. 'My heart, it weeps like a river,' she said, 'for the pain we have caused you.'"[189] The regretful Ifé indirectly acknowledges her past uncritical loyalty to those aspects of Haitian culture that oppress women and girls. Wishing to make amends, she, as Mildred Mortimer notes, seeks to bring Sophie "under the protection of the mother deity, Erzulie as symbol of ideal motherhood," in effect asking the younger woman "to reconstruct her Haitian heritage by retaining its spirituality and discarding the negative oppressive elements."[190] Back in Providence, Sophie indeed takes Ifé's statue of Erzulie to one of her group therapy sessions, "ponder[ing] what it meant in terms of [her] family."[191] Albeit a step on her journey rather than its completion, this healing encounter with Ifé is one of the reasons why Sophie, after her return to the United States, spontaneously starts to call Haiti "home," which as a young adult she has never done before.[192]

In *Sleep On, Beloved*, Grandma Nedd's terminal illness signifies an irreversible loss for Suzanne, emphasizing for her that she no longer has a home in Jamaica, which she, as a Caribbean diasporan living in Canada, has previously envisioned to be her true homeland. The mortality of the matriarch looms over *Breath, Eyes, Memory* as well, but here the dynamics triggered by the proximity of death instead emphasize Sophie's reconnection with Haiti. Ifé, still in charge of herself and her life, puts her final affairs in order while both of her daughters are in Dame Marie. This process, which in Danticat's treatment highlights the novel's pivotal motif of land, celebrates the Caco family's close ties to the Haitian homeland: at Ifé's suggestion, she and her daughters go to "see the notary about the land papers."[193] Significantly, they equally divide the family property between Martine, Atie, Sophie, and Brigitte—the implication being that all four heiresses, including US-born Brigitte, will always have a place to return to, a piece of land to which they belong and which belongs to them, in Haiti. This scene, with its strong emphasis on the importance of being rooted in one's ancestral land, now seems particularly poignant in light of Danticat's reflections, in *Create Dangerously*, on Haiti as "slippery ground" after the 2010 earthquake and in light of the news trickling from Haiti suggesting that, because an unknown number of land title records were destroyed during the disaster, land title disputes might hinder postquake reconstruction efforts for years to come.[194]

After the difficult but liberating discussion about "testing," followed by the democratic division of the family's land, the reconciled Martine and Sophie return to the United States, where Martine faces a new challenge: she unexpectedly finds herself pregnant. Martine is a breast cancer survivor who has gone through a double mastectomy, another variety of trauma related to her womanhood. Metaphorically, her breastlessness poignantly alludes to her past inability to nurture Sophie during the years when the child lived in Haiti while Martine was working hard in New York to secure a financial future for them both (and for Ifé and Atie, too). The dutiful immigrant mother judges herself harshly. Despite her recent reconciliation with Sophie, she sees herself as a failed parent and refuses to "fail" another child. She despairs completely and takes her own life by stabbing herself seventeen times in the abdomen.[195] The Caco women's family name denotes a scarlet bird, and when such a bird dies, "there is," according to Atie's storytelling, "always a rush of blood that rises to its neck and the wings, they look so bright, you would think of them on fire."[196] As critics have noted, Martine indeed dies a Caco death (the historical Cacos were fighters, as mentioned, revolutionaries during the US occupation of Haiti).[197] But her suicide, a horrifying bloodbath, is, of course, a tragic and deliberately subversive variation on that motif.

Sophie returns to Haiti for a second time sooner than intended, in order to bury Martine there. She decides that Martine, who for two decades had the will to survive and support her family while bearing her burdens, will be buried with the honors of a fighter against gender violence. As if mocking the denigrating words of the rapist, whose cruel verbal abuse Martine still heard in her head shortly before her death,[198] Sophie chooses a bright red dress and red accessories as the clothing that her mother will wear during her final journey. Instead of marking the shame of a fallen woman, the color scarlet here serves as the color worn by a woman warrior, a brave Caco fighter. Through this bold sartorial choice, Sophie defiantly reverses the roles of oppressor and victim and creates her own version of Erzulie-inspired spirituality, just as Ifé had encouraged her to do: "She [Martine] would look like a Jezebel, hotblooded Erzulie who feared no men, but rather made them her slaves, raped *them*, and killed *them*."[199] Though initially aghast at the sight of her daughter's body being wrapped in red,[200] Ifé indicates her approval in a language that spiritually places both Martine and Sophie within the continuum of all Caco women, living and dead: "There is a place where women are buried in clothes the color of flames, where we drop coffee on the ground for those who went ahead, where the daughter is never fully a woman until her mother has passed on before her."[201]

The night before Martine's funeral, Sophie articulates for herself the relationship between land, mother-daughter connection, storytelling, and Haitian traditional songs in terms that are so strong as to be almost essentialist: "I realized that it was neither my mother nor my Tante Atie who had given all the mother-and-daughter motifs to all the stories they told and all the songs they sang. It was something that was essentially Haitian. Somehow, early on, our song makers and tale weavers had decided that we were all daughters of this land."[202] Earth, soil, and land are also powerfully present in the narrative of the burial itself, as is the motif of the Caco family as a circle of women who share a common heritage: "My grandmother threw the first handful of dirt on the coffin as it was lowered onto the ground. Then Tante Atie, and then me. I threw another handful for my daughter who was not there, but was part of this circle of women from whose gravestones our names had been chosen."[203]

As dirt is being shoveled onto the coffin, grief-stricken Sophie runs from the graveyard down the hill into the cane field where the sixteen-year-old Martine had been traumatized for life. Having been told by her therapist that she and Martine should visit the cane field together as part of their shared search for inner peace,[204] Sophie now creates her own version of that envisioned visit. She "attack[s] the cane," symbolically seeking to eradicate all forms of black women's captivity through an active fight: "I took off my shoes and began to beat a cane stalk. I pounded it until it began to lean over.... I pulled at it, yanking it from the ground."[205] As Sophie physically struggles to overcome the oppressive power that the cane field has, in multiple ways, had over generations of Caco women, she hears Ifé shout a question echoing female street vendors' concern about each other's burdens: *"Ou libéré?"*[206] Atie then shouts the same words, but the phrase rolls off her tongue as an affirmative exclamation, not as a question: *"Ou libéré!"*[207] In the midst of her grief, Sophie begins to experience the liberation that she has yearned for—not because the one who used to "test" her is gone, but because of her now deeply felt connection with her family's circle of women and their rootedness in Haiti, symbolized by their jointly owned piece of land, and because of her developing ability to carry this connection and rootedness with her wherever she goes.

As befits the novel's strong focus on land and on the complex yet possible relationship between the Haitian homeland and diaspora, the word "place" is repeated several times on the final page of the novel's last chapter. This repetition is in close dialogue with the novel's title: Sophie comes, in her words, from "a place where breath, eyes, and memory are one, a place from which you carry your past like the hair on your head."[208] This "place," real and/or remembered, here operates as a *lieu de mémoire*, a site of memory, to evoke Pierre Nora's famous term.[209] The novel's final meditation on "place,"[210] however deeply inspired it is by actual Haitian soil, powerfully demonstrates that the "place" that Sophie and Ifé refer to is a site that in part exists in their imagination/*memory*. This site is sustained for them by the communal and familial storytelling, which acts as a repository for the community's and family's lived experience—referred to by the title's *breath*—and which constantly interprets and reinterprets what the participant-witnesses' *eyes* have seen. (Such a repository is extremely important in the Caco family and in the novel's Haiti in general because, due to political violence, "people can disappear into thin air. All traces lost except in the vivid eyes of one's memory.")[211] This is why "breath, eyes, and memory" indeed "are one" in this "place" or site.[212]

What happens, then, when the "place" no longer exists and the land has, in the wake of a major earthquake, become "slippery ground" or even "sacred ground" saturated with anonymous human remains? What kind of "place" does a migrant then go to, in order to "return"? In *Create Dangerously*, Danticat, commenting on the calling of the immigrant artist/writer, offers one answer to this difficult question:

> The immigrant artist shares with all other artists the desire to interpret and possibly remake his or her own world. So though we may not be creating as dangerously as our forebears—though we are not risking torture, beatings, execution, though exile does not threaten us into perpetual silence—still, while we are at work bodies are littering the streets somewhere. People are buried under rubble somewhere. Mass graves are being dug somewhere. Survivors are living in make-shift tent cities and refugee camps somewhere, shielding their heads from the rain, closing their eyes, covering their ears, to shut out the sounds of military "aid" helicopters. And still, many are reading, and writing, quietly, quietly.[213]

For a reader/writer, as Danticat's reflection suggests, the site of memory created by reading/writing is a "place" to go to, even in the wake of unimaginable disasters that may destroy the very land that people used to walk on. To say this is not to privilege reading/writing over lived experience, but to emphasize that the written word can testify to the importance of individual lives and places even after they have changed for the long term, have altered irrevocably, or have been permanently obliterated.

The books and essays that Danticat has published since her first novel reveal her commitment to continuing the process of reimagining her Haitian heritage in dialogue with her own migrant experiences and those of other members of the Haitian diaspora. Danticat, as evidenced by the subtitle of *Create Dangerously*, tends to refer to herself as an "immigrant" rather than as a "diasporan" or a "diasporic individual"—in contrast to Caryl Phillips, for example, who in his essays often explicitly does the latter (while also using the lexicon of exile and migrancy). Danticat's 2001 introduction to *The Butterfly's Way: Voice from the Haitian Dyaspora in the United States*, in which she notes that in Haiti being called a *Dyaspora* often means being told that the addressee has lived overseas too long to truly understand Haitian life any more,[214] explains why she refers to herself as a diasporic individual less frequently than many other African-descended writers do: in Haiti the term is used, pejoratively, to refer to a semi-outsider who is no longer in touch with her Haitian roots and has lost her alleged ethnocultural "authenticity." Danticat's linguistic preference, "immigrant," also underscores that she has emphatically embraced the calling of being a Haitian-born writer in the United States: she sees the task of educating Americans about Haiti's past and present as part of her vocation, and she stays focused on these two countries and their complicated relationship.[215] In addition to her creative work as a writer of fiction and nonfiction, Danticat has, as Brinda Mehta summarizes, used her fame and visibility "to denounce police brutality against Haitians," to speak out against "human rights abuses in Haiti and the Dominican Republic," to advocate for "immigration reform and bilingual education," and to partake "in community outreach and cultural awareness programs to create a sense of identity and belonging among diasporic communities in the United States."[216] Because of her primary focus on US-Haitian relations, Danticat frequently uses the word "diaspora" in reference to the *Haitian* diaspora rather than to the *African* diaspora at large.

Nevertheless, although Danticat focuses on the US-Haiti axis and primarily uses the term "diaspora" to refer to Haitian expatriates in the United States and beyond, her writing is permeated with material that reveals the utmost importance of Africa, Africanity, and the African diaspora for her thought. Such material is present in *Breath, Eyes, Memory* as well. For example, when Haitian American Sophie and her future husband, African American Joseph, meet for the first time, Joseph points out that their shared African heritage—rather than, for example, their newly shared Americanness—is what they, although they are strangers to each other, have in common.[217] Also, when Martine, her partner Marc, Sophie, and Joseph all gather together for the first (and last) time, Marc exclaims, "We are all African."[218] The group sings African American spirituals, and Marc recognizes the direct kinship between "Oh Mary, Don't You Weep" and the Voudou song "Erzulie, Don't You Weep."[219] Linking the Virgin Mary with Erzulie, Christianity with Voudou, and the West with an Africa memoried by black diasporans, this scene brings together connections formed around the symbolic homeland of Africa ("We are all African"), from which the first-generation slaves were uprooted violently (hence the need for consolation, "don't you weep") with lateral diasporic connectivity, because the similarity between the two songs suggests a flow of black cultural influences across national borders. As James Clifford writes in *Routes*, "the transnational connections linking diasporas need not be articulated primarily through a real or symbolic homeland. . . . Decentered, lateral connections may be as important as those formed around a teleology of origin/return."[220] In *Breath, Eyes, Memory*, Danticat emphasizes the importance of both the symbolic homeland and the lateral connections rather than choosing, or asking the reader to choose, between the two.

Shortly before her death, Martine expresses the wish that the spiritual "Sometimes I Feel Like a Motherless Child" be sung at her funeral.[221] By articulating a diasporic individual's longing for the symbolic motherland that she paradoxically envisions both as a lost mother and as a source of solace, Martine implicitly requests to be reunited with her "Mother Africa" in death. The presence of Africa in Danticat's literary imagination and in her characters' diasporic imaginary is, indeed, the most evident in the spiritual belief of the novel's Dame Marie community that their dead will go to "Guinea."[222] While the villagers literally use the name "Guinea" to refer to the hill where their graveyard is located,[223] their spiritual conviction transcends the local geography by suggesting that their dead join their African ancestors: in death, the diasporans' exile is over, and they return to where their forebears came from. For the Caco women, the existence of "Guinea" in their midst serves as a constant reminder of their diasporic (be)longing, which mandates an ever-continuing dialectic between adaptation and resistance in their New World lives.

Conclusion

A State of Independence, *Sleep On, Beloved*, and *Breath, Eyes, Memory*—each of which focuses on a different Caribbean national background while portraying a black Caribbean migration experience—all depict, briefly or extensively, diasporans' return trips back to the Caribbean. This chapter has shown, first, that regardless of whether such returns are cast as emotionally significant "homecomings," as disappointing visits, or as complex combinations of the two, they play a pivotal role in how the three novels' main characters interpret their pasts and envision their futures as members of their families, of two nations, of the Caribbean diaspora, and—crucially, from the perspective of this book—of the African diaspora. Second, this chapter has emphasized that while Phillips, Foster, and Danticat are all generations removed from their African origins (although Phillips, who in 1990 acted as a visiting lecturer at the University of Ghana, has been to Africa on several occasions), each of the three novels engages Africa, thereby signaling its status as a participant in the project of writing the African diaspora (to riff on Homi Bhabha's famous concept of "writing the nation").[224] In *A State of Independence*, such engagement may seem fleeting. Yet, Bertram's reflections on abandoned sugar mills as emblems of the difficulty of appropriately commemorating slavery resonate with Keith Sandiford's 2011 commentary on the close connection between the ocean and sugar in the Caribbean Atlantic and black Atlantic imaginaries[225]—a connection that, obviously, points to Africa as the source of the slave labor used on sugar plantations.

"Caribbean identity" cannot, of course, be automatically equated with "African diasporic identity," due to the complex history of the Caribbean and the resulting ethnoracial and cultural diversity and creolization characterizing the region. As Judith A. Byfield, Denzer LaRay, and Anthea Morrison point out in discussing the region's past, "African descent did not encompass the full range of West Indian identity formation," and "Africanness sometimes existed in tension with national identities that crystallized over time."[226] Furthermore, the extent to which contemporary black Caribbean diasporans in North America highlight the African diasporic dimension of their identities in their daily lives and cultural practices varies immensely from group to group and from individual to individual. However, all three novels examined in this chapter deliberately situate themselves in the tradition of African diasporic writing: they not only acknowledge black Caribbean diasporans' historical connection with Africa but also weave this connection into their narratives of black diasporic identity and its formation.

In the introduction to this book, I quoted the conclusion at which Saidiya Hartman arrives, in the end of *Lose Your Mother*, about her personal relationship to her African heritage: "The legacy that I chose to claim was articulated in the ongoing struggle to escape, stand down, and defeat slavery in all of its myriad forms. . . . It was a dream of autonomy rather than nationhood."[227] When Danticat's Sophie, after losing her mother, directs her grief and anger into beating the cane field in Dame Marie, she, too, seeks to "defeat slavery in all of its myriad forms." Having given Martine back to Haitian soil and to "Guinea," Sophie decides, after all, not to lose either her mother(land) or herself to any legacy of oppression (racial, sexual, economic, or cultural), but to live as a black woman in the New World, as an African-descended Haitian in the United States—in touch with her multiple heritages and aware that she is entitled to both connection and autonomy, both rootedness and freedom. In a 2000 essay titled "AHA!" Danticat, in a similar vein, writes that being an "*AHA*, African-Haitian-American," means living out "the following elements: African to acknowledge our ancestral roots deep in the African continent; Haitian, because of course most of us were either born in Haiti or were first generation born of Haitian parents; and American because we were from the

Americas, living in the other 'America,' the United States of America."[228] In *Sleep On, Beloved*, Foster's Suzanne reaches a very similar, though less analytically articulated, conclusion regarding her African- and Jamaican-descended life in Canada. In "Necessary Journeys" (2004), Phillips, too, writes about his "triple heritage of journeying: British, African diasporan, Caribbean."[229] His rendering of Bertram's existential processes in *A State of Independence* is in dialogue with his own connectedess with this "triple heritage." Phillips, Foster, and Danticat all acknowledge the importance of at least three contexts,[230] Africa included, that define their diasporic consciousness, and each writer approaches the African diaspora as a condition whereby movement, migration, accommodation, resistance, and black agency produce fluid identities that draw on "journeying," hybridity, process, and change.

Epilogue

As noted at the beginning of this book, secular culture plays a crucial role in producing and reproducing the African diasporic imaginary—that is, in keeping alive the sense that there *is* something that can be called a black diasporic community and something that can be called a black diasporic identity, however nonnormatively defined. Concerned with one type of cultural production, this book has analyzed a selection of contemporary fiction by writers of the old Anglophone African diaspora in the West: novels depicting movement, migration, and dislocation in various stages and settings of black Atlantic history. These novels reimagine the lives of uprooted groups and individuals of African descent on the Atlantic rim and, in so doing, actively contribute to the transnational formation of black diasporic identity/consciousness—a formation that is an ongoing sociocultural process, neither new nor finished.

I have stressed, from the outset, that the old Anglophone African diaspora in the West is characterized by considerable ethnic, national, socioeconomic, sociocultural, religious, and political diversity, as well as by markedly different interplays of race, class, and gender in different geographical locations and microcontexts. Black diasporic sensibilities perpetually renew and transform themselves in response to the limitless variety of life experiences in the diaspora. Nevertheless, rather than merely emphasizing black diversity for its own sake, I have repeatedly brought the discussion back to the original propellers of the old African diaspora, in order to underscore the coexistence of past and present in diasporic identification and consciousness. More specifically, this book's diasporic hermeneutics have highlighted, first, the historical origin of the old African diaspora in the Middle Passage and slavery and, second, the cultural mediation of the collective memory of this ur-event. The emphasis on the old African diaspora's origin in involuntary displacement (that is, an emphasis on an *event*, rather than on geographically locatable "roots" or on cultural "authenticity") has enabled me to ground my approach to diaspora in a racially antiessentialist understanding of black diasporic identity formation and to focus on the commemoration and reimagining of the historical urexperience of uprooting in cultural production—here, in black Anglophone fiction.

As my readings of such novels as Johnson's *Middle Passage* and Hill's *The Book of Negroes* have demonstrated, fictional Middle Passage narratives on the one hand mourn the individual and collective lives and memories that were lost as a result of the Atlantic slave trade as well as depict the emergence of a racialized and pejoratively understood "blackness" in the Americas and Europe. On the other hand, they celebrate black agency and highlight the innovative strategies of survival, acclimatization, and resistance developed by enslaved Africans and their descendants. These themes, in modified yet recognizable forms, are also powerfully present in the novels about later black migrations analyzed in this book: even though such works as Lamming's *The Emigrants*, Phillips's *The Final Passage*, and Foster's *Sleep On, Beloved* are not about the Middle Passage per se, they nevertheless briefly reference Africa, the Middle Passage, and the early African presence in the New World. They thereby highlight their participation in the project of writing the African diaspora, to echo and modify Homi Bhabha's famous concept of "writing the nation."[1] For example, one of Lamming's minor characters refers to the hopeful West Indian migrants journeying to England in the early 1950s as "a bit o' cargo" crowded together in the tightly packed dormitories of an emigrant ship (a reference to the circumstances on slave ships). Phillips's Leila Preston nostalgically reflects, upon leaving the West Indies, on the breadfruit trees that for her represent continuity with her and her fellow black Caribbeans' African past. Foster's Ona Nedd ponders the connections between the Middle Passage and her own migration to Toronto when she flies over the Atlantic rim following the burial of her mother in Jamaica. As these and the other references to Africa, the Middle Passage, and the early African presence in the Americas discussed in chapters 3, 4, and 5 indicate, the novels in question depict twentieth-century black transnational migrations (the movement of black labor, in particular) as taking place in dialogue with sociopolitical and sociocultural developments that are connected with the legacy of the colonialist and imperialist exploitation of black labor.

Paul C. Johnson's *Diaspora Conversions*, which I referenced while discussing diasporic religiosity, articulates insights relevant to the theorization of diaspora that deserve to be highlighted here. Johnson "views diasporas as not simply determined by biological descent or by historical fiat, but rather as a possible subject position . . . , a way of seeing adopted to varying degrees."[2] This view, which emphasizes self-identification and choice, resonates with the obvious fact that not every single black-authored novel published in the contemporary Anglophone world identifies itself as diasporic. That is, not every black novel either alludes to the Middle Passage and enslavement or applies some other strategy signaling African diasporic self-identification, such as an emphasis on lateral black diasporic connectivity. However, the novels analyzed in this book do so. In different ways and "to varying degrees," they place themselves within an African diasporic framework and orient themselves toward what Johnson calls a "diasporic horizon."[3] At times, they accomplish this goal by depicting diasporic religiosity and by using the idiom of spirituality. Danticat's *Breath, Eyes, Memory*, in which a Haitian cemetery is named "Guinea"—a reference to the religious hope that African diasporans will be united with their ancestors after death—is a case in point, as is the explicit evocation of "Mother Africa" as a source of nurture and spiritually conceived pan-Africanism in Jamaican Pocomania services in *Sleep On, Beloved*.

While the term "diasporic horizon" is relevant in connection with diasporic religiosity, it can also be applied to secular contexts. As Johnson points out, the term "horizon" suggests an orientation toward the future as well as the past: "By naming a horizon of expectation, they [diasporas] provide solidarity, purpose, identity, and futurity."[4] He goes on to note that diasporic mobilization, including such activities as religious rituals, fund-raising, and campaigning, takes place "[a]gainst this horizon."[5] In recent years, "mobilization" has, indeed, emerged as a key concept in diaspora studies,[6] in part because of Martin Sökefeld's influential 2006 argument that "the formation of diaspora is not a 'natural' consequence of migration but that specific processes of mobilization have to take place for a diaspora to emerge."[7] Although for Sökefeld "mobilization" is a concept primarily related to social and political life and movements, the *cultural* mediation of diasporic memory can be interpreted as yet another type of "mobilization" that also allows a diasporic consciousness to emerge and develop. Indeed, Sökefeld himself concedes that "it is difficult conceptually to separate diaspora as social form from diaspora as a type of consciousness."[8] Emphasizing the latter, Aisha Khan remarks, "Diaspora is a particular kind of historical experience[:] . . . the very fact of uprootedness has shaped the sense of self of entire communities. A consciousness thus emerges among members of a community who in everyday discourse and practice memorialize their displacement."[9] In addition to "everyday discourse and practice," diasporic displacement can also be effectively memorialized and reimagined in and through fiction, as this book has emphasized, and in and through other literary, visual, and performing arts.

In the introduction, I quoted from Dionne Brand's self-designed epigraph to *A Map to the Door of No Return*: "There are maps to the Door of No Return.... But to the Door of No Return which is illuminated in the consciousness of Blacks in the Diaspora there are no maps."[10] Indeed, the science of cartography cannot, in itself, say much about black diasporic consciousness; rather, black "exiles must make their own maps," to summon again Derek Walcott's memorable line from *Midsummer*.[11] This book has shown that historically oriented fiction that is interested in both the empirical realities and the existential dimensions of the African diasporic experience is extremely well suited for such "map-making." In the novels discussed here, such "maps" focus on routes and passages rather than on "roots" as guarantors of alleged cultural authenticity. This focus on passages, to quote Gilroy, "break[s] the simple sequence of explanatory links between place, location, and consciousness."[12] In Gilroyan hermeneutics, such a dismantling of allegedly self-evident associative links between place and identity is a crucial aspect of the work that diaspora does. That is, the theoretical concept and empirical reality of diaspora serves as a critique *both* of any idealization of ethnoracially homogeneous nation-states (whether such idealization is derived from nineteenth-century national romanticism or from other sources) *and* of the kind of nostalgia for roots that characterizes ahistorical, romantic varieties of Afrocentrism.

My "cartographical" project in this book has been an open-ended process of mapping out some of the terrain of the literary expressions that black Anglophone novelists have given to diasporic identity/consciousness in recent decades. By way of conclusion, two final comments that point to possible paths for future scholarship are in order. My first comment concerns the relationship between the old and new African diasporas in the Western world: not only are the "new African diasporas" in the West producing new writers from their midst, but some novelists of the older African and African Caribbean diasporas in Europe and North America have also begun actively conversing with the stories and histories of newly diasporic Africans. Caryl Phillips's *A Distant Shore* is a prime example of such a dialogue. True, African characters have been present in Caribbean-born writers' post–World War II novels about black immigrants in Britain from the outset: both George Lamming's *The Emigrants* and Sam Selvon's *The Lonely Londoners* offered brief glimpses into the experience of Nigerians in London. However, they almost exclusively focused on rather spectacular Nigerian men, such as Lamming's elusive and enigmatic mathematical genius/nightclub manager Azi and Selvon's happy-go-lucky womanizer, Cap(tain). In *A Distant Shore*, Phillips significantly expands and deepens this tradition by telling the tragic story of a West African male—both a victim of and a participant in the violence tearing his country apart—who tries to establish a new life for himself in England but loses his battle against racist expectations concerning blackness in general and black manhood in particular. Phillips's *Foreigners*, with its narrative of the fate of David Oluwale, also focuses on a newly diasporic African's struggle in England. Lawrence Hill's *The Illegal*, a 2015 novel about a marathon runner of African descent who leaves his home country to escape political oppression, exemplifies a similar trend in black Canadian writing. These new lateral developments in the cultural production of the African diaspora offer important opportunities for scholars studying contemporary debates over whether black solidarity exists in the twenty-first-century world. As Patrick Manning observes in *The African Diaspora*, today the "need for community faces its greatest contradiction in the expanding economic inequality among humans,"[13] and it is clear that members of the African diaspora also experience such growing divisions among themselves. However, although such challenges are tangible and real, some of the diaspora's recent literary production actively supports, through empathetic storytelling, black solidarity across ethnicity, social class, and the division between the old and new African diasporas.

Second, black diaspora studies operate at the intersection of race-based and transnational approaches. These two types of approaches may occasionally be in productive conflict with each other because transnational approaches ask questions about equality, solidarity, and alliance-formation in ways that both converse with and, at times, transcend racialization studies. It is hardly a coincidence that Paul Gilroy, who made the term "Black Atlantic" famous and is one of the founders of black diaspora studies, in *Against Race* writes about his utopian longing for a postracial era, or that Caryl Phillips, one of the most emphatically diasporic black writers of our era, frequently portrays interracial friendships and relationships in his fiction. It is an important part of the work of scholars to study and articulate the meanings of various existential, cultural, and socioeconomic classifications—such as "race"—that have come into existence either outside or within academia. Relatedly, we must continue to interrogate and reevaluate the past and present usefulness of such categories and constructs and pose for ourselves the critical question of whether our work perhaps at times contributes to their persistence. We must address these questions continuously because societies and cultures are always in a state of flux, always transforming themselves. Such changes now in part occur in response to opportunities for transnational communication through digital media, which place more people in informal contact with each other than has ever been the case before, thus facilitating transformative encounters and alliances among strangers across national and ethnoracial borders in ways that were unimaginable just a few decades ago.

Notes

Introduction: Passages to (Be)Longing

1. Hill, *The Book of Negroes*, 301, 318.
2. Winfried Siemerling locates Aminata's home village in Niger but does not offer any evidence to substantiate this claim (*The Black Atlantic Reconsidered*, 171). My suggestion that the novel's Bayo is located in what is now known as Mali is supported by Hill's thanks, in the acknowledgments section of *The Book of Negroes*, to Valentin Vydrine, who "answered many questions to do with languages and ethnic groups in the West African country now known as Mali" (482), and by his remarks in interviews ("Projecting History Honestly," 315; "A Person of Many Places," 304). The novel's Bayo is fictional, but Hill's commentary on its approximate whereabouts places it in Mali.
3. This book indeed focuses on the Atlantic world, rather than, for example, including Afro-Asian sites.
4. I acknowledge, of course, that the history of the Western world has known early, including pre-Columbian, black travelers and migrants whose identity positions cannot be characterized by alluding to the Middle Passage. See, for example, Peter Fryer's discussion of the first black people in Britain (*Staying Power*, chapter 1), which opens with a mention of black soldiers in the Roman imperial army. See also my brief discussion of new African diasporas under the heading "Language, Geography, and the Old and New African Diasporas" in this introduction.
5. Khan, "Dark Arts and Diaspora," 43.
6. Ibid.; italics added.
7. Warner-Lewis, "Cultural Reconfigurations," 19.
8. See my brief discussion of "collective memory" under the heading "Diaspora, Collective Memory, and Cultural Mediation" in this introduction. For a thorough critical overview of the emergence of "memory" and "collective memory" as key concepts in the historically oriented humanities, see chapter 5 of Kerwin Lee Klein's *From History to Theory* (112–37), an earlier version of which was published as "On the Emergence of *Memory* in Historical Discourse" in *Representations* 69 (Winter 2000): 127–50.

9. As for recent scholarly works on black diasporic fiction, the subtitle of Heather Russell's *Legba's Crossing: Narratology in the African Atlantic* (2009) may, at first sight, suggest an overlap with my book. However, Russell examines African American and African Caribbean novels; black Canada and black Britain are beyond the purview of her study. Also, her primary focus—narratology, broadly (and in part metaphorically) understood—is very different from mine. In *At Home In Diaspora* (2005), Wendy W. Walters, in turn, analyzes "black international writing," as the subtitle of her book indicates. Of the five authors whom she studies, two are African American (Richard Wright and Chester Himes), two are Caribbean-born and US-based (Michelle Cliff and Caryl Phillips), and one is a Swiss-born Francophone cosmopolitan, of Cameroonian descent, living in Paris (Simon Njami). Despite the obvious intellectual resonance between her methodology and mine, Walters's main goals and foci differ from mine both in *At Home In Diaspora* and in her 2013 book, *Archives of the Black Atlantic*, which is a nuanced exploration of African-descended literary authors' treatment of history, with an emphasis on these writers' "skeptical" and revisionary use of "dominant archives" (2). Neither black Britain nor black Canada is part of the scope of either study; instead, both include at least one African-born Francophone author. Also, *Archives of the Black Atlantic* analyzes both fiction and poetry. My book, in turn, concentrates on black *Anglophone* diasporic *novels*; is structured as a chronological narrative, with respect to the depicted eras; and focuses on literary representations of, and contributions to, black diasporic identity formation.

10. This trend is, I repeat, no categorical rule because, as a group, black diasporic novelists of course write for any number of purposes, including entertainment, the novel being a vastly diverse genre in terms of both form and content. Nevertheless, the frequent references in black historical fiction to how the "black Atlantic" came into being constitute an important phenomenon that should not be overlooked in discussions of contemporary literary constructions of black diasporic identity.

11. See B. Anderson, *Imagined Communities*.

12. Appadurai, *Modernity at Large*, 161.

13. Sökefeld, "Mobilizing in Transnational Space," 266–67.

14. M. Wright, *Becoming Black*, 1.

15. Sidbury, *Becoming African in America*, 6.

16. Ibid., 6–7.

17. Ibid.

18. Ibid., 7; italics added.

19. For a more detailed discussion of *Jazz*'s treatment of war, see Valkeakari, "Beyond the Riverside," 149–52.

20. For Du Bois's famous definition of double consciousness, see *The Souls of Black Folk*, 10–11. Gilroy inserted Du Bois's concept into the subtitle of his 1993 classic, *The Black Atlantic: Modernity and Double Consciousness*. Samir Dayal used the term "diasporic double consciousness," in this exact form, in his 1996 essay, "Diaspora and

Double Consciousness," while discussing the contributions of Gilroy and others to theorizing diaspora: "There is a strategic value in cultivating a diasporic double consciousness" (47). Dayal elaborated on his use of the term as follows: "Doubleness as I am conceptualizing it is less a 'both/and' and more a 'neither just this/nor just that.' My attempt here is to conceive doubleness negatively, to explode the positive and equilibristic constructions of diaspora around the desire for belonging" (47).

21. I here allude to the term "fictions of belonging," the main title of Gerard Carruthers's 2005 article that discusses national identity and the novel in Ireland and Scotland.

22. Gilroy, "Diaspora and the Detours of Identity," 329.

23. See, for example, Davies and M'Bow, "Towards African Diaspora Citizenship," and the conclusion titled "Igniting Diaspora Citizenship" in Daniel, *Caribbean and Atlantic Diaspora Dance*, 189–95.

24. Workplace, family, and place of worship are examples of "microcontexts" in the sense intended here.

25. Stephens, *Black Empire*, 13.

26. Walvin, *Making the Black Atlantic*, x.

27. According to the sociologist Rubén G. Rumbaut's influential definition, a 1.5-generation immigrant arrives in the receiving society under age eighteen. See, for example, Rumbaut, "Severed or Sustained Attachments?" 49.

28. See Koser, ed., *New African Diasporas*. For edited volumes that specifically focus on African-descended people in Europe, see, for example, *Africa in Europe*, edited by Rosenhaft and Aitken, and *Black Europe and the African Diaspora*, edited by Hine, Keaton, and Small.

29. As Stéphane Dufoix remarks in *Diasporas*, "starting in the 1970s, this ancient word ["diaspora"] underwent an amazing inflation that peaked in the 1990s, by which time it was being applied to most of the world's peoples" (1). Even if Dufoix's statement may seem slightly hyperbolical, the gist of it—the claim that there has been an exponential increase in the popularity and use of "diaspora"—is inarguable. Scholars have both noticed and significantly contributed to this development. In his 2005 landmark article, "The 'Diaspora' Diaspora," Rogers Brubaker provocatively argued that the proliferation of meanings applied to "diaspora" in both non-academic and academic forums had resulted in a "'diaspora' diaspora," that is, in "a dispersion of the meanings of the term in semantic, conceptual, and disciplinary space" (1). Considering these developments, it is no wonder that "diaspora studies," in a comparative sense, has become an interdisciplinary academic field in its own right. The 1991 launching of the journal *Diaspora: A Journal of Transnational Studies* was a major milestone in the field's evolution, and institutional academic units focusing on comparative diasporas have also begun to emerge; the University of Toronto, for example, is currently home to a Centre for Diaspora and Transnational Studies.

30. Braziel and Mannur, "Nation, Migration, Globalization," 2.

31. Cohen, *Global Diasporas* (2nd ed., 2008), chapter 1 (1–19).

32. See, for example, ibid., 2–4, 39–40. Cohen also uses the term "victim diaspora" extensively in the first edition (1997) of his book.

33. Cohen, *Global Diasporas* (2nd ed., 2008), 1.

34. Ibid. Political, ideological, or conceptual differences at times prevent scholars from agreeing unanimously on which diasporas should "qualify" as victim diasporas. As Cohen notes, the Palestinian diaspora is a case in point.

35. Ibid., 1–2, 4–11.

36. Ibid., 1–2; see also 9–11.

37. Ibid., 12.

38. Ibid., 2, 11–14. For Cohen's proposal for the defining characteristics of diasporas, see 161–62.

39. Campt and D. Thomas, "Gendering Diaspora," 2.

40. Ibid., 1, 2.

41. Ibid., 3; italics added.

42. Gilroy, *Against Race*, 124.

43. G. Fabre and Benesch, "Introduction: The Concept of African Diaspora(s)," xviii. Cohen, too, somewhat wryly asserts in the second edition of *Global Diasporas* that the bare basic parameters of the "victim diaspora" model offer "too narrow an interpretation even of the experience of the paradigmatic case, the Jewish people" (159). He had already made the same point, a little more cautiously, in the first edition of *Global Diasporas* (xi).

44. I am aware that it has become something of an industry to criticize *The Black Atlantic* for everything that it does not do. For example, *The Black Atlantic* does not focus on Africa, nor does it discuss the old Francophone, Hispanophone, Lusophone, or Dutch-speaking African diasporas, or a particularly wide range of the new African diasporas either. (For more comprehensive critiques, see, for example, Braziel, *Duvalier's Ghosts*, chapter 1; Durán-Almarza, "Introduction," 1–2; Fraile-Marcos, "M/Othering Black Female Subjectivity," 184. See also Gikandi's and Dayan's well-known concerns referenced in my chapter 1, paragraph 4 and notes 11 and 12. For a recent book-length essay collection that evaluates *The Black Atlantic* and its legacy, see *New Perspectives on the Black Atlantic*, edited by Ledent and Cuder-Domínguez.) Raising important issues, criticisms of Gilroy's book have advanced academic dialogue about the African diaspora. At times, however, they seem to attack *The Black Atlantic* for failing to deliver what it does not promise. While Gilroy "heuristically" (3) and tentatively proposes the term "the black Atlantic world" (3), he is clear, from the outset (4, 15, 17, 19), about African America, the (Anglophone) Caribbean and black Britain/Europe being the main geographical foci of *The Black Atlantic*. The book does not attempt to cover everything or offer a large survey; instead, it focuses on "figures who begin as African-Americans or Caribbean people and are then changed into

something else which evades those specific labels and with them all fixed notions of nationality and national identity" (19).

45. See, in particular, Clifford, *Routes*.

46. See Clifford, "Introduction: The Pure Products Go Crazy." Williams's poem "The pure products of America / go crazy" was originally published in Williams, *Spring and All*, 64–71.

47. For a longer discussion of Gilroy's reflections on racial essentialism, antiessentialism, and "anti-antiessentialism" in *There Ain't No Black in the Union Jack*, *The Black Atlantic*, and *Small Acts*, see Valkeakari, "Between Camps: Paul Gilroy and the Dilemma of Race," 22–25.

48. See, for example, Gilroy, *The Black Atlantic*, 80.

49. Ibid., xi; italics in the original.

50. See Jones, "The Changing Same (R&B and New Black Music)."

51. Gilroy, *The Black Atlantic*, 102.

52. Ibid., 81.

53. Edwards, *The Practice of Diaspora*, 13.

54. Ibid., 13–14.

55. Ibid., 13.

56. For works with a strong and explicitly elaborated focus on the fluidity and malleability of "race" and racial formations, see, for example, Appiah, *In My Father's House*; Gilroy, *Against Race*; Guterl, *The Color of Race in America*; Roediger, *How Race Survived U.S. History*; Roediger and Esch, *The Production of Difference*; and such important works in whiteness studies (which some of the above-mentioned titles also in part represent) as Jacobson, *Whiteness of a Different Color*; Painter, *The History of White People*; Roediger, *Colored White*; and Roediger, *Working toward Whiteness*.

57. The current main trend in discussions of "blackness" is, indeed, to highlight and celebrate the vast diversity that characterizes the world's diasporic black populations both within and between the various groups. In the United States, such books as *Thirteen Ways of Looking at Black Man* (1997), by Henry Louis Gates Jr., and *Black Cool: One Thousand Streams of Blackness* (2012), edited by Rebecca Walker, exemplify this trend. So does *Who's Afraid of Post-Blackness: What It Means to Be Black Now* (2011), by the popular cultural critic and television personality Touré [Neblett], *if* this (US) "post-blackness" is understood, as Touré does, as not leaving behind "blackness" itself but, instead, as "leaving behind the vision of Blackness as something narrowly definable" and as "embracing every conception of Blackness as legitimate" (Touré, *Who's Afraid of Post-Blackness*, 12). Michael Eric Dyson performs a linguistic and interpretive act identical with Touré's when he says, in his introduction to Touré's book, that "post-Black ... doesn't signify the end of Blackness" but "points, instead, to the end of the reign of a narrow, single notion of Blackness" ("Tour(é)ing Blackness," xv).

58. Dalton, *Racial Healing*, 108.

59. For a longer meditation on *There Ain't No Black in the Union Jack*, *The Black Atlantic*, and *Against Race*, see Valkeakari, "Between Camps: Paul Gilroy and the Dilemma of Race."

60. The fundamental problem with the concept of race is the historical baggage that it carries: in the Western world, the history of the idea of "race" is more or less identical with the history of racism. For book-length elaborations of this argument, see, for example, Hannaford, *Race*, and Fredrickson, *Racism*. See also the American Anthropological Association's "Statement on 'Race.'" For an overview of the rise of the idea of race in colonial Virginia (a context highly relevant for the early development of race-thinking in what is now the United States), see Roediger, *How Race Survived*, chapter 1.

61. See, for example, Gilroy, *Postcolonial Melancholia*, 9.

62. For a book-length study on the genealogy of "yellowness" as a racial term, see Keevak, *Becoming Yellow*. For a corresponding treatment of "redness," see, for example, Goddard, "I Am a Red-Skin."

63. Gilroy argues in *Against Race* that even empowering and celebratory uses of "blackness," let alone of "whiteness," contribute to the existence of the racial fault line (12–13).

64. Brand, epigraph to *A Map to the Door of No Return*.

65. Khan, "Dark Arts and Diaspora," 44.

66. See note 8 above.

67. Klein, *From History to Theory*, 123.

68. Ibid.

69. As Eyerman notes in *Cultural Trauma* (5), in cultural sociology the roots of this approach to memory lie in Émile Durkheim's notion of collective consciousness. Halbwachs, who perished at the Buchenwald concentration camp in 1945, was the most prominent second-generation Durkheimian sociologist developing the notion of collective memory. See Halbwachs, *The Collective Memory*; and Halbwachs, *On Collective Memory*.

70. Eyerman, *Cultural Trauma*, 5. As he acknowledges, Eyerman here references the title of Paul Connerton's 1989 book, *How Societies Remember*.

71. Eyerman, *Cultural Trauma*, 1.

72. Ibid.

73. Ibid., 3.

74. To add a quick caveat, during the twentieth century—its early decades, in particular—the relationship of African American collective identity formation and culture with slavery was, in my view, a more complicated process than Eyerman acknowledges. (See Berlin, Favreau, and Miller's "Introduction: Slavery as Memory and History" for an overview of what these three scholars aptly term the "struggle over slavery's memory" [xv] in US academic historiography and in American society at large.) To give just one example, the first African American neo-slave narrative,

Margaret Walker's *Jubilee*, was not published until 1966. As this late date suggests, in many African American circles slavery was long viewed as a topic to move on from rather than to dwell upon. However, in the 1970s and the '80s, *Roots: The Saga of an American Family* (1976; adapted as a popular television series in the late 1970s), by the late Alex Haley, and the Pulitzer Prize-winning *Beloved* (1987), by the 1993 Nobel Laureate Toni Morrison, accomplished a great deal by successfully reminding both black and white Americans that the shame associated with slavery should not be projected on the *victims* of the institution. These cultural products for their part paved the way for more open discussions in public and political forums about the ever-present legacies of slavery in the Western Hemisphere. At the same time, they facilitated conversations among African Americans about the role and locus of early black Atlantic history in contemporary African American identity formation in ways that had not been particularly popular even during the civil rights movement or in its immediate aftermath, let alone during the earlier decades of the twentieth century. Saidiya Hartman, for example, in *Lose Your Mother* recalls the silence about slavery at a Black Power summer camp that she attended as a schoolgirl: "The counselors taught us to disdain property, perform the Black Power handshake, and march in strict formation, but they never mentioned the Middle Passage or chattel persons" (11).

75. Eyerman, *Cultural Trauma*, 6.
76. Ibid., 4.
77. C. Phillips, *The European Tribe*, 99.
78. M. Wright, "Middle Passage Blackness," 217.
79. Ibid., 220.
80. Keizer, *Black Subjects*, 11; italics added.
81. Guridy, *Forging Diaspora*, xi.
82. Carby, "Becoming Modern Racialized Subjects," 631, 632. For a more detailed discussion of Equiano in the same article, see 629–35.
83. Althusser, "Ideology and Ideological State Apparatuses," 170.
84. As Stuart Hall observed in "The Problem of Ideology" (36), Althusser "put on the agenda the whole neglected issue of how ideology becomes internalized, how we come to speak 'spontaneously,' within the limits of the categories of thought which exist outside us and which can more accurately be said to think us."
85. Butler, *Bodies That Matter*, 123.
86. Ibid., 124.
87. M. Wright, "Middle Passage Blackness," 220.
88. Hall, "Cultural Identity and Diaspora," 244.
89. Gilroy, *Against Race*, 123; italics added.
90. Hall, "Negotiating Caribbean Identities," 9.
91. Edwards, "The Uses of 'Diaspora,'" 29.
92. For example, Frazier opened *The Negro Church in America* (1964; copyrighted in 1963) by stating that "because of the manner in which the Negroes were captured in

Africa and enslaved, they were practically stripped of their social heritage" (1), and by arguing that the mechanisms of "selection [of Africans] for the slave markets tended to reduce to a minimum the possibility of the retention and the transmission of African culture" (1). This statement stands in rather stark contrast to W.E.B. Du Bois's identification of the black church as the core of the surviving African heritage on American soil in *The Philadelphia Negro* (1899), although it must be added that for Du Bois, at the time he wrote the book, "the church really represented *all* that was left of African tribal life, and was the *sole* expression of the organized efforts of the slaves" (*The Philadelphia Negro*, 197; italics added). For a brief but relevant discussion of Frazier's antisurvivalist position in *The Negro Church in America* and beyond, see Holloway, introduction to *Africanisms in American Culture*, ix.

93. The title of the 1990 essay collection *Africanisms in American Culture*—a book that opens with the editor Joseph E. Holloway's survey of earlier works addressing the same topic and with a brief synopsis of the Herskovits-Frazier debate (see also Dimock, "African, Caribbean, American," 38–39, for such a synopsis)—is indicative not only of that single volume's content and approach, but also of a more comprehensive development in the humanities and social sciences within African American and American studies in recent decades. As Michael A. Gomez wrote in 2000, "There is little doubt that the old debate over Africanisms between Melville Herskovits and E. Franklin Frazier has long been settled in favor of the former. The evidence of a continuing African culture in North America, albeit changing and reconfiguring, is simply overwhelming" ("Preacher-Kings," 502).

94. Mbembé remarks in "African Modes of Self-Writing": "The extreme case of South Africa (and other settler colonies) has long led people, both in the West and Africa, to think that the polar opposition between blacks and whites summed up by itself the whole racial question in Africa. . . . In fact—no matter what definition one gives the notion—the racial unity of Africa has always been a myth. But this myth is currently imploding under the impact of internal (as well as external) factors connected with African societies' linkages to global cultural flows" (264).

95. For a book-length scholarly survey and sharp critique of Afrocentrism, see Howe, *Afrocentrism*.

96. As Howe reminds us in *Afrocentrism* (106), "something describable as a literary Afrocentrism" manifested itself in the Black Aesthetic of the Black Arts movement (the artistic counterpart of the Black Power movement of the late 1960s and early 1970s), even though the term "Afrocentrism" was not yet in vogue at the time. For a discussion of the earlier ancestors of Afrocentrism, such as Ethiopianism and pan-Africanism, see, for example, Howe, *Afrocentrism*, part 1 (19–121). In its heyday, Afrocentrism was especially prominent in the United States, but it also existed in the African diaspora beyond US borders; one of its main thinkers, Cheikh Anta Diop (1923–86), was Senegalese, influential in Francophone West Africa as well as in the Francophone black diaspora (in France, in particular). Afrocentrism, too, is now usually regarded

as part of the history of the development of black/Africana studies rather than representing the field's current mainstream, although it would be a mistake to assume that the movement is dead.

97. Although this maternal term, "Mother Africa," now sounds archaic, it is still relevant to discussions of diaspora conceived as orphanhood, as, for example, the title of Hartman's *Lose Your Mother* indicates. One of my primary sources, Cecil Foster's *Sleep On, Beloved*, uses the term explicitly (5).

98. Hughes, *The Big Sea*, 103.

99. Hughes, "Afro-American Fragment."

100. R. Wright, *Black Power*. For a longer discussion of Wright's book, see Schramm, *African Homecoming*, 13–15. See also Gaines, *American Africans in Ghana*, 54–68; Gates, *Tradition and the Black Atlantic*, 7–9; and Gilroy, *The Black Atlantic*, 150–51.

101. Hall, "Negotiating Caribbean Identities," 11.

102. Trouillot, *Silencing the Past*, xix.

103. Ibid., 27.

104. See Hall, "Negotiating Caribbean Identities," 9.

105. Hartman, *Lose Your Mother*, 5, 7.

106. Ibid., 235.

107. Hughes, "Afro-American Fragment," 129.

108. Morrison, *Song of Solomon*, 299–304.

109. See note 97 above.

110. Hartman, *Lose Your Mother*, 234.

111. Diagne, "Keeping Africanity Open."

112. For a book that focuses more systematically on "the place of Africa in the writings and arguments of black diasporic writers and thinkers" (7), see Goyal, *Romance, Diaspora, and Black Atlantic Literature*.

113. Hughes, "Afro-American Fragment," 129.

114. Caryl Phillips was born in St. Kitts and raised and educated in England, and he has mainly been based in the United States since the early 1990s. In addition to his academic appointments in the States, he has also taught at universities in Ghana, Sweden, Singapore, Barbados, and India.

115. See Danticat, "AHA!," especially 39–40.

116. See Danticat, *Create Dangerously*, which carries the subtitle *The Immigrant Artist at Work*.

117. Baldwin, "Autobiographical Notes," 8.

118. Castle, "Don't Pick Up." Castle acknowledges Ian Watt (*Rise of the Novel*) and Tony Tanner (*Adultery in the Novel*) as particularly important commentators on the role of orphanhood in Anglophone novels.

119. See note 9 above.

120. Walters, *Archives of the Black Atlantic*, 1.

121. Gilroy, *Against Race*, 2.

122. Ibid., 122.

Chapter 1. An African American Journey to Black Diasporic Consciousness: Charles Johnson's *Middle Passage*

1. Diedrich, Gates, and Pedersen, "The Middle Passage between History and Fiction," 8. Historian Colin A. Palmer notes that the term "Middle Passage" was probably first deployed by English traders in the eighteenth century ("The Middle Passage," 53). The word "middle" refers to the second leg of what is often visualized as the triangular trade that took ships "from England to Africa, from Africa to the Americas (carrying slaves), and from the Americas back to England" (Webster, "The *Zong* in the Context of the 18th-Century Slave Trade," 286, n2).

2. Diedrich, Gates, and Pedersen, "The Middle Passage between History and Fiction," 8.

3. See, in particular, Roach, *Cities of the Dead: Circum-Atlantic Performance*.

4. Diedrich, Gates, and Pedersen, "The Middle Passage between History and Fiction," 9.

5. Ibid., 8.

6. I use the term "Middle Passage novels" to refer to works of long fiction that converse intimately with the genre of the neo-slave narrative but mainly focus on Africans' forced transatlantic crossings rather than on their lives at New World destinations. Ashraf Rushdy, among others, classifies Johnson's *Middle Passage* as a neo-slave narrative (*Neo-Slave Narratives*, 221–26). I agree that it is possible to think of some Middle Passage novels as forming a distinct category of neo-slave narratives. *Middle Passage*—with its black protagonist's first-person narration that utilizes tropes typical of antebellum slave narratives (such as the connection, established through Rutherford's log, between literacy/writing and freedom)—is an excellent candidate for inclusion in such a category. George Lamming's *Natives of My Person*, in turn (briefly discussed in chapter 4), is an example of a *modified* Middle Passage novel that cannot be primarily classified as a neo-slave narrative drawing from the conventions of antebellum slave narratives because black characters are almost completely absent from the text.

7. For a collection of essays focusing on the philosophical aspects of Johnson's oeuvre, see *Charles Johnson: The Novelist as Philosopher*, edited by Conner and Nash.

8. Gilroy, *The Black Atlantic*, 4.

9. Ibid.

10. See my introduction, note 44.

11. Gikandi, "Introduction," 3. The paraphrased aspects of Gikandi's comments draw on Joan Dayan, "Paul Gilroy's Slaves, Ships, and Routes: The Middle Passage as Metaphor," *Research in African Literatures* 27.4 (Winter 1996): 7–14.

12. Gikandi, "Introduction," 3.

13. Gilroy, *The Black Atlantic*, 4.

14. Bakhtin, *The Dialogic Imagination*, 426; quoted in Gilroy, *The Black Atlantic*, 225n2.

15. Byrd, *Charles Johnson's Novels*, 103.

16. See note 11 above.

17. See, for example, C. Johnson, *Middle Passage*, 66.

18. The comic aspects of Johnson's novel cannot be understood correctly without scrutinizing who is the target of his ironic humor. More often than not, the joke is on Rutherford; it is never on the abused Allmuseri. The novel's comic and ironic dimensions are in dialogue with *Invisible Man*, which Ellison once called "one long, loud rant, howl and laugh" ("Change the Joke and Slip the Yoke," 111): as Ellison's narrator-protagonist tells the story of his "black and blue" existence in a blues voice, he ridicules not only the deceptive schemes of his various "benefactors," but also many of his own past actions. Johnson's Rutherford is another antihero-cum-narrator who retrospectively chuckles at the errors of his youth while narrating his largely tragic, yet in part humorously rendered, life story.

19. Conner, "To Utter the Holy," 58.

20. *Benito Cereno*, first serialized in *Putnam's Monthly* in 1855, was republished in *The Piazza Tales*, a collection of Melville's stories, the following year. The edition that I cite reprints the 1856 version of the text. *Middle Passage* converses with a variety of antecedents, as several critics have observed; Nash (*Charles Johnson's Fiction*, 130–31; 199–200, n1), for example, mentions Melville, Saul Bellow, Olaudah Equiano, James Baldwin, Conrad's sea stories, Homer's *Odyssey*, and Swift's *Gulliver's Travels*. The list could easily be expanded to include, for example, Ellison's *Invisible Man*. I here focus solely on *Benito Cereno*, the role of which as a precursor of *Middle Passage* has not, in my view, been studied sufficiently. Among the critics who most substantially discuss *Benito Cereno* as a subtext of *Middle Passage* are Barbara Z. Thaden ("Charles Johnson's *Middle Passage* as Historiographic Metafiction"), Helen Lock ("The Paradox of Slave Mutiny"), and Deborah Baker Wyrick ("Johnson's Battle of the Books"). What my contribution adds to their analyses is a focus on the important role of perception in both *Benito Cereno* and *Middle Passage*. Secondarily, I also read Johnson's García as a refashioned Cereno.

21. The subtitle of Byrd's *Charles Johnson's Novels* is *Writing the American Palimpsest*, and "palimpsest" is his key metaphor for Johnson's use of intertextuality.

22. C. Johnson, interview by Irene Wanner, 163. Johnson has characterized the Allmuseri as a group "counterpoised to the materialism of the West" and as "the most spiritual tribe imaginable" (C. Johnson, interview by Marian Blue, 135). Johnson's approach to the Allmuseri is idealizing, and he freely admits to having wanted to create "a whole tribe of Mother Teresas and Gandhis" (135). However, he also remarks: "I made up very little. I just borrowed from different third world cultures to create a composite tribe that I wanted to be as non-Western in its values as possible" (136).

23. See, for example, Byrd, *Charles Johnson's Novels*, 111, and Jordan, *African American Servitude*, 153.

24. Jonathan Little (*Charles Johnson's Spiritual Imagination*, 141–42) borrows this term from the Buddhist scholar Hajimi Nakamura.

25. For a relevant discussion of what "emptiness" signifies in Johnson's Buddhist approach, see Gary Storhoff, *Understanding Charles Johnson*, 20–21. Storhoff, a self-identified Buddhist, quotes Dale S. Wright's statement that "the concept of 'emptiness' derives from, and eventually encompasses, the key elements in Buddhist contemplative practice: impermanence, dependent origination, and no self" (Wright, *Philosophical Meditations on Zen Buddhism*, 51; qtd. in Storhoff, *Understanding Charles Johnson*, 21). Storhoff elaborates: "For Johnson, an experiential understanding of emptiness leads to a release from the desires for things in the world around us, even a desire for a unique identity. As protagonists are freed from desire in Johnson's fiction, they are liberated from the hold things have over them, including the hold of their own individuality.... Johnson ... sees the acceptance of emptiness as redemptive. All things are empty; 'emptiness' is a universal descriptor" (20). Storhoff observes the similarity of this view on emptiness with Emerson's "transparent eyeball" and Sartre's "nothingness" and goes on to say that in Johnson's fiction emptiness "represent[s] an openness and radical indeterminacy, a rejection of an entirely definite or self-enclosed nature" (20). Storhoff notes that emptiness enables what Thich Nhat Hanh calls "interbeing" (21; see also note 62 below), and he proceeds to argue that "Johnson's work moves relentlessly toward the concept of emptiness" (21). This argument certainly applies to *Middle Passage* and its ending.

26. C. Johnson, *Middle Passage*, 79.

27. Ibid., 36.

28. Ibid., 136.

29. Johnson has expressed his deep admiration for Ellison and *Invisible Man* numerous times in speech and in writing. For example, when he received the National Book Award for *Middle Passage* on November 27, 1990, he read a tribute to Ellison as part of his acceptance speech.

30. In the epigraph to *Invisible Man*, Ellison quotes the question that the American captain Delano asks his mentally and physically broken Spanish colleague at the end of *Benito Cereno* (103): "'You are saved,' cried Captain Delano, more and more astonished and pained; 'you are saved: what has cast such a shadow upon you?'" Cereno's reply, which Ellison leaves invisible, is "The Negro" (103). For a comparative discussion of *Middle Passage* and *Invisible Man*, see Little, *Charles Johnson's Spiritual Imagination*, 136, 155–58.

31. To quote just one relevant example, Johnson referred to "the remarkable passages on 'history' and perception in Ellison's *Invisible Man*" when interviewed by Boccia (615). See also note 29 above.

32. See also Thaden, "Charles Johnson's *Middle Passage* as Historiographic Metafiction," 762. The African names originate from one of the depositions appended to *Benito Cereno*'s historical antecedent, Amasa Delano's *A Narrative of Voyages and Travels, in the Northern and Southern Hemispheres: Comprising Three Voyages round the World; Together with a Voyage of Survey and Discovery, in the Pacific Ocean and Oriental Islands*, published in Boston in 1817. For the authoritative modern edition, see Delano, *Delano's Voyages of Commerce and Discovery*.

33. C. Johnson, *Middle Passage*, 173. While this line can be read as referring either to Delano's *Voyages* or to Melville's *Benito Cereno* or to both, it seems likely that many or most contemporary American literary authors and readers who are aware of Delano's *Voyages* have discovered the text after first reading *Benito Cereno*.

34. Ellison, *Invisible Man*, 439.

35. See note 20 above.

36. Scudder, "Melville's *Benito Cereno* and Captain Delano's *Voyages*." See also notes 32 and 33 above. Although Melville's fictionalized tale in part differs from Amasa Delano's historical account, especially in its characterization of the individuals involved and in its depiction of the final encounter between the two captains in the climax's aftermath, the narrative's main outline is the same in both works. One of the main differences is that the *post factum* relationship between the two captains is polite, conciliatory, and poignant in *Benito Cereno*, whereas in *Voyages* the "generous" Delano takes legal action against the "ungrateful" Cereno. For a more thorough comparison, see Stuckey and Leslie, "Aftermath." For a recent discussion of the insurrection on the *Tryal*, see Taylor, *If We Must Die*, 139–43.

37. More specifically, *Benito Cereno* addresses, as Eric Sundquist notes, what Melville in the mid-nineteenth century identified as the crisis of both slavery and slave rebellion: "If Melville's tale presents no clear solution to the problems of racism and bondage, it nevertheless stands forth like Aranda's skeleton, a figurehead of revolution and slavery in stunning crisis" (*To Wake the Nations*, 139).

38. C. Johnson, *Middle Passage*, 35–36.

39. Because Johnson's postmodern narrative abounds with paradoxes, grim ironies, and hilarious tongue-in-cheek moments, it is befitting that the character made to bear the burden of both the presidential and vice-presidential family names associated with the racist anti-Indian law of 1830 is Jackson Calhoun, Rutherford's kind and generous older brother, the least power-hungry of all of the novel's Americans.

40. For a reading of *Benito Cereno* that focuses on the *San Dominick*, looking at "the slave ship as a distinct cultural artifact" and as a "space . . . curated by the insurgent Africans," see I. Wilson, *Specters of Democracy*, 126–44 (127, 128).

41. Trouillot, *Silencing the Past*, 73.

42. Melville, *Benito Cereno*, 38.

43. Ibid., 103.

44. See note 30 above.

45. Melville, *Benito Cereno*, 104.

46. C. Johnson, *Middle Passage*, 43.

47. Ibid., 206.

48. Ibid., 209.

49. Melville, *Benito Cereno*, 104.

50. See C. Johnson, *Middle Passage*, 65.

51. C. Johnson, interview by Jonathan Little, 99.

52. Johnson said in a 1996 interview with Michael Boccia, "As a phenomenologist, I cannot help but believe that consciousness is primary for all 'experience'—that the nature of the *I* is the deepest of mysteries, and that all other questions arise from this primordial one, *What am I?*" (615; italics in the original).

53. C. Johnson, interview by Jonathan Little, 101.

54. Ibid., 102.

55. C. Johnson, interview by Jim McWilliams, 296; italics in the original. He continued, "There's no contradiction, at least not for the Buddhadharma, which emphasizes the interdependence of all things and avoids dualism" (296).

56. C. Johnson, Preface to *Turning the Wheel*, xvi.

57. Storhoff's summary of these pivotal teachings of Buddhism (*Understanding Charles Johnson*, 17–18) is to the point: "Johnson's work revolves around Buddhism's central doctrine: All things are in constant flux.... The seminal Buddhist concept of dependent origination (partitya samutpada) explains how things are transient, and how things eventually become what they fleetingly are. According to this concept, all people, thoughts, and objects are incessantly changing because they depend, at the very moment they come into existence and from that point thereafter, on other things, which are also changing because they too are dependent on other things, and so on ad infinitum.... Because of dependent origination, all things exist in a relational matrix throughout history."

58. See Olson, *The Different Paths of Buddhism*, 54.

59. Ibid., 165.

60. I write "partial" rather than "complete" expression, because the narrative does not go so far as to explicitly repudiate the dualism between eternalism and nihilism (although it does emphatically renounce dualism in general; see C. Johnson, *Middle Passage*, 98). This choice is in keeping with Johnson's general disinclination to write about such topics as eternity, rebirth, or afterlife. When he discusses Buddhism in essays and interviews, Johnson interests himself in its potential to help individuals liberate themselves from the shackles of self-centeredness in *this* life and *this* world.

61. C. Johnson, *Middle Passage*, 2.

62. Thich Nhat Hahn, a Vietnamese-born monk (whom Martin Luther King unsuccessfully nominated for the 1967 Nobel Peace Prize) and the founder of the Buddhist Order of Interbeing, coined the term "interbeing" to articulate the intercon-

nectedness of the universe and the profound interdependence of all things. Storhoff elaborates on interbeing as follows: "[R]eality is composed of interpenetrating and contingent elements brought together in an instant of time, only to slide immediately into a slightly different configuration. Interbeing points Johnson . . . meditatively to the Oneness of the world" (*Understanding Charles Johnson*, 21). Johnson, aware of King's admiration for Nhat Hahn, has repeatedly articulated his profound appreciation of Nhat Hahn's disposition and teachings.

63. C. Johnson, "Philosophy and Black Fiction," 84.

64. Johnson lays out his understanding of the fundamentals of Buddhism in concise form in "Reading the Eightfold Path," an educational meditation included in *Turning the Wheel* (3–33). He quotes the Four Noble Truths of Buddhism in the form conveyed by an English translation of the sloka written by Ashvaghosa around 100 C.E.: "This is pain, this also is the origin of pain in the world of living beings; this also is the stopping of pain; this is that course that leads to the stopping" (*Turning the Wheel*, 4). In fact, "suffering" is a more frequent translation than "pain" in this context. As Storhoff points out (without explicitly evoking Johnson's preferred translation), "Pain, of course, is unavoidable in life; but Buddhists make a distinction between pain and suffering, the latter connoting an emotional attachment to or intemperate craving for the things we desire" (*Understanding Charles Johnson*, 21).

65. C. Johnson, "Reading the Eightfold Path," 4; italics in the original.

66. C. Johnson, *Middle Passage*, 113. Jackson's St. Francis-like qualities are further affirmed by his love of birds and by the trusting and affectionate response that he receives from them (112), just as the Catholic saint allegedly did.

67. Ibid., 116.

68. Ibid., 117.

69. Ibid., 109.

70. Ibid., 61.

71. Ibid., 5. For an article-length analysis that focuses on Isadora's role in the novel, see Muther, "Isadora at Sea."

72. Ibid., 7.

73. C. Johnson, "The Philosopher and the American Novel," 59.

74. C. Johnson, *Middle Passage*, 3; italics in the original.

75. Ibid., 46.

76. C. Johnson, "Reading the Eightfold Path," 6.

77. Ibid., 7.

78. C. Johnson, *Middle Passage*, 46.

79. Ibid., 20.

80. Melville, *Moby-Dick*, 70. Rudolph Byrd also briefly notes this moment of intertextuality (*Charles Johnson's Novels*, 110).

81. Johnson, as mentioned earlier, also subtly evokes the Native American predicament by setting his novel in the year of the passage of the Indian Removal Act and by

creating the full name of a minor character out of the last names of President Jackson and Vice President Calhoun. See note 39 above.

82. C. Johnson, *Middle Passage*, 21.

83. See ibid., 38.

84. O'Keefe, "Reading Rigor Mortis," 635.

85. Falcon is "a patriot whose burning passion [is] the manifest destiny of the United States to Americanize the entire planet" (C. Johnson, *Middle Passage*, 30). Even his name, as critics have noted, suggests a miniscule version of the American eagle, the guardian of the Republic, and his birthday, including the year, is the same as that of the United States (49).

86. C. Johnson, *Middle Passage*, 33.

87. O'Keefe, "Reading Rigor Mortis," 640.

88. C. Johnson, *Middle Passage*, 46.

89. Ibid., 87.

90. Ibid., 150–51.

91. O'Keefe, "Reading Rigor Mortis," 640.

92. During the ocean voyage, Falcon articulates some pivotal truth claims that Rutherford revisits and re-examines repeatedly on his journey toward mental freedom. In particular, Falcon's rugged meditation on dualism, that "bloody structure of the mind" which is "a transcendental Fault, a deep crack in consciousness itself" (C. Johnson, *Middle Passage*, 98), anticipates Rutherford's transformation because Falcon here critiques what the younger man also ends up rejecting—that is, dualism in any form that results in a conceptual distinction between "me" and "you" and between "us" and "them" (a distinction facilitating, or even necessitating, the concepts of the "Other" and the "enemy"). Slavery, Falcon freely admits, is one manifestation of this "deeper, ontic wound" (98). Johnson's choice of the bigoted Falcon as the utterer of these insights in itself critically interrogates one type of dualism, namely, any simplistic and unproblematized division of human beings into the inherently good and the inherently wicked. This narrative strategy of making a repulsive character speak words of wisdom echoes the episode in Twain's *Huckleberry Finn* (156–62) in which Colonel Sherburn executes a drunken man in cold blood, is faced by a lynch mob seeking revenge, and then perceptively criticizes mob mentality as he addresses the crowd that pursues him.

93. C. Johnson, *Middle Passage*, 35. This reference to Jonah serves as an allusion both to *Moby-Dick*'s chapter 9, "The Sermon," and to the "Blackness of Blackness" homily in the prologue to *Invisible Man*.

94. C. Johnson, *Middle Passage*, 66.

95. As Equiano writes, he "used frequently to have different cargoes of new negroes in [his] care for sale" while laboring for a master named Robert King, who was a Philadelphia Quaker and a prominent merchant (*The Interesting Narrative*, 77).

96. Ibid.

97. For a useful summary and analysis of the existential and political navigations characterizing the (almost startlingly entrepreneurial) middle section of Equiano's narrative, see Baker, *Blues, Ideology*, 35.

98. C. Johnson, *Middle Passage*, 66.

99. Ibid.

100. Ibid.

101. Ibid., 43.

102. Nash (*Charles Johnson's Fiction*, 136) refers to Henry Louis Gates Jr.'s discussion of the Esu-Elegbara myth in *The Signifying Monkey*, especially to Gates's treatment of the term *ng'ang'ama* (18), which resonates with "Ngonyama." Wyrick, on the other hand, reads the name as "an anagram of 'agony man,' the existentially distressed leader of the slave rebellion whose soul is scarred by the need to harness violence in the service of freedom" ("Johnson's Battle of the Books," 2).

103. C. Johnson, *Middle Passage*, 76.

104. Ibid., 109.

105. Ibid., 146.

106. Ibid., 140; italics in the original.

107. Ibid., 144.

108. D. Scott, "Interrogating Identity," 652.

109. C. Johnson, *Middle Passage*, 124.

110. Ibid., 167–71.

111. C. Johnson, "Philosophy and Black Fiction," 82.

112. See, for example, C. Johnson, *Middle Passage*, 78.

113. C. Johnson, *Middle Passage*, 204.

114. Ibid., 179; italics in the original.

115. Ibid., 187.

116. Ibid., 209.

117. Ibid., 140.

118. Ibid., 179.

119. C. Johnson, interview by Jim McWilliams, 295.

120. See, for example, C. Johnson, *Middle Passage*, 98.

121. Carby, "Becoming Modern Racialized Subjects," 625.

122. Rediker, *The Slave Ship*, 10.

123. C. Johnson, "Novelists of Memory," 101.

124. See, for example, C. Johnson, *Being and Race*, 5–7, and the above quotation from C. Johnson, "Novelists of Memory," 101. Conner and Nash, too, observe that Johnson's foundational artistic-cum-philosophical position—according to which "to perceive, to philosophize, and to create artistically are essentially the same action, and they depend on the ability to shed our pre-judgments and see the world anew"—is articulated "in opposition to the ideologies of Afrocentrism, Negritude, and the Black Aesthetic" ("Introduction," xxvi).

125. C. Johnson, "Philosophy and Black Fiction," 80.
126. Ibid., 82.
127. C. Johnson, "Whole Sight," 90.
128. Selzer, *Charles Johnson in Context*, 157.
129. Ibid., 159.
130. Ibid., 161.
131. Ibid., 168.
132. Ibid.
133. Ibid., 6.
134. Ibid.
135. Ibid.
136. Ibid.
137. In "Cosmopolitan Patriots" (22)—his 1997 response to "Patriotism and Cosmopolitanism," Martha Nussbaum's now-canonical 1994 *Boston Review* essay on cosmopolitanism—Appiah still preferred the term "rooted" cosmopolitanism when referring to the same moral and political position that he in his 2006 book calls "partial cosmopolitanism."
138. Appiah, *Cosmopolitanism*, xv.
139. This view of cosmopolitanism echoes literary-historical discussions of Anglo-American high modernism. Amanda Anderson, however, usefully complicates any simplistic understanding of the Victorian and high modernist ideal of detachment by addressing Victorian intellectuals' "ambivalence and uncertainty" about this ideal (*The Powers of Distance*, 3).
140. Appiah, *Cosmopolitanism*, xviii.
141. E. Brown, "Hellenistic Cosmopolitanism," 555.
142. Ibid. In "Nussbaum's Concept of Cosmopolitanism" (52), Naseem and Hyslop-Margison use the term "robust" cosmopolitanism when they refer to what Eric Brown calls "strict" cosmopolitanism.
143. Shapcott, *International Ethics*, 50–51. Shapcott's benevolent definition of anticosmopolitanism presumes that both "cosmopolitans and anti-cosmopolitans sit within a common horizon and tradition of thinking that is anchored in the twin pillars of liberty and equality" (ix). However, many other scholars use "anticosmopolitanism" to denote philosophical and political positions that do not build on either liberty or equality; see, for example, Beck, *The Cosmopolitan Vision*, 111. When Shapcott juxtaposes cosmopolitans and anticosmopolitans, he focuses on a much narrower debate or political phenomenon than Beck does.
144. Appiah, *Cosmopolitanism*, xv.
145. Ibid., xv–xvii.
146. See my introduction, note 91.
147. Forrest, *There is a Tree*, 20.

Chapter 2. Early Black Atlantic Crossings: Lawrence Hill's *The Book of Negroes*

1. Born in Newmarket, in the Greater Toronto Area, in 1957, Hill is the son of American immigrants (an African American father and a white American mother) who, concerned about hostility toward interracial couples in the pre–civil rights United States, in 1953 moved to Canada the day after they were married in Washington, D.C., and later on had and raised their children in their adopted country. Hill's 2001 memoir, *Black Berry, Sweet Juice: On Being Black and White in Canada*, discusses Canadian attitudes toward biracial identity and mixed cultural heritage. His fictional writings include four novels to date. The first, *Some Great Thing* (1992), about a biracial journalist working for a Winnipeg newspaper, was followed by *Any Known Blood* (1997), a story of five generations of fictive Langston Canes, whose black and mixed-race family history traverses the US-Canada border. *The Book of Negroes*, marking Hill's breakthrough as a bestselling novelist in Canada and beyond, goes further back in time than his previous works of fiction and portrays the black diasporic experience on a broader canvas. (For a discussion of *The Book of Negroes* as a bestseller, see Medovarski, "Currency and Cultural Consumption," 9.) Hill's fourth novel, *The Illegal* (2015), is about a young marathon runner of African descent who leaves his home country to flee political oppression.

2. Both the original Canadian edition, by HarperCollins Canada, and the first US edition, by Norton, were published in 2007. Norton not only considered Hill's original title (which reproduces the title of a 1783 British naval ledger) too documentary, but also worried about the potential of the word "Negroes" to offend American readers. Norton therefore requested that Hill come up with an alternate title for the US edition (Hill, "Projecting History Honestly," 319; Hill, "Why I'm Not Allowed My Book Title"). For this reason, the novel initially appeared in the United States as *Someone Knows My Name*. However, Norton re-released it as *The Book of Negroes* after the US television network BET purchased the Canadian six-part TV miniseries *The Book of Negroes*, adapted from Hill's work, which first aired in the United States in February 2015 (see Hill, "What I Learned").

In another reaction to the novel's original title, in June 2011 a small group of Dutch protesters of Surinamese descent, calling themselves the "Federation for Honour and Reparation of Slavery in Surinam," were so upset by the use of "Negroes" in the title of the Dutch translation (*Het negerboek*) that they publicly burned the novel's cover. For news coverage of the incident, see, for example, Hickman, "Dutch Group Burns the Cover." Not surprisingly, Hill was less than pleased. Informed of the group's intention beforehand, he commented on the planned protest in advance in an opinion piece in the *Toronto Star* ("What Lawrence Hill Tells Dutch Group"). Afterward, he addressed the incident by writing a short publication titled *Dear Sir, I Intend to Burn Your Book*.

3. Walters, *Archives of the Black Atlantic*, 3.

4. See my introduction, note 2.

5. Hill, "Conversation," 16.

6. Black Loyalism and its repercussions are also the subject of another 2007 novel, *Not with Silver*, by Nigerian British Simi Bedford. *The Book of Negroes* pursues historical accuracy more ambitiously than *Not with Silver* and therefore offers more material for a discussion of the possibilities and limits of historical fiction. George Elliott Clarke's 2005 *George and Rue*—which offers a fictionalized rendering of the true story of George and Rufus Hamilton, black Canadian brothers (Clarke's cousins), who in 1949 murdered a cab driver in New Brunswick and were subsequently executed—more briefly references the history of British-minded African Americans by evoking black refugees from the War of 1812 who escaped to the British and were relocated to Nova Scotia. Clarke's and the Hamilton brothers' ancestors were among these migrants. Clarke comments, in his unpaginated "Author's Note to the U.S. Edition [of *George and Rue*]," on African Canadian history in Nova Scotia, "Although our ancestors had physical freedom, they were forced to work like slaves, basically, for that was their function in the Nova Scotian economy and society, and it remained our reality, until well into the 1960s. (Nova Scotia is a displaced Mississippi.)" See also Clarke's verse play *Beatrice Chancy*, set in Annapolis Valley, Nova Scotia, in 1801.

7. See Hill, *Book of Negroes*, 481.

8. Berlin, review, 398. See also, for example, Schama, *Rough Crossings*, 449, 451.

9. While both monographs are of a high standard, they are by no means identical. E. Wilson's book focuses on the years 1792–1808, the latter date marking the year when the Sierra Leone Company was dissolved and Sierra Leone became a colony of the British Crown. J. Walker covers more history, starting in 1783 (and dealing in depth with the Nova Scotia experience, which Wilson describes rather briefly) and ending in 1870. For more detailed comparisons, see Leo Spitzer's and Peter J. Duignan's reviews, each of which discusses both books.

10. For a longer list of relevant works, see "Further Reading" in Schama, *Rough Crossings*, 449–51.

11. Schama, *Rough Crossings*, 11. Schama uses the phrase to refute it, not to agree with it.

12. See, for example, J. Walker, *The Black Loyalists*, ix; E. Wilson, *The Loyal Blacks*, 178.

13. In addition to Hill's more detailed approach to history, another significant difference between his novel and Johnson's is that while *Middle Passage* is set in a two-month time frame (the duration of the depicted slave ship experience) and describes the protagonist's journey into black diasporic consciousness in highly philosophical terms, *The Book of Negroes* covers Aminata's life from adolescence to the eve of her death and accomplishes this task through first-person narration in which the main mode is psychological rather than philosophical.

14. Carby, "Becoming Modern Racialized Subjects," 625.

15. Walters, *Archives of the Black Atlantic*, 1.

16. As is often the case with historical fiction, Hill's narrative is heavily invested in what he in an interview calls his protagonist's long-term "emotional survival" (Hill, "His Novel Takes Him Back," F1). Hill, in fact, gave Aminata the middle name of his eldest daughter in order to put himself in a mental place where he could create an emotionally credible character. Also, the novel's events begin with Aminata's abduction from her home village when she is eleven, the same age that Geneviève Aminata Hill was at the time when her father started to write *The Book of Negroes*. As Hill freely admits, "I asked myself, 'What if this were my daughter? How would she have survived?' . . . I tried to think of Aminata as my child" ("His Novel Takes Him Back," F1). See also Hill, "A Person of Many Places," 301.

17. Hill, "A Person of Many Places," 308.

18. See Wood, *Blind Memory*, especially chapter 1.

19. Among the few analyses of *The Book of Negroes* published to date are Andrea Medovarski's "Currency and Cultural Consumption" and Winfried Siemerling's discussion of the novel in *The Black Atlantic Reconsidered* (170–85; see also 20–24, 26, 27, 353).

20. Hill, *The Book of Negroes*, 475. Moreover, for Hill's acknowledgment of the importance of early black Nova Scotian texts for his writing process, see Hill, "Conversation," 17, 20.

21. Hill, *The Book of Negroes*, 4.

22. Andrews, "The Representation of Slavery," 80. Andrews here builds on his *To Tell a Free Story* (1986) and on Robert Stepto's groundbreaking *From Behind the Veil* (1979), the pioneering study of the connection of literacy and freedom in African American antebellum slave narratives.

23. See note 2 above.

24. Kline, "From Slavery to Freedom."

25. Hill, *The Book of Negroes*, 66.

26. Ibid., 72.

27. Ibid., 3.

28. Eakin, introduction to *American Autobiography*, 8.

29. Hill, *The Book of Negroes*, 4.

30. This publication was titled *Some MEMOIRS of the LIFE of JOB, the SON of SOLOMON the High Priest of Boonda in Africa; Who was a Slave about two Years in Maryland; and afterwards being brought to England, was set free, and sent to his native Land in the Year 1734* (London: Printed for Richard Ford, 1734). Austin's discussion of Diallo in *African Muslims in Antebellum America* (50–62) includes a summary and analysis of the memoir. (For shorter discussions, see also Turner, *Islam in the African-American Experience*, 25–26; Curtin, *Muslims in America*, 1–4; and Diouf, *Servants of Allah*, especially 11–12, 36–37, 88–89, 135–36, 164–66.) For a brief précis of pre-1990s scholarship on Diallo, including Henry Louis Gates Jr.'s contributions, see Judy, *(Dis)*

Forming the American Canon, 22–23. Judy's incomplete reference to *Fortunate Slave* by "Foster" Grant (23) alludes to *The Fortunate Slave: An Illustration of African Slavery in the Early Eighteenth Century* by Douglas Grant. See, in particular, chapter 4 of *The Fortunate Slave*.

31. The first paragraph of Haley's *Roots*, which depicts Kunta Kinte's birth, includes the following reflection, attributable to two elderly women acting as midwives: "According to the forefathers, a boy firstborn presaged special blessings of Allah not only upon the parents but also upon the parents' families" (1). The narrative then further highlights Kunta's Islamic heritage by depicting the call, heard throughout the village, "to the first of the five daily prayers that had been offered up to Allah for as long as anyone living could remember" (1–2). See also J. Smith, *Islam in America*, 78. In the 2013 interview with Siemerling, Hill acknowledged having read *Roots* "at least twice" (Hill, "Conversation," 20).

32. Hill has worked as a Canadian Crossroads International volunteer in Mali, Niger, and Cameroon (Hill, "A Person of Many Places," 306), all countries where Islam is a strong presence. See also Hill, *Black Berry, Sweet Juice*, section entitled "Allah's Blessing" (63–75). The book that emerged from Hill's collaboration with Joshua Key, a young white man from Oklahoma who fought in the war in Iraq for seven months in 2003 (*The Deserter's Tale: The Story of an Ordinary Soldier Who Walked Away from the War in Iraq*, 2007), is also worth mentioning in this connection. Key, disillusioned by the war's realities, deserted the US army while on leave. After fourteen months in hiding, he and his family sought asylum in Canada. Hill wrote down Key's story after a series of in-depth interviews. *The Deserter's Tale* on one level represents, by its very existence, a complication to any simplistic anti-Muslim master narrative circulating in North America.

33. The four plainclothes police officers who fired forty-one bullets at Diallo during the incident later said that they had stopped him because he fit the description of a rape case suspect. As he reached his wallet to show identification, the officers, according to their statements, believed that Diallo was reaching for a firearm and gunned him down. They were prosecuted for second-degree murder but were acquitted. For news coverage of the incident and its aftermath, see, for example, Medaglia, "Diallo Cousin Still Fights for a Foothold."

34. Rushdy, *Neo-Slave Narratives*, 7.

35. Baldwin, "Nobody Knows My Name," 208.

36. Hill, *The Book of Negroes*, 4, 56–57.

37. Ibid., 1.

38. Ibid., 101.

39. Hill, "Projecting History Honestly," 315.

40. In his thorough 2005 biography of Equiano, Vincent Carretta famously posits that if the relevant baptismal and naval records are accurate, Equiano was born in South Carolina around 1747 (*Equiano, the African*, xiv–xv, 2). John Bugg's strong criticism of

Carretta's position in "The Other Interesting Narrative" resulted in a *PMLA* "Forum" exchange between these two scholars in March 2007 (Carretta and Bugg, "Deciphering the Equiano Archives"). Although a detailed discussion of Equiano falls beyond the scope of this book, I would like to note that Cathy N. Davidson, in discussing the controversy over Equiano's birthplace, proposes that we should perhaps read his narrative as a novel ("Olaudah Equiano," 25). Although I am highly appreciative of most aspects of Davidson's essay, I find her suggestion regarding genre problematic, given that the debate about *The Interesting Narrative*'s historical truthfulness only concerns its first two chapters. Besides, deliberate narrative construction is not unique to fiction. Autobiography, too, always entails a process of construction (identity construction, a fashioning of the self) instead of detailing everything that has taken place in an individual's life. Any autobiographer is, as John Sturrock observes, "the interpreter of his life" ("Theory Versus Autobiography," 25–26). Autobiographers selectively focus on those moments and events of their lives that are important for their overall interpretations of themselves, and any memoir necessarily entails a narrative of selfhood, the deliberate narrative construction of a textual self (a written self, a self on the page), a narrated identity formation. The presence of such a construction in a book does not, per se, make the book a novel.

41. Hill, *The Book of Negroes*, 4.
42. See, for example, ibid., 409, 434, 443–44.
43. Folkenflik, "Introduction: The Institution of Autobiography," 15.
44. See note 40 above.
45. When Johnson's Allmuseri first board the *Republic*, they see the white crew as "savages" with cannibalistic appetites (*Middle Passage*, 65)—an allusion to *The Interesting Narrative*'s Middle Passage section (38–42, especially 38–39). Moreover, as mentioned in the previous chapter, Rutherford's inner torment over his indirect participation in the slave trade can be read as alluding to the distress that Equiano experienced when temporarily working on slave ships.
46. Alternatively, to apply Hazel Carby's train of thought in "Becoming Modern Racialized Subjects" (630–31) to *The Book of Negroes*, Aminata can, metaphorically, be thought of as Equiano's lost sister. The sister was kidnapped with Equiano from their home village and shared some of his journey from the African inland to the coast. However, the two were forcibly separated twice during the long trek, and after the second separation she disappeared permanently from his life (Equiano, *The Interesting Narrative*, 32–36). Carby comments on the sister's role in Equiano's text: "Standing only as a severed last link with family and the place from which Equiano came, the figure of 'sister' is not a subject in her own right but merely register of, or signifier for, Equiano's condition as singular, abducted male, an orphan who will be reborn in the course of the narrative" ("Becoming Modern Racialized Subjects," 630–31). In *The Book of Negroes* it is the "sister," Aminata, rather than a male figure, who is "reborn" as a diasporic subject in the narrative's course.

47. Hill, *The Book of Negroes*, 13.
48. Ibid.
49. Ibid., 20.
50. Ibid.
51. Ibid., 11.
52. As Austin notes, "It is not yet possible to tell how many Muslims were in West Africa or were taken out of it in the era of the international slave trade" (*African Muslims in Antebellum America*, 22). According to Austin's boldest estimate, "there may have been about forty thousand African Muslims in the colonial and pre-Civil War territory making up the United States before 1860" (22). He admits, however, that the figure may be inaccurate, and he looks forward to future scholarship that "will lead to better figures and descriptions" (23).
53. Ibid., 23. For another important scholarly discussion of Arabic literacy among early African Muslims in America, see Diouf, *Servants of Allah*, chapter 4.
54. Austin, *African Muslims in Antebellum America*, 23.
55. Ibid., 12.
56. Hill, *The Book of Negroes*, 22.
57. Ibid., 112.
58. See note 45 above.
59. Equiano, *The Interesting Narrative*, 77.
60. Hill, *The Book of Negroes*, 81.
61. Ibid., 86.
62. Ibid., 81.
63. Ibid., 80.
64. Ibid., 93.
65. G. Fabre, "The Slave Ship Dance"; see especially 38–40.
66. Hill, *The Book of Negroes*, 16. Through the character of Fomba, Hill demonstrates his awareness of African slavery, primarily depicting it as a prisoner-of-war phenomenon, just as Equiano did (*The Interesting Narrative*, 26), rather than as an ideological institution that states the innate superiority of one ethnoracial group over another.
67. Hill, *The Book of Negroes*, 105.
68. Carby, "Becoming Modern Racialized Subjects," 632.
69. Hill, *The Book of Negroes*, 104–5.
70. Ibid., 106, 122.
71. Ibid., 107.
72. Ibid., 108.
73. Ibid., 105.
74. Ibid., 110.
75. Ibid., 131.
76. Ibid., 111.

77. Ibid.
78. Ibid., 110.
79. Ibid., 114.
80. Ibid., 112.
81. Ibid., 106.
82. Hill, "Projecting History Honestly," 311–12.
83. Hill, *The Book of Negroes*, 118.

84. Hill's implication that Aminata effortlessly stays fluent in Fulfude and Bamanankan throughout her life, despite having few opportunities to speak these languages in her adulthood (with the exception of her encounters with her husband, Chekura), may seem overly idealistic in light of what we know about migrants' difficulties in keeping alive languages that they cannot actively speak in their new environments. Hill, however, all along portrays Aminata as an exceptionally active and talented language learner rather than as an average "student."

85. For a book-length history of the Jewish presence in colonial and antebellum Charleston, see Hagy, *This Happy Land*.

86. Hill, *The Book of Negroes*, 205.

87. As Frederick Douglass mentioned in his 1845 *Narrative* (38), the social norms of city life imposed constraints on those urban slaveholders who did not wish to appear cruel or negligent in the eyes of their nonslaveholding neighbors.

88. See, for example, Hill, *The Book of Negroes*, 187.
89. See, for example, ibid., 199.
90. See also Sollors's brief but illuminating discussion of Equiano's reading (Sollors, introduction, xvi–xix).
91. Hill, *The Book of Negroes*, 164–65.
92. Ibid., 204.
93. See, for example, ibid., 189.
94. Douglass, *Narrative*, 68.
95. Ibid., 97.
96. JanMohamed and Lloyd, preface, ix.
97. Hill, *The Book of Negroes*, 188.
98. Ibid., 189.
99. Ibid., 209.
100. See my chapter 3, note 158.
101. Hill, *The Book of Negroes*, 205.
102. Ibid., 209–10.
103. Ibid., 165; italics in the original.
104. Ibid., 203.
105. Ibid.
106. Ibid.
107. Ibid.

108. Ibid., 205.
109. Ibid.; italics in the original.
110. Ibid., 209.
111. Ibid., 212.
112. Ibid., 213.
113. Ibid., 165.
114. E. Wilson (*The Loyal Blacks*, 62) and Schama (*Rough Crossings*, 112) both confirm that many of New York's black people found their way to this district.
115. In discussing the "Rebuilding after the fire of 1776" in *The Historical Atlas of New York City*, Eric Homberger says that Canvas Town consisted of "shanties and huts made of old ships' canvas and spars *erected in the burnt-out areas*" (56, italics added). E. Wilson agrees: "Much of the devastated area was never rebuilt [after the 1776 fire]. Sailcloth was stretched between skeletal walls and chimney stacks, and temporary huts, roofed in canvas, were hastily erected. In this 'Canvas Town' were crowded many of the black refugees ... up to the British departure in 1783" (*The Loyal Blacks*, 62). According to Mark Caldwell, too, "Canvas Town, or (its alternate name) Topsail Town, rose as a chaos of shanties almost overnight from the smoking wreckage" (*New York Night*, 50). See also Abbott, "The Neighborhoods of New York," 41; Barck, *New York City during the War for Independence*, 82; Carp, "The Night the Yankees Burned Broadway," 475 and n7, 475–76; and Foote, *Black and White Manhattan*, 216. To mention three landmark buildings that play a role in *The Book of Negroes*, the 1776 fire destroyed Trinity Church, but St. Paul's Chapel survived, as did Fraunces Tavern, which was George Washington's favorite establishment in New York City.
116. Dunlap, *History of the New Netherlands*, 2:79.
117. Ibid.; italics added. Also quoted in Caldwell, *New York Night*, 50.
118. See Hill, *The Book of Negroes*, 206.
119. Ibid., 252.
120. Ibid., 311.
121. Hill focuses on Black Loyalists, but he also paints sympathetic portraits of some black New Yorkers who sided with the patriots. Notably, he fictionalizes the tavern keeper Samuel "Black Sam" Fraunces, a historical figure who became chief steward in George Washington's presidential household after the war (see also note 115 above). It must be added, however, that Fraunces's racial ancestry has historically been an enigma. He has been portrayed, visually as well as verbally, as white, black, and biracial. Today, many believe that he was of mixed (black and white) West Indian origin (see, for example, Horton, "From Class to Race," 59). Both Schama and Hill choose to count Fraunces among "black" New Yorkers. In *The Book of Negroes* Sam, whose unselfish assistance is crucial for Aminata's survival in New York City in the early days of her fugitive existence, at the war's end tries to persuade her to stay in the emerging United States (303). However, his words fail to convince her.
122. Schama, *Rough Crossings*, 7.

123. Ibid., 8.

124. Ibid., 5.

125. Carretta, *Equiano the African*, 203.

126. Ibid.

127. See Fryer, *Staying Power*, 113–32. In the early 1770s, news seems to have trickled across the Atlantic into America's black communities about two court cases tried in London that each resulted in the victory of a (former) slave and his abolitionist defense counsel: through the decisions in the Jonathan Strong case of 1767 and the more extensively publicized James Somerset case of 1772, the court in effect ruled that a person first enslaved in a British colony and then physically brought to Britain could neither be forced to return to his site of slavery overseas nor be sold to another slaveholder to be taken overseas. Although each of these rulings was only concerned with the individual case before the court, they (especially the Somerset case) were widely interpreted as pronouncing slavery illegal on British soil (Schama, *Rough Crossings*, 18). No wonder then, as Schama notes, that a 1774 Philadelphia pamphlet by "Freeman" joyously informed American slaves that they could have freedom just by "setting foot on that happy Territory where slavery is forbidden to perch" (quoted in *Rough Crossings*, 18).

128. See Dunmore, Proclamation.

129. Quoted in Schama, *Rough Crossings*, 8.

130. E. Wilson, *The Loyal Blacks*, 25–27.

131. This is Schama's term; see *Rough Crossings*, 77.

132. Ibid., 7.

133. J. Walker, *The Black Loyalists*, 3.

134. E. Wilson, *The Loyal Blacks*, 21; 37, n9. The figures that Schama and Carretta offer are in the same ballpark. Schama's estimate falls somewhere between eighty thousand and one hundred thousand (*Rough Crossings*, 8), and Carretta also speaks of "perhaps as many as one hundred thousand" (*Equiano the African*, 203).

135. Jasanoff, *Liberty's Exiles*, 352. See also Pybus, "Jefferson's Faulty Math," cited in Jasanoff, *Liberty's Exiles*, 352; 420n4.

136. J. Walker, *The Black Loyalists*, 3; E. Wilson, *The Loyal Blacks*, 1; Carretta, *Equiano the African*, 203; Jasanoff, *Liberty's Exiles*, 8.

137. Schama, *Rough Crossings*, 132.

138. Ibid., 153; Jasanoff, *Liberty's Exiles*, 352. In addition to Nova Scotia, Loyalists, black and white, were evacuated from New York and other cities to several other locations as well. For the dispersal of the Black Loyalists across the Atlantic world as a result of the evacuations of 1783, see Pulis, ed., *Moving On: Black Loyalists in the Afro-Atlantic World*. See also Craton, "Loyalists Mainly to Themselves," which discusses the Black Loyalist migration to the Bahamas.

139. Hill, *The Book of Negroes*, 268.

140. Ibid.

141. Ibid., 279–80; italics in the original. The novel quotes the proclamation's core verbatim (cf. Schama, *Rough Crossings*, 100).

142. Hill, *The Book of Negroes*, 280.

143. Quoted from US Department of State, "Preliminary Articles of Peace," 99; italics added. See also Hill, *The Book of Negroes*, 282–83.

144. Hill, *The Book of Negroes*, 283.

145. J. Walker (*The Black Loyalists*, 12) adds, "There is considerable difficulty in establishing the total number of Black Loyalists who took refuge in Nova Scotia during and after the War for Independence. The 'Book of Negroes' . . . listed a total of 3,000, inspected in New York between 26 April and 30 November 1783, bound for Nova Scotia. Others may well have gone the same route either before or after the roll was taken."

146. As E. Wilson puts it in *The Loyal Blacks*, the British chose Nova Scotia as a destination for Loyalists "not because it was ideal, but because it was nearby and thinly settled" (71).

147. Hill, *The Book of Negroes*, 285.

148. J. Walker, *The Black Loyalists*, 10; see also Schama, *Rough Crossings*, 151.

149. J. Walker, *The Black Loyalists*, 11; Schama, *Rough Crossings*, 146–49.

150. For a published edition of the "Book of Negroes," see Hodges, ed., *The Black Loyalist Directory*. For more information about editions and for a digital version of the text, see *Nova Scotia*, http://novascotia.ca/archives/virtual/africanns/BN.asp, a website developed by Nova Scotia Communities, Culture, and Heritage.

151. Hill, *The Book of Negroes*, 473.

152. Frey, *Water from the Rock*, 193.

153. Hill, "Freedom Bound," 22.

154. Schama, *Rough Crossings*, 151.

155. Hill, "Freedom Bound," 22.

156. Schama, *Rough Crossings*, 6.

157. Hill, *The Book of Negroes*, 294.

158. Ibid.

159. Hill, "Projecting History Honestly," 316–17. Katherine McKittrick makes a similar point about the paucity of scholarship on slavery in Canada (*Demonic Grounds*, 97).

160. See, for example, J. Walker, *The Black Loyalists*, chapters 2–3; E. Wilson, *The Loyal Blacks*, chapters 5–6; Schama, *Rough Crossings*, chapter 8.

161. For the relevant historical background, see, for instance, J. Walker, *The Black Loyalists*, chapter 2; and E. Wilson, *The Loyal Blacks*, chapter 6.

162. For discussions of the black Nova Scotians' religious life, see, for example, J. Walker, *The Black Loyalists*, chapter 4; and E. Wilson, *The Loyal Blacks*, chapter 7. The anthology *"Face Zion Forward"* contains texts by John Marrant (Huntingdonian), David George (Baptist), and Boston King (Methodist), among others. The book opens

with an excellent introduction by Joanna Brooks and John Saillant to Black Loyalists' religiosity. Also, chapters 3 and 4 of James Sidbury's *Becoming African in America* frequently address Black Loyalists' religious institutions in Nova Scotia and Sierra Leone.

163. On Wilkinson, see, for instance, J. Walker, *The Black Loyalists*, 73; and E. Wilson, *The Loyal Blacks*, 124.

164. Hill, *The Book of Negroes*, 319, 350.

165. See J. Walker, *The Black Loyalists*, 73.

166. Hill, *The Book of Negroes*, 319.

167. Ibid., 326.

168. Ibid.

169. For depictions of the historical riot, see, for example, J. Walker, *The Black Loyalists*, 48–49; Schama, *Rough Crossings*, 238. See also note 199 below.

170. The life of Thomas Peters is described, for example, in Fyfe, *A History of Sierra Leone*, 32–34, 36, 41–42; and, more extensively, in various chapters and passages in J. Walker, *The Black Loyalists*; E. Wilson, *The Loyal Blacks*; and Schama, *Rough Crossings*. In each case, see the book's index, entry "Peters, Thomas," for relevant page numbers.

171. For a book-length study on John Clarkson, see E. Wilson, *John Clarkson and the African Adventure*. As with Thomas Peters, John Clarkson's life is also discussed in Fyfe, *A History of Sierra Leone*; J. Walker, *The Black Loyalists*; E. Wilson, *The Loyal Blacks*; and Schama, *Rough Crossings*. In each case, see the book's index entry "Clarkson, John" for relevant page numbers.

172. Carretta, *Equiano the African*, 223, 228–35.

173. E. Wilson, *The Loyal Blacks*, 178–79; Schama, *Rough Crossings*, 219; 255; 441, n49. Wilson notes the importance of this detail for her entire project: "[I]n after years, it was passed off as fortuitous that Peters reached London just as Sharp's modest St. George's Bay Company was undergoing its metamorphosis into the Sierra Leone Company. The thesis of this entire study is that the black Americans who went to Sierra Leone acted knowingly at every stage" (*The Loyal Blacks*, 178).

174. Hill, *The Book of Negroes*, 359.

175. Ibid., 370, 371.

176. The definitive work of the history of Sierra Leone is Fyfe, *A History of Sierra Leone*. For the historical experience of the Black Loyalists and their descendants in Sierra Leone, see also, for instance, J. Walker, *The Black Loyalists*, chapters 7–15; and E. Wilson, *The Loyal Blacks*, chapters 12–19.

177. Hill, *The Book of Negroes*, 378–79.

178. Ibid., 377–78.

179. Ibid., 378.

180. Falconbridge, *Narrative of Two Voyages*, 82. As Fyfe sarcastically notes, these words "long served the English public as a motto for Sierra Leone" (*A History of Sierra Leone*, 40).

181. Hill, *The Book of Negroes*, 384.
182. Ibid., 409.
183. Ibid., 391.
184. Ibid., 436.
185. Ibid., 233.
186. See, for example, Fyfe, *A History of Sierra Leone*, 24–25; Carretta, *Equiano the African*, 232.
187. Hill, *The Book of Negroes*, 393.
188. Ibid., 385.
189. Ibid., 394.
190. Ibid., 438–39.
191. Ibid., 442–43.
192. Ibid., 100–101.
193. Douglass, *My Bondage and My Freedom*, 367.
194. Ibid. For a longer discussion of this subject, see Sundquist, "Frederick Douglass: Literacy and Paternalism."
195. Hill, *The Book of Negroes*, 5.
196. Baker, foreword, xiii.
197. Hill, "Projecting History Honestly," 316. Hill also said in the same interview: "I wouldn't like it if a historian came behind me and said, 'This is preposterous. The things that Hill is having take place in this novel are utterly impossible, never happened and never could have happened.' It doesn't matter so much if they never happened, but I would like them to be plausible and make sense" (316).
198. Ibid.
199. For example, Hill changes the date of Nova Scotia's first race riot from 1784 (not 1783, as he argues in "A word about history" [473], his afterword to *The Book of Negroes*) to 1787. (For references to the correct date, July 26, 1784, see J. Walker, *The Black Loyalists*, 48; Schama, *Rough Crossings*, 238.) Also, in the novel Thomas Peters dies a heroic death at the hands of slave traders in Sierra Leone while defending captured Africans, but in actuality his death did not have such a heroic dimension. Peters died of an illness in June 1792, soon after two dramatic, unrelated events: he clashed with Clarkson on leadership issues and was convicted, by an all-black jury, of theft. (See, for example, Schama, *Rough Crossings*, 334–43, 348–49; Sidbury, *Becoming African in America*, 102–103.) In his afterword to the novel, Hill, to his credit, acknowledges these changes. He also mentions his fictional extension of John Clarkson's stay in Sierra Leone and the historical impossibility of a private individual like Aminata having been hired as a "Book of Negroes" scribe ("A word about history," in *The Book of Negroes*, 473).
200. At times, Hill's important emphasis on black agency makes him vulnerable to the temptation of overreaching and stretching credibility. For example, the novel has several episodes in which white individuals, including powerful white men, take time

for lengthy conversations and sophisticated debates with Aminata. Her discussion with William Armstrong, the second in command on Bance Island, is a case in point (Hill, *The Book of Negroes*, 417–22). Such passages contain intriguing writing but also give rise to critical questions, because in the novel's historical contexts race, gender, and social class determined the parameters of any individuals' interactions with each other far more rigidly than is the case in much of today's world. It is, of course, difficult to say with certainty that a given dialogue or event in *The Book of Negroes* would have been absolutely impossible in the life of a black slave woman or a free black woman in the eighteenth or early nineteenth century. It is unlikely, however, that one person would have experienced *everything* that Hill's Aminata experiences, including her long string of mutually respectful encounters with powerful white men. Also, surviving all the migrations that she survives would have required an extraordinarily strong health in the depicted era. Aminata is best viewed as a composite character who embodies various aspects of the experiences of early diasporic black people.

201. Hill, "Projecting History Honestly," 316; italics added.

202. See note 200 above.

203. As Davidson writes, the "hybrid form" ("Olaudah Equiano," 19) of Equiano's narrative replicates the multiplicity (which Davidson prefers to term the "profound uncertainty") of his selfhood: "The text combines (in unequal parts) slave narrative, sea yarn, military adventure, ethnographic reportage, historical fiction, travelogue, picaresque saga, sentimental novel, allegory, tall tale, pastoral origins myth, gothic romance, conversion tale, and abolitionist tract, with different features coming to the fore at different times, and the mood vacillating accordingly" (19).

204. Wimbush, "Reading Darkness," 13.

205. Keizer, *Black Subjects*, 51. Keizer argues, however, that Johnson's negative depictions of women in *Middle Passage* and his other tales of slavery are "driven by the Enlightenment and post-Enlightenment philosophies that the author engages in his works on slavery," rather than stemming from misogyny (51).

206. For a thorough discussion of ideologies of womanhood during slavery, see chapter 2 of Carby, *Reconstructing Womanhood* (20–39).

207. Cheyette, *Diasporas of the Mind*, xiii.

208. Ibid.

209. In using the terminological dichotomy of the "victim" and "celebratory" diasporas, I again summon Cheyette's lexicon; see *Diasporas of the Mind*, xiii.

Chapter 3. War, Trauma, Displacement, Diaspora: Toni Morrison's and Caryl Phillips's African American Soldiers

1. For my use of the term "Middle Passage novel," see chapter 1, note 6.

2. Diedrich, Gates, and Pedersen, "The Middle Passage between History and Fiction," 8.

3. See Forrest, *There Is a Tree* 20, 21, 23. For a longer discussion of this scene, see

Valkeakari, *Religious Idiom and the African American Novel*, 120–21. Forrest's first three novels were published with Toni Morrison serving as his editor at Random House.

4. For a longer analysis of Morrison's treatment of war in her first seven novels (including *Paradise*, which Morrison initially called *War*), see my 2003 article "Beyond the Riverside." I have also touched on the war motif in *Paradise* in the section of *Religious Idiom and the African American Novel* (194–200) that discusses how, in that novel, Morrison deploys both religious idiom and the discourse of war while narrating various types of othering, exclusion, and exceptionalism.

5. See Butler, *Frames of War*.

6. Such recent essay collections as *The Future of Trauma Theory*, edited by Gert Buelens, Sam Durrant, and Robert Eaglestone, and *Trauma in Contemporary Literature*, edited by Marita Nadal and Mónica Calvo, offer substantive contributions to the field and helpful overviews of the current state of the intersectionality of literary and trauma studies.

7. Caruth, introduction to "Trauma and Experience," 5.

8. I here align myself with Saidiya Hartman's provocative and poignant use of the term "collateral damage": "Historians still debate whether twelve million or sixty million had been sentenced to death to meet the demands of the transatlantic commerce in black bodies. Impossible to fathom was that all this death had been incidental to the acquisition of profit and to the rise of capitalism. Today we might describe it as collateral damage. The unavoidable losses created in pursuit of the greater objective. Death wasn't a goal of its own but just a by-product of commerce, which has had the lasting effect of making negligible all the millions of lives lost.... [T]he Atlantic trade created millions of corpses, but as a corollary to the making of commodities. To my eyes this lack of intention didn't diminish the crime of slavery but from the vantage of judges, juries, and insurers exonerated the culpable agents" (*Lose Your Mother*, 31).

9. Although much of Gilroy's scholarly production is directly concerned with "race," he strives to find alternative discourses and, most importantly, seeks to remain outside or "between" what he terms "camps"—that is, outside or between social formations marked by "the confluence of 'race' and 'nation' in the service of authoritarian ends" (Gilroy, "Between Camps," 7). He thinks of "camps" as "locations in which particular versions of solidarity, belonging, kinship and identity have been devised, practiced and policed" (12)—"policed" being the key word. Although such "camps" cannot always be straightforwardly equated with nation-states, Gilroy, combining his pervasive critique of racisms with his equally fierce critique of nationalisms, connects "camp" formation with "[t]he racialisation of the nation state" and underscores camps' "hierarchical and regimented qualities" (6, 7). These are the types of structures that he wishes to remain "between" and transcend, being intellectually invested in transnational social and cultural formations, especially diaspora.

10. See my chapter 2, note 67.

11. See, for example, C. Phillips, "Water," 165.

12. In a 1976 interview with Robert Stepto, Morrison commented on the environs of the "small river town in Ohio" (Morrison, "Intimate Things," 12) in which she had set *Sula*: "Ohio is right on the Kentucky border, so there's not much difference between it and the 'South.' It's an interesting state from the point of view of black people because it is right there by the Ohio river, in the south, and at its northern tip is Canada" (12).

13. Such connotations are, of course, evident in *Beloved* as well, given what happens to Sethe and her family soon after they "cross the river."

14. Lentz-Smith, *Freedom Struggles*, 4.

15. Ibid., 5.

16. Ibid.

17. Du Bois, *The Souls of Black Folk*, 17.

18. Du Bois, "Close Ranks," 115.

19. Du Bois, "Returning Soldiers," 127. Mark Braley's "The Sweetness of His Strength" (2001) includes a brief survey of scholarly contributions (by Elliott M. Rudwick, Mark Ellis, David Levering Lewis, and William Jordan) to the debate over Du Bois's stance on war (99).

20. Randolph and Owen, "Who Shall Pay for the War?" 118.

21. Ibid.

22. Morrison, "Unspeakable Things Unspoken," 26. Morrison first presented "Unspeakable Things Unspoken" as the Tanner Lecture on Human Values at the University of Michigan on October 7, 1988.

23. Ibid.

24. My phrase, "the rise of a proud New Negro militancy," is not intended to suggest that the "New Negro" trope and sensibility suddenly emerged, out of nowhere, as late as 1919. For a history of the New Negro trope, see Gates and Jarrett's introduction to *The New Negro*.

25. McKay, "If We Must Die"; Hughes, "I Too."

26. Patricia Hunt is correct in suggesting that "*war* and *men* [are] as central to this novel *[Sula]* as *peace* and *women*" ("War and Peace," 444; italics in the original). Elizabeth B. House's argument that Morrison's narrative of Shadrack "establishes most of the imagery patterns with which she structures *Sula*" similarly underscores the veteran's importance in the novel in its entirety ("*Sula*: Imagery," 102). The encounter between Shadrack and Sula after Chicken Little's drowning—including Shadrack's much-discussed utterance "always," which Sula recalls at the moment of her death—further highlights Shadrack's significance (see Baker, *Workings of the Spirit*, 148–49; Dubey, "No Bottom and No Top," 76; House, "*Sula*: Imagery," 102; Matus, *Toni Morrison*, 64–65). While Shadrack's and Plum Peace's psychological postwar battles are the most prominent aspect of Morrison's allusions to the Great War in *Sula*, the war is also referenced in the scene, set in 1920, in which Helene and Nel Wright meet African American veterans who are "still in their shit-colored uniforms and peaked

caps" (21)—an allusion to the veterans' marginalized socioeconomic status back in the United States. Chuck Jackson, in "A Headless Display," goes so far as to link Morrison's treatment of soldiers in *Sula* to the lynching narrative tradition.

27. For a longer discussion of the biblical resonances of Shadrack's name, see Hunt, "War and Peace," 449–50.

28. PTSD was first included in the American Psychiatric Association's *Diagnostic and Statistical Manual of Mental Disorders* (*DSM*) in 1980—that is, following the publication of *Sula* and prior to the appearance of *Tar Baby*. The inclusion of PTSD in the *DSM* largely, though not solely, resulted from research on posttraumatic symptom clusters displayed by American veterans of the Vietnam War (see, for example, Luckhurst, *The Trauma Question*, 59–64). However, as Luckhurst reminds us, "In the 1990s, shell shock was absorbed into PTSD," and World War I was thus "retrofit[ted] ... with modern trauma theory" (53). It is this now widely accepted "retrofitting" that justifies my somewhat anachronistic usage of PTSD to describe the post–World War I condition of Shadrack.

29. See Caruth, introduction to "Trauma and Experience," 5.

30. Ibid.

31. Medallion is a poignantly ironic name for the fictional hometown of Shadrack, an undecorated soldier who returns from the war with no medals and no glory (see also Grewal, *Circles of Sorrow*, 56).

32. With its simultaneously warm and ironic folkloric story of how the Bottom got its name ("it's high up in the hills . . . , but when God looks down, it's the bottom, . . . the bottom of heaven—the best land there is"; Morrison, *Sula*, 5), *Sula*'s opening highlights the importance of a sense of place and, ultimately, of rootedness. It is true, of course, as Trudier Harris has pointed out, that Morrison's etiological anecdote fits "a classic tale cycle of the black man being duped by the white man" (*Fiction and Folklore*, 55): according to this story of origin, a white farmer tricked his manumitted slave into accepting the Bottom's hilly, infertile land as payment for onerous chores, and in the novel's present the Bottom's African Americans are powerfully aware of what Philip Page terms "the racial division of the land" (*Dangerous Freedom*, 62). However, their resilience has largely reversed the joke, as Harris observes, and "the black folks create reasonably happy lives for themselves in a place almost animate in its influence upon them" (*Fiction and Folklore*, 56).

33. Morrison, *Sula*, 14.

34. Mott, *War Neuroses*, 80. See also Luckhurst, *The Trauma Question*, 50.

35. Morrison, *Sula*, 12.

36. Ibid., 10.

37. Ibid., 12.

38. Bouson, *Quiet as It's Kept*, 51.

39. Morrison, *Sula*, 173.

40. Caruth, *Literature in the Ashes of History*, 76. She quotes Derrida's *Mal d'Archive: Une impression freudienne*, "Prière d'insérer," 1 (Paris: Galilée, 1995).

41. Caruth, ibid. She again quotes Derrida from the source identified in note 40 above.

42. Caruth, ibid.

43. Ibid.

44. Luckhurst, *The Trauma Question*, 97.

45. Whitehead, *Trauma Fiction*, 4.

46. Luckhurst, *The Trauma Question*, 87.

47. Ibid., 97; italics added.

48. Morrison, *Sula*, 7.

49. Ibid.

50. Ibid., 156.

51. Ibid., 61.

52. Ibid.

53. Ibid., 61, 62.

54. Ibid., 61.

55. A peculiar combination of repetition compulsion, death drive, and search for atonement, Shadrack's morbid festival—intended as a collective coping mechanism—dedicates one day a year to the fear of death, so that the entire community can then be done with it and focus on other things for the rest of the year. The hyperbolic word "National" in the title of this holiday, National Suicide Day, can be understood as having multiple levels of meaning. First, it reflects Shadrack's peculiar but genuine attempt to be part of the community by doing good to others: in his view, he is helping all willing members of the community, not just himself, to cope with their shared mortality. Second, the social connotations of the word "National" reveal the otherwise isolated Shadrack's need for an annual communal validation of his chosen coping mechanism—and, by extension, of his existence. Third, the adjective "National" also functions as Morrison's ironic joke highlighting the "organized, public madness" of the mentally broken private, as she writes in "Unspeakable Things Unspoken" (26). Fourth, it is significant that when the people of the Bottom start to feel at ease with the celebration, they drop the qualifier "National," indicating an intimate, familiar relationship with what they have adopted as theirs (see Morrison, *Sula*, 16).

56. Morrison, *Sula*, 158.

57. Ibid.

58. Ibid., 14.

59. Ibid., 161.

60. McKee, "Spacing and Placing Experience," 39.

61. Morrison, *Sula*, 161.

62. Grewal, *Circles of Sorrow*, 45.

63. Morrison, *Sula*, 159. Matus, too, associates Shadrack with a "latter-day Pied Piper" (*Toni Morrison*, 58).

64. To clarify, the people of the Bottom neither cure nor abandon Shadrack after his return from the war. Instead, they tolerate his presence in the physical and mental space that he establishes for his broken self on the margins of the community. See also note 55 above.

65. Luckhurst, *The Trauma Question*, 87.

66. Ibid.

67. Ibid.

68. Ibid., 91.

69. Ibid.

70. Ibid.

71. Ibid., 91–97.

72. Caruth, *Unclaimed Experience*, 5.

73. Luckhurst, *The Trauma Question*, 93.

74. Morrison, *Sula*, 13.

75. As for Woolfian allusions in *Sula*, it is noteworthy that the mentally isolated and fragile Shadrack begins his post-hospitalization existence with a "plunge" (11)—a word that subversively evokes the "plunge" that Woolf's suicidal World War I veteran Septimus Warren Smith takes in *Mrs. Dalloway* as he leaps from a windowsill onto the street below. In the very opening of Woolf's novel, Mrs. Dalloway's exclamation, "What a plunge" (3), foreshadows Septimus's lethal leap out of the window onto the street. While a "plunge" typically suggests a powerful movement of the entire body, in *Sula* it refers, ironically, to the four steps that the released, but hardly cured, Shadrack cautiously takes from the hospital door to the grass that he needs to cross in order to reach the gate that opens up to the outside world—a representation of the enormous challenge that the young veteran faces as he prepares to begin the journey toward post-rehabilitation normalcy (10). Briefly connecting with some still-existing modicum of independence and assertiveness within his fractured psyche, Shadrack is momentarily drawn to the idea of "a direction of one's own" (10; another Woolfian allusion), but after the initial "leap" or "plunge" that takes him to the edge of the grass to be crossed, he immediately "los[es] his way" (11). Lorie Watkins Fulton reads *Mrs. Dalloway* and *Sula* together in "A Direction of One's Own." For a shorter comparative discussion of these two novels, see Grewal, *Circles of Sorrow*, 56–58. Morrison wrote her 1955 master's thesis at Cornell on alienation in Faulkner and Woolf, and *Mrs. Dalloway* was one of the works she examined.

76. Morrison, *Sula*, 13.

77. Luckhurst, *The Trauma Question*, 1.

78. The most thorough book-length study of African American soldiers in Vietnam to date is James E. Westheider's *The African American Experience in Vietnam: Brothers*

in Arms (2008). Its chapter 2 (17–38) focuses on the draft and its impact on African Americans.

79. Examples of influential scholarly books on American literary and cinematic representations of the Vietnam War and its veterans that overlook *Tar Baby* include *American Literature and the Experience of Vietnam*, by Philip D. Beidler (which, admittedly, appeared in 1982, only one year after *Tar Baby*'s publication); *American Myth and the Legacy of Vietnam*, by John Hellmann (1986); *Search and Clear: Critical Responses to Selected Literature and Films of the Vietnam War*, edited by William J. Searle (1988); *Fourteen Landing Zones: Approaches to Vietnam War Literature*, edited by Philip K. Jason (1991); *Re-Writing America: Vietnam Authors in Their Generation*, by Beidler (1991); *Vietnam War Stories: Innocence Lost*, by Tobey C. Herzog (1992); *Fighting and Writing the Vietnam War*, by Donald Ringnalda (1994); and *Friendly Fire: American Images of the Vietnam War*, by Katherine Kinney (2000).

80. Morrison, *Sula*, 11. See note 75 above.

81. Ibid., 12.

82. Morrison, *Tar Baby*, 1.

83. Morrison's narrative seems inconsistent in its representation of whether Son and Cheyenne were actually married, unless her terminology refers to a common-law marriage. On the one hand, Son "went to Eloe, *married* Cheyenne, left the set early when a fistfight broke out and found his sleeping *wife* sleeping with a teenager" (Morrison, *Tar Baby*, 224; italics added). Son also tells Ondine that he used to be married (161), and in Eloe Son's friend Soldier mentions to Jadine that Son "was married before" (254). On the other hand, Son was a "man without human rites: unbaptized, uncircumcised, minus puberty rites or the formal rites of manhood. *Unmarried* and undivorced. He had attended no funeral, *married in no church*, raised no child" (165–66; italics added).

84. Morrison, *Tar Baby*, 2.

85. Ibid.

86. Ibid., 1.

87. Ibid., 2.

88. Ibid., 8.

89. See note 32 above.

90. Sharpe, "The Middle Passages of Black Migration," 25–26.

91. Morrison, *Beloved*, 315.

92. American Psychiatric Association, *DSM-5*, 271, 275. I quote and cite the most recent edition of the *DSM*, whose language is the most current. The definition of PTSD has expanded since the publication of *DSM-III* in 1980 (the edition available at the time when Morrison wrote *Tar Baby*), but differences between the third, fourth, and fifth editions do not affect the substantive points that I make in my discussion of the novel.

93. To give just one example, in chapter 5 the sight of his future girlfriend Jadine's fur coat, made from the skins of ninety brutally slaughtered baby seals, stops Son in his tracks. Having sneaked into her empty bedroom at L'Arbe de la Croix in broad daylight, he finds himself staring at the luxurious coat. Spread across Jadine's bed, it resembles, in Son's eyes, a herd of creatures that have just been killed. Seized by intrusive memories, Son simultaneously has flashbacks both to what he saw during his eight-year period as an unlicensed crewman at sea and to his earlier experiences in Vietnam: "[L]ambs, chickens, tuna, *children*—he had seen them all die by the ton" (Morrison, *Tar Baby*, 131; italics added). See also note 106 below.

94. Morrison, *Tar Baby*, 137.

95. Ibid., 136–37.

96. Ibid., 137; italics added.

97. Shadrack's sense of guilt, which exceeds mere "survivor's guilt," is palpably present in the narrative of his hospitalization. During his psychotic breaks, Shadrack believes that whenever he attempts to mobilize his hands (the hands of a soldier, an intended killer), they start growing uncontrollably, obeying a will of their own. This frightening hallucination, indicative of his internal conflicts and of his post-battlefield fear of the uncontrollable and unexpected, makes him rave madly as he attempts to protect the hospital staff from his "monstrous hand[s]" and "his terrible fingers" (Morrison, *Sula*, 9). Tragically, Shadrack finds relief in a straitjacket (9) because this device, by preventing his hands from doing "deadly" deeds, establishes order and peace in his life, temporarily making him feel that he is where he should be—in a safe niche, in his place in the world.

98. See, for example, Fassin and Rechtman, *The Empire of Trauma*, 88–97, 280. See also Luckhurst, *The Trauma Question*, 59–65.

99. Fassin and Rechtman, *The Empire of Trauma*, 21.

100. Morrison, *Tar Baby*, 166.

101. See Luckhurst, *The Trauma Question*, 1.

102. Morrison, *Tar Baby*, 166.

103. Ibid.

104. Ibid., 138.

105. Schreiber, *Race, Trauma, and Home*, 107.

106. On the night of Son's arrival on Isle des Chevaliers, memories of Vietnam again surface when he tries to orient himself in an unfamiliar environment: "An old dread of mines chilled him—stopped him dead and he had to remind himself several times that this was the Caribbean" (Morrison, *Tar Baby*, 134). The war memories "kept him up all night, practically" (136), in the form of intrusive recollections causing insomnia.

107. Morrison, *Tar Baby*, 305.

108. Ibid., 300.

109. Ibid., 305–6.

110. Lee, "Missing Peace," 571.
111. Morrison, *Tar Baby*, 152, 153.
112. Ibid., 153.
113. Ibid., 306.
114. Ibid., 167.
115. Ibid., 167–68.
116. Schreiber, *Race, Trauma, and Home*, 1.
117. Morrison, *Tar Baby*, 168.
118. Ibid., 167.
119. Ibid.
120. Ibid.

121. As Raphael Dalleo observes, "African Americans simultaneously find themselves members of the black diaspora and citizens of U.S. Empire. . . . [A]t times, African Americans have been able to reap the benefits of imperial privilege, even as the racist logic of American Empire repeatedly returns to definitions of blacks as a group regarded as—and often, legally treated as—a foreign body within the United States" ("Introduction").

122. See, for example, Page, *Dangerous Freedom*, 125.

123. Ibid.

124. For a brief but illuminating discussion of scholarship on *Tar Baby* from the perspective of critics' treatment of blackness, see Krumholz, "Blackness and Art," 263–65.

125. Ibid., 264.

126. Ibid., 265.

127. See Paquet, "The Ancestor as Foundation."

128. Valerian and Margaret's last name is Street (suggesting rerouting), but their privileged exilic condition has nothing to do with the life on the street. Valerian is named after a Roman emperor, as he points out to Son (Morrison, *Tar Baby*, 146). The white patriarch reigns over what Son ironically thinks of as a "plantation" (219), complete with black servants and a hierarchical approach to human relationships. Valerian pompously rules under the sign of the cross, no less, the symbol of the Christian/colonial conquest: his mansion on Isle des Chevaliers is called L'Arbe de la Croix. (For a discussion of the possible significance of the misspelling of *l'arbre* in the mansion's name, see Mayberry, *Can't I Love*, 122–23.) The company he keeps also affirms Morrison's characterization of Valerian as a "colonialist" figure: his only friend in the French Caribbean, Dr. Michelin, a dentist, has been "expelled from Algeria" (Morrison, *Tar Baby*, 15), harbors racist attitudes toward people of color/colonial subjects, and in the Caribbean refuses to accept black patients (15).

129. Morrison, *Tar Baby*, 132.

130. Ibid.

131. Ibid., 139–40.

132. Ibid., 140.
133. Ibid., 61, 163. See also Du Bois, *The Philadelphia Negro*.
134. Morrison, *Tar Baby*, 163.
135. Ibid., 161.
136. Ibid., 164.
137. Ibid., 202–5.
138. Ibid., 205.
139. Ibid., 105–7.
140. Ibid., 105, 107.
141. Zauditu-Selassie, *African Spiritual Traditions*, 115.
142. Paquet, "The Ancestor as Foundation," 509.
143. Ibid.
144. Morrison, *Tar Baby*, 152.
145. Paquet, "The Ancestor as Foundation," 513.
146. Morrison, *Tar Baby*, 299.
147. Ibid., 300.
148. Ibid., 288–90.
149. Ibid., 299.
150. Ibid., 306.
151. Caruth, *Unclaimed Experience*, 11; italics in the original.
152. Ibid., 5.
153. Ibid., 4.
154. See my introduction, note 8.
155. Ibid. In chronicling the rise of "memory" in the historically oriented humanities, Klein offers remarks on the conceptual genealogies and usages of "identity" and "trauma."
156. Young, *At Memory's Edge*, 1.
157. Hirsch, *The Generation of Postmemory*, 5.
158. Michael Rothberg includes a discussion of Caryl Phillips's work in *Multidirectional Memory*, a 2009 study reading representations of the cultural memory of the Holocaust and colonialism/decolonization in conjunction with each other. Arguing strongly and convincingly against the view that a "competition of victims" must necessarily ensue when "memories of slavery and colonialism bump up against memories of the Holocaust in contemporary multicultural societies," Rothberg proposes that collective memory should not be thought of "as *competitive* memory—as a zero-sum struggle over scarce resources," but instead should be viewed "as *multidirectional*: as subject to ongoing negotiation, cross-referencing, and borrowing" (*Multidirectional Memory*, 2, 3). Hirsch's term "connective histories" resonates with Rothberg's "multidirectional memory" and is in part inspired by it, as she acknowledges (*The Generation of Postmemory*, 21): Hirsch, too, is driven by the question of "how to account for contiguous or intersecting histories without allowing them to occlude or erase each

other, how to turn competitive or appropriative memory into more capacious transnational memory work" (20). For an essay that analyzes Phillips's *Higher Ground* and *The Nature of Blood* from the perspective of black-Jewish relations and connective diasporas, see Craps, "Linking Legacies of Loss." For a book chapter that reads *The Nature of Blood* in conjunction with trauma theory, see Whitehead, *Trauma Fiction*, chapter 4 (89–116).

159. C. Phillips, "Water," 163.
160. Ibid.
161. Rice, *Creating Memorials*, 166.
162. Ibid., 166–67.
163. For a book-length treatment of African American troops in Britain during World War II, see Graham Smith, *When Jim Crow Met John Bull*. See also Reynolds, *Rich Relations*, chapters 14 (216–237) and 18 (302–24); and Carby, "Becoming Modern Racialized Subjects," 641–50.
164. See my chapter 1, note 6.
165. C. Phillips, *Crossing the River*, 159.
166. In discussing romantic relationships between African American GIs and white British women and the responses of British society to the biracial children of such unions, Graham Smith remarks wryly, "The near-universal hostility towards interracial sexual relations in Britain before and during the war varied only in the vehemence of its expression. It cut across all shades of political opinion and class to such an extent that it was accepted as a fact of life that needed little or no explanation" (*When Jim Crow Met John Bull*, 188). For a longer discussion of the topic, see his chapter 8, 187–216.
167. C. Phillips, *Crossing the River*, 228.
168. G. Smith, *When Jim Crow Met John Bull*, 206. For a more detailed treatment of wartime mixed marriages, see 204–7.
169. C. Phillips, *Crossing the River*, 227.
170. Ibid., 229.
171. Ibid., 224.
172. Ibid., 232.
173. As Graham Smith reminds us, "At some point in 1944 or 1945 Somerset County Council made a unique decision: to take into care all brown babies who came to its attention" (*When Jim Crow Met John Bull*, 212). For a longer discussion of this decision and its consequences, see *When Jim Crow Met John Bull*, 212–16. Phillips's story is set in Yorkshire, but the Somerset example is nevertheless illuminating.
174. C. Phillips, *Crossing the River*, 228.
175. Ibid., 1.
176. Ibid.
177. Griffin, review of *Crossing the River*, 45.
178. Gilroy, *The Black Atlantic*, 49.

179. C. Phillips, "Water," 165, 166; italics added.
180. C. Phillips, *Crossing the River*, 235.
181. C. Phillips, "Spectral Triangle," 4. Also quoted in Rice, *Creating Memorials*, 170.
182. See also Griffin, review of *Crossing the River*, 45.
183. Fassin and Rechtman, *The Empire of Trauma*, 20.
184. LaCapra, *Writing History, Writing Trauma*, xiii.
185. Ibid., 13, 14.
186. C. Phillips, "Water," 164.

Chapter 4. Journeys to the Heart of Empire after World War II: George Lamming's, Caryl Phillips's, and Andrea Levy's Caribbean Migrants

1. Gilroy, *There Ain't No Black*, 17.
2. Ibid., 13.
3. See, for example, ibid., 158.
4. Ball, *Imagining London*, 15. Gikandi writes, in describing the intellectual process that resulted in *Maps of Englishness*, that he "began to ponder on ways in which cultures produced on the margins of a dominant discourse might actually have the authority not only to subvert the dominant but also to transform its central notions" (*Maps of Englishness*, xv). Baucom, in turn, argues that "we should read imperialism not simply as the history of England's expansion and contraction but as the history of a cultivated confusion," because "[t]he empire . . . is less a place where England exerts control than the place where England loses command of its own narrative of identity" (*Out of Place*, 3).
5. Ball, *Imagining London*, 15.
6. I here quote the title of Jopi Nyman's *Under English Eyes*.
7. Carby, "Becoming Modern Racialized Subjects," 624, 625.
8. Pirker, *Narrative Projections*, 9.
9. Ibid., 11.
10. Ibid.
11. Both Phillips and Levy subversively utilize maternal idiom and imagery while portraying the mother country's reception of postwar Caribbean migrants, as my analyses of *The Final Passage* and *Small Island* will demonstrate.
12. As Hazel Carby remarks, African Caribbean diasporic intellectuals "consistently engage and reproduce the past in the present, narrating the continuous and to-be-continued struggle with the historical forces and legacy of colonialism" ("Postcolonial Translations," 222). In this chapter, my analyses of novels will detect a similar trend in fiction.
13. D. Thomas, *Modern Blackness*, 4.
14. McKay, "Old England," 64.
15. Ibid., 63.
16. See my discussion in the next paragraph.

17. McKay, "Claude MacKay [*sic*] Describes His Own Life."

18. Ibid., 275.

19. McKay, "Old England," 63.

20. McKay, *A Long Way from Home*, 66. McKay initially resorts to the cautious metaphor of an inhospitable climate ("the English as a whole were a strangely unsympathetic people, as coldly chilling as their English fog"), but toward the end of the travelogue he becomes more outspoken about the gravity of English racism and offers such tangible examples as the effects of racial discrimination on London housing (67; 303–4).

21. Ibid., 300.

22. Since the 1954 publication of *The Emigrants*, the tradition of giving expression to the first-generation black Caribbean immigrant experience in postwar Britain through the medium of the novel has perhaps most famously been continued by Sam(uel) Selvon's *The Lonely Londoners* (1956), Phillips's *The Final Passage*, and Levy's *Small Island*. The literary legacy of Indo-Caribbean Selvon, who died in 1994, is evoked frequently and sympathetically by his black Caribbean colleagues, participants in what Phillips has aptly termed the "creolising Caribbean consciousness" ("Introduction: The Gift of Displacement," 133). Among the less-remembered works in the same thematic category are, for example, *Because They Know Not* (1959) by Jamaican A. G. (Alvin Gladstone) Bennett, in which the protagonist returns to Jamaica and becomes a successful politician there; the three London novels by the white English writer Colin MacInnes (*City of Spades*, 1957; *Absolute Beginners*, 1959; and *Mr. Love and Justice*, 1960), which depict black immigration, the emerging youth culture, and the transformation of London into a multiethnic metropolis in an entertaining mode; and *Moses Ascending* (1975), the first of Selvon's two sequels to *The Lonely Londoners*. Also, several other novels could be mentioned here that do not, however, quite qualify as works depicting the *first-generation* West Indian immigrant experience in *postwar* Britain. For example, Jean Rhys's *Voyage in the Dark* was published in 1934, before the *Windrush* moment. *White Teeth* (2000) by Zadie Smith, the daughter of a Jamaican-born mother and an English father, is, in turn, an inherently multicultural and hybrid novel that addresses the black Caribbean experience without making it the narrative's sole focus. Not unlike *White Teeth*, Andrea Levy's first three novels—*Every Light in the House Burnin'* (1994), *Never Far from Nowhere* (1996), and *Fruit of the Lemon* (1999)—study the black Caribbean immigration experience from the perspective of the children of first-generation migrants. Caryl Phillips's *In the Falling Snow* (2009) offers a contemporary glimpse into the lives of the British-born son and grandson of a first-generation West Indian male migrant.

23. My brief contextualization of this chapter's primary sources within the worlds depicted in Lamming's *Natives of My Person* and, to a lesser degree, in Phillips's *Cambridge* resonates with Nana Wilson-Tagoe's 1998 comment that "the [black Caribbean] writer's imaginative relationship to Africa and the ancestor" involves "mature

and subtle probing into the ways in which an African consciousness modified and transformed itself in the physical and psychological situation of slavery and colonialism" (*Historical Thought*, 253). I will keep this contextualization short because various critics have already analyzed the significant, albeit often complex, role of Africa in the diasporic visions laid out, for example, in *The Pleasures of Exile*, Lamming's 1960 essay collection in which he, in "The African Presence," discusses his encounter with Africa and with the African dimension of his diasporic subjectivity during his 1958 trip to Ghana and Nigeria; in *The Atlantic Sound*, Phillips's 2000 circum-Atlantic travelogue; and in *The New World Order*, Phillips's 2001 essay collection, which includes his often-quoted statement that he would like his "ashes to be scattered in the middle of the Atlantic Ocean at a point equidistant between Britain, Africa and North America" ("Conclusion: The 'High Anxiety' of Belonging," 304). For a discussion that focuses on Lamming's visit to Africa, see Schwartz, "Locating Lamming," 14–15. For relevant secondary sources regarding Phillips, see, for example, Ledent, "Ambiguous Visions of Home"; Pirker, "A Black Atlantic Agenda," 197–207; and Ward, "The Cloud of Ambivalence."

24. Lamming, *The Pleasures of Exile*, 15.

25. See, for example, Paquet, *The Novels of George Lamming*, 2–3; C. Alexander, "Rivers to Cross," 60; Forbes, *From Nation to Diaspora*, 159, 235; J. D. Brown, *Migrant Modernism*, 82; Simoes da Silva, *The Luxury of Nationalist Despair*, 5–6. Multiple other citations could easily be included in this list because, as Simoes da Silva points out—exaggerating only slightly—"almost every critic of Lamming's work" summons his use of the Caliban-Prospero trope (*The Luxury of Nationalist Despair*, 5–6).

26. Paquet, *The Novels of George Lamming*, 31–47.

27. In addition to Paquet's analysis cited in note 26 above, for substantive discussions of *The Emigrants* see, for example, Gikandi, *Writing in Limbo*, 89–98; C. Alexander, "Rivers to Cross," 59–63; Nair, *Caliban's Curse*, 15, 44, 50, 55, 57–61, 63–66, 68, 71–73, 75, 79, 81, 87, 126, 128, 130; Simoes da Silva, *The Luxury of Nationalist Despair*, 103–26; Procter, *Dwelling Places*, 31–45 (a discussion that, notably, includes a detailed analysis of the significance of physical spaces in the novel); Wheat, "Examining Colonialism and Exile"; Ellis, "Foreign Bodies"; and Guarducci, "Only the Ship Remained."

28. In addition to Gikandi's analysis of Lamming's relationship with modernism in *Writing in Limbo*, J. Dillon Brown has discussed the same topic in chapter 3 of *Migrant Modernism* (73–102). For an earlier version of the chapter, see J. D. Brown, "Exile and Cunning."

29. Philip Nanton's essay "On Knowing and Not Knowing George Lamming" is a rare exception in Lamming scholarship in that it discusses, albeit briefly (57–60), Sartrean influences among the "[c]onstituent elements of Lamming's style" (52). For brief mentions of Lamming's interest in existentialism, see Chamberlain, "The 'Consolation of Freedom,'" 79; Chamberlain, "George Lamming," 179; Schwarz, "Locating Lamming," 12; and Schwarz, "C.L.R. James and George Lamming," 66.

30. Pratt, *Imperial Eyes*, 7.
31. Carby, "Becoming Modern Racialized Subjects," 641.
32. See my chapter 3, note 2.
33. See my introduction, note 81.
34. Gilroy, *Postcolonial Melancholia*, 2.
35. Dawson, *Mongrel Nation*, 17.
36. Stephens, *Black Empire*, 2.
37. In the context discussed by Stephens, the second journey is "from the colony to America" (*Black Empire*, 2) rather than to England, but the logic is the same.
38. Eliot, "Little Gidding," part 5, 208.
39. For a more detailed analysis of *Cambridge*, see, for example, Ledent, *Caryl Phillips*, 80–106.
40. See, for example, Thiong'o, "Freeing the Imagination," 100.
41. Ibid.
42. C. Phillips, "Following On," 235–36. In 1999, Belinda Edmonson suggested, while discussing Phillips's 1995 interview with Jenny Sharpe (C. Phillips, "Of This Time"), that "[i]nterestingly, Phillips does not claim exile writers such as Lamming and James as part of [the black British] narrative tradition" (*Making Men*, 173, n26). In that particular interview, Phillips indeed discussed how the literary production of African American writers, particularly Richard Wright, inspired his early formation as a writer. More recently, however, he has also stressed the importance of selected Caribbean influences for his self-understanding as a literary artist and diasporic intellectual, as "Following On"—with its emphasis on Lamming, Selvon, and James, in particular—clearly indicates.
43. Lamming, *Natives of My Person*, 17.
44. Ibid.
45. Ibid., 135.
46. For Edward Said's thoughtful commentary on Conrad's much-discussed novella and its ambiguities regarding imperialism, see *Culture and Imperialism*, 25–26.
47. Lamming, *Natives of My Person*, 106.
48. Ibid., 103.
49. Ibid., 104.
50. Ibid., 109–10.
51. Ibid., 111.
52. Ibid., 135–36.
53. See my chapter 3, note 8.
54. Lamming, *Natives of My Person*, 351.
55. Paul, *Whitewashing Britain*, 9.
56. Ibid., 16; italics added.
57. Arana and Ramey, introduction," 1.
58. Carby, foreword, xv–xvi.

59. See E. Powell, "Rivers of Blood." Fomenting fear and hatred, Powell argued that black immigrants might soon organize "to consolidate their members, to agitate and campaign against their fellow citizens, and to overawe and dominate the rest with the legal weapons which the ignorant and ill-informed have provided" (18). The Virgilian allusion adorned the very climax of his speech: "As I look ahead, I am filled with foreboding. Like the Roman, I seem to see 'the River Tiber foaming with much blood'" (18).

60. Lamming, *The Emigrants*, 43.

61. Paquet, *The Novels of George Lamming*, 32. Paquet, too, quotes Lilian's mention of the "bit o' cargo."

62. Lamming, *The Emigrants*, 65.

63. Ibid., 65–66.

64. Klein, *From History to Theory*, 84.

65. This parenthetical clarification is included in Robert F. Brown and Peter C. Hodgson's English translation.

66. Hegel, *Lectures*, 196, 197.

67. Klein, *From History to Theory*, 84. For Hegel's elaboration of his understanding of historiography being a prerequisite for a people becoming "world-historical" (*Lectures*, 191), see *Lectures*, 133–34.

68. Lamming, *In the Castle of My Skin*, 30–31.

69. Ibid., 42.

70. Lamming, "George Lamming Talks to Caryl Phillips."

71. Ibid., 12.

72. Ibid.

73. Lamming, *The Emigrants*, 50.

74. Lamming, "George Lamming Talks to Caryl Phillips," 14.

75. For more information about the West Indies Federation, see, for example, Rogoziński, *A Brief History of the Caribbean*, 321–23. The West Indies Federal Archives Center is located on the Cave Hill campus of the University of the West Indies in Barbados.

76. For a longer discussion of Lamming's support of the federation and his disappointment over its collapse, see Chamberlain, "The 'Consolation of Freedom,'" 79–86.

77. Lamming, *The Emigrants*, 66.

78. See, for example, Lamming, "George Lamming Talks to Caryl Phillips," 13–14, and Lamming, *The Emigrants*, 131.

79. McKay, *A Long Way from Home*, 67.

80. Ibid.

81. Boehmer, *Empire, the National, the Postcolonial*, 153.

82. Ibid.

83. See Høgsbjerg, *C.L.R. James in Imperial Britain*, especially 71, 74, 79–81, 86–88.

84. Thiong'o, "Freeing the Imagination," 100.

85. Lamming, "The Sovereignty of the Imagination," 104.

86. Ibid., 111; italics in the original.

87. R. Wright, introduction. As for Wright's relationship with *French* existentialism specifically, it is true that Michel Fabre argues, in "Richard Wright and the French Existentialists" (1978), that Heidegger, Nietzsche, Kierkegaard, and Dostoevsky were more significant existentialist influences on Wright than were the French giants. (Nevertheless, Fabre [41–43] does note Wright's appreciation of Sartre and the dialogue that Wright's *The Outsider* conducts with Camus's *L'Étranger*.) Other critics, too, have reminded us of the foundational importance of Wright's *American* experience for the formation of his black exilic existentialism (see Gates and McKay, "Richard Wright," 1379). Lamming, in any case, drank deeply from the wells of French existentialism during his formative years as a novelist and has explicitly said so.

88. Høgsbjerg, *C.L.R. James in Imperial Britain*, 82–84.

89. Joyce, "What We Do," 601.

90. Griswold, "Fabrication of Meaning," 1114–15.

91. Thornber, "Early Twentieth-Century Intra-East Asian Literary Contact Nebulae," 751. Thornber defines "artistic contact nebulae" as "spaces where dancers, dramatists, musicians, painters, sculptors, writers, and other artists from cultures, societies, or nations in unequal power relationships grapple with and transculturate one another's creative output" (751).

92. Lamming, "The Sovereignty of the Imagination," 111–12.

93. Ellison, "Change the Joke," 111–12.

94. Ibid., 112.

95. Eventually, the question of the relationship between intellectualism and political action famously contributed to the fallout between Sartre and Algerian-born Camus: Sartre became an increasingly vocal supporter of openly expressed left-wing political commitments, whereas Camus, at least according to many of his critics, went in a different direction, particularly during the Algerian war of independence—a cause with which Frantz Fanon, another important intellectual and political influence on Lamming, became deeply involved. (For Lamming's remarks on his interest in Fanon, see, for example, "The Sovereignty of the Imagination," 175.) However, in *Albert Camus the Algerian: Colonialism, Terrorism, Justice* (2007), David Carroll thoroughly revisits Camus's relationship to politics, French colonialism, and Algeria. Carroll's Camus is considerably more radical, or at least morally more committed and coherent, than the Camus of most scholars in recent decades. Carroll writes that during his research he "became convinced that what is most interesting in Camus' writings and missing from the picture of the 'colonialist Camus' constructed by his most militant postcolonial critics is what Camus himself called 'the Algerian' in him. Not a *French* Algerian in him who wanted Algeria to remain French at any costs, but rather the Algerian part of him" (xiii).

96. See note 95 above.

97. For the sake of terminological convenience, I treat Camusian absurdism as a branch of existentialism—a common practice among scholars despite Camus's well-known desire to see his absurdism as distinct from existentialism.

98. Robinson, "Theorizing Politics after Camus," 1.

99. Lamming, "The Sovereignty of the Imagination," 112.

100. The narrator soon disappears from the text as narrator, although he briefly resumes this capacity at the beginning of the novel's final section. He can, with some minor reservation, be identified with the character Collis.

101. As Paquet points out, Lamming here "takes advantage of the traditional route stops to extend the novel's frame of reference to the French-speaking Caribbean as well" (*The Novels of George Lamming*, 31).

102. See Lamming, *The Emigrants*, 15.

103. See ibid., 274–75.

104. See, for example, ibid., 18.

105. However, despite these similarities, *The Emigrants*' parallelism with *The Stranger* neither aims at any formulaic imitation nor is carried all the way through the end. At the conclusion of *The Stranger*, Meursault's indifferent, laissez-faire nihilism is overcome by a new defiant, absurdist stance—an existential position at which he arrives after being subjected to the objectifying Look of others (a Sartrean notion adopted by Camus) during his trial in court. This new position enables Meursault, even while imprisoned, to mentally embrace his radical existential freedom, to appreciate the life that he still has left as worth being lived to its fullest, and to face his imminent death boldly, without fear. The ending of *The Emigrants*, in turn, focuses on intersubjectivity, the subject-object relation, and the dialectic of recognition in a Hegelian, Sartrean, and Fanonian vein rather than embracing Camus's defiant absurdism (which was, more specifically, the position of the *young* Camus) in any triumphant manner. Ambiguous and open, the conclusion of *The Emigrants* gives expression to a complex process of African Caribbean adaptation to an unwelcoming Britain—a dually diasporic process that will continue in generations to come.

106. The term "*no-THING*" permeates the thoughts of the Grenadian character Higgins as he prepares to set foot in England in the aftermath of a major disappointment (Lamming, *The Emigrants*, 106–7). During the voyage, he unexpectedly discovered that the cooking school in Liverpool that he had intended to attend in order to qualify for the British job market had just closed down. Higgins fears that his emigration might turn into an all-encompassing nothingness annihilating his very existence, which indeed becomes his fate as he mentally falls apart in his new environment soon after arrival. Lamming's rendering of Higgins's mental soliloquy on the ship, after the collapse of what had seemed a solid education plan, employs such existentially laden key words as "meaning," "actions," and "something other than *no-THING*."

107. See, for example, Fanon, *Black Skin, White Masks*, 112, 116.

108. Ibid., 216–17.

109. Lamming, *The Emigrants*, 28–32.

110. In this early scene of the novel, the objectifying gaze is neither a racializing gaze nor a sexualizing gaze, as both subjects are heterosexual black males from Barbados (who are approximate equals in terms of social class as well, although Dickson perceives himself to be superior). Rather than focusing on racially or sexually based objectification, this scene illustrates the vicious and endless Sartrean circle in which *any* subject, mentally stripped naked and ashamed when confronted by the other's objectifying Look, seeks in turn to objectify the other by his own gaze. Martin Jay has aptly called this approach Sartre's "uncompromisingly relentless demonization of *le regard*" (*Downcast Eyes*, 275). It was this aspect of Sartre's theory of the basic dynamics of human intersubjectivity that prompted him to include the famous line "Hell is—other people!" in his play *No Exit* (45). Collis and Dickson's Sartrean (or, hellish) encounter early in the voyage may seem to call into question any possibility of a positive West Indian community formation en route to England, but Lamming counters the failed Collis-Dickson connection with moments of more successful bonding among other emigrants on the ship. However, England in many ways turns out to be "hell itself" (Lamming, *The Emigrants*, 50); from *this* point of view, the Collis-Dickson encounter serves as a foreshadowing of what is to come.

111. Fanon, *Black Skin, White Masks*, 110. Fanon here draws from Du Bois's well-known definition of double consciousness, the "sense of always looking at one's self through the eyes of others" (*The Souls of Black Folk*, 11), as well as conducts a dialogue with Sartre's concept of the Look—which, in turn, converses with Hegel's dialectic of recognition. As James H. Nichols discusses Du Bois's and Fanon's intellectual backgrounds in his 2007 book (mainly devoted to Alexandre Kojève, one of the best-known twentieth-century commentators on Hegel's philosophy, including the master-slave dialectic), he evokes the teaching of "all of the great phenomenologists," who, according to his summary, acknowledge that "as embodied consciousness we have at least three different perspectives on the world: the dimension of seeing, the dimension of being seen, and the dimension of being conscious of being seen by others" (Nichols, *Alexandre Kojève*, 108). What distinguished the first "black" phenomenologies and existentialisms from their "white" predecessors was, as Nichols observes, the serious attention that the latter gave to questions of race, racialization, and racism (106).

112. Lamming, *The Emigrants*, 138–48.

113. Ibid., 204.

114. Ibid., 266.

115. Ibid.

116. Ibid., 267.

117. See, for example, M. Collins, "Pride and Prejudice," for an article-length analysis of "the dissonance between black and white perceptions of West Indian men" in postwar Britain (393).

118. Dryden, *The Modern Gothic*, 39.

119. Lamming, *The Emigrants*, 237.

120. Lamming, *The Pleasures of Exile*, 36–37.

121. Nair, *Caliban's Curse*, 27.

122. Helgerson uses the term "printed voyage" in "Camões, Hakluyt, and the Voyages of Two Nations," 27. Quoted in Nair, *Caliban's Curse*, 28; see also 149n2.

123. See Hall, "Race, Articulation and Societies Structured in Dominance"; quoted in Gilroy, *There Ain't No Black*, 30.

124. Gilroy, *The Black Atlantic*, 85.

125. See, for example, Durán-Almarza, "Introduction," 1–2.

126. Forbes, *From Nation to Diaspora*, 216.

127. Lamming, "The Sovereignty of the Imagination," 102.

128. See especially Lamming, *The Emigrants*, 281.

129. Ibid., 23.

130. Ibid., 24.

131. Ibid., 275.

132. Campt and D. Thomas, "Gendering Diaspora," 2.

133. C. Phillips, "Rites of Passage," 79.

134. P. Powell, "A Search for Caribbean Masculinities."

135. C. Phillips, interview by Kay Saunders, 4.

136. C. Phillips, *The Final Passage*, 138–39.

137. Ibid., 140–42.

138. Ibid., 161–62.

139. Ibid., 177.

140. C. Phillips, interview by Kay Saunders, 6.

141. Ibid., 5.

142. Ibid.

143. Ibid.

144. If there is any modernist doubling in *The Final Passage*, then Bradeth and his partner, Millie, serve as doubles for Michael and Leila.

145. C. Phillips, *The Final Passage*, 20.

146. Ibid., 125.

147. Ibid., 127.

148. Ibid., 125.

149. Ibid.

150. Ibid.

151. Ibid., 69.

152. Ibid., 124.

153. Ibid., 131.

154. Ibid., 20, 95.

155. Ibid., 123.

156. Ibid., 129.

157. Ibid., 182.

158. Eliot, "Little Gidding," part 5, 208. In *The Emigrants*, Lamming's Faulknerian/Joycean modernist style abounds with what J. Dillon Brown has termed the "tactical difficulties" (see the subtitle of "Exile and Cunning") of a strategically cunning exilic author fluent in the nuances of Prospero's language. In *The Final Passage* Phillips, by contrast, opts for a stylistically rather straightforward narrative, except for the nonlinear chronological organization of the novel's five sections, whose circular significance is discussed in Ledent, *Caryl Phillips*, 19–24.

159. See my discussion above of *The Emigrants*' veiled reference to Hegel's notion that peoples without historiography, or without the kind of historiography that met his standards, failed to qualify as "world-historical." Furthermore, in a segment of *The Final Passage* that converses with Lamming's rendering of Barbadian schoolchildren's classroom experiences in *In the Castle of My Skin*, Leila thinks back to her exposure to history on her native island: "At school her teachers had ... done their best to confuse what little history of the island there was, and she had never really worked out for herself the relationship between the English, the Irish, the French, the Portuguese, the Africans and so on" (171). The Prestons and their fellow islanders of African descent are hardly historyless, but Phillips does cast them as people who are out of touch with their collective past because their history has been systematically rendered absent in imperial historiography.

160. Gikandi, *Writing in Limbo*, 1.

161. Despite Gikandi's critique of Gilroy's partly metaphorical and epistemological treatment of the slave ship (see my chapter 1, paragraph 4, and notes 11 and 12), both scholars' definitions of when "modernity" began are the same and are in line with most historians' consensus on this matter. I, too, here again use "modernity"—in the vein of Gilroy, Gikandi, and others—in the sense of the era inaugurated, both historically and paradigmatically, by Columbus's "discovery" of the New World.

162. C. Phillips, *The Final Passage*, 18.

163. Ibid.

164. Ibid., 169–70.

165. Levy, *Small Island*, 196.

166. Stephens, *Black Empire*, 2.

167. Levy, *The Long Song*, 141–42.

168. Tölölyan, "Restoring the Logic of the Sedentary," 137.

169. C. Alexander and Knowles, introduction, 7.

170. Jaggi, "Englishmen Born and Bred," 4. Also quoted in Arana, "Sea Change," 21.

171. Lang, "Enthralling," 123–24; 139, n1, n2.

172. Carby, "Becoming Modern Racialized Subjects," 641.

173. Noble, *Jamaica Airman*, 7.

174. For a discussion of similar disappointments among historical Caribbean RAF recruits, see Murray, *Lest We Forget*, 28–29.

175. Levy, "Empire's Child," interview by Bonnie Greer.

176. For a historical note recording a brief training period for some Caribbean RAF recruits at "Camp Patrick Henery [sic] in Newport News, Virginia," see Murray, *Lest We Forget*, 41.

177. Rice, *Creating Memorials*, 173.

178. Levy, *Small Island*, 129.

179. Ibid., 132.

180. Ibid., 139.

181. Ibid.

182. Ibid.

183. Ibid., 141–42. For a longer discussion of Levy's treatment of space, geography, and cartography in *Small Island*, see David James, *Contemporary British Fiction*, 152–55.

184. Levy, *Small Island*, 138.

185. Ibid.

186. Carby, foreword, xv–xvi.

187. Indeed, part of the irony embedded in the novel's title is that Jamaicans have traditionally thought of other West Indians, rather than themselves, as coming from *small* islands. Another part of the irony is that in this novel postwar Great Britain finds itself, as Cynthia James notes, "reduced to a small island with its loss of world power and post-war ruin" ("You'll Soon Get Used to Our Language").

188. C. James, "You'll Soon Get Used to Our Language."

189. Ibid.

190. Levy, *Small Island*, 7.

191. C. James, "You'll Soon Get Used to Our Language."

192. For an analysis of *Small Island* that focuses on the novel's "attempt to use sexuality as a site upon which to intervene in English history and force new narratives about race to the fore," see Poon, "Intimate Arrangements" (130).

193. As Michael Perfect notes, Hortense "unknowingly adopts a child that is both biologically linked to her *and* is the son of the person with whom she was first in love" ("Fold the Paper and Pass It On," 39).

194. Levy, *Small Island*, 518–22.

195. Ibid., 527.

196. Ibid., 521.

197. Levy, "Empire's Child," interview by Bonnie Greer.

198. Levy, *Small Island*, 522.

199. See G. Smith, *When Jim Crow Met John Bull*, 209–12.

200. Muños-Valdivieso, "Metaphors of Belonging," 99.

201. Ibid., 108.

202. McLeod, "Postcolonial Fictions of Adoption," 45.
203. Ibid.

Chapter 5. Roots, Routes, and Returns: Caryl Phillips's, Cecil Foster's, and Edwidge Danticat's Caribbean Returnees

1. D. Walcott, *Midsummer*, part 1, VII.
2. Stein, *Black British Literature*, 4.
3. McKay, "To a Friend," 18.
4. McKay, "I Shall Return," 168. Quoted with permission of the literary representative of the estate of Claude McKay.
5. Paquet, *Caribbean Autobiography*, 87.
6. Marshall, *Praisesong for the Widow*, 209.
7. For a more detailed discussion of *Praisesong for the Widow* that specifically focuses on diasporic identity, see McGill, *Constructing Black Selves*, 98–116.
8. Marshall, *Brown Girl, Brownstones*, 185.
9. For a more thorough analysis of *Brown Girl, Brownstones*, see, for example, Hathaway, *Caribbean Waves*, 86–118.
10. Brand, *In Another Place, Not Here*, 14, 15.
11. For recent longer analyses of *In Another Place, Not Here*, see Vedal's "Immigrant Desire" and Visvis's "Traumatic Forgetting." Vedal juxtaposes African diasporic trauma with what she sees as Canadian society's ideological conflation of safety and whiteness, and she reads Brand's novel through the lens of this critical juxtaposition. Visvis, in turn, examines the relationship between traumatic forgetting and spatial tropes in the novel.
12. See my introduction, note 27.
13. See my chapter 4, note 168.
14. Foster, *Sleep On, Beloved*, 5. See also my introduction, note 97.
15. See A. J. Seymour, "The Novel in the British Caribbean," part 3, 239–40; cited in Sáez, "Postcoloniality, Atlantic Orders," 17.
16. Sáez, "Postcoloniality, Atlantic Orders," 17.
17. Ibid.
18. Ibid., 18.
19. Ibid.
20. Ibid.
21. J. D. Brown, "A State of Interdependence," 89.
22. Ibid., 103.
23. Ibid., 85; italics added.
24. For a detailed discussion of the relationship between St. Kitts and the island featured in *A State of Independence*, see Sáez, "Postcoloniality, Atlantic Orders," 24–25.
25. C. Phillips, "St Kitts," 136.

26. C. Phillips, *A State of Independence*, 145.
27. Varela-Zapata, "Translating One's Own Culture," 398.
28. C. Phillips, *A State of Independence*, 18.
29. Ibid.
30. Ibid.
31. Ibid., 19.
32. Ibid.
33. Ibid., 10.
34. Ibid., 157.
35. C. Phillips, *The Final Passage*, 171.
36. C. Phillips, *A State of Independence*, 63.
37. For a longer discussion of this scene and its implications, see Ledent, *Caryl Phillips*, 46.
38. C. Phillips, *A State of Independence*, 86.
39. Ibid., 136; italics added.
40. Ibid., 136.
41. C. Phillips, "Extravagant Strangers," 296.
42. C. Phillips, *A State of Independence*, 112.
43. Ibid., 103.
44. Ibid., 158.
45. J. D. Brown, "A State of Interdependence," 89.
46. See, in particular, ibid., 101–2.
47. C. Phillips, interview by Kay Saunders, 3–4; italics added.
48. J. D. Brown, "A State of Interdependence," 102.
49. Ibid., 89.
50. Ibid., 91.
51. Ibid., 89.
52. Saunders in C. Phillips, interview by Kay Saunders, 3; italics added.
53. C. Phillips, interview by Kay Saunders, 3.
54. C. Phillips, *A State of Independence*, 70, 76.
55. Ibid., 76.
56. Sáez, "Postcoloniality, Atlantic Orders," 23. See also J. D. Brown, "A State of Interdependence," 87.
57. See note 56 above. See also J. D. Brown, "A State of Interdependence," 103n1.
58. C. Phillips, *A State of Independence*, 127.
59. Rahbek, "Caryl Phillips's *A State of Independence*," 81.
60. Phillips, in fact, confirms Bertram's paternity in the interview by Kay Saunders, 7.
61. Ibid.
62. Offering a different reading, Nyman argues that Bertram's "attempt to reconnect with Patsy . . . is doomed to be merely temporary" (*Home, Identity, Mobility,*

38). In my view, this interpretation, particularly the powerfully pessimistic term "doomed," requires more textual evidence than Nyman provides.

63. C. Phillips, interview by Kay Saunders, 9.

64. For a succinct discussion of this notion, see, for example, Mardorossian, *Reclaiming Difference*, 116.

65. C. Phillips, *A State of Independence*, 145.

66. Ibid., 11.

67. Ibid., 158.

68. Foster is the son of parents who emigrated from Barbados to Britain when he was a young child, leaving him in the care of relatives. He writes about this experience in his 1998 memoir, *Island Wings*. The generational shift in migration destinations exhibited by Foster's family history—that is, his parents going to Britain and him selecting North America—was typical; see, for example, Foster, *A Place Called Heaven*, 35–36. Regarding the same pattern with Jamaican migrants, see note 69 below.

69. As Elaine Bauer and Paul Thompson write in *Jamaican Hands across the Atlantic*, "the main destination [of Jamaican migrants overseas] for the first postwar decades was Britain, but from the 1970s it switched to North America. Migrants to Britain came above all in the 1950s and 1960s. With the increasing restrictiveness of British immigration policy and the converse opening up of the United States and Canada to West Indian migrants, North America became and has remained the main destination" (16). Heron, too, writes, "Mass migration from the Caribbean was deliberately stopped by British immigration policy in 1962. Consequently, significant migrant flows to England shifted to the U.S. and, for the first time, to Canada which also liberalized its immigration policies in the early 1960s" (*Occupational Attainment*, 6).

70. Davies, *Black Women, Writing, and Identity*, 113.

71. R. Walcott, "Towards a Methodology," 242.

72. Ibid., 242–43.

73. Ibid., 243.

74. Foster writes more about the Caribana festival, its history, and its cultural politics in chapters 10 ("Caribana Dreams") and 11 ("Caribana Crisis") of *A Place Called Heaven*, his 1996 nonfiction book, which, as its subtitle indicates, focuses on *The Meaning of Being Black in Canada*.

75. *Sleep On, Beloved* has received very little critical attention. Among the few published articles on this novel are Reckley's "Barriers, Boundaries, and Alienation" (24, 27–30) and N. Thomas's "Cecil Foster's *Sleep On, Beloved*."

76. Daenzer, "An Affair between Nations," 82. See also note 69 above.

77. Foster, *Sleep On, Beloved*, 69–72.

78. Ibid., 70.

79. For a longer discussion of the Second Domestic Scheme, see Calliste, "Canada's Immigration Policy."

80. N. Thomas, "Cecil Foster's *Sleep On, Beloved*," 490.

81. Foster, *Sleep On, Beloved*, 69–70; italics added.

82. Also, as a newly arrived migrant Ona attends the services of the Spiritual Baptist Church in Toronto. As Carol B. Duncan notes, the first Spiritual Baptist Churches emerged in Toronto in the mid-1970s (*This Spot of Ground*, 76). This historical detail further confirms that Ona immigrates through the FDM, not through the Second Domestic Scheme, which had been discontinued in January 1968; see Calliste, "Canada's Immigration Policy," 113.

83. Daenzer, "An Affair between Nations," 81.

84. Ibid.

85. Foster, *Sleep On, Beloved*, 70.

86. Stasiulis and Bakan, *Negotiating Citizenship*, 49.

87. Ibid.

88. Ibid.

89. Ibid.

90. Ibid.

91. Foster, *Sleep On, Beloved*, 207.

92. Duncan, *This Spot of Ground*, 92n3. Barry Chevannes distinguishes between the terms "[Jamaican] Revival" and "[Jamaican] Revivalism," using "Revivalism" to refer "not only [to] the rituals generally associated with the Revival religion," but also, more comprehensively, to "the complex of beliefs and values" underlying the Revival tradition (*Rastafari*, 22). Duncan, in part drawing on Chevannes, elaborates on the relationship between Jamaican Revivalism and Pocomania in order to describe the latter: "Revivalism is characterized by a belief in a hierarchical spirit world over which presides 'Massa God' of the Christian tradition. Included here also are spirit beings in Caribbean folk tradition such as 'jumbies,' as well as the spirits of ancestors and other dead. The spirit world can intervene in human affairs and humans can also interact with the spirit world. Pocomania . . . shares the worldview of Revivalism. It is characterized, however, by an emphasis on connections with ancestors who act as intermediaries in the world of human affairs for their descendants" (*This Spot of Ground*, 92n3).

93. Foster, *Sleep On, Beloved*, 5.

94. P. Johnson, *Diaspora Conversions*, 2.

95. Foster, *Sleep On, Beloved*, 3; italics in the original.

96. Ibid., 3–4.

97. Ibid., 5.

98. Ibid., 9.

99. Ibid., 5.

100. Ibid., 6.

101. Ibid., 5.

102. Ibid., 4.

103. Ibid.

104. Ibid.
105. Ibid.
106. Ibid.
107. Ibid.
108. Ibid., 5.
109. Ibid., 56.
110. Ibid., 21.
111. Duncan, *This Spot of Ground*, xi. Duncan describes the diversity of contemporary black Canadian religiosity as follows: "The assumption of a black, Protestant Christian monolith is seriously challenged by the presence of a black Catholic tradition and black Muslims, Jews, Buddhists and practitioners of traditional African and African-Caribbean religions including Orisha, Spiritual Baptists and Jamaican Revival in Canada" ("Religion, Spirituality, and Migration," 146).
112. Duncan, "Religion, Spirituality, and Migration," 146–47.
113. Duncan, *This Spot of Ground*, 3.
114. Foster, *Sleep On, Beloved*, 106.
115. Ibid., 291.
116. Ibid.
117. Ibid., 293.
118. Ibid., 296.
119. Ibid., 293, 294.
120. Ibid., 297.
121. Ibid.
122. Ibid., 302.
123. Ibid.
124. Ibid., 304.
125. Ibid., 23.
126. Ibid., 24.
127. Ibid., 23–24.
128. Ibid., 249.
129. Ibid., 250.
130. Ibid., 251.
131. Ibid., 255–56.
132. See ibid., 49, 263.
133. Ibid., 265.
134. Ibid., 266.
135. Ibid., 325.
136. Ibid., 324–25.
137. Ibid., 325.
138. Ibid., 325.
139. Munro, "Inside Out," 13. The article includes a brief biography of Danticat.

140. Davies, *Black Women, Writing, and Identity*, 115.

141. On the first anniversary of the earthquake, in January 2011, the Haitian government offered the figure of 316,000 as the official death toll of the quake (see Archibold, "Haiti"), without explaining how it had arrived at this estimate. A draft of a US government report dated May 31, 2011, suggests lower numbers for both the dead and the displaced than the estimates offered by the Haitian government (see Archibold, "U.S. Reduces Estimates"). In 2012, Laurent Dubois, a leading historian of Haiti, wrote that the quake "killed upwards of 230,000 people and left millions homeless" (*Haiti: The Aftershocks*, 3). Whatever the exact death toll, there is no doubt that the quake was a major disaster with dire humanitarian consequences. 142. Dubois, *Haiti: The Aftershocks*, 244–48, 269–74.

143. Ibid.

144. Danticat, *Create Dangerously*, 158.

145. Ibid.

146. Ibid., 157–58.

147. To be exact, the text of *Breath, Eyes, Memory* leaves the rapist's identity unknown, not only in terms of his face and name, but also in terms of whether he was a Tonton Macoute: "My [Sophie's] father might have been a *Macoute*" (139). However, in *Create Dangerously* Danticat unequivocally states that Martine was "raped by a brutal Tonton Macoute whose face she never sees" (32). In Danticat's imagination, the rapist seems to have been a Macoute all along, but her novel forces the reader to struggle with the same uncertainty that Martine has to live with.

148. Francis, "Silences Too Horrific To Disturb," 78; italics in the original.

149. In *Create Dangerously*, Danticat confirms that she intended Atie's love for Louise to be read as more than just friendly affection (even though Atie's same-sex attraction is rendered so subtly that critics often miss or doubt it): "Atie Caco, Martine's sister, harbors a secret unrequited love for another woman" (32). In "Neocolonialism, Queer Kinship, and Diaspora," Meg Wesling includes *Breath, Eyes, Memory* in her sophisticated discussion of "queer diaspora" but does not specifically identify Atie's love for Louise as romantic and erotic (666). Although *Breath, Eyes, Memory* is one of the two primary sources that Wesling reads closely, she only mentions Louise in one paragraph and even then refrains from offering an interpretation of the nature of Atie and Louise's "close attachment" (666). Instead, she argues that in this novel "[i]t is not same-sex erotic desire, but the complex relation between state power, gendered violence, and familial attachments that . . . form a queer model of kinship that attends to the circumstances of diaspora" (650).

150. As Patricia Hill Collins writes, "'othermothers,' women who assist bloodmothers by sharing mothering responsibilities, traditionally have been central to the institution of Black motherhood" ("The Meaning of Motherhood," 47).

151. Danticat, *Breath, Eyes, Memory*, 11.

152. Ibid., 11–12.

153. Ibid., 12.
154. Ibid., 11.
155. Dubois, *Haiti: The Aftershocks*, 33.
156. Ibid.
157. Dubois and Jenson, "Haiti Can Be Rich Again."
158. Danticat, *Breath, Eyes, Memory*, 151, 200.
159. Wesling, "Neocolonialism, Queer Kinship, and Diaspora," 664.
160. Danticat, *Breath, Eyes, Memory*, 46–47.
161. Ibid., 29.

162. Kincaid, *Lucy*, 29–30. Neither Wordsworth's name nor the poem's title is explicitly mentioned in *Lucy*, but the reference is obvious.

163. In this comically rendered scene of *Small Island*, the young Hortense attempts to teach her grandmother, Miss Jewel, to recite "I wandered lonely as a Cloud," in order to encourage the illiterate peasant woman "to speak properly as the King of England does" (43). The project fails rather spectacularly. Levy's joke is neither on Hortense nor on Miss Jewel, but on the politics of colonial education.

164. Danticat, *Breath, Eyes, Memory*, 21.

165. Several critics have noted the importance of oral tradition, as epitomized by Ifé and Atie's storytelling, for the novel as a whole. For example, Mildred Mortimer comments on it as follows: "Grandma Ifé is aware of the socioeconomic changes taking place around her, yet is firmly anchored to rural Caribbean tradition, particularly Caribbean tales and legend. Sustained by the oral tradition of which they have both become artful performers, Grandma Ifé and her daughter Atie tell stories that—for the brief duration of the tale—transform their rural Haitian landscape into a 'magic kingdom.' ... [T]hey open the child's world to imaginative space. Here, fluid boundaries separate the real and the imaginary" (*Writing from the Hearth*, 173). For a reading that examines the Haitian oral storytelling tradition in conjunction with the silence of the traumatized in *Breath, Eyes, Memory*, see Sarthou, "Unsilencing Défilés Daughters."

166. Danticat, *Breath, Eyes, Memory*, 21.
167. S. Alexander, *African Diasporic Women's Narratives*, 109.
168. Danticat, *Breath, Eyes, Memory*, 61.
169. Ibid., 28.
170. Ibid., 31.
171. Ibid.
172. Ibid., 43–44.
173. Ibid., 65.
174. Ibid.
175. S. Alexander, *African Diasporic Women's Narratives*, 110.
176. Davies, *Black Women, Writing, and Identity*, 115.
177. Danticat, *Breath, Eyes, Memory*, 154.

178. Ibid., 80, 88.
179. Ibid., 89.
180. Francis, "Silences Too Horrific To Disturb," 80.
181. Danticat, *Breath, Eyes, Memory*, 206.
182. Ibid., 201.
183. Ibid., 23.
184. Ibid., 162.
185. Ibid., 170.
186. Ibid.
187. Mardorossian, "Danticat and Caribbean Women Writers," 42.
188. Danticat, *Breath, Eyes, Memory*, 156–57.
189. Ibid., 157.
190. Mortimer, *Writing from the Hearth*, 180.
191. Danticat, *Breath, Eyes, Memory*, 202.
192. Ibid., 195.
193. Ibid., 164.
194. See *HaitiLibre*, "Haïti—Reconstruction."
195. Danticat, *Breath, Eyes, Memory*, 224.
196. Ibid., 150.
197. See, for example, H. Scott, *Caribbean Women Writers*, 40.
198. Danticat, *Breath, Eyes, Memory*, 217.
199. Ibid., 227.
200. Ibid., 231.
201. Ibid., 234.
202. Ibid., 230.
203. Ibid., 232–33.
204. Ibid., 211.
205. Ibid., 233.
206. Ibid.
207. Ibid.
208. Ibid., 234.
209. For a book-length collection of essays that link Nora's term—which he introduced and developed in the multivolume *Les Lieux de Mémoire*—to the African American experience, see *History and Memory in African-American Culture*, edited by G. Fabre and O'Meally. For an English translation of Nora's introduction to *Les Lieux de Mémoire*, see Nora, "Between Memory and History" (also reprinted in G. Fabre and O'Meally's essay collection, 284–300). For a reading that brings together *Breath, Eyes, Memory* and Toni Morrison's 1987 essay "The Site of Memory," see Rossi, "'Let the Words Bring Wings to Our Feet,'" 208.
210. Danticat, *Breath, Eyes, Memory*, 233–34.
211. Ibid., 170.

212. Ibid., 234.
213. Danticat, *Create Dangerously*, 18.
214. Danticat, introduction to *The Butterfly's Way*, xiv–xv. See also *Create Dangerously*, 49–51.
215. Obviously, to highlight Danticat's chosen focus (that is, the combined focus of Haiti and the United States) is not to call into question the existence of even more comprehensively global perspectives that inform her thinking. Such perspectives are evident, for example, in the following passage from *Create Dangerously*: "I am an immigrant and hopefully an artist, an immigrant artist at work. Even though there is probably no such thing as an immigrant artist in this globalized age, when Algeria and Haiti and even ancient Greece and Egypt are only a virtual visit away. Even without globalization, the writer bound to the reader, under diabolic, or even joyful, circumstances inevitably becomes a loyal citizen of the country of his readers" (15).
216. Mehta, *Notions of Identity, Diaspora, and Gender*, 13.
217. Danticat, *Breath, Eyes, Memory*, 72.
218. Ibid., 214.
219. Ibid., 215.
220. Clifford, *Routes*, 249–50.
221. Danticat, *Breath, Eyes, Memory*, 215.
222. See, for example, ibid., 104.
223. See, for example, ibid., 174.
224. See Bhabha, "DissemiNation," 297.
225. Sandiford, *Theorizing a Colonial Caribbean-Atlantic Imaginary*, 2.
226. Byfield, LaRay, and A. Morrison, introduction, 2.
227. See my introduction, note 110.
228. Danticat, "AHA!" 39–40; italics in the original. See also Mardorossian's discussion of the same quotation in "Danticat and Caribbean Women Writers" (46–47) and Régine Michelle Jean-Charles's engagement with "AHA!" in "Danticat and the African American Women's Literary Tradition" (52).
229. C. Phillips, "Necessary Journeys," 125.
230. As noted earlier, Phillips has primarily been based in the United States since the 1990s; hence my phrase "at least three contexts."

Epilogue

1. See my chapter 5, note 224.
2. P. Johnson, *Diaspora Conversions*, 2–3.
3. P. Johnson, "On Leaving and Joining Africanness," 174.
4. P. Johnson, *Diaspora Conversions*, 37.
5. Ibid.
6. See Cohen, *Global Diasporas* (2nd ed., 2008), 13.
7. Sökefeld, "Mobilizing in Transnational Space," 265.

8. Ibid.
9. Khan, "Dark Arts and Diaspora," 43.
10. See my introduction, note 64.
11. See my chapter 5, note 1.
12. Gilroy, *Against Race*, 123.
13. Manning, *The African Diaspora*, 350.

Bibliography

Abbott, Carl. "The Neighborhoods of New York: 1760–1775." *New York History* 55 (January 1974): 35–54.

Alexander, Claire. "'Rivers to Cross': Exile and Transformation in the Caribbean Migration Novels of George Lamming." In *Writing Across Worlds: Literature and Migration*, edited by Russell King, John Connell, and Paul White, 57–69. London: Routledge, 1995.

Alexander, Claire, and Caroline Knowles. Introduction. In *Making Race Matter*, edited by Alexander and Knowles, 1–16.

———, eds. *Making Race Matter: Bodies, Space and Identity*. Houndmills, England: Palgrave Macmillan, 2005.

Alexander, Simone A. James. *African Diasporic Women's Narratives: Politics of Resistance, Survival, and Citizenship*. Gainesville: University Press of Florida, 2014.

Althusser, Louis. "Ideology and Ideological State Apparatuses (Notes towards an Investigation)." In *Lenin and Philosophy and Other Essays*, by Louis Althusser, translated by Ben Brewster, 127–86. New York: Monthly Review Press, 1971.

American Anthropological Association. "Statement on 'Race.'" May 17, 1998. http://www.aaanet.org/stmts/racepp.htm.

American Psychiatric Association. *Diagnostic and Statistical Manual of Mental Disorders*, 5th ed. Arlington: American Psychiatric Association, 2013.

Anderson, Amanda. *The Powers of Distance: Cosmopolitanism and the Cultivation of Detachment*. Princeton, N.J.: Princeton University Press. 2001.

Anderson, Benedict. *Imagined Communities: Reflections on the Origin and Spread of Nationalism*. Rev. ed. London: Verso, 1991.

Andrews, William L. "The Representation of Slavery and the Rise of Afro-American Literary Realism, 1865–1920." In *African American Autobiography: A Collection of Critical Essays*, edited by William L. Andrews, 77–89. Englewood Cliffs, N.J.: Prentice-Hall, 1993.

———. *To Tell a Free Story: The First Century of Afro-American Autobiography, 1760–1865*. Urbana: University of Illinois Press, 1986.

Appadurai, Arjun. *Modernity at Large: Cultural Dimensions of Globalization*. Minneapolis: University of Minnesota Press, 1996.

Appiah, Kwame Anthony. *Cosmopolitanism: Ethics in a World of Strangers*. New York: Norton, 2006.

———. "Cosmopolitan Patriots." In Nussbaum et al., 21–29.

———. *In My Father's House: Africa in the Philosophy of Culture*. New York: Oxford University Press, 1992.

Arana, R. Victoria. "Sea Change: Historicizing the Scholarly Study of Black British Writing." In *Black British Writing*, edited by Arana and Ramey, 19–45.

Arana, R. Victoria, and Lauri Ramey. Introduction. In *Black British Writing*, edited by Arana and Ramey, 1–7.

———, eds. *Black British Writing*. Houndmills, England: Palgrave Macmillan, 2004.

Archibold, Randal C. "Haiti: Quake's Toll Rises to 316,000." *New York Times*, January 13, 2011. http://www.nytimes.com/2011/01/14/world/americas/14briefs-Haiti.html?scp=1&sq=Haiti:%20Quake's%20Toll%20Rises&st=cse.

———. "U.S. Reduces Estimates of Homeless in Haiti Quake." *New York Times*, May 31, 2011. http://www.nytimes.com/2011/06/01/world/americas/01haiti.html?scp=1&sq=%2522US%20Reduces%20Estimates%2522&st=cse.

Austin, Allan D. *African Muslims in Antebellum America: Transatlantic Stories and Spiritual Struggles*. New York: Routledge, 1997.

Baker, Houston A., Jr. *Betrayal: How Black Intellectuals Have Abandoned the Ideals of the Civil Rights Era*. New York: Columbia University Press, 2008.

———. *Blues, Ideology, and Afro-American Literature: A Vernacular Theory*. Chicago: University of Chicago Press, 1984.

———. Foreword. In *Race and Displacement*, edited by Marouan and Simmons, vii–xiv.

———. *Workings of the Spirit: The Poetics of Afro-American Women's Writing*. Chicago: University of Chicago Press, 1991.

Bakhtin, Mikhail M. *The Dialogic Imagination*. Edited and translated by Michael Holquist. Austin: University of Texas Press, 1981.

Baldwin, James. "Autobiographical Notes." 1955. In Baldwin, *Collected Essays*, 5–9.

———. *Collected Essays*. Edited by Toni Morrison. Library of America series 98. New York: Literary Classics of the United States, 1998.

———. "Nobody Knows My Name: A Letter from the South." 1959. In Baldwin, *Collected Essays*, 197–208.

Ball, John Clement. *Imagining London: Postcolonial Fiction and the Transnational Metropolis*. Toronto: Toronto University Press, 2004.

Barck, Oscar Theodore. *New York City during the War for Independence, with Special Reference to the Period of British Occupation*. 1931. Port Washington, N.Y.: Ira J. Friedman, 1966.

Baucom, Ian. *Out of Place: Englishness, Empire, and the Locations of Identity*. Princeton, N.J.: Princeton University Press, 1999.

Bauer Elaine, and Paul Thompson. *Jamaican Hands across the Atlantic*. Kingston, Jam.: Ian Randle, 2006.

Beck, Ulrich. *The Cosmopolitan Vision* [*Kosmopolitische Blick oder: Krieg ist Frieden.*] 2004. Translated by Ciaran Cronin. Cambridge, England: Polity Press, 2006.

Beidler, Philip D. *American Literature and the Experience of Vietnam*. Athens: University of Georgia Press, 1982.

———. *Re-Writing America: Vietnam Authors in Their Generation*. Athens: University of Georgia Press, 1991.

Bennett, A[lvin] G[ladstone]. *Because They Know Not*. London: Phoenix Press, 1959.

Berlin, Ira. *Many Thousands Gone: The First Two Centuries of Slavery in North America*. Cambridge, Mass.: Belknap Press of Harvard University Press, 1998.

———. Review of *The Black Loyalists: The Search for a Promised Land in Nova Scotia and Sierra Leone, 1783–1870*, by James W. St. G. Walker. *William and Mary Quarterly*, 3rd series, 35.2 (April 1978): 396–98.

Berlin, Ira, Marc Favreau, and Steven F. Miller. "Introduction: Slavery as Memory and History." In *Remembering Slavery: African Americans Talk About Their Personal Experiences of Slavery and Emancipation*, edited by Ira Berlin, Marc Favreau, and Steven F. Miller, xv–xlix. New York: New Press, in association with the Library of Congress, 2007.

Bhabha, Homi K. "DissemiNation: Time, Narrative, and the Margins of the Modern Nation." In *Nation and Narration*, edited by Homi K. Bhabha, 291–322. London: Routledge, 1990.

Boehmer, Elleke. *Empire, the National, and the Postcolonial, 1890–1920: Resistance in Interaction*. Oxford: Oxford University Press, 2002.

Bouson, J. Brooks. *Quiet as It's Kept: Shame, Trauma, and Race in the Novels of Toni Morrison*. Albany: State University of New York Press, 2000.

Braley, Mark. "'The Sweetness of His Strength': Du Bois, Teddy Roosevelt, and the Black Soldier." In *W.E.B. Du Bois and Race: Essays Celebrating the Centennial Publication of The Souls of Black Folk*, edited by Chester J. Fontenot Jr. and Mary Alice Morgan, 97–121. Macon, Ga.: Mercer University Press, 2001.

Brand, Dionne. *In Another Place, Not Here*. 1996. New York: Grove Press, 1997.

———. *A Map to the Door of No Return: Notes to Belonging*. Toronto: Doubleday Canada, 2001.

Braziel, Jana Evans. *Duvalier's Ghosts: Race, Diaspora, and U.S. Imperialism in Haitian Literatures*. Gainesville: University Press of Florida, 2010.

Braziel, Jana Evans, and Anita Mannur. "Nation, Migration, Globalization: Points of Contention in Diaspora Studies." In *Theorizing Diaspora*, edited by Braziel and Mannur, 1–22.

———, eds. *Theorizing Diaspora: A Reader*. Malden, Mass.: Blackwell, 2003.

Brooks, Joanna, and John Saillant. Introduction to *"Face Zion Forward": First Writers of the Black Atlantic, 1785–1798*, edited by Joanna Brooks and John Saillant, 3–33. Boston: Northeastern University Press, 2002.

Brown, Eric. "Hellenistic Cosmopolitanism." In *A Companion to Ancient Philosophy*, edited by Mary Louise Gill and Pierre Pellegrin, 549–58. Malden, Mass.: Blackwell, 2006.

Brown, J. Dillon. "Exile and Cunning: The Tactical Difficulties of George Lamming." *Contemporary Literature* 47.4 (Winter 2006): 669–94.

———. *Migrant Modernism: Postwar London and the West Indian Novel*. Charlottesville: University of Virginia Press, 2013.

———. "A State of Interdependence: Caryl Phillips and the Postwar World Order." *Ariel: A Review of International English Literature* 44:2–3 (April–July 2013): 85–111.

Brubaker, Rogers. "The 'Diaspora' Diaspora." *Ethnic and Racial Studies* 28:1 (January 2005), 1–19.

Buelens, Gert, Sam Durrant, and Robert Eaglestone, eds. *The Future of Trauma Theory: Contemporary Literary and Cultural Criticism*. London: Routledge, 2014.

Bugg, John. "The Other Interesting Narrative: Olaudah Equiano's Public Book Tour." *PMLA* 121.5 (October 2006): 1424–42.

Butler, Judith. *Bodies That Matter: On the Discursive Limits of "Sex."* New York: Routledge, 1993.

———. *Frames of War: When Is Life Grievable?* London: Verso, 2009.

Byfield, Judith A., LaRay Denzer, and Anthea Morrison. Introduction to *Gendering the African Diaspora: Women, Culture, and Historical Change in the Caribbean and Nigerian Hinterland*, edited by Judith A. Byfield, LaRay Denzer, and Anthea Morrison, 1–17. Bloomington: Indiana University Press, 2010.

Byrd, Rudolph P. *Charles Johnson's Novels: Writing the American Palimpsest*. Bloomington: Indiana University Press, 2005.

———, ed. *I Call Myself an Artist: Writings by and about Charles Johnson*. Bloomington: Indiana University Press, 1999.

Caldwell, Mark. *New York Night: The Mystique and Its History*. New York: Scribner, 2005.

Calliste, Agnes. "Canada's Immigration Policy and Domestics from the Caribbean: The Second Domestic Scheme." In *The Social Basis of Law: Critical Readings in the Sociology of Law*, 2nd ed., edited by Elizabeth Comack and Stephen Brickey, 136–68. Halifax, Nova Scotia: Garamond Press, 1991.

Campt, Tina, and Deborah A. Thomas. "Gendering Diaspora: Transnational Feminism, Diaspora and Its Hegemonies." *Feminist Review* 90 (2008): 1–8.

Camus, Albert. *The Stranger [L'Étranger]*. 1942. Translated by Matthew Ward. New York: Vintage, 1989.

Carby, Hazel V. "Becoming Modern Racialized Subjects: Detours through Our Pasts to Produce Ourselves Anew." *Cultural Studies* 23.4 (July 2009): 624–57.

———. Foreword. In *Making Race Matter*, edited by Alexander and Knowles, xii–xvii.

———. "Postcolonial Translations." *Ethnic and Racial Studies* 30.2 (March 2007): 213–34.

———. *Reconstructing Womanhood: The Emergence of the Afro-American Woman Novelist*. 1987. New York: Oxford University Press, 1989.
Carp, Benjamin L. "The Night the Yankees Burned Broadway: The New York City Fire of 1776." *Early American Studies* 4.2 (Fall 2006): 471–511.
Carretta, Vincent. *Equiano the African: Biography of a Self-Made Man*. Athens: University of Georgia Press, 2005.
Carretta, Vincent, and John Bugg. "Deciphering the Equiano Archives." *PMLA* 122.2 (March 2007): 571–73.
Carroll, David. *Albert Camus the Algerian: Colonialism, Terrorism, Justice*. New York: Columbia University Press, 2007.
Carruthers, Gerard. "Fictions of Belonging: National Identity and the Novel in Ireland and Scotland." In *A Companion to the British and Irish Novel, 1945–2000*, edited by Brian W. Shaffer, 112–27. Malden, Mass.: Blackwell, 2005.
Caruth, Cathy. Introduction to "Trauma and Experience." In *Trauma: Explorations in Memory*, edited by Cathy Caruth, 3–12. Baltimore: Johns Hopkins University Press, 1995.
———. *Literature in the Ashes of History*. Baltimore: Johns Hopkins University Press, 2013.
———. *Unclaimed Experience: Trauma, Narrative, and History*. Baltimore: Johns Hopkins University Press, 1996.
Castle, Terry. "Don't Pick Up: Why Kids Need to Separate from Their Parents." *Chronicle Review*, May 6, 2012. http://chronicle.com/article/The-Case-for-Breaking-Up-With/131760/.
Chamberlain, Mary. "The 'Consolation of Freedom': Reflections on Nationalist Hopes." In *The Locations of George Lamming*, edited by Schwarz, 49–66.
———. "George Lamming." In *West Indian Intellectuals in Britain*, edited by Bill Schwarz, 175–95. Manchester: Manchester University Press, 2003.
Chevannes, Barry. *Rastafari: Roots and Ideology*. Syracuse, N.Y.: Syracuse University Press, 1994.
Clarke, George Elliott. *Beatrice Chancy*. Victoria, BC: Polestar, 1999.
———. *George and Rue*. 2005. New York: Carroll and Graf, 2006.
Clifford, James. "Introduction: The Pure Products Go Crazy." In *The Predicament of Culture: Twentieth-Century Ethnography, Literature, and Art*, by James Clifford, 1–18. Cambridge, Mass.: Harvard University Press, 1988.
———. *Routes: Travel and Translation in the Late Twentieth Century*. Cambridge, Mass.: Harvard University Press, 1997.
Cohen, Robin. *Global Diasporas: An Introduction*. (1st ed., Seattle: University of Washington Press, 1997.) 2nd rev. ed., London: Routledge, 2008.
Collins, Marcus. "Pride and Prejudice: West Indian Men in Mid-Twentieth-Century Britain." *Journal of British Studies* 40.3 (July 2001): 391–418.
Collins, Patricia Hill. "The Meaning of Motherhood in Black Culture and Black

Mother-Daughter Relationships." In *Double Stitch: Black Women Write about Mothers and Daughters*, edited by Patricia Bell-Scott, Beverly Guy-Sheftall, Jacqueline Jones Royster, Janet Sims-Wood, Miriam DeCosta-Willis, and Lucie Fultz, 42–60. Boston: Beacon Press, 1991.

Conner, Marc C. "To Utter the Holy: The Metaphysical Romance of *Middle Passage*." In *Charles Johnson*, edited by Conner and Nash, 57–81.

Conner, Marc C., and William R. Nash. "Introduction: Charles Johnson and Philosophical Black Fiction." In *Charles Johnson*, edited by Conner and Nash, xi–xxxvii.

———, eds. *Charles Johnson: The Novelist as Philosopher*. Jackson: University Press of Mississippi, 2007.

Connerton, Paul. *How Societies Remember*. Cambridge: Cambridge University Press, 1989.

Conrad, Joseph. *Heart of Darkness*. 1899. In *"Heart of Darkness" and Selections from "The Congo Diary,"* introduction by Caryl Phillips, 1–96. New York: Modern Library, 1999.

Craps, Stef. "Linking Legacies of Loss: Traumatic Histories and Cross-Cultural Empathy in Caryl Phillips's *Higher Ground* and *The Nature of Blood*." In *Caryl Phillips*, edited by Ledent and Tunca, 155–73.

Craton, Michael. "Loyalists Mainly to Themselves: The 'Black Loyalist' Diaspora to the Bahamas, 1783–c. 1820." In *Working Slavery, Pricing Freedom: Perspectives from the Caribbean, Africa and the African Diaspora*, edited by Verene A. Shepherd, 44–68. New York: Palgrave, 2002.

Curtin, Edward E., IV. *Muslims in America: A Short History*. Oxford: Oxford University Press, 2009.

Daenzer, Patricia M. "An Affair between Nations: International Relations and the Movement of Household Service Workers." In *Not One of the Family: Foreign Domestic Workers in Canada*, edited by Abigail B. Bakan and Daiva Stasiulis, 81–118. Toronto: University of Toronto Press, 1997.

D'Aguiar, Fred. *Feeding the Ghosts*. London: Chatto and Windus, 1997.

Dalleo, Raphael. "Introduction." *Anthurium* 11.1, article 1 (May 2014). http://scholarlyrepository.miami.edu/anthurium/vol11/iss1/1.

Dalton, Harlon L. *Racial Healing: Confronting the Fear between Blacks and Whites*. New York: Doubleday, 1995.

Daniel, Yvonne. *Caribbean and Atlantic Diaspora Dance: Igniting Citizenship*. Urbana: University of Illinois Press, 2011.

Danticat, Edwidge. "AHA!" In *Becoming American: Personal Essays by First Generation Immigrant Women*, edited by Meri Nana-Ama Danquah, 39–44. New York: Hyperion, 2000.

———. 1994. *Breath, Eyes, Memory*. New York: Vintage, 1998.

———. *Create Dangerously: The Immigrant Artist at Work*. Princeton, N.J.: Princeton University Press, 2010.

———. Introduction to *The Butterfly's Way: Voices from the Haitian Dyaspora in the United States,* edited by Edwidge Danticat, ix–xvii. New York: Soho Press, 2001.

Davidson, Cathy N. "Olaudah Equiano, Written by Himself." *Novel* 40.1–2 (Fall 2006–Spring 2007): 18–51.

Davies, Carol Boyce. *Black Women, Writing, and Identity: Migrations of the Subject.* London: Routledge, 1994.

Davies, Carol Boyce, and Babacar M'Bow. "Towards African Diaspora Citizenship: Politicizing an Existing Global Geography." In *Black Geographies and the Politics of Place,* edited by McKittrick and Woods, 14–45.

Dawson, Ashley. *Mongrel Nation: Diasporic Culture and the Making of Postcolonial Britain.* Ann Arbor: University of Michigan Press, 2007.

Dayal, Samir. "Diaspora and Double Consciousness." *Journal of the Midwest Modern Language Association* 29.1 (Spring 1996): 46–62.

Dayan, Joan. "Paul Gilroy's Slaves, Ships, and Routes: The Middle Passage as Metaphor." *Research in African Literatures* 27.4 (Winter 1996): 7–14.

Defoe, Daniel. 1719. *Robinson Crusoe.* London: Penguin Classics, 2001.

Delano, Amasa. *Delano's Voyages of Commerce and Discovery: Amasa Delano in China, the Pacific Islands, Australia, and South America, 1789–1807.* 1817. Stockbridge, Mass.: Berkshire House, 1994.

Diagne, Souleymane Bachir. "Keeping Africanity Open." *Public Culture* 14.3 (Fall 2002): 621–23.

Diedrich, Maria, Henry Louis Gates Jr., and Carl Pedersen. "The Middle Passage between History and Fiction: Introductory Remarks." In *Black Imagination and the Middle Passage,* edited by Diedrich, Gates, and Pedersen, 5–13.

———, eds. *Black Imagination and the Middle Passage.* New York: Oxford University Press, 1999.

Dimock, Wai Chee. "African, Caribbean, American: Black English as Creole Tongue." In *Transforming Diaspora: Communities beyond National Boundaries,* edited by Robin E. Field and Parmita Kapadia, 37–64. Madison, N.J.: Fairleigh Dickinson University Press, 2011.

Diouf, Sylviane A. *Servants of Allah: African Muslims Enslaved in the Americas.* New York: New York University Press, 1998.

Douglass, Frederick. *Autobiographies.* Edited by Henry Louis Gates Jr. New York: Library of America, 1996.

———. *My Bondage and My Freedom.* 1855. In Douglass, *Autobiographies,* 103–452.

———. *Narrative of the Life of Frederick Douglass, an American Slave. Written by Himself.* 1845. In Douglass, *Autobiographies,* 1–102.

Dryden, Linda. *The Modern Gothic and Literary Doubles: Stevenson, Wilde, and Wells.* Houndmills, England: Palgrave Macmillan, 2003.

Dubey, Madhu. "'No Bottom and No Top': Oppositions in *Sula.*" 1994. In *Toni Morrison: Contemporary Critical Essays,* edited by Linden Peach, 70–88. New York: St. Martin's Press, 1998.

Dubois, Laurent. *Haiti: The Aftershocks of History*. New York: Metropolitan Books/ Henry Holt, 2012.

Dubois, Laurent, and Deborah Jenson. "Haiti Can Be Rich Again." *New York Times*, January 8, 2012. http://www.nytimes.com/2012/01/09/opinion/haiti-can-be-rich-again.html.

Du Bois, W.E.B. "Close Ranks." *Crisis*, July 16, 1918. In *If We Must Die*, edited by Stanford, 115.

———. *The Philadelphia Negro*. Philadelphia: University of Pennsylvania, 1899.

———. "Returning Soldiers." *Crisis*, May 18, 1919. In *If We Must Die*, edited by Stanford, 127–28.

———. *The Souls of Black Folk*. 1903. Edited by Henry Louis Gates Jr. and Terri Hume Oliver. New York: Norton, 1999.

Dufoix, Stéphane. *Diasporas [Les diasporas]*. 2003. Translated by William Rodarmor, with a foreword by Roger Waldinger. Berkeley: University of California Press, 2008.

Duignan, Peter J. Review of *The Black Loyalists*, by James W. St. G. Walker, and *The Loyal Blacks*, by Ellen Gibson Wilson. *Journal of Southern History* 43:2 (May 1977): 287–88.

Duncan, Carol B. "Religion, Spirituality, and Migration in Canada." In *Multiple Lenses: Voices from the Diaspora Located in Canada*, edited by David Divine, 142–47. Newcastle, England: Cambridge Scholars Publishing, 2007.

———. *This Spot of Ground: Spiritual Baptists in Toronto*. Waterloo, Canada: Wilfrid Laurier University Press, 2008.

Dunlap, William. *History of the New Netherlands, Province of New York, and State of New York, to the Adoption of the Federal Constitution*. Vol. 2: 1840. New York: Burt Franklin, 1970.

Dunmore, John Murray, Fourth Earl of [Governor of Virginia]. Proclamation, November 7, 1775. Early American Imprints, series I: Evans, 1639–1800, no. 14592. Available at http://www.encyclopediavirginia.org/Lord_Dunmore_s_Proclamation_1775.

Durán-Almarza, Emilia María. "Introduction: (E)ngendering the Black Atlantic." In *Diasporic Women's Writing*, edited by Durán-Almarza and Álvarez-López, 1–11.

Durán-Almarza, Emilia María, and Esther Álvarez-López, eds. *Diasporic Women's Writing of the Black Atlantic: (E)ngendering Literature and Performance*. New York: Routledge, 2014.

Dyson, Michael Eric. "Tour(é)ing Blackness." In *Who's Afraid of Post-Blackness*, by Touré, xi–xviii.

Eakin, John Paul. Introduction to *American Autobiography: Retrospect and Prospect*, edited by John Paul Eakin, 3–22. Madison: University of Wisconsin Press, 1991.

Edmonson, Belinda. *Making Men: Gender, Literary Authority, and Women's Writing in Caribbean Narrative*. Durham, N.C.: Duke University Press, 1999.

Edwards, Brent Hayes. *The Practice of Diaspora: Literature, Translation, and the Rise of Black Internationalism*. Cambridge, Mass.: Harvard University Press, 2003.

———. "The Uses of 'Diaspora.'" In *African Diasporas in the New and Old Worlds*, edited by Fabre and Benesch, 3–38.

Eliot, T. S. "Little Gidding." In *Collected Poems, 1909–1962*, 200–209. New York: Harcourt, Brace and World, 1963.

Ellis, David. "'Foreign Bodies': George Lamming's *The Emigrants*." *Comparative Critical Studies* 9.2 (2012): 213–25.

Ellison, Ralph. "Change the Joke and Slip the Yoke." 1958. In *The Collected Essays of Ralph Ellison*, edited by John F. Callahan, 100–112. New York: Modern Library, 1995.

———. *Invisible Man*. New York: Random House, 1952.

Equiano, Olaudah. *The Interesting Narrative of the Life of Olaudah Equiano, or Gustavus Vassa, the African*. 1789. Edited by Werner Sollors. New York: Norton, 2001.

Eyerman, Ron. *Cultural Trauma: Slavery and the Formation of African American Identity*. Cambridge: Cambridge University Press, 2001.

Fabre, Geneviève, "The Slave Ship Dance." In *Black Imagination and the Middle Passage*, edited by Diedrich, Gates, and Pedersen, 33–46.

Fabre, Geneviève, and Klaus Benesch. "Introduction: The Concept of African Diaspora(s)." In *African Diasporas in the New and Old Worlds*, edited by Fabre and Benesch, xiii–xxi.

———, eds. *African Diasporas in the New and Old Worlds: Consciousness and Imagination*. Amsterdam: Rodopi, 2004.

Fabre, Geneviève, and Robert O'Meally, eds. *History and Memory in African-American Culture*. New York: Oxford University Press, 1994.

Fabre, Michel. "Richard Wright and the French Existentialists." *MELUS* 5.2 (Summer 1978): 39–51.

Falconbridge, Anna Maria. *Narrative of Two Voyages to the River Sierra Leone during the Years 1791-1792-1793*. In *Narrative*, by Anna Maria Falconbridge, and *An Account of the Slave Trade on the Coast of Africa*, by Alexander Falconbridge, edited by Christopher Fyfe, 6–163. Liverpool: Liverpool University Press, 2000.

Fanon, Frantz. *Black Skin, White Masks* [*Peau noire, masques blancs*]. 1952. Translated by Charles Lam Markmann. New York: Grove Press, 1967.

Fassin, Didier, and Richard Rechtman. *The Empire of Trauma: An Inquiry into the Condition of Victimhood* [*L'empire du traumatisme: Enquête sur la condition de victime*]. 2007. Translated by Rachel Gomme. Princeton, N.J.: Princeton University Press, 2009.

Folkenflik, Robert. "Introduction: The Institution of Autobiography." In *The Culture of Autobiography*, edited by Folkenflik, 1–20.

———, ed. *The Culture of Autobiography: Constructions of Self-Representation*. Stanford, Calif.: Stanford University Press, 1993.

Foote, Thelma Wills. *Black and White Manhattan: The History of Racial Formation in Colonial New York City.* Oxford: Oxford University Press, 2004.

Forbes, Curdella. *From Nation to Diaspora: Samuel Selvon, George Lamming and the Cultural Performance of Gender.* Kingston, Jam.: University of the West Indies Press, 2005.

Forrest, Leon. *The Bloodworth Orphans.* 1977. Chicago: Another Chicago Press, 1987.

———. *There Is a Tree More Ancient than Eden.* 1973. Chicago: Another Chicago Press, 1988.

Foster, Cecil. *Blackness and Modernity: The Colour of Humanity and the Quest for Freedom.* Montreal: McGill-Queen's University Press, 2007.

———. *Genuine Multiculturalism: The Tragedy and Comedy of Diversity.* Montreal: McGill-Queen's University Press, 2014.

———. *Island Wings: A Memoir.* Toronto: HarperCollins, 1998.

———. *A Place Called Heaven: The Meaning of Being Black in Canada.* Toronto: HarperCollins, 1996.

———. *Sleep On, Beloved.* New York: Ballantine Books, 1995.

Fraile-Marcos, Ana María. "M/Othering Black Female Subjectivity across the Black Atlantic in the Novels of Maryse Condé, Edwidge Danticat, and Elizabeth Nunez." In *Diasporic Women's Writing*, edited by Durán-Almarza and Álvarez-López, 183–201.

Francis, Donette A. "'Silences Too Horrific To Disturb': Writing Sexual Histories in Edwidge Danticat's *Breath, Eyes, Memory*." *Research in African Literatures* 35.2 (Summer 2004): 75–90.

Frazier, E. Franklin. *The Negro Church in America.* New York: Schocken Books, 1964.

Fredrickson, George M. *Racism: A Short History.* Princeton, N.J.: Princeton University Press, 1992.

Frey, Sylvia R. *Water from the Rock: Black Resistance in a Revolutionary Age.* Princeton, N.J.: Princeton University Press, 1991.

Fryer, Peter. *Staying Power: The History of Black People in Britain.* London: Pluto Press, 1984.

Fulton, Lorie Watkins. "'A Direction of One's Own': Alienation in *Mrs. Dalloway* and *Sula*." *African American Review* 40.1 (Spring 2006): 67–77.

Fyfe, Christopher. *A History of Sierra Leone.* 1962. London: Oxford University Press, 1968.

Gaines, Kevin. *American Africans in Ghana: Black Expatriates and the Civil Rights Era.* Chapel Hill: University of North Carolina Press, 2006.

Gates, Henry Louis, Jr. *The Signifying Monkey: A Theory of African-American Literary Criticism.* New York: Oxford University Press, 1988.

———. *Thirteen Ways of Looking at Black Man.* New York: Random House, 1997.

———. *Tradition and the Black Atlantic: Critical Theory in the African Diaspora.* New York: BasicCivitas, 2010.

Gates, Henry Louis, Jr., and Gene Andrew Jarrett. Introduction to *The New Negro: Readings on Race, Representation, and African American Culture, 1892–1938*, edited by Henry Louis Gates Jr. and Gene Andrew Jarrett, 1–20. Princeton, N.J.: Princeton University Press, 2007.

Gates, Henry Louis, Jr., and Nellie Y. McKay. "Richard Wright." In *The Norton Anthology of African American Literature*, edited by Henry Louis Gates Jr. and Nellie Y. McKay, 1376–80. New York: Norton, 1997.

Gikandi, Simon. "Introduction: Africa, Diaspora, and the Discourse of Modernity." *Research in African Literatures* 27.4 (Winter 1996): 1–6.

———. *Maps of Englishness: Writing Identity in the Culture of Colonialism*. New York: Columbia University Press, 1996.

———. *Writing in Limbo: Modernism and Caribbean Literature*. Ithaca: Cornell University Press, 1992.

Gilroy, Paul. *Against Race: Imagining Political Culture Beyond the Color Line*. Cambridge, Mass.: Belknap Press of Harvard University Press, 2000.

———. "Between Camps: Race and Culture in Postmodernity. An Inaugural Lecture Given by Professor Paul Gilroy on 4 March 1997." Inaugural Lecture series. London: Goldsmiths College, University of London, 1997.

———. *The Black Atlantic: Modernity and Double Consciousness*. 1993. Cambridge, Mass.: Harvard University Press, 1999.

———. "Diaspora and the Detours of Identity." In *Identity and Difference*, edited by Kathryn Woodward, 299–343. London: Sage, in association with Open University, 1997.

———. *Postcolonial Melancholia*. New York: Columbia University Press, 2005.

———. *Small Acts: Thoughts on the Politics of Black Cultures*. London: Serpent's Tail, 1993.

———. *"There Ain't No Black in the Union Jack": The Cultural Politics of Race and Nation*. 1987. Chicago: University of Chicago Press, 1991.

Goddard, Ives. "'I Am a Red-Skin': The Adoption of a Native American Expression (1769–1826)." *European Review of Native American Studies* 19.2 (2004): 1–20.

Gomez, Michael A. "The Preacher-Kings: W.E.B. Du Bois Revisited." In *African Americans and the Bible*, edited by Wimbush, 501–13.

Goyal, Yogita. *Romance, Diaspora, and Black Atlantic Literature*. Cambridge: Cambridge University Press, 2010.

Grant, Douglas. *The Fortunate Slave: An Illustration of African Slavery in the Early Eighteenth Century*. London: Oxford University Press, 1968.

Grewal, Gurleen. *Circles of Sorrow, Lines of Struggle: The Novels of Toni Morrison*. Baton Rouge: Louisiana State University Press, 1998.

Griffin, Farah Jasmine. Review of *Crossing the River*, by Caryl Phillips. *Boston Review* 19.3–4 (June–September, 1994): 45–46.

Griswold, Wendy. "The Fabrication of Meaning: Literary Interpretation in the United States, Great Britain, and the West Indies." *American Journal of Sociology* 92.5 (March 1987): 1077–1117.

Guridy, Frank Andre. *Forging Diaspora: Afro-Cubans and African Americans in a World of Empire and Jim Crow*. Chapel Hill: University of North Carolina Press, 2010.

Guterl, Matthew Pratt. *The Color of Race in America, 1900–1940*. Cambridge, Mass.: Harvard University Press, 2001.

Hagy, James William. *This Happy Land: The Jews of Colonial and Antebellum Charleston*. Tuscaloosa: University of Alabama Press, 1993.

HaitiLibre. "Haïti—Reconstruction: Les problèmes fonciers entravent la reconstruction." July 6, 2010. http://www.haitilibre.com/article-544-haiti-reconstruction-les-problemes-fonciers-entravent-la-reconstruction.html. [Unauthorized, anonymous English translation: "Haiti: Land Ownership Questions Hinder Reconstruction." http://lo-de-alla.org/2010/07/haiti-land-ownership-questions-hinder-reconstruction/.]

Halbwachs, Maurice. *The Collective Memory* [*La Mémoire collective*]. 1950. Translated by Francis J. Ditter Jr. and Vida Yazdi Ditter. New York: Harper and Row, 1980.

———. *On Collective Memory* [*Les cadres sociaux de la mémoire*]. 1952. Edited and translated by Lewis A. Coser. Chicago: University of Chicago Press, 1992.

Haley, Alex. *Roots: The Saga of an American Family*. Garden City, N.Y.: Doubleday, 1976.

Hall, Stuart. "Cultural Identity and Diaspora." 1990. In *Theorizing Diaspora*, edited by Braziel and Mannur, 233–46.

———. "Negotiating Caribbean Identities." *New Left Review* 209 (1995): 3–14.

———. "The Problem of Ideology: Marxism without Guarantees." 1986. In *Stuart Hall: Critical Dialogues in Cultural Studies*, edited by David Morley and Kuan-Hsing Chen, 25–46. London: Routledge, 1996.

———. "Race, Articulation, and Societies Structured in Dominance." In *Sociological Theories: Race and Colonialism*, 305–45. Paris: UNESCO, 1980.

Hannaford, Ivan. *Race: The History of an Idea in the West*. Baltimore: Johns Hopkins University Press, 1996.

Harris, Trudier. *Fiction and Folklore: The Novels of Toni Morrison*. Knoxville: University of Tennessee Press, 1991.

Hartman, Saidiya. *Lose Your Mother: A Journey along the Atlantic Slave Route*. New York: Farrar, Straus and Giroux, 2007.

Hathaway, Heather. *Caribbean Waves: Relocating Claude McKay and Paule Marshall*. Bloomington: Indiana University Press, 1999.

Hegel, Georg Wilhelm Friedrich. *Lectures on the Philosophy of World History*. Vol. 1, *Manuscripts of the Introduction and the Lectures of 1822–3*. Edited and translated by Robert F. Brown and Peter C. Hodgson, with the assistance of William G. Geuss. Oxford: Clarendon Press, 2011.

Helgerson, Richard. "Camões, Hakluyt, and the Voyages of Two Nations." In *Colo-

nialism and Culture, edited by Nicholas B. Dirks, 27–64. Ann Arbor: University of Michigan Press, 1992.

Hellmann, John. *American Myth and the Legacy of Vietnam*. New York: Columbia University Press, 1986.

Henry, Frances. *The Caribbean Diaspora in Toronto: Learning to Live with Racism*. Toronto: Toronto University Press, 1994.

Heron, Melonie P. *The Occupational Attainment of Caribbean Immigrants in the United States, Canada, and England*. New York: LFB Scholarly Publishing, 2001.

Herskovits, Melville J. *The Myth of the Negro Past*. New York: Harper and Brothers, 1941.

Herzog, Tobey C. *Vietnam War Stories: Innocence Lost*. London: Routledge, 1992.

Hickman, Angela. "Dutch Group Burns the Cover of Lawrence Hill's Novel *The Book of Negroes*." *National Post*, June 22, 2011. http://arts.nationalpost.com/2011/06/22/writers-union-decries-planned-book-burning-as-censorship-at-its-worst/.

Hill, Lawrence. *Any Known Blood*. 1997. Toronto: HarperCollins, 2007.

———. *Black Berry, Sweet Juice: On Being Black and White in Canada*. Toronto: HarperCollins, 2001.

———. *The Book of Negroes*. Toronto: HarperCollins, 2007.

———. "A Conversation with Lawrence Hill." Interview by Winfried Siemerling. *Callaloo* 36.1 (Winter 2013): 5–26.

———. *Dear Sir, I Intend to Burn Your Book: An Anatomy of a Book Burning*. Edmonton: University of Alberta Press, 2013.

———. "Freedom Bound." *The Beaver: Canada's History Magazine*, February–March 2007, 16–23.

———. "His Novel Takes Him Back to Roots of His Ancestry. Interview by David Mehegan." *Boston Globe*, November 14, 2007.

———. *The Illegal*. Toronto: HarperCollins, 2015.

———. "'A Person of Many Places': Lawrence Hill in Conversation with Pilar Cuder-Domínguez." Interview by Pilar Cuder-Domínguez. In *New Perspectives on the Black Atlantic*, edited by Ledent and Cuder-Domínguez, 295–310.

———. "Projecting History Honestly: An Interview with Lawrence Hill." Interview by Jessie Sagawa. *Studies in Canadian Literature/Études en littérature canadienne* 33.1 (2008): 307–22.

———. "What I Learned about Language When I Titled My Novel *The Book of Negroes*." *Slate*, February 13, 2015. http://www.slate.com/blogs/lexicon_valley/2015/02/13/negro_may_not_be_pc_but_the_book_of_negroes_is_the_best_name_for_my_novel.html.

———. "What Lawrence Hill Tells Dutch Group Planning to Burn His Book." *Toronto Star*, June 20, 2011. http://www.thestar.com/entertainment/article/1012068-what-lawrence-hill-tells-dutch-group-planning-to-burn-his-book?bn=1.

———. "Why I'm Not Allowed My Book Title." *Guardian*, May 20, 2008. http://www.theguardian.com/books/booksblog/2008/may/20/whyimnotallowedmybooktit.

Hine, Darlene Clark, Trica Danielle Keaton, and Stephen Small. *Black Europe and the African Diaspora*. Urbana: University of Illinois Press, 2009.

Hirsch, Marianne. *The Generation of Postmemory: Writing and Visual Culture after the Holocaust*. New York: Columbia University Press, 2012.

Hodges, Graham Russell, ed. *The Black Loyalist Directory: African Americans in Exile after the American Revolution*. New York: Garland, 1996.

Høgsbjerg, Christian. *C.L.R. James in Imperial Britain*. Durham, N.C.: Duke University Press, 2014.

Holloway, Joseph E. Introduction to *Africanisms in American Culture*, edited by Joseph E. Holloway, ix–xxi. Bloomington: Indiana University Press, 1991.

Homberger, Eric. *The Historical Atlas of New York City: A Visual Celebration of Nearly 400 Years of New York City's History*. New York: Henry Holt, 1994.

hooks, bell, and Cornel West. *Breaking Bread: Insurgent Black Intellectual Life*. Boston: South End Press, 1991.

Horton, Lois E. "From Class to Race in Early America: Northern Post-Emancipation and Racial Reconstruction." In *Race and the Early Republic: Racial Consciousness and Nation-Building in the Early Republic*, edited by Michael A. Morrison and James Brewer Stewart, 55–74. Lanham, Md.: Rowman and Littlefield, 2001.

House, Elizabeth B. "*Sula*: Imagery, Figurative Language, and Symbols." In *Approaches to Teaching the Novels of Toni Morrison*, edited by Nellie Y. McKay and Kathryn Earle, 99–105. New York: Modern Language Association, 1997.

Howe, Stephen. *Afrocentrism: Mythical Pasts and Imagined Homes*. London: Verso, 1998.

Hughes, Langston. "Afro-American Fragment." 1930. In Hughes, *Collected Poems*, 129.

———. *The Big Sea: An Autobiography*. 1940. New York: Hill and Wang, 1993.

———. *The Collected Poems of Langston Hughes*, 1994. Edited by Arnold Rampersad and David Roessel. New York: Vintage, 1995.

———. "I, Too." 1925. In Hughes, *Collected Poems*, 46.

Hunt, Patricia. "War and Peace: Transfigured Categories and the Politics of *Sula*." *African American Review* 27.3 (Fall 1993): 443–59.

Jackson, Chuck. "A 'Headless Display': *Sula*, Soldiers, and Lynching." *Modern Fiction Studies* 52.2 (Summer 2006): 374–92.

Jacobson, Matthew Frye. *Whiteness of a Different Color: European Immigrants and the Alchemy of Race*. Cambridge, Mass.: Harvard University Press, 1998.

Jaggi, Maya. "Englishmen Born and Bred . . . Almost: A New Generation of British-Born Black and Asian Writers Is Emerging." *Mail & Guardian Review of Books: Literary Supplement to the Mail & Guardian* 13.7 (February 21–27, 1997): 4–5.

James, C.L.R. *The Black Jacobins: Toussaint L'Ouverture and the San Domingo Revolution*. 1938. New York: Vintage, 1989.

James, Cynthia. "'You'll Soon Get Used to Our Language': Language, Parody and West Indian Identity in Andrea Levy's *Small Island*." *Anthurium* 5.1, article 3 (Spring 2007). http://scholarlyrepository.miami.edu/anthurium/vol5/iss1/3.

James, David. *Contemporary British Fiction and the Artistry of Space: Style, Landscape, Perception*. London: Continuum, 2008.

JanMohamed, Abdul, and David Lloyd. Preface to *The Nature and Context of Minority Discourse*, edited by Abdul JanMohamed and David Lloyd, ix–xi. New York: Oxford University Press, 1990.

Jasanoff, Maya. *Liberty's Exiles: American Loyalists in the Revolutionary World*. New York: Knopf, 2011.

Jason, Philip K., ed. *Fourteen Landing Zones: Approaches to Vietnam War Literature*. Iowa City: University of Iowa Press, 1991.

Jay, Martin. *Downcast Eyes: The Denigration of Vision in Twentieth-Century Thought*. Berkeley: University of California Press, 1993.

Jean-Charles, Régine Michelle. "Danticat and the African American Women's Literary Tradition." In *Edwidge Danticat*, edited by Munro, 52–69.

Johnson, Charles. *Being and Race: Black Writing since 1970*. Bloomington: Indiana University Press, 1988.

———. "Being and Race: An Interview with Charles Johnson." By George Myers Jr. 1988. In C. Johnson, *Passing the Three Gates*, 34–41.

———. "An Interview with Charles Johnson." By Marian Blue. 1993. In C. Johnson, *Passing the Three Gates*, 123–41.

———. "An Interview with Charles Johnson." By Michael Boccia. *African American Review* 30.4 (Winter 1996): 611–18.

———. "An Interview with Charles Johnson." By Jonathan Little. 1993. In C. Johnson, *Passing the Three Gates*, 97–122.

———. "An Interview with Charles Johnson." By Jim McWilliams. 2003. In C. Johnson, *Passing the Three Gates*, 271–99.

———. "Interviews with Northwest Writers: Charles Johnson." By Irene Wanner. 1993/1994. In C. Johnson, *Passing the Three Gates*, 159–91.

———. *Middle Passage*. 1990. New York: Plume, 1991.

———. "Novelists of Memory." 1989. In *Charles Johnson's Novels*, edited by Byrd, 97–107.

———. *Passing the Three Gates: Interviews with Charles Johnson*. Edited by Jim McWilliams. Seattle: University of Washington Press, 2004.

———. "The Philosopher and the American Novel: Q & A at the California State Library." 1991. In C. Johnson, *Passing the Three Gates*, 53–67.

———. "Philosophy and Black Fiction." 1980. In *Charles Johnson's Novels*, edited by Byrd, 79–84.

———. Preface to *Turning the Wheel*. In C. Johnson, *Turning the Wheel*, xiii–xviii.
———. "Reading the Eightfold Path." In C. Johnson, *Turning the Wheel*, 3–33.
———. *Turning the Wheel: Essays on Buddhism and Writing*. New York: Scribner, 2003.
———. "Whole Sight: Notes on New Black Fiction." 1980. In *Charles Johnson's Novels*, edited by Byrd, 85–90.
Johnson, Paul C. *Diaspora Conversions: Black Carib Religion and the Recovery of Africa*. Berkeley: University of California Press, 2007.
———. "On Leaving and Joining Africanness through Religion: The 'Black Caribs' Across Multiple Diasporic Horizons." *Journal of Religion in Africa* 37 (2007): 174–211.
Jones, LeRoi [Amiri Baraka]. "The Changing Same (R&B and New Black Music)." 1966. In *Black Music*, by Leroi Jones [Amiri Baraka], 180–211. New York: William Morrow, 1967.
Jordan, Margaret I. *African American Servitude and Historical Imaginings: Retrospective Fiction and Representation*. Houndmills, England: Palgrave Macmillan, 2004.
Joyce, Joyce Ann. "'What We Do and Why We Do What We Do': A Diasporic Commingling of Richard Wright and George Lamming." *Callaloo* 32.2 (2009):593–604.
Judy, Ronald A. T. *(Dis)Forming the American Canon: African-Arabic Slave Narratives and the Vernacular*. Minneapolis: University of Minnesota Press, 1993.
Keevak, Michael. *Becoming Yellow: A Short History of Racial Thinking*. Princeton, N.J.: Princeton University Press, 2001.
Keizer, Arlene R. *Black Subjects: Identity Formation in the Contemporary Narrative of Slavery*. Ithaca: Cornell University Press, 2004.
Key, Joshua, and Lawrence Hill. *The Deserter's Tale: The Story of an Ordinary Soldier Who Walked Away from the War in Iraq*. New York: Atlantic Monthly Press, 2007.
Khan, Aisha. "Dark Arts and Diaspora." *Diaspora: A Journal of Transnational Studies* 17.1 (Spring 2008): 40–63.
Kincaid, Jamaica. *Lucy*. 1991. London: Picador, 1994.
Kinney, Katherine. *Friendly Fire: American Images of the Vietnam War*. Oxford: Oxford University Press, 2000.
Klein, Kerwin Lee. *From History to Theory*. Berkeley: University of California Press, 2011.
Kline, Nancy. "From Slavery to Freedom." Review of *Someone Knows My Name* [*The Book of Negroes*], by Lawrence Hill. *New York Times*, January 20, 2008. http://www.nytimes.com/2008/01/20/books/review/Kline-t.html.
Koser, Khalid, ed. *New African Diasporas*. London: Routledge, 2003.
Krumholz, Linda. "Blackness and Art in Toni Morrison's *Tar Baby*." *Contemporary Literature* 49.2 (2008): 263–92.
LaCapra, Dominick. *Writing History, Writing Trauma*. Baltimore: Johns Hopkins University Press, 2001.

Lamming, George. *The Emigrants.* 1954. Ann Arbor: University of Michigan Press, 1994.
———. "George Lamming Talks to Caryl Phillips." Interview by Caryl Phillips. *Wasafiri* 26 (Autumn 1997): 10–17.
———. *In the Castle of My Skin.* New York: McGraw-Hill, 1953.
———. *Natives of My Person.* 1971. London: Allison and Busby, 1986.
———. *The Pleasures of Exile.* 1960. Ann Arbor: University of Michigan Press, 1992.
———. "The Sovereignty of the Imagination: An Interview with George Lamming." By David Scott. *Small Axe* 6.2 (September 2002): 72–200.
Lang, Anouk. "'Enthralling but at the Same Time Disturbing': Challenging the Readers of *Small Island.*" *Journal of Commonwealth Literature* 44.2 (2009): 123–40.
Ledent, Bénédicte. "Ambiguous Visions of Home: The Paradoxes of Diasporic Belonging in Caryl Phillips's *The Atlantic Sound.*" *EnterText* 1.1 (Winter 2000): 198–211.
———. *Caryl Phillips.* Manchester: Manchester University Press, 2002.
Ledent, Bénédicte, and Pilar Cuder-Domínguez, eds. *New Perspectives on the Black Atlantic: Definitions, Readings, Practices, Dialogues.* Bern: Peter Lang, 2012
Ledent, Bénédicte, and Daria Tunca, eds. *Caryl Phillips: Writing in the Key of Life.* Amsterdam: Rodopi, 2012.
Lee, Rachel. "Missing Peace in Toni Morrison's *Sula* and *Beloved.*" *African American Review* 28.4 (Winter 1994): 571–83.
Lentz-Smith, Adriane. *Freedom Struggles: African Americans and World War I.* Cambridge, Mass.: Harvard University Press, 2009.
Levy, Andrea. "Empire's Child: Bonnie Greer Meets Andrea Levy." By Bonnie Greer. *Guardian*, January 31, 2004. http://www.guardian.co.uk/books/2004/jan/31/fiction.race.
———. *Every Light in the House Burnin'.* London: Headline Review, 1994.
———. *Fruit of the Lemon.* London: Headline Review, 1999.
———. *The Long Song.* London: Headline Review, 2010.
———. *Never Far from Nowhere.* London: Headline Review, 1996.
———. *Small Island.* London: Headline Review, 2004.
Lifton, Robert Jay. *Home from the War: Vietnam Veterans: Neither Victims nor Executioners.* New York: Simon and Schuster, 1973.
Little, Jonathan. *Charles Johnson's Spiritual Imagination.* Columbia: University of Missouri Press, 1997.
Lock, Helen. "The Paradox of Slave Mutiny in Herman Melville, Charles Johnson, and Frederick Douglass." *College Literature* 30.4 (Fall 2003): 54–70.
Luckhurst, Roger. *The Trauma Question.* London: Routledge, 2008.
MacInnes, Colin. *Absolute Beginners.* 1959. In MacInnes, *Omnibus.*
———. *City of Spades.* 1957. In MacInnes, *Omnibus.*
———. *The Colin MacInnes Omnibus. His Three London Novels: City of Spades, Absolute Beginners, Mr. Love and Justice.* London: Allison and Busby, 1985. [Novels paginated separately.]

———. *Mr. Love and Justice*. 1960. In MacInnes, *Omnibus*.

Manning, Patrick. *The African Diaspora: A History through Culture*. New York: Columbia University Press, 2009.

Mardorossian, Carine M. "Danticat and Caribbean Women Writers." In *Edwidge Danticat*, edited by Munro, 39–51.

———. *Reclaiming Difference: Caribbean Women Rewrite Postcolonialism*. Charlottesville: University of Virginia Press, 2005.

Marouan, Maha, and Merinda Simmons, eds. *Race and Displacement: Nation, Migration, and Identity in the Twenty-First Century*. Tuscaloosa: University of Alabama Press, 2013.

Marshall, Paule. *Brown Girl, Brownstones*. 1959. New York: Feminist Press at the City University of New York, 1981.

———. *Praisesong for the Widow*. New York: Plume, 1983.

Matus, Jill. *Toni Morrison*. Manchester: Manchester University Press, 1998.

Mayberry, Susan Neal. *Can't I Love What I Criticize? The Masculine and Morrison*. Athens: University of Georgia Press, 2007.

Mbembé, Achille. "African Modes of Self-Writing." Translated by Steven Rendall. *Public Culture* 14.1 (Winter 2002): 239–73.

McGill, Lisa D. *Constructing Black Selves: Caribbean American Narratives and the Second Generation*. New York: New York University Press, 2005.

McKay, Claude. *Banana Bottom*. 1933. San Diego: Harvest/Harcourt Brace, 1961.

———. "Claude MacKay [sic] Describes His Own Life: A Negro Poet." *Pearson's Magazine* 39 (September 1918): 275–76.

———. *Complete Poems*. Edited by William J. Maxwell. Urbana: University of Illinois Press, 2004.

———. "I Shall Return." 1920. In *Complete Poems*, by Claude McKay, 167–68.

———. "If We Must Die." 1919. In *Complete Poems*, by Claude McKay, 177–78.

———. *A Long Way from Home*. 1937. San Diego: Harcourt Brace Jovanovich, 1970.

———. *My Green Hills of Jamaica and Five Jamaican Short Stories*. Kingston, Jam.: Heinemann Educational Books (Caribbean), 1979.

———. "Old England." In *Songs of Jamaica*, by Claude McKay, with an introduction by Walter Jekyll, 63–65. Kingston, Jam.: Aston W. Gardner, 1912.

———. "To a Friend." 1912. In *Complete Poems*, by Claude McKay, 18.

McKee, Patricia. "Spacing and Placing Experience in Toni Morrison's *Sula*." In *Toni Morrison: Critical and Theoretical Approaches*, edited by Nancy J. Peterson, 37–62. Baltimore: Johns Hopkins University Press, 1997.

McKittrick, Katherine. *Demonic Grounds: Black Women and the Cartographies of Struggle*. Minneapolis: University of Minnesota Press, 2006.

McKittrick, Katherine, and Clyde Woods, eds. *Black Geographies and the Politics of Place*. Cambridge, Mass.: South End Press, 2007.

McLeod, John. "Postcolonial Fictions of Adoption." *Critical Survey* 18.2 (2006): 45–55.

———. *Postcolonial London: Rewriting the Metropolis*. London: Routledge, 2004.
Medaglia, Angelica. "Diallo Cousin Still Fights for a Foothold." *New York Times*, July 31, 2007. http://www.nytimes.com/2007/07/31/nyregion/31diallo.html?ref=%20amadou_diallo&_r=0.
Medovarski, Andrea. "Currency and Cultural Consumption: Lawrence Hill's *The Book of Negroes*." *Studies in Canadian Literature/Études en littérature canadienne* 38.2 (2013): 9–30.
Mehta, Brinda. *Notions of Identity, Diaspora, and Gender in Caribbean Women's Writing*. Houndmills, England: Palgrave Macmillan, 2009.
Melville, Herman. *Benito Cereno*. 1856. In *"Bartleby" and "Benito Cereno,"* by Herman Melville, 35–104. New York: Dover, 1990.
———. *Moby-Dick*. 1851. 2nd Norton ed. New York: Norton, 2002.
Metzgen, Humphrey, and John Graham. *Caribbean Wars Untold: A Salute to the British West Indies*. Kingston, Jam.: University of West Indies Press, 2007.
Morrison, Toni. *Beloved*. 1987. New York: Vintage/Random House, 2004.
———. *The Bluest Eye*. 1970. New York: Knopf, 2000.
———. *Conversations with Toni Morrison*. Edited by Danille Taylor-Guthrie. Jackson: University Press of Mississippi, 1994.
———. "Intimate Things in Place: A Conversation with Toni Morrison." 1976/1977. Interview by Robert Stepto. In Morrison, *Conversations*, 10–29.
———. *Jazz*. 1992. London: Picador, 1993.
———. *Paradise*. New York: Knopf, 1998.
———. "The Site of Memory." In *Inventing the Truth: The Art and Craft of Memoir*, edited by William Zinsser, 101–24. Boston: Houghton Mifflin, 1987.
———. *Song of Solomon*. 1977. New York: Vintage, 2004.
———. *Sula*. 1973. New York: Plume, 1982.
———. *Tar Baby*. 1981. New York: Knopf, 1998.
———. "This Side of 'Paradise.'" Morrison Defends Herself from Criticism against Her New Novel." Interview by Anna Mulrine. *U.S. News*, January 19, 1998. http://www.usnews.com/usnews/culture/articles/980119/archive_003034.htm.
———. "Unspeakable Things Unspoken: The Afro-American Presence in American Literature." *Michigan Quarterly Review* 28.1 (Winter 1989): 1–34.
Mortimer, Mildred P. *Writing from the Hearth: Public, Domestic, and Imaginative Space in Francophone Women's Fiction of Africa and the Caribbean*. Lanham, Md.: Lexington Books, 2007.
Mott, Frederick Walker. *War Neuroses and Shell Shock*. London: Henry Frowde and Hodder and Stoughton, 1919.
Muños-Valdivieso, Sofía. "Metaphors of Belonging in Andrea Levy's *Small Island*." In *Metaphor and Diaspora in Contemporary Writing*, edited by Jonathan P. A. Sell, 99–116. Houndmills, England: Palgrave Macmillan, 2012.

Munro, Martin. "Inside Out: A Brief Biography of Edwidge Danticat." In *Edwidge Danticat*, edited by Munro, 13–25.

———, ed. *Edwidge Danticat: A Reader's Guide*. Charlottesville: University of Virginia Press, 2010.

Murray, Robert N. *Lest We Forget: The Experiences of World War II Westindian Ex-Service Personnel*. Nottingham: Nottinghamshire Westindian Combined Ex-Services Association, 1996.

Muther, Elizabeth. "Isadora at Sea: Misogyny as Comic Capital in Charles Johnson's *Middle Passage*." *African American Review* 30.4 (Winter 1996): 649–58.

Nadal, Marita, and Mónica Calvo, eds. *Trauma in Contemporary Literature: Narrative and Representation*. London: Routledge, 2014.

Nair, Supriya. *Caliban's Curse: George Lamming and the Revisioning of History*. Ann Arbor: University of Michigan Press, 1996.

Nanton, Philip. "On Knowing and Not Knowing George Lamming: Personal Style and Metropolitan Influences." In *The Locations of George Lamming*, edited by Schwarz, 49–66.

Naseem, M. Ayaz, and Emery J. Hyslop-Margison. "Nussbaum's Concept of Cosmopolitanism: Practical Possibility or Academic Delusion?" *Paideusis* 15.2 (2006): 51–60.

Nash, William R. *Charles Johnson's Fiction*. Urbana: University of Illinois Press, 2003.

Nichols, James H., Jr. *Alexandre Kojève: Wisdom at the End of History*. Lanham, Md.: Rowman and Littlefield, 2007.

Noble, E. Martin. *Jamaica Airman: A Black Airman in Britain, 1943 and After*. London: New Beacon Books, 1984.

Nora, Pierre. "Between Memory and History: *Les lieux de mémoire*." Translated by Marc Roudebush. *Representations* 26 (Spring 1989): 7–25.

———. *Les lieux de mémoire*. Paris: Éditions Gallimard, 1984–92.

Nussbaum, Martha C. "Patriotism and Cosmopolitanism." 1994. In Nussbaum et al., 2–17.

Nussbaum, Martha C., Kwame Anthony Appiah, Benjamin R. Barber, et al. *For Love of Country: Debating the Limits of Patriotism*, edited by Joshua Cohen. Boston: Beacon, 1996.

Nyman, Jopi. *Home, Identity, and Mobility in Contemporary Diasporic Fiction*. Amsterdam: Rodopi, 2009.

———. *Under English Eyes: Constructions of Europe in Early Twentieth-Century British Fiction*. Amsterdam: Rodopi, 2000.

O'Keefe, Vincent A. "Reading Rigor Mortis: Offstage Violence and Excluded Middles 'in' Johnson's *Middle Passage* and Morrison's *Beloved*." *African American Review* 30.4 (Winter 1996): 635–47.

Olson, Carl. *The Different Paths of Buddhism: A Narrative-Historical Introduction*. New Brunswick: Rutgers University Press, 2005.

Page, Philip. *Dangerous Freedom: Fusion and Fragmentation in Toni Morrison's Novels.* Jackson: University Press of Mississippi, 1995.

Painter, Nell Irvin. *The History of White People.* New York: Norton, 2010.

———. Review of *Many Thousands Gone: The First Two Centuries of Slavery in North America,* by Ira Berlin. *African American Review* 34.3 (Autumn 2000): 515–17.

Palmer, Colin A. "The Middle Passage." In *Captive Passage: The Transatlantic Slave Trade and the Making of the Americas,* compiled and edited by The Mariners' Museum, Newport News, Va., 53–75. Washington, D.C.: Smithsonian Institution Press, 2002.

Paquet, Sandra Pouchet. "The Ancestor as Foundation in *Their Eyes Were Watching God* and *Tar Baby.*" *Callaloo* 13.3 (Summer 1990): 499–515.

———. *Caribbean Autobiography: Cultural Identity and Self-Presentation.* Madison: University of Wisconsin Press, 2002.

———. *The Novels of George Lamming.* London: Heinemann, 1982.

Paul, Kathleen. *Whitewashing Britain: Race and Citizenship in the Postwar Era.* Ithaca: Cornell University Press, 1997.

Perfect, Michael. "'Fold the Paper and Pass It On': Historical Silences and the Contrapuntal in Andrea Levy's Fiction." *Journal of Postcolonial Writing* 46.1 (February 2010): 31–41.

Phillips, Caryl. *The Atlantic Sound.* 2000. New York: Vintage International, 2001.

———. *Cambridge.* 1991. London: Picador, 1992.

———. *Colour Me English: Selected Essays.* London: Harvill Secker, 2011.

———. "Conclusion: The 'High Anxiety' of Belonging." 2000. In C. Phillips, *A New World Order,* 303–9.

———. *Conversations with Caryl Phillips.* Edited by Reneé T. Schatteman. Jackson: University Press of Mississippi, 2009.

———. *Crossing the River.* 1993. London: Picador, 1994.

———. *A Distant Shore.* New York: Knopf, 2003.

———. *The European Tribe.* 1987. New York: Vintage, 2000.

———. *The Final Passage.* 1985. New York: Vintage, 1995.

———. "Following On: The Legacy of Lamming and Selvon." 1998. In C. Phillips, *A New World Order,* 232–38.

———. *Foreigners.* New York: Knopf, 2007.

———. *Higher Ground: A Novel in Three Parts.* 1989. New York: Penguin Books, 1990.

———. *In the Falling Snow.* New York: Knopf, 2009.

———. Interview by Kay Saunders. 1986. In C. Phillips, *Conversations,* 3–10.

———. "Introduction: The Gift of Displacement." In C. Phillips, *A New World Order,* 129–34.

———. *The Lost Child.* New York: Farrar, Straus and Giroux, 2015.

———. *The Nature of Blood.* London: Faber and Faber, 1997.

———. "Necessary Journeys." 2004. In C. Phillips, *Colour Me English,* 123–31.

———. *A New World Order: Essays.* 2001. New York: Vintage, 2002.

———. "Of This Time, of That Place: A Conversation with Caryl Phillips." Interview by Jenny Sharpe. 1995. In C. Phillips, *Conversations,* 27–35.

———. "Rites of Passage." 2001. Interview by Maya Jaggi. In C. Phillips, *Conversations,* 77–86.

———. "Spectral Triangle." Interview by Maya Jaggi. *Guardian,* May 5, 1993, 4.

———. *A State of Independence.* 1986. New York: Vintage, 1995.

———. "St Kitts: 19 September 1983." 1983. In C. Phillips, *A New World Order,* 135–43.

———. "Water." 1993. In C. Phillips, *Colour Me English,* 163–66.

Phillips, Mike, and Trevor Phillips. *Windrush: The Irresistible Rise of Multi-Racial Britain.* 1998. London: HarperCollins, 1999.

Pirker, Eva Ulrike. "A Black Atlantic Agenda: Artistic/Narrative Strategies in Caryl Phillips's *The Atlantic Sound* and Isaac Julien's *Paradise Omeros*." In *New Perspectives on the Black Atlantic,* edited by Ledent and Cuder-Domínguez, 195–216.

———. *Narrative Projections of a Black British History.* New York: Routledge, 2011.

Poon, Angelia. "Intimate Arrangements: Race, Sex, and the English Nation in Andrea Levy's *Small Island*." In *Sexuality and Contemporary Literature,* edited by Joel Gwynne and Angelia Poon, 127–45. Amherst, N.Y.: Cambria Press, 2012.

Powell, Enoch. "Rivers of Blood." Speech delivered at the annual general meeting of the West Midlands Area Conservative Political Centre, Birmingham, England, April 20, 1968. *Occidental Quarterly: Western Perspectives on Man, Culture, and Politics* 1.1 (Fall 2001). http://www.toqonline.com/archive/2001/fall-01/.

Powell, Patricia. "A Search for Caribbean Masculinities." *Anthurium* 10.2, article 21 (2013). http://scholarlyrepository.miami.edu/anthurium/vol10/iss2/21.

Pratt, Mary Louise. *Imperial Eyes: Travel Writing and Transculturation.* 2nd rev. ed. New York: Routledge, 2008.

Procter, James. *Dwelling Places: Postwar Black British Writing.* Manchester: Manchester University Press, 2003.

———, ed. *Writing Black Britain, 1948–1998: An Interdisciplinary Anthology.* Manchester: Manchester University Press, 2000.

Pulis, John W., ed. *Moving On: Black Loyalists in the Afro-Atlantic World.* New York: Garland, 1999.

Pybus, Cassandra. *Epic Journeys of Freedom: Runaway Slaves of the American Revolution and Their Global Quest for Liberty.* Boston: Beacon Press, 2006.

———. "Jefferson's Faulty Math." *William and Mary Quarterly* 62.2 (April 2005): 243–64.

Rahbek, Ulla. "Caryl Phillips's *A State of Independence*: Character, Country, Conflict." In *Bridges across Chasms: Towards a Transcultural Future in Caribbean Literature,* edited by Bénédicte Ledent, 79–88. Liege: L3-Liege, Language, Literature, 2004.

Randolph, Asa Philip, and Chandler Owen. "Who Shall Pay for the War?" *Messenger,* November 1917. In *If We Must Die,* edited by Stanford, 118.

Reckley, Ralph, Sr. "Barriers, Boundaries and Alienation: Caribbean Women in the Novels of Cecil Foster." *The Middle-Atlantic Writers Association Review* 13.1 (June 1998): 24–30.

Rediker, Marcus. *The Slave Ship: A Human History*. New York: Viking, 2007.

Reynolds, David. *Rich Relations: The American Occupation of Britain, 1942–1945*. New York: Random House, 1995.

Rhys, Jean. *Voyage in the Dark*. 1934. London: Andre Deutsch, 1967.

Rice, Alan. *Creating Memorials, Building Identities: The Politics of Memory in the Black Atlantic*. Liverpool: Liverpool University Press, 2010.

Ringnalda, Donald. *Fighting and Writing the Vietnam War*. Jackson: University Press of Mississippi, 1994.

Roach, Joseph. *Cities of the Dead: Circum-Atlantic Performance*. New York: Columbia University Press, 1996.

Robinson, Christopher C. "Theorizing Politics after Camus." *Human Studies* 32.1 (March 2009): 1–18.

Roediger, David R. *Colored White: Transcending the Racial Past*. Berkeley: University of California Press, 2002.

———. *How Race Survived U.S. History: From Settlement and Slavery to the Obama Phenomenon*. London: Verso, 2008.

———. *Working toward Whiteness: How America's Immigrants Became White: The Strange Journey from Ellis Island to the Suburbs*. New York: Basic Books, 2005.

Roediger, David R., and Elizabeth D. Esch, *The Production of Difference: Race and the Management of Labor in U.S. History*. New York: Oxford University Press, 2012.

Rogoziński, Jan. *A Brief History of the Caribbean: From the Arawak and Carib to the Present*. Rev. ed. New York: Plume, 2000.

Rosenhaft, Eve, and Robbie Aitken, eds. *Africa in Europe: Studies in Transnational Practice in the Long Twentieth Century*. Liverpool: Liverpool University Press, 2013.

Rossi, Jennifer C. "'Let the Words Bring Wings to Our Feet': Negotiating Exile and Trauma through Narrative in Danticat's *Breath, Eyes, Memory*." *Obsidian III: Literature in the African Diaspora* 6:2–7:1 (Fall/Winter 2005–Spring/Summer 2006): 203–19.

Rothberg, Michael. *Multidirectional Memory: Remembering the Holocaust in the Age of Decolonization*. Stanford, Calif.: Stanford University Press, 2009.

Ruffin, Kimberly N. "'A Realm of Monuments and Water': Lorde-ian Erotics and Shange's African Diaspora Cosmopolitanism." In *Black Geographies and the Politics of Place*, edited by McKittrick and Woods, 137–53.

Rumbaut, Rubén G. "Severed or Sustained Attachments? Language, Identity, and Imagined Communities in the Post-Immigrant Generation." In *The Changing Face of Home: The Transnational Lives of the Second Generation*, edited by Peggy Levitt and Mary C. Waters, 43–95. New York: Russell Sage Foundation, 2002.

Rushdy, Ashraf H. A. *Neo-Slave Narratives: Studies in the Social Logic of a Literary Form.* New York: Oxford University Press, 1999.
Russell, Heather. *Legba's Crossing: Narratology in the African Atlantic.* Athens: University of Georgia Press, 2009.
Sáez, Elena Machado. "Postcoloniality, Atlantic Orders, and the Migrant Male in the Writings of Caryl Phillips." *Small Axe* 9.1 (March 2005): 17–39.
Said, Edward W. *Culture and Imperialism.* 1993. New York: Vintage Books, 1994.
Sandiford, Keith. *Theorizing a Colonial Caribbean-Atlantic Imaginary: Sugar and Obeah.* New York: Routledge, 2011.
Sarthou, Sharrón Eve. "Unsilencing Défilés Daughters: Overcoming Silence in Edwidge Danticat's *Breath, Eyes, Memory* and *Krik?Krak!*" *Global South* 4:2 (Fall 2010): 99–123.
Sartre, Jean-Paul. *Being and Nothingness* [*L'Être et le néant*, 1943]. Translated by Hazel E. Barnes. New York: Washington Square Press, 1992.
———. *No Exit* [*Huis Clos*, 1945]. Translated by Stuart Gilbert. New York: Vintage International, 1989.
Schama, Simon. *Rough Crossings: Britain, the Slaves, and the American Revolution.* New York: HarperCollins, 2006.
Schramm, Katharina. *African Homecoming: Pan-African Ideology and Contested Heritage.* Walnut Creek, Calif.: Left Coast Press, 2010.
Schreiber, Evelyn Jaffe. *Race, Trauma, and Home in the Novels of Toni Morrison.* Baton Rouge: Louisiana State University Press, 2010.
Schwarz, Bill. "C.L.R. James and George Lamming: The Measure of Historical Time." *Small Axe* 7.2 (September 2003): 39–70.
———. "Locating Lamming." In *The Locations of George Lamming*, edited by Bill Schwarz, 1–25. Oxford, England: Macmillan Caribbean, 2007.
———, ed. *The Locations of George Lamming*, Oxford, England: Macmillan Caribbean, 2007.
Scott, Daniel M., III. "Interrogating Identity: Appropriation and Transformation in *Middle Passage*." *African American Review* 29.4 (Winter 1995): 645–55.
Scott, Helen. *Caribbean Women Writers and Globalization: Fictions of Independence.* Aldershot, England: Ashgate, 2006.
———. "*Ou libéré?* History, Transformation, and the Struggle for Freedom in Edwidge Danticat's *Breath, Eyes, Memory*." In *Ecrire en pays assiégé, Haïti: Writing under Siege*, edited by Marie-Agnès Sourieau and Kathleen M. Balutansky, 459–78. Amsterdam: Rodopi, 2004.
Scudder, Harold H. "Melville's *Benito Cereno* and Captain Delano's *Voyages*." *PMLA* 43 (June 1928): 502–32.
Searle, William J., ed. *Search and Clear: Critical Responses to Selected Literature and Films of the Vietnam War.* Bowling Green, Ohio: Bowling Green State University Popular Press, 1988.

Selvon, Sam[uel]. *The Lonely Londoners*. 1956. New York: Longman, 1985.

———. *Moses Ascending*. 1975. London: Penguin, 2008.

Selzer, Linda Furgerson. *Charles Johnson in Context*. Amherst: University of Massachusetts Press, 2009.

Seymour, A. J. "The Novel in the British Caribbean." Part 3. *BIM* 11.44 (January–June 1967): 238–42.

Shapcott, Richard. *International Ethics: A Critical Introduction*. Cambridge, England: Polity Press, 2010.

Sharpe, Jenny. "The Middle Passages of Black Migration." In *New Routes for Diaspora Studies*, edited by Sukanya Banerjee, Aims McGuinness, and Steven C. McKay, 25–43. Bloomington: Indiana University Press, 2012.

Sidbury, James. *Becoming African in America: Race and Nation in the Early Black Atlantic*. Oxford: Oxford University Press, 2007.

Siemerling, Winfried. *The Black Atlantic Reconsidered: Black Canadian Writing, Cultural History, and the Presence of the Past*. Montreal: McGill-Queen's University Press, 2015.

Simoes da Silva, A. J. *The Luxury of Nationalist Despair: George Lamming's Fiction as Decolonizing Project*. Amsterdam: Rodopi, 2000.

Smith, Graham. *When Jim Crow Met John Bull: Black American Soldiers in World War II Britain*. 1987. New York: St. Martin's Press, 1988.

Smith, Jane I. *Islam in America*. 2nd ed. New York: Columbia University Press, 2010.

Smith, Zadie. *White Teeth*. New York: Vintage, 2000.

Sökefeld, Martin. "Mobilizing in Transnational Space: A Social Movement Approach to the Formation of Diaspora." *Global Networks* 6.3 (2006): 265–83.

Sollors, Werner. Introduction to *Interesting Narrative of the Life of Olaudah Equiano*. In Equiano, ix–xxxi.

Spitzer, Leo. Review of *The Loyal Blacks*, by Ellen Gibson Wilson, and *The Black Loyalists*, by James W. St. G. Walker. *American Historical Review* 82.4 (October 1977): 1066–67.

Stanford, Karin L., ed. *If We Must Die: African American Voices on War and Peace*. Lanham, Md.: Rowman and Littlefield, 2008.

Stasiulis, Daiva K., and Abigail B. Bakan. *Negotiating Citizenship: Migrant Women in Canada and the Global System*. 2003. Toronto: University of Toronto Press, 2005.

Stein, Mark. *Black British Literature: Novels of Transformation*. Columbus: Ohio State University Press, 2004.

Stephens, Michelle Ann. *Black Empire: The Masculine Global Imaginary of Caribbean Intellectuals in the United States, 1914–1962*. Durham, N.C.: Duke University Press, 2005.

Stepto, Robert B. *From Behind the Veil: A Study of Afro-American Narrative*. 2nd ed. Urbana: University of Illinois Press, 1991.

Storhoff, Gary. *Understanding Charles Johnson*. Columbia: University of South Carolina Press, 2004.

Stuckey, Sterling, and Joshua Leslie. "Aftermath: Captain Delano's Claim against Benito Cereno." *Modern Philology* 85.3 (February 1988): 265–87.

Sturrock, John. "Theory versus Autobiography." In *The Culture of Autobiography*, edited by Folkenflik, 21–37.

Sundquist, Eric J. "Frederick Douglass: Literacy and Paternalism." *Raritan* 6:2 (Fall 1986): 108–24.

———. *To Wake the Nations: Race in the Making of American Literature*. Cambridge, Mass.: Belknap Press of Harvard University Press, 1993.

Tanner, Tony. *Adultery in the Novel*. Baltimore: Johns Hopkins University Press, 1979.

Taylor, Eric Robert. *If We Must Die: Shipboard Insurrections in the Era of the Atlantic Slave Trade*. Baton Rouge: Louisiana State University Press, 2006.

Thaden, Barbara Z. "Charles Johnson's *Middle Passage* as Historiographic Metafiction." *College English* 59.7 (November 1997): 753–66.

Thiong'o, Ngũgĩ wa. "Freeing the Imagination: George Lamming's Aesthetics of Decolonization." *Transition* 100 (2009): 164–69.

Thomas, Deborah A. *Modern Blackness: Nationalism, Globalization, and the Politics of Culture in Jamaica*. Durham, N.C.: Duke University Press, 2004.

Thomas, Nigel G. "Cecil Foster's *Sleep on, Beloved*: A Depiction of the Consequences of Racism in Canadian Immigration Policy." *Journal of Black Studies* 38.3 (January 2008): 484–501.

Thornber, Karen L. "Early Twentieth-Century Intra-East Asian Literary Contact Nebulae: Censored Japanese Literature in Chinese and Korean." *Journal of Asian Studies* 68.3 (August 2009): 749–75.

Tölölyan, Khachig. "Restoring the Logic of the Sedentary to Diaspora Studies." In *Les diasporas: 2000 ans d'histoire*, edited by Lisa Anteby-Yemeni, William Berthomière, and Gabriel Sheffer, 137–48. Rennes, France: Presses Universitaires de Rennes, 2005.

Touré. *Who's Afraid of Post-Blackness: What It Means to Be Black Now*. New York: Free Press, 2011.

Trouillot, Michel-Rolph. *Silencing the Past: Power and the Production of History*. Boston: Beacon Press, 1995.

Turner, Richard Brent. *Islam in the African-American Experience*. Bloomington: Indiana University Press, 1997.

Twain, Mark. *Adventures of Huckleberry Finn*. 1884/1885. 3rd Norton ed. New York: Norton, 1999.

US Department of State. "Preliminary Articles of Peace," November 30, 1782. In *Treaties and Other International Acts of the United States of America*, vol. 2, edited by Hunter Miller, 96–107. Washington, D.C.: Government Printing Office, 1931.

Valkeakari, Tuire. "Between Camps: Paul Gilroy and the Dilemma of Race." In *Post-

National Enquiries: Essays on Ethnic and Racial Border Crossings, edited by Jopi Nyman, 8–29. Newcastle, England: Cambridge Scholars Publishing, 2009.

———. "Beyond the Riverside: War in Toni Morrison's Fiction." *Atlantic Literary Review* 4.1–2 (January–March and April–June 2003): 133–64.

———. "The Politics of Perception in Herman Melville's *Benito Cereno* and Charles Johnson's *Middle Passage*," *Studies in American Fiction* 33:2 (Autumn 2005): 229–50.

———. *Religious Idiom and the African American Novel, 1952–1998*. Gainesville: University Press of Florida, 2007.

Varela-Zapata, Jesús. "Translating One's Own Culture: Coming Back from the Metropolis in Caryl Phillips's *A State of Independence*." In *Translating Cultures*, edited by Isabel Carrera Suárez, Aurora García Fernández, and M. S. Suárez Lafuente, 397–406. Oviedo, Spain, and Hebden Bridge, England: KRK/Dangaroo, 1999.

Vedal, Lauren. "Immigrant Desire: Contesting Canadian Safety and Whiteness in Dionne Brand's *In Another Place, Not Here*." In *Race and Displacement*, edited by Marouan and Simmons, 69–81.

Visvis, Vikki. "Traumatic Forgetting and Spatial Consciousness in Dionne Brand's *In Another Place, Not Here*." *Mosaic: A Journal for the Interdisciplinary Study of Literature* 45:3 (September 2012): 115–31.

Walcott, Derek. *Midsummer*. New York: Farrar, Straus and Giroux, 1984.

Walcott, Rinaldo. "Towards a Methodology for Reading Hip Hop in Canada." In *Ebony Roots, Northern Soil: Perspectives on Blackness in Canada*, edited by Charmaine A. Nelson, 238–253. Newcastle, England: Cambridge Scholars Publishing, 2010.

Walker, James W. St. G. *The Black Loyalists: The Search for a Promised Land in Nova Scotia and Sierra Leone, 1783–1870.* 1976. Toronto: University of Toronto Press, 1992.

Walker, Margaret. *Jubilee*. 1966. Boston: Houghton Mifflin, 1999.

Walker, Rebecca, ed. *Black Cool: One Thousand Streams of Blackness*. Berkeley, Calif.: Soft Skull Press, 2012.

Walters, Wendy W. *Archives of the Black Atlantic: Reading between Literature and History*. New York: Routledge, 2013.

———. *At Home in Diaspora: Black International Writing*. Minneapolis: University of Minnesota Press, 2005.

Walvin, James. *Making the Black Atlantic: Britain and the African Diaspora*. London: Cassell, 2000.

Wambu, Onyekachi, ed. *Empire Windrush: Fifty Years of Writing about Black Britain*. London: Victor Gollancz, 1998.

Ward, Abigail. "'The Cloud of Ambivalence': Exploring Diasporan Identity in Caryl Phillips's *The Atlantic Sound* and *A New World Order*." In *Caryl Phillips*, edited by Ledent and Tunca, 191–212.

Warner-Lewis, Maureen. "Cultural Reconfigurations in the African Caribbean." In *The African Diaspora: African Origins and New World Identities*, edited by Isidore

Okpewho, Carole Boyce Davies, and Ali A. Mazrui, 19–27. Bloomington: Indiana University Press, 1999.

Watt, Ian. *The Rise of the Novel: Studies in Defoe, Richardson and Fielding*. Berkeley: University of California Press, 1957.

Webster, Jane. "The *Zong* in the Context of the Eighteenth-Century Slave Trade." *Journal of Legal History* 28.3 (December 2007): 285–98.

Wesling, Meg. "Neocolonialism, Queer Kinship, and Diaspora: Contesting the Romance of the Family in Shani Mootoo's *Cereus Blooms at Night* and Edwidge Danticat's *Breath, Eyes, Memory*." *Textual Practice* 25:4 (2011), 649–70.

Westheider, James E. *The African American Experience in Vietnam: Brothers in Arms*. Lanham, Md.: Rowman and Littlefield, 2008.

Wheat, Celeste. "Examining Colonialism and Exile in George Lamming's *In the Castle of My Skin* (1953), *The Emigrants* (1954), and *The Pleasures of Exile* (1960)." *Journal of Colonialism and Colonial History* 10.3 (Winter 2009). http://o-muse.jhu.edu.helin.uri.edu/journals/journal_of_colonialism_and_colonial_history/v010/10.3.wheat.html.

Whitehead, Anne. *Trauma Fiction*. Edinburgh: Edinburgh University Press, 2004.

Williams, William Carlos. *Spring and All*. Paris: Contact, 1923.

Wilson, Ellen Gibson. *John Clarkson and the African Adventure*. London: Macmillan, 1980.

———. *The Loyal Blacks*. New York: Capricorn Books, 1976.

Wilson, Ivy G. *Specters of Democracy: Blackness and the Aesthetics of Politics in the Antebellum U.S.* Oxford: Oxford University Press, 2011.

Wilson-Tagoe, Nana. *Historical Thought and Literary Representation in West Indian Literature*. Gainesville: University Press of Florida; Barbados: Press University of the West Indies; Oxford: James Currey, 1998.

Wimbush, Vincent L. "Reading Darkness, Reading Scriptures." In *African Americans and the Bible*, edited by Wimbush, 1–43.

———, ed. *African Americans and the Bible: Sacred Texts and Social Textures*. New York: Continuum, 2000.

Wood, Marcus. *Blind Memory: Visual Representations of Slavery in England and America 1780–1865*. New York: Routledge, 2000.

Woolf, Virginia. *Mrs. Dalloway*. 1925. New York: Harcourt, Brace and World, 1953.

Wordsworth, William. "I Wandered Lonely as a Cloud." In *Poems, in Two Volumes, and Other Poems, 1800–1807*, edited by Jared Curtis, 207–8. Ithaca: Cornell University Press, 1983.

Wright, Dale S. *Philosophical Meditations on Zen Buddhism*. Cambridge: Cambridge University Press, 1998.

Wright, Michelle M. *Becoming Black: Creating Identity in the African Diaspora*. Durham, N.C.: Duke University Press, 2004.

———. "Middle Passage Blackness and Its Diasporic Discontents: The Case for a Post-War Epistemology." In *Africa in Europe*, edited by Rosenhaft and Aitken, 217–33.

———. *Physics of Blackness: Beyond the Middle Passage Epistemology*. Minneapolis: University of Minnesota Press, 2015.

Wright, Richard. *Black Power: A Record of Reactions in a Land of Pathos*. New York: Harper, 1954.

———. Introduction to *In the Castle of My Skin* by George Lamming, v–viii. New York: McGraw-Hill, 1953.

———. *Outsider*. New York: Harper, 1953.

Wyrick, Deborah Baker. "Charles Johnson's Battle of the Books." *Postscript* 11 (1994): 1–9.

Young, James E. *At Memory's Edge: After-Images of the Holocaust in Contemporary Art and Architechture*. New Haven, Conn.: Yale University Press, 2000.

Zauditu-Selassie, K. *African Spiritual Traditions in the Novels of Toni Morrison*. Gainesville: University Press of Florida, 2009.

Index

Abolitionism, in *The Book of Negroes*, 1, 64–67, 69–70, 73, 90–91, 93, 95–96

Absurdism, 276n97, 276n105

Achebe, Chinua, 9

Adichie, Chimamanda Ngozi, 9

Africa, 5; black diasporic identity and, 21; in *The Book of Negroes*, 1, 63–65, 69, 71–72, 76–77, 84, 91–96, 229n2; in *Breath, Eyes, Memory*, 182, 219–20; imperial cartographies of, 81–83; Lamming in, 271n23; Liberia, founding of, 99; racial diversity in, 236n94; return and, 21–27; in *Sleep On, Beloved*, 181–82, 195–96; in *A State of Independence*, 181, 219–20. *See also* Ghana (Gold Coast); Mali; "Mother Africa"; Sierra Leone, in *The Book of Negroes*; Sierra Leone Company

African American fiction, as black diasporic fiction, 2–4. *See also The Bloodworth Orphans; Middle Passage; Sula; Tar Baby; There Is a Tree More Ancient than Eden*

African Americans, as members of the black Atlantic diaspora, 2

African Caribbean: diaspora as part of the black Atlantic diaspora, 2; identity as creolized Caribbean identity, 220; usage of, vii–viii. *See also* Barbados/Barbadian; *Breath, Eyes, Memory; The Emigrants; The Final Passage;* Haiti; *In the Castle of My Skin;* Jamaica; McKay, Claude; *Sleep On, Beloved; A State of Independence;* St. Kitts; *Tar Baby;* West Indian

African diasporas (black diasporas): Anglophone, 2, 7–9, 180; Dutch-speaking, 7, 232n44; Francophone, 8, 9, 112, 152, 180, 230n9, 232n44, 267n128, 276n101; Hispanophone, 7, 232n44; Lusophone, 7, 232n44; old and new, 2, 7–9. *See also* Black Atlantic diaspora (African Atlantic diaspora); Black diasporic identity formation, communal and individual; Black diasporic memory

Africanisms (African survivalisms), 21–22, 53

Africanist diasporic spirituality: in *Breath, Eyes, Memory*, 182, 219, 224; in *Sleep On, Beloved*, 194–200, 224, 284n92

Africanist turn, in scholarship, 22

Africanity (Africanness), 26–27

African Muslims in Antebellum America (Austin), 72

"Afro-American Fragment" (Hughes), 23–24

Afrocentrism, 22, 56, 236n96

Against Race (Gilroy), 11, 14, 32, 226

Alexander, Simone A. James, 209–10

Algeria, 267n128, 275n95, 289n215

Althusserianism, radicalization and, 19–20, 235n84

American Africans in Ghana (Gaines), 22

Anderson, Benedict, 4

Andrews, William L., 66

Anticolonialism, 3–4, 101, 140, 149–50, 270n12; in *Natives of My Person*, 135–36, 140–43

Anticosmopolitanism, 58–59

Antiessentialism. *See* Racial antiessentialism

Appadurai, Arjun, 4

Appiah, Kwame Anthony, 57; *Cosmopolitanism*, 58–59

Archives of the Black Atlantic (Walters), 29, 62, 230n9

322 · Index

At Home in Diaspora (Walters), 230n9
Atlantic slave trade, 1, 4, 15, 18, 21, 27, 36, 223; in *The Book of Negroes*, 64, 66–70, 72–76, 84, 92, 94–95, 223; as catalyst for black Atlantic diaspora, 4–5, 11–12, 35–36; in *Crossing the River*, 99–100, 102, 125, 127–28; in *Middle Passage*, 26–27, 36–42, 44, 48–53, 223. *See also* Abolitionism, in *The Book of Negroes*
At Memory's Edge (Young), 123
Austin, Allan D., 72, 252n52
"Autobiographical Notes" (Baldwin), 28

Bakan, Abigail B., 193–94
Baker, Houston A., Jr., 57, 96, 245n97, 261n26
Baldwin, James: "Autobiographical Notes," 28; "Nobody Knows My Name," 68–69
Ball, Clement, *Imagining London*, 132
Baraka, Amiri (LeRoi Jones), 13
Barbados/Barbadian, 4, 133, 146–48, 151–52, 154–55, 177–79, 190, 194, 203, 237n144, 274n75, 277n110, 279n159, 283n68
Baucom, Ian, *Out of Place*, 132, 270n4
Becoming African in America (Sidbury), 5
Becoming Black (Wright, M.), 5
Bedford, Simi, *Not With Silver*, 248n6
Being and Race (Johnson, C.), 43
Beloved (Morrison), 74, 107, 110, 113, 118, 129, 205, 235n74
Benesch, Klaus, 11–12
Benito Cereno (Melville), 36–37, 239n20; Delano in, 40–41, 241n36; *Middle Passage* and, 37–42; *Narrative of Voyages and Travels* and, 39–40; perception in, 37–42; transformation in, 41
ben Solomon, Job. *See* Diallo, Ayuba Suleiman
Berlin, Ira, 63, 234n74
The Big Sea (Hughes), 23
Black agency, diaspora-making and, 19, 138
Black Arts movement, 56, 236n96
The Black Atlantic (Gilroy), 12–13, 127–28; criticisms of, 157, 232n44; gender in, 157; *Middle Passage* and, 34–35; slave-ship in, 34–35
Black Atlantic diaspora (African Atlantic diaspora): colonialism, imperialism, slavery, and slave trade as catalysts for, 4–5, 11–12, 35–36; old Anglophone, definition of, 2. *See also* African diasporas (black diasporas)
Black Britishness, 131–33, 167, 173–75; Gilroy on, 131
Black Canadians, 2; diasporic culture and, 191, 202–3
Black diasporas. *See* African diasporas (black diasporas)
Black diasporic fiction, Anglophone, 3, 230n9
Black diasporic identity formation, communal and individual, 3–6, 222–23
Black diasporic memory, 2–3. *See also* Collective memory
Black Empire (Stephens), 8, 139, 166
Black Loyalists, in *The Book of Negroes*, 63–64; Dunmore's proclamation, 85–87; evacuation of, 86–87; in Nova Scotia, 63, 88–91; in Sierra Leone, 1, 63–64, 84, 91–96
The Black Loyalists (Walker, J.), 63–64, 85, 87, 91, 248n9, 256n145
Blackness, 5, 9, 18–21. *See also* Racial antiessentialism; *Sula*; *Tar Baby*
Black Power (Wright, R.), 23
Black Power movement, 56
Black Skin, White Masks (Fanon), 153–54, 277n111
Black Subjects (Keizer), 18, 97, 259n205
Black Women, Writing, and Identity (Davies), 190, 204, 210–11
The Bloodworth Orphans (Forrest), 128
The Bluest Eye (Morrison), 110
Bodies That Matter (Butler), 19–20
Boehmer, Elleke, 149
"Book of Negroes," 1, 87, 247n2
The Book of Negroes (Hill), 1, 30–31, 229n2; abolitionism in, 1, 64–67, 69–70, 73, 90–91, 93, 95–96; Africa in, 65, 76–77, 91–96; American Revolutionary War in, 83–87; Black Loyalism in, 1, 63–64, 84–96; circum-Atlantic perspective in, 62–63; freedom in, 64, 66, 70, 77, 79, 81–90, 92, 94–95, 98; gender in, 65, 70–72, 86, 97; historical accuracy and, 96–97, 258n197, 258nn199–200; "home" in, 1, 94–96, 98; imperialism in, 81–83; *Interesting Narrative* and, 66, 69–70, 72–73, 93, 97; Judaism in, 79–80; language as motif in, 77, 253n84; literacy in, 78–81; *Middle Passage* and,

97, 248n13; Middle Passage narrative in, 72–74; midwifery in, 71, 74, 84; religion in, 70–72, 75, 77, 78–81, 93; sexual violence in, 72–73, 78; slave market in, 76; slavery in, 3, 68–69, 78–81, 95; slave-ship in, 73, 251n45; title, 1, 87, 247n2
Bouson, J. Brooks, 106
Brand, Dionne, 15, 225; *In Another Place, Not Here*, 179–80; *A Map to the Door of No Return: Notes to Belonging*, 15, 225
Braziel, Jana Evans, 10
Breath, Eyes, Memory (Danticat), 3, 9, 204–19; Africa in, 182, 219–20; community in, 207–8; daffodil imagery in, 209–10; Duvalier regime in, 204, 206–11; food in, 208; gender in, 204, 206, 211–13; "home" in, 210–11, 216; intergenerational reconciliation in, 206–7, 212–14; land in, 208–10, 212, 214–17; return narratives in, 180–81, 212–16; sexual violence in, 206, 209, 212–13, 215, 286n147; *Sleep On, Beloved* and, 214
Britain: Atlantic slave trade and, 85; as empire and post-empire, 131; history of black people in, 131, 229n4; Mckay on, 133–35; post–World War II anti-immigration rhetoric, 144. *See also* Anticolonialism; Black Britishness; British Nationality Act (1948); *The Emigrants*; *The Final Passage*; *Natives of My Person*; *Small Island*; Windrush moment
British Nationality Act (1948), 133, 143–44, 171
Brown, J. Dillon, 136, 183, 186–89, 272n28, 272n158, 279n158
Brown Girl, Brownstones (Marshall), 178–79
Brubaker, Rogers, "The 'Diaspora' Diaspora," 231n29
Buddhism, 36–37; Johnson, C., and, 44, 240n25, 242n55, 242n57, 243n64; in *Middle Passage*, 43–47, 55
Bugg, John, 250n40
Butler, Judith, 101; *Bodies That Matter*, 19–20
Byrd, Rudolph P., 35–36, 243n80

Cambridge (Phillips, C.), 125–26, 139, 271n23
Campt, Tina, 11, 160
Camus, Albert, 205, 275n97; *The Stranger*, 152–53, 275n87, 275n95, 276n105

Canada: Canadian-based African Caribbean identity and black Canadian identity in *Sleep On, Beloved*, 190–92, 202–4; Caribana festival, 191, 202–3; Caribbean domestic workers in, 192–94; FDM, 192–94; LCP, 192–93; policy of multiculturalism in, 191; slavery in, 88. *See also* Black Canadians; Black Loyalists, in *The Book of Negroes*; Foster, Cecil; Hill, Lawrence; Methodism; Nova Scotia; *Sleep On, Beloved*; Spiritual Baptist Church, in *Sleep On, Beloved*
Canvas Town, New York City, 83–84, 254n115
Carby, Hazel, 56, 64, 74, 132, 138, 251n46; on African Caribbean diasporic intellectuals' critique of colonialism, 270n12; on black troops in Britain during World War II, 138, 168; on British Nationality Act (1948), 144, 171; on Equiano and racialization, 19; on Equiano's lost sister, 251n46
Caribbean identity as creolized identity, 220. *See also* African Caribbean; Barbados/Barbadian; *Breath, Eyes, Memory*; *The Emigrants*; *The Final Passage*; Haiti; *In the Castle of My Skin*; Jamaica; McKay, Claude; *Sleep On, Beloved*; *A State of Independence*; St. Kitts; *Tar Baby*; West Indian
Carretta, Vincent, 85, 250n40, 255n134
Cartography and maps, literal and metaphorical, 116, 140, 170, 177, 197, 225; in *The Book of Negroes*, 79, 81–83
Caruth, Cathy, 16, 31, 102; *Literature in the Ashes of History*, 107; *Unclaimed Experience*, 122–23
Castle, Terry, 29
Charles Johnson in Context (Selzer), 57–58
Cheyette, Brian, 98
Children, as motif in black diasporic literature: adopted, 172–75, 204; biracial, 127, 172–75. *See also* Family formation, as symbolic of diasporic community formation in host society; "Mother Africa"; Orphanhood, as metaphor for diasporic condition
Clarke, George Elliott, 248n6
Clarkson, John, 66, 90–93, 95, 257n171
Clifford, James, 12, 33, 218
"Close Ranks" (Du Bois), 104–5
Cohen, Robin: *Global Diasporas*, 10, 232n43; on phases of diaspora studies, 10

Collective memory: in *Crossing the River*, 127–28; cultural mediation of, 2–3, 16–17, 229n8; Eyerman on, 16–17

Colonialism, 9, 49, 95, 124, 145–46; British, 132–36, 146–47, 149–50; as catalyst for black Atlantic diaspora, 4–5, 11–12, 35–36; French, 137, 152, 275n95; French existentialism and, 137, 152, 275n95; neocolonialism, 186–88, 192–93. *See also* Anticolonialism; *Natives of My Person*

Connective diasporas, 80, 124, 268n158

Conner, Marc C., 36

Contact nebulae, Thornber on, 150–51, 275n91

Contact zones, Pratt on, 137, 150–51

Cosmopolitanism, 27–28; anticosmopolitanism, 58–59; diasporic consciousness and, 28, 57–59; in *Middle Passage*, 57–59; partial, 58–59, 246n137; Stoic, 58

Cosmopolitanism (Appiah), 58–59

Create Dangerously (Danticat), 204–5, 214, 217, 286n149

Crossing the River (Phillips, C.), 3, 31; African American soldiers in, 6–7, 100–101, 123–28; collective memory in, 127; displacement in, 125; interracial marriage in, 126; Middle Passage in, 124–25; orphanhood in, 127–28; trauma in, 99–100

"Crossing the river" trope, as Middle Passage reference, 103; in *Sula*, 107–9

Cultural hybridity, 12, 20

Cultural Trauma (Eyerman), 16–17, 234n69

Daenzer, Patricia M., 192–93

D'Aguiar, Fred, 18

Dalleo, Raphael, 267n121

Dalton, Harlon L., 14

Danticat, Edwidge, 7; *Create Dangerously*, 204–5, 214, 217, 286n149; on Haitian heritage, 217–18; on immigrant artists, 217, 289n215; on immigrant identity, 27, 218. See also *Breath, Eyes, Memory*

Davies, Carol Boyce, *Black Women, Writing, and Identity*, 190, 204, 210–11

Dawson, Ashley, 139

Dayal, Samir, on diasporic double consciousness, 7, 230n20

Defoe, Daniel, 28–29

Delano, Amasa: in *Benito Cereno*, 40–41, 241n36; *Narrative of Voyages and Travels*, 39–40

Derrida, Jacques, 107

Diallo, Ayuba Suleiman (Job ben Solomon), 68, 249n30, 250n33

Diaspora: concepts of, 2, 6, 10–12, 231n29; cosmopolitanism and, 28, 57–58; empire/imperialism and, 10–11, 131–37, 139–47, 150, 155, 158, 161–64, 171–72, 175; globalization and, 11–12; Jewish, 2, 10, 78–80, 124, 232n43, 268n158; phases of scholarship on, 10; queer, 286n149; war and, 31, 100–103, 122–25, 129–30. *See also* African diasporas (black diasporas); Black Atlantic diaspora (African Atlantic diaspora); Black diasporic identity formation, communal and individual; Black diasporic memory; Connective diasporas; Diaspora citizenship; Diaspora making; Diasporic double consciousness; Diasporic horizon; Diasporic religion, Johnson, P. C., on; Displacement; Victim diaspora

Diaspora citizenship, 7

Diaspora Conversions (Johnson, P. C.), 223–24

"The 'Diaspora' Diaspora" (Brubaker), 231n29

Diaspora making: black agency and, 19, 138; Guridy on, 19, 138

Diasporas (Dufoix), 231n29

Diasporas of the Mind (Cheyette), 98

Diasporic double consciousness, 7, 82, 230n20

Diasporic horizon, 224

Diasporic religion, Johnson, P. C., on, 196–97, 224

Díaz, Junot, 9

Diedrich, Maria, 33, 99–100

Diop, Cheikh Anta, 236n96

Displacement: diaspora and, 6–7, 11, 31; war and, 100

A Distant Shore (Phillips, C.), 124, 225–26

Domestic workers, Caribbean, 192–94, 198–99

Double consciousness: diasporic, 7, 82, 230n20; DuBois on, 230n20, 277n111

Douglass, Frederick, 66–67, 253n87

Dryden, Linda, 155

Dubois, Laurent, 208, 286n141

Du Bois, W.E.B., 7, 44, 154, 235n92; "Close

Ranks," 104–5; *The Souls of Black Folk*, 104, 230n20, 277n111
Dufoix, Stéphane, *Diasporas*, 231n29
Duncan, Carol B., 196, 198, 284n82, 284n92, 286n111
Dunlap, William, 83

Education: cultural mediation and, 3, 16, 134, 146; as motif in *The Book of Negroes*, 77–82
Edwards, Brent Hayes: *The Practice of Diaspora*, 13; "The Uses of 'Diaspora,'" 21, 59
Eliot, T. S., 29, 151; "Little Gidding," 140, 164
Ellison, Ralph, 151; *Invisible Man*, 38–39, 65, 239n18, 239n20, 240nn29–31
The Emigrants (Lamming), 3, 27, 31, 133, 143–50, 225–26; African Caribbean diaspora in, 138; "Another Time," 148; "A Voyage," 144–45, 148; existentialism and, 137, 150–56; gender and, 157–59; migrants in, 147; nothingness in, 153; "Rooms and Residents," 147–48; *Small Island* and, 171; *The Stranger* and, 152–53, 276n105
Empire/imperialism: diaspora and, 10–11, 131–37, 139–47, 150, 155, 158, 161–64, 171–72, 175; neo-empire, 116–17
Engels, Friedrich, 46
Equiano, Olaudah, 11, 19, 51, 66, 69–73, 90–91, 93, 97, 235n82, 239n20, 244n95, 245n97, 250n40, 251nn45–46, 252n66, 253n90. See also *Interesting Narrative*
Ethnocultural heritage, race and, 14
The European Tribe (Phillips, C.), 17
Exile literature, as distinct from immigrant literature, 27
Eyerman, Ron, 16–17, 234n69

Fabre, Geneviève, 11–12, 74
Family formation, as symbolic of diasporic community formation in host society, 165–77, 203–4, 218. See also Children, as motif in black diasporic literature; "Mother Africa"; Orphanhood, as metaphor for diasporic condition
Fanon, Frantz, 275n95; *Black Skin, White Masks*, 153–54, 277n111
Fassin, Didier, 114, 129
FDM. See Foreign Domestic Movement program

Feeding the Ghosts (D'Aguiar), 18
Feminism/feminist, black, 97, 207
The Final Passage (Phillips, C.), 3, 31, 133, 279n158; African Caribbean diaspora in, 138; gender in, 137, 160–65; mother country in, 164–65; sections of, 160–61
Folkenflik, Robert, 70
Forbes, Curdella: on Lamming, Selvon, and gender, 157; *From Nation to Diaspora*, 157
Foreign Domestic Movement program (FDM), 192–94
Forging Diaspora (Guridy), 19
Forrest, Leon, 101, 115, 128
Foster, Cecil, 283n68; on multiculturalism, 191. See also *Sleep On, Beloved*
Foucault, Michel, 23, 64
Francis, Donette A., 206, 211–12
Frazier, E. Franklin, 21–22; Herskovits and, 21–22, 236n93; *The Negro Church in America*, 236n92
Freedom Struggles (Lentz-Smith), 104
French existentialism: *The Emigrants* and, 137, 150–56; Lamming on, 151, 275n87; Wright, R., and, 150, 275n87. See also Camus, Albert; Sartre, Jean-Paul
Frey, Sylvia R., 63
From Nation to Diaspora (Forbes), 157
Fryer, Peter, *Staying Power*, 131–32, 229n4
Fyfe, Christopher, 257n176, 257n180, 257nn170–71

Gaines, Kevin, 22
Garvey, Marcus, 22
Gates, Henry Louis, Jr., 33, 57, 100, 245n102, 249n30
Gender: in *The Black Atlantic*, 157; in *The Book of Negroes*, 70–72, 86, 97; in *Breath, Eyes, Memory*, 204, 206, 211–13; in Caribbean societies, 161; diaspora and, 11; in *The Emigrants*, 157–59; in *The Final Passage*, 137, 160–65; *Middle Passage* and, 97, 259n205; mother country as gendered concept/motif, 130, 162–65, 170–71, 270n11; Phillips, C., on, 161–62; Powell, P., on, 161; in *Small Island*, 137, 166. See also Feminism/feminist, black; Masculinism/masculinist
The Generation of Postmemory (Hirsch), 123–24

Geography, African diasporas and, 2, 7–9
George and Rue (Clarke), 248n6
Ghana (Gold Coast), 22–24, 58, 149, 219, 237n114, 272n23
Ghosts, in trauma novel, 110
Gikandi, Simon, 136, 164, 279n161; on Gilroy, 34–35; *Maps of Englishness*, 132, 270n4
Gilroy, Paul, 7, 226; *Against Race*, 11, 32; *The Black Atlantic*, 12–13, 34–35, 127–28, 157, 232n44; on diaspora, 21; on gender, 157; *Postcolonial Melancholia*, 138–39; on racial antiessentialism, 12–14, 260n9; *There Ain't No Black in the Union Jack*, 131
Global Diasporas (Cohen), 10
Globalization, diaspora and, 11–12
Great Migration, 6
Griffin, Farah, 127
Griswold, Wendy, 150
"Guinea": in *The Book of Negroes*, 81–82; in *Breath, Eyes, Memory*, 182, 219–20, 224
Guridy, Frank A.: on diaspora making, 19, 138; *Forging Diaspora*, 19, 138

Haiti: in *Breath, Eyes, Memory*, 180, 204–19; Ceremony of Souls, 151; Danticat on, 217–18; diaspora/*Dyaspora*, 217–18; Dubois on, 205, 208, 286n141; Duvalier regime, 204, 206, 211; earthquake (2010), 204–6, 214, 216–17, 286n141; Revolution, 23, 39–40, 150
Halbwachs, Maurice, 16, 234n69
Haley, Alex, *Roots*, 68, 234n74, 250n31
Hall, Stuart, 12, 64, 157, 235n84; "Cultural Identity and Diaspora," 20; "Negotiating Caribbean Identities," 21, 23–24
Hartman, Saidiya, *Lose Your Mother*, 23–25, 64, 220, 234n74, 237n97
Haunting, in trauma novel, 110
Hegel, G.W.F., 153–54, 277n111; *Lectures on the Philosophy of World History*, 146, 274n67, 279n159
Herskovits, Melville J.: Frazier and, 21–22, 236n93; *The Myth of the Negro Past*, 22
Hill, Lawrence, 247n1; on historical accuracy, 96–97, 258n197, 258n199; *The Illegal*, 226, 247n1; Islam and, 250n32. See also *The Book of Negroes*; Mali
Hirsch, Marianne, 123–24

Historical accuracy: Hill on, 96–97, 258n197, 258n199; of *Interesting Narrative*, 250n40
Historical fiction, 28–30
History to Theory (Klein), 16
Holloway, Joseph E., 236nn92–93
Holocaust studies, 17, 102, 123, 268n158
hooks, bell, 57
Hughes, Langston: "Afro-American Fragment," 23–24; *The Big Sea*, 23; "I, Too," 105

"I, Too" (Hughes), 105
Identity: black British, 173; black diasporic memory and, 33; Caribbean, 203, 220; family and, 165–74; gender and, 71; name and, 67; in *Small Island*, 165–74; in *Song of Solomon*, 67; transnational, 3; trauma and, 114; West Indian, 148. See also Black diasporic identity formation, communal and individual
"If We Must Die" (McKay), 105
Imaginary, African diasporic, 2
Imagined communities, 4
Imagining London (Ball), 132
Immigrant literature, 27
Imperialism. See Empire/imperialism
In Another Place, Not Here (Brand), 179–80
Indian Removal Act, 243n81
In the Castle of My Skin (Lamming), 146, 150, 279n159
Interbeing, 242n62
Interesting Narrative (Equiano), 19, 97, 251n46; *The Book of Negroes* and, 66, 69–70, 72–73, 93, 97; historical accuracy of, 250n40; Middle Passage and, 51; Middle Passage in, 73
Interracial relationships, 126, 172, 269n166
In the Falling Snow (Phillips, C.), 175
Invisible Man (Ellison), 38, 240n29; *Middle Passage* and, 240n30
Islam/Muslims: in *The Book of Negroes*, 65–68, 72, 75, 79–80, 93; Hill and, 250n32; in *Roots*, 68, 250n31

Jackson, Andrew, 40, 243n81
Jamaica: gender roles in, 161; Powell, P., on, 161; RAF volunteers in World War II, 168, 170–71; *Sleep On, Beloved* and, 190–204; *Small Island* and, 169–70. See also McKay, Claude

James, C.L.R., 140, 149–50, 273n42
Jasanoff, Maya, 63, 85–86
Jazz (Morrison), 6, 114
Jewish diaspora, 2, 10, 78–80, 124, 232n43, 268n158
Johnson, Charles: *Being and Race*, 43; Buddhism and, 44, 240n25, 242n55, 242n57, 243n64; on diaspora, 55–57; on Ellison, 38–39; on Melville, 39; "Novelists of Memory," 34, 56, 245n124; "Philosophy and Black Fiction," 45–46, 56; on racial antiessentialism, 55–57; *Turning the Wheel*, 44, 48. See also *Middle Passage*
Johnson, Paul C., 196; *Diaspora Conversions*, 223–24
Jones, LeRoi (Amiri Baraka), 13

Karenga, Maulana, 22
Keizer, Arlene R., *Black Subjects*, 18, 97, 259n205
Khan, Aisha: on diaspora as literal and symbolic community formation, 2; on diaspora as uprootedness, 15, 224; on distinction between diaspora and migration, 15
King, Martin Luther, Jr., 44
Klein, Kerwin Lee, 16, 146, 229n8, 268n155
Kline, Nancy, 67
Koser, Khalid, 9
Kreyòl, 9
Krumholz, Linda, 117, 267n124
Kwanzaa, 22

LaCapra, Dominick, 129–30
Lamming, George: in Africa, 271n23; on African diaspora, 136, 139; on African diasporic consciousness, 149–50; on French existentialism, 151, 275n87; on imperialism, 140; *In the Castle of My Skin*, 146, 150, 279n159; Phillips, C., and, 140–41, 273n42; *The Pleasures of Exile*, 136; scholarship on, 136–37, 272n25, 272nn27–29; Wright, R., and, 150. See also *The Emigrants*; *Natives of My Person*
Land, in *Breath, Eyes, Memory*, 208–10, 212, 214–17
LCP. *See* Live-In Caregiver Program
Lectures on the Philosophy of World History (Hegel), 146, 274n67, 279n159
Legba's Crossing (Russell), 230n9

Lentz-Smith, Adriane, 104
Levy, Andrea: on black Englishness as Englishness, 167; father as *Windrush* passenger, 138; *The Long Song*, 136; on parents' lives in England, 270n11. See also *Small Island*
Liberia, founding of, 99
Lifton, Robert Jay, 113–14
Literacy, freedom and, 66, 77, 82, 238n6, 249n22
Literature in the Ashes of History (Caruth), 107
Little, Jonathan, 43–44
Live-In Caregiver Program (LCP), 192–93
The Lonely Londoners (Selvon), 174, 225–26, 271n22
The Long Song (Levy), 136
A Long Way from Home (McKay), 149, 271n20
Lose Your Mother (Hartman), 23–25, 64, 220, 234n74, 237n97
The Loyal Blacks (Wilson), 63, 254n114, 256n146, 257n173
Luckhurst, Roger: on trauma fiction, 109–10; *The Trauma Question*, 107, 109–11, 114, 262n28

Making the Black Atlantic (Walvin), 88
Mali: in *The Book of Negroes*, 1, 229n2; Hill as international volunteer in, 250n32
Manning, Patrick, 226
Mannur, Anita, 10
Maps. *See* Cartography and maps, literal and metaphorical
Maps of Englishness (Gikandi), 132, 270n4
A Map to the Door of No Return (Brand), 15, 225
Mardorossian, Carine M., 213, 283n64, 289n228
Marshall, Paule: *Brown Girl, Brownstones*, 178–79; *Praisesong for the Widow*, 178
Masculinism/masculinist, 11, 137, 157, 160, 161
Master-slave dialectic, 150, 277n111
McKay, Claude: *Banana Bottom*, 177–78; on Britishness, 135, 272n20; "If We Must Die," 105; "I Shall Return," 177; *A Long Way from Home*, 135, 149, 271n20; *My Green Hills of Jamaica*, 177–78; on nationalism and transnationalism, 135; "Old England," 133–34; "To a Friend," 177
McLeod, John, 174

Melville, Herman: *Benito Cereno*, 36–42, 239n20; Johnson, C., on, 39; *Moby-Dick*, 49

Memory studies, in the humanities, 102, 123, 229n8

Methodism: in *The Book of Negroes*, 89–90; Moses Wilkinson and Black Loyalists in Nova Scotia, 89–90

Middle Passage, 238n1; in African American history, 22; black diasporic identity and, 5–6; in *The Book of Negroes*, 72–74; in *Cambridge*, 139; in *Crossing the River*, 124–25; in *The Emigrants*, 144–45; epistemology, 18–21, 60; in *In Another Place, Not Here*, 179; in *Interesting Narrative*, 73; in *Natives of My Person*, 141; Phillips, C., on, 125; in *Praisesong for the Widow*, 178; sensibility, 99–100; slave-ship dance, 73–74; in *Sula*, 129; in *Tar Baby*, 112, 114, 129; terror and, 50; transnational identity and, 3

Middle Passage (Johnson, C.), 3, 30, 32; Atlantic slave trade in, 36, 49–50; *Benito Cereno* and, 37–42; *The Black Atlantic* and, 34–35; *The Book of Negroes* and, 97, 248n13; Buddhism in, 43–47, 55; cosmopolitanism and, 57–59; diasporic existence as continuing journey in, 53–55; dualism and, 244n92; gender and, 97, 259n205; humor in, 239n18; *Interesting Narrative* and, 51; intertextual sources, 39; *Invisible Man* and, 240n30; narrative of diasporic subjectivity in, 34; perception in, 36–46, 49, 51–52; phenomenology in, 43–46; slavery in, 4, 46–48; slave-ship in, 35, 37–38, 48–49; transformation in, 36, 38, 41–42, 45, 50

Middle Path (Middle Way): in Buddhism, 44–45; in *Middle Passage*, 45

Midsummer (Walcott, D.), 177, 225

"Mobilizing in Transnational Space" (Sökefeld), 4–5

Moby-Dick (Melville), 49

Modernism, 137, 164–65, 246n139, 272n28

Modernity, 2, 5–6, 12, 19, 30–31, 34–35, 70, 96–97, 101–3, 105, 107, 109, 128–29, 131, 137, 164–65, 279n161

Modernity at Large (Appadurai), 4

Morrison, Toni: *Beloved*, 74, 107, 110, 113, 118, 129, 205, 235n74; *The Bluest Eye*, 110; *Jazz*, 6, 114; *Song of Solomon*, 24–25, 67; trauma fiction, 110; "Unspeakable Things Unspoken," 105; war motif, 260n4, 261n26. See also *Sula*; *Tar Baby*

"Mother Africa," 23, 25, 29, 182, 195–96, 219–20, 224, 237n97. See also Orphanhood, as metaphor for diasporic condition

Mother country, (England/Britain) as gendered concept/motif, 133, 270n11; in *The Final Passage*, 162–65; in *Small Island*, 170–71

Multiculturalism, Canadian policy of, 191

Multidirectional Memory (Rothberg), 268n158

Muños-Valdivieso, Sofía, 173

Munro, Martin, 204

The Myth of the Negro Past (Herskovits), 22

Nair, Supriya, 136, 156

Narrative of Voyages and Travels (Delano), 39–40

Narrative Projections of a Black British History (Pirker), 133

Natives of My Person (Lamming): captured Africans in, 142; critique of colonialism and imperialism in, 135–36, 140–43; gender in, 143; modified Middle Passage motif in, 141; Phillips, C., on, 140

Ndibe, Okey, 9

The Negro Church in America (Frazier), 236n92

Neo-empire, 116–17, 186–88

Neo-slave narrative: *The Book of Negroes* as, 30, 62, 75, 77, 79, 97; *Jubilee* as, 234n74; *Middle Passage* as, 35, 238n6; Rushdy on, 68. See also *Beloved*; *Roots*

New Negro, 105–6, 261n24

Nhat Hahn, Thich, 44, 242n62

Nkrumah, Kwame, 22–23

"Nobody Knows My Name" (Baldwin), 68–69

Nora, Pierre, 216

Nothingness, in Sartrean existentialism and *The Emigrants*, 153, 276n106

Not With Silver (Bedford), 248n6

Nova Scotia: as Black Loyalists' destination in *The Book of Negroes*, 63, 88–91; slavery in, 88

"Novelists of Memory" (Johnson, C.), 34, 56, 245n124

Nyman, Jopi, 270n6, 282n62

Objectification, 155, 209, 277n110; racial and sexual, 159
O'Keefe, Vincent A., 49
Oral tradition/storytelling, in *Breath, Eyes, Memory*, 206, 209, 214–16, 287n165
Origins, of African diaspora/diasporans, 3, 10–12, 15, 22, 25, 32, 36, 53, 69, 76–77, 105, 175, 177, 196, 219, 222; Edwards on, 13, 21, 59; Gilroy on, 11–12, 36
Orphanhood, as metaphor for diasporic condition, 29, 127–28. *See also* "Mother Africa"
Out of Place (Baucom), 132
Owen, Chandler, 105

Paquet, Sandra Pouchet, 117–18, 120, 136, 145, 178, 274n61
Paris Peace Treaty (1783), 86–87; Provisional (1782), 86–87
Paul, Kathleen, *Whitewashing Britain*, 143–44
Pedersen, Carl, 33, 100
Perception: in *Benito Cereno*, 37–42; characteristics of, 38; in *Middle Passage*, 36–46, 49, 51–52; phenomenology and, 43
Peters, Thomas, 90–91, 93, 257n173, 258n199
Phenomenology: Husserlian, 43; in *Middle Passage*, 43–46; perception and, 43
Phillips, Caryl, 237n114; *The Atlantic Sound*, 271n33; *Cambridge*, 125–26, 139–40, 271n23; on C.L.R. James, Lamming, and Selvon, 140, 273n42; connective diasporas and, 124, 268n158; *A Distant Shore*, 124, 225–26; *The European Tribe*, 17; on exile and migrancy, 27; *Foreigners*, 124, 226; on gender in Caribbean societies, 161–62; *Higher Ground*, 124; influences, 273n42; *In the Falling Snow*, 175; *The Lost Child*, 124; modernism and, 164–65, 189, 278n144; *The Nature of Blood*, 124; *The New World Order*, 271n23; on old and new African Diasporas, 124; "Water," 125, 127, 130. *See also Crossing the River*; *The Final Passage*; *A State of Independence*
Phillips, Mike and Trevor, 132–33
"Philosophy and Black Fiction" (Johnson, C.), 45–46, 57
Pirker, Eva Ulrike, 133
Planetary humanism, Gilroy on, 32
The Pleasures of Exile (Lamming), 136; Phillips, C., on, 140

Pocomania (Pukumina), 182, 284n92; in *Sleep On, Beloved*, 194–200, 224, 284n92
Postmemory, 123–24
Posttraumatic stress disorder (PTSD), 102, 262n28; definition, 265n92; in *Sula*, 102–3, 105–11; in *Tar Baby*, 113–14; trauma fiction and, 110; Vietnam War and, 114
Powell, Enoch, "Rivers of Blood" speech, 144, 274n59
Powell, Patricia, "A Search for Caribbean Masculinities," 161
The Practice of Diaspora (Edwards), 13
Praisesong for the Widow (Marshall), 178
Pratt, Mary Louise, on contact zones, 137, 150
Procter, James, 133, 136, 272n27
PTSD. *See* Posttraumatic stress disorder
Pybus, Cassandra, 63, 86, 255n135

Queer diaspora, 286n149

Race: in Africa, 236m94; relation to racism in the West, 234n60. *See also* Althusserianism, radialization and; Blackness; Racial antiessentialism; Racism; Whiteness studies
Racial antiessentialism, 12–16, 223; Gilroy on, 12–14, 260n9; in *Middle Passage*, 55–57
Racism, 4, 9, 12, 14, 18–19, 56, 60, 68, 133–35, 138–39, 144–45, 169–70, 234n60, 241n37, 260n9, 271n20, 277n111
Rahbek, Ulla, 189
Randolph, Asa Philip, 105
Rechtman, Richard, 114, 129
Recognition, dialectic of, 19, 52, 152–55, 276n105, 277nn110–11
Rediker, Marcus, 56
Religion. *See* Africanist diasporic spirituality; Buddhism; Diasporic religion, Johnson, P. C., on; Islam/Muslims; Methodism; Pocomania (Pukumina); Spiritual Baptist Church, in *Sleep On, Beloved*
Return to Africa/Africanity, 21–27; in *The Book of Negroes*, 1, 81–82, 91–95, 98; Hartman on, 23–25; in *Middle Passage*, 26–27, 53–54
Revolutionary War, American, 2, 47, 63, 86–87; slavery and, 85–87. *See also* Black Loyalists, in *The Book of Negroes*; Paris Peace Treaty (1783)
Rice, Alan, 125, 169

Roots (Haley), 68, 234n74, 250n31
Rothberg, Michael, on multidirectional collective memory, 268n158
Rough Crossings (Schama), 63, 85, 88, 91, 254n114, 254n121, 255n127, 255n131, 255n134
Rumbaut, Rubén G., 181, 231n27
Rushdy, Ashraf H. A., 68, 238n6
Russell, Heather, 230n9

Sáez, Elena Machado, on *A State of Independence*, 182–83, 188
Sagawa, Jessie, 76–77
Sartre, Jean-Paul, 150–54, 240n25, 272n29, 275n87, 275n95, 276n105, 277nn110–11
Saunders, Kay, 161, 186
Schama, Simon, *Rough Crossings*, 63, 85, 88, 91, 254n114, 254n121, 255n127, 255n131, 255n134
Schreiber, Evelyn Jaffe, 114, 116
Selvon, Sam(uel), 137, 147, 149, 157, 174, 273n42; *The Lonely Londoners*, 174, 225–26, 271n22
Selzer, Linda Furgerson, 57–58
Sexual violence: in *The Book of Negroes*, 72–73, 78; in *Breath, Eyes, Memory*, 206, 209, 212–13, 215, 286n147; slavery and, 78
Sharpe, Jenny, 112–13
Sidbury, James, 5
Siemerling, Winfried, 62, 229n2, 249n19
Sierra Leone, in *The Book of Negroes*, 1, 63–64, 69, 71, 84, 91–96
Sierra Leone Company, 90–91, 93–94, 248n9, 257n173
Silencing the Past (Trouillot), 23, 40, 64
Slave market, in *The Book of Negroes*, 76
Slave narratives, 66–67; neo-slave narratives, 35, 68, 238n6
Slavery: American Revolutionary War and, 85–87; black Atlantic diaspora and, 4; black diasporic identity and, 5–6; in *The Book of Negroes*, 3, 68–69, 78–81, 95; collective memory and, 15, 17, 234n74; cultural mediation and, 17; in *Middle Passage*, 46–48; religious slaveholders and, 79; urban, 253n87. See also Abolitionism, in *The Book of Negroes*; Atlantic slave trade
The Slave Ship (Rediker), 56
Slave-ships, 34–35; in *The Book of Negroes*, 73, 251n45; in *Middle Passage*, 35, 37–38, 48–49;
sexual exploitation of African women on, 73; *Tryal* insurrection, 39
Sleep On, Beloved (Foster), 3, 190–204; Africa in, 181–82, 221; *Breath, Eyes, Memory* and, 214; Canadian-based African Caribbean identity and black Canadian identity in, 190–92, 202–4; Caribana festival, 191, 202–3; domestic worker narrative in, 192–94; Pocomania (Pukumina) in, 194–200, 224, 284n92; return narratives in, 180–81, 195–96; Spiritual Baptist Church in, 198–99, 284n82
Small Island (Levy), 3, 31, 133; adoption narrative in, 172–75, 204; African Caribbean diaspora in, 138; biracial child in, 172–75, 204; *The Emigrants* and, 168, 171; family and identity formation in, 165–74; gender in, 137, 166; Jamaican RAF volunteers in World War II, 168, 170–71; mother country in, 170–71
Smith, Graham, 126, 269n163, 269n166, 269n173
Smith, Zadie, *White Teeth*, 138, 271n22
Sökefeld, Martin, 224; "Mobilizing in Transnational Space," 4–5
Song of Solomon (Morrison), 24–25, 67
The Souls of Black Folk (Du Bois), 104, 230n20, 277n111
Soyinka, Wole, 9
Spiritual Baptist Church, in *Sleep On, Beloved*, 198–99, 284n82
Stasiulis, Daiva K., 193–94
A State of Independence (Phillips, C.), 3, 180, 182–90; Africa in, 181, 219–20; Brown, J. D., on, 183, 186–89; exile in, 189; interdependence in, 189; return narrative in, 182–83; Sáez on, 182–83, 188; United States in, 187–88
Staying Power (Fryer), 131–32, 229n4
Stein, Mark, 177
Stephens, Michelle Ann, *Black Empire*, 8, 139, 166
Stepto, Robert, 249n22, 261n12
St. Kitts, 125, 160, 183, 186–87, 237n114, 281n24
Storhoff, Gary, 240n25, 242n57, 242n62, 243n64
Stowe, Harriet Beecher, 65
The Stranger (Camus), 152–53, 275n87, 275n95,

276n105; *The Emigrants* and, 152–53, 276n105
Sula (Morrison), 3, 6–7, 31; African American veteran in, 105–11; blackness in, 110–11; "crossing the river" trope in, 103, 107–9; diasporic qualities of, 31, 101–3, 122–23, 129–30; guilt in, 266n97; *Mrs. Dalloway* and, 264n75; *Tar Baby* and, 112, 113; trauma and PTSD in, 102–3, 105–11, 122–23. *See also* Displacement; War, diaspora and; World War I
Sundquist, Eric J., 241n37, 258n194

Tar Baby (Morrison), 3, 6–7, 31; African American veteran in, 111–15; blackness in, 117–19; Caribbean in, 112–13; class in, 119; diasporic qualities of, 31, 101–4, 122–23, 129–30; Middle Passage references in, 112–14, 129; mythic structure of, 115; *Sula* and, 112, 113; transnational black communion in, 103, 111–23; trauma and PTSD in, 102–3, 113–14, 122–23; whiteness in, 117–18. *See also* Vietnam War; War, diaspora and
Terror, as defining feature of slave trade and slavery, Gilroy on, 11–12, 35–36
Theorizing Diaspora (Braziel, Mannur), 10
There Ain't No Black in the Union Jack (Gilroy), 131
There Is a Tree More Ancient than Eden (Forrest), 101, 115
Thiong'o, Ngũgĩ wa, 140, 149
Thomas, Deborah A., 11, 160; on British imperialism, 134
Thomas, Nigel H., 192, 283n75
Thornber, Karen L., on contact nebulae, 150–51, 275n91
Tölölyan, Khachig, 167
Transformation, 226–27; in *Benito Cereno*, 41; in *Middle Passage*, 36, 38, 41–42, 45, 50
Trauma. *See* Displacement; Posttraumatic stress disorder; Trauma theory; Ur-trauma, of the African diaspora
The Trauma Question (Luckhurst), 107, 109–11, 114, 262n28
Trauma theory, 16–17, 31, 102, 107, 110, 113–14, 122–23, 260n6
Trouillot, Michel-Rolph, 23, 40, 64

Tryal insurrection, 39
Turning the Wheel (Johnson, C.), 44, 48

Unclaimed Experience (Caruth), 122–23
United States, as neocolonial and neoimperialist power, 116–17, 186–88. *See also* Revolutionary War, American
"Unspeakable Things Unspoken" (Morrison), 105
Ur-trauma, of the African diaspora, 3, 7, 31, 99, 102, 107, 109, 122, 129, 222

Victim diaspora (forced diaspora, classical diaspora, prototypical diaspora), 10–11, 19, 222, 232n34; black agency and, 18–21, 25, 60–61, 98, 223, 232n43
Vietnam War: African American veteran, PTSD and, 114; scholarship on American literary and cinematic representations of, 265n79; in *Tar Baby*, 111–23

Walcott, Derek, 177, 225
Walcott, Rinaldo, 191
Walker, James W. St. G., *The Black Loyalists*, 63–64, 85, 87, 91, 248n9, 256n145
Walker, Margaret, *Jubilee*, 234n74
Walters, Wendy W.: *Archives of the Black Atlantic*, 29, 62, 64, 230n9; *At Home in Diaspora*, 230n9
Walvin, James, 8
War, diaspora and, 31, 100–103, 122–25, 129–30. *See also* Revolutionary War, American; Vietnam War; World War I; World War II
Warner-Lewis, Maureen, 2
"Water" (Phillips, C.), 125, 127, 130
West, Cornel, 57
West Indian: identity formation, 148, 156, 220; usage of, vii–viii. *See also* African Caribbean
West Indies, Federation of, viii, 148, 274n75
Whitehead, Anne, 107
Whiteness. *See* Racial antiessentialism; *Tar Baby*; Whiteness studies
Whiteness studies, 233n56
White Teeth (Smith, Z.), 138, 271n22
Whitewashing Britain (Paul), 143–44
Wilson, Ellen Gibson, *The Loyal Blacks*, 63, 254n114, 256n146, 257n173

Wilson-Tagoe, Nana, 271n23
Windrush, SS Empire, 132, 138, 173
Windrush moment, 132–33; fiction post-, 31–32, 130, 135–38, 144, 149, 155–57, 159–60, 167–68, 271n22
Woolf, Virginia, 29, 111, 264n75
World War I: for African American soldiers, 104; African American veteran in *Sula*, 105–11
World War II: African American soldier in *Crossing the River*, 124–27, 129–30; Jamaican RAF volunteers in *Small Island*, 138, 168–71

Wright, Michelle M.: *Becoming Black*, 5; on Middle Passage epistemology, 18, 20
Wright, Richard, 230n9, 273n42; *Black Power*, 23; French existentialism and, 150, 275n87
Writing History, Writing Trauma (LaCapra), 129–30

Young, James E., 123

Zauditu-Selassie, K., 120

Tuire Valkeakari, professor of English at Providence College in Providence, Rhode Island, is the author of *Religious Idiom and the African American Novel, 1952–1998*. Her articles have appeared in numerous scholarly journals, including *MELUS, Studies in American Fiction, Studies in Canadian Literature/Études en Littérature Canadienne, Atlantic Literary Review,* and *Atlantis*, and in various essay collections.